50

Also press — c

paternal grandr

OWAIN, uncle of RHY) AP THOMA)

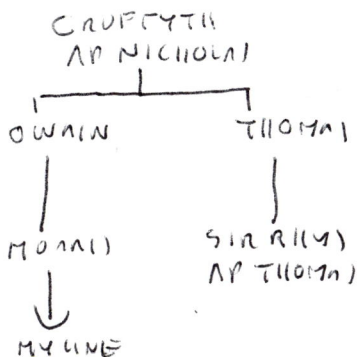

GRUFFYTH
AP NICHOLA)
├── OWAIN
│   │
│   MOAA()
│   ↓
│   MY LINE
└── THOMA)
      │
      SIR RHY)
      AP THOMA)

Sir Rhys ap Thomas
and his Family

Sir Rhys ap Thomas and his Family

A Study in the Wars of the Roses and Early Tudor Politics

RALPH A. GRIFFITHS

CARDIFF

UNIVERSITY OF WALES PRESS

1993

© Ralph A. Griffiths, 1993

British Library Cataloguing-in-Publication Data
A catalogue record for this book is available from the British Library

ISBN 0-7083-1218-7

Jacket design by Design Principle, Cardiff
Typeset by Megaron, Cardiff
Printed in Great Britain by the Cromwell Press, Melksham, Wiltshire

For Glanmor Williams
and in memory of
Alun Davies

Contents

Illustrations

Foreword

This book has two distinct and related parts. The first deals with one of the most prominent and influential families to emerge in Wales between the conquests of Edward I and the Acts of Union of Henry VIII. The fortunes of this family, which in the person of Rhys ap Thomas took a decisive role in Henry Tudor's enterprise in 1485, were a touchstone of political, dynastic and social developments in England and Wales during the Wars of the Roses and the Tudor century that followed. The second part of the book is an edition of the early seventeenth-century Life of Sir Rhys ap Thomas and his immediate forebears. This is perforce based on a version published in 1796, for the original manuscript – if it still survives – has not come to light despite hopes kept alive as the eye scanned lists and catalogues in various libraries and archives during three decades. It is now reasonably safe to proceed *faute de mieux*. The two parts of the book are intimately connected. Sir Rhys ap Thomas and his kinsfolk so dominated large parts of Wales – especially the south and west – during the fifteenth and early sixteenth centuries that their attitudes and actions were of direct importance to Lancastrian, Yorkist and Tudor monarchs and to the substantial section of the Anglo-Welsh and Marcher aristocracy that was prominent at court and in the country before Wales was united with the English realm. Although a few of the material possessions of Sir Rhys's family happily still survive, the greater part of its archive has regrettably perished, so that the existence of a version of the family's perception of its own history is a special boon.

This book touches on a number of English and Welsh historical themes which have long interested me. My efforts to explore them were encouraged at an earlier stage by the late Margaret Sharp, Charles Ross and S. B. Chrimes, and also by Colin Richmond, David Morgan and the friendly fifteenth-century historians who have met regularly since 1970. In studying the Welsh dimension in particular, I have learnt much from

Brynmor Pugh, and from the small group of later medieval historians in the University of Wales led by Glanmor Williams and Rees Davies, in whose company I have studied this period in Wales's history which, until the twentieth century, was commonly squeezed into a few sentences between stirring accounts of Owain Glyndŵr's activities, Henry Tudor's celebrated march, and what was perceived to be the enlightened authoritarianism of King Henry VIII.

In preparing this study, I have received help from a number of quarters and from many friends and colleagues. Among the University of Wales's corps of Welsh literary scholars, the following have identified and explained literary allusions: Dafydd Bowen, Eleri Davies, Hywel T. Edwards, Geraint Gruffudd, Dafydd Johnston and Peredur Lynch. Likewise, my colleagues, Ceri Davies and Eddie Owens, readily placed their knowledge of classical literature at my disposal. Gwynedd Pierce and Brian Ll. James explained references to a Glamorgan place-name; and the late Isobel Westcott took me further than anyone else was able to do towards an explanation of a particularly elusive seventeenth-century English literary allusion. Various historical references were generously contributed by Ian Arthurson, Caroline Barron, Mark Ballard, Peter Begent, Margaret Condon, Wil Griffith, Steven Gunn, John Law, Rhys Robinson and Roger Turvey. Donald Moore and Jack Spurgeon were helpful with, respectively, pictures and buildings connected with Sir Rhys ap Thomas's family; other items were made accessible through the good offices of Alison Allan, T. Alun Davies, Roy Saer and especially Arwel Lloyd Hughes, at the Welsh Folk Museum at St Fagans. The maps were expertly prepared by Guy Lewis. The present Lord Dynevor, Sir Rhys's descendant, has shown a friendly interest over many years.

It is a pleasure to record, once again, the generous support of the Council of the University College of Swansea and of the British Academy, and the assistance of the archivists and librarians of a number of institutions, in facilitating the research on which this book is based. In bringing it to publication, I have appreciated the care and thoroughness of the University of Wales Press (especially of Ceinwen Jones) and of the proof-reader, Henry Maas. Above all, my debt is greatest – as often in the past – to Glanmor Williams, who read and improved the entire manuscript.

University College of Swansea   June 1993

Abbreviations

Acts PC	*Acts of the Privy Council of England*
Arch. Camb.	*Archaeologia Cambrensis* (London, 1846–)
Bartrum, *300–1400*	P. C. Bartrum, *Welsh Genealogies, AD 300–1400* (8 vols., Cardiff, 1974)
Bartrum, *1400–1500*	P. C. Bartrum, *Welsh Genealogies, 1400–1500* (18 vols., Aberystwyth, 1983)
BBCS	*Bulletin of the Board of Celtic Studies* (Cardiff, 1921–)
Bindoff, *HC*	S. T. Bindoff (ed.), *History of Parliament: The Commons, 1509–1558* (3 vols., London, 1982)
BL	British Library
CAD	*Calendars of Ancient Deeds*
Cal. Papal Reg.	*Calendars of the Papal Registers*
Campbell, *Materials*	W. Campbell (ed.), *Materials for a History of the Reign of Henry VII* (2 vols., Rolls Series, 1877)
Carms. Antiquary	*The Carmarthenshire Antiquary* (Carmarthen, 1941–)
CCL	Cardiff Free Central Library
CCR	*Calendars of the Close Rolls*
CFR	*Calendars of the Fine Rolls*
Clark, *Cartae*	G. T. Clark (ed.), *Cartae et alia Munimenta quae ad Dominium de Glamorgancia pertinent* (6 vols., Cardiff, 1893–1910)
Companion to Welsh Lit.	M. Stephens (ed.), *The Oxford Companion to the Literature of Wales* (Oxford, 1986)
CP	G. E. Cockayne, *The Complete Peerage of England, Scotland, Ireland, Great Britain and*

	the United Kingdom (12 vols. in 13, London 1910–59)
CPR	*Calendars of the Patent Rolls*
CR	*The Cambrian Register* (3 vols., London, 1795–1818)
CRO	Carmarthen Record Office
CSP, Dom.	*Calendars of the State Papers, Domestic*
CSP, Span	*Calendars of State Papers, Spanish*
DNB	L. Stephens and S. Lee (eds.), *The Dictionary of National Biography* (63 vols., London, 1885–1900; reprinted Oxford, 1921–2)
DWB	J. E. Lloyd and R. T. Jenkins (eds.), *The Dictionary of Welsh Biography down to 1940* (London, 1959)
Dwnn	Lewys Dwnn, *Heraldic Visitations of Wales*, ed. S. R. Meyrick (2 vols., Llandovery, 1846)
EETS	Early English Text Society
EHR	*English Historical Review* (London, 1886–)
Foedera	T. Rymer (ed.), *Foedera, conventiones, literae . . .* (10 vols., The Hague, 1739–45)
Geiriadur	*Geiriadur Prifysgol Cymru* (Cardiff, 1950–)
Griffiths, *Principality of Wales*	R. A. Griffiths, *The Principality of Wales in the Later Middle Ages*, Vol. I: *South Wales, 1277–1536* (Cardiff, 1972)
Griffiths, 'Wales and the March'	R. A. Griffiths, 'Wales and the March', in S. B. Chrimes, C. D. Ross and R. A. Griffiths (eds.), *Fifteenth-Century England, 1399–1509* (Manchester, 1972), pp. 145–72
Harleian 433	R. Horrox and P. W. Hammond (eds.), *British Library, Harleian MS 433* (4 vols., Gloucester, 1979–83)
Hasler, *HC*	P. W. Hasler (ed.), *History of Parliament: The Commons, 1558–1603* (3 vols., London, 1981)
HMC	*Historical Manuscripts Commission*
JHSCW	*Journal of the Historical Society of the Church in Wales* (1947–)
Leland, *Collectanea*	J. Leland, *De Rebus Britannicis Collectanea* (16 vols., London, 1715)
Lemprière	F. A. Wright (ed.), *Lemprière's Classical Dictionary* (new edn., London, 1879)
Le Neve	*J. Le Neve's Fasti Ecclesiae Anglicanae, 1300–1541*, ed. B. Jones (12 vols., London, 1962–7)

Limbus	G. T. Clark, *Limbus Patrum Morganiae et Glamorganiae* (London, 1886)
LP, Henry VIII	*Letters and Papers, Foreign and Domestic, of the Reign of Henry VIII*
MSS in the Welsh Language	*Historical Manuscripts Commission: Reports on Manuscripts in the Welsh Language* (2 vols., London, 1898–1910)
Mynegai	*Mynegai i Farddoniaeth Gaeth y Llawysgrifau* (13 vols., Cardiff, 1978)
NLW	National Library of Wales, Aberystwyth
NLWJ	*National Library of Wales Journal* (Aberystwyth, 1939–)
OED	*Oxford English Dictionary* (2nd edn., 20 vols., Oxford, 1989)
PBA	*Proceedings of the British Academy* (London, 1903–)
PRO	Public Record Office, London
RCAHM	*Royal Commission on Ancient and Historical Monuments*
RP	*Rotuli Parliamentorum* (6 vols., London, 1767)
RS	Rolls Series
SR	*The Statutes of the Realm* (11 vols., Record Commission, 1810–28; reprinted 1963)
TCASFC	*Transactions of the Carmarthenshire Antiquarian Society and Field Club* (Carmarthen, 1905–39)
THSC	*Transactions of the Honourable Society of Cymmrodorion* (London, 1893–)
THSLC	*Transactions of the Historic Society of Lancashire and Cheshire* (Liverpool, 1848–)
TRHS	*Transactions of the Royal Historical Society* (London, 1872–)
Wedgwood, *HP*	J. C. Wedgwood, *History of Parliament, 1439–1509: Biographies of Members of the Commons House* (London, 1936)
Williams, *Welsh Church*	G. Williams, *The Welsh Church from Conquest to Reformation* (2nd edn., Cardiff, 1976)
WHR	*Welsh History Review* (Cardiff, 1960–)
WRO	Worcester Record Office
WWHR	*West Wales Historical Records* (14 vols., Carmarthen, 1910–29)

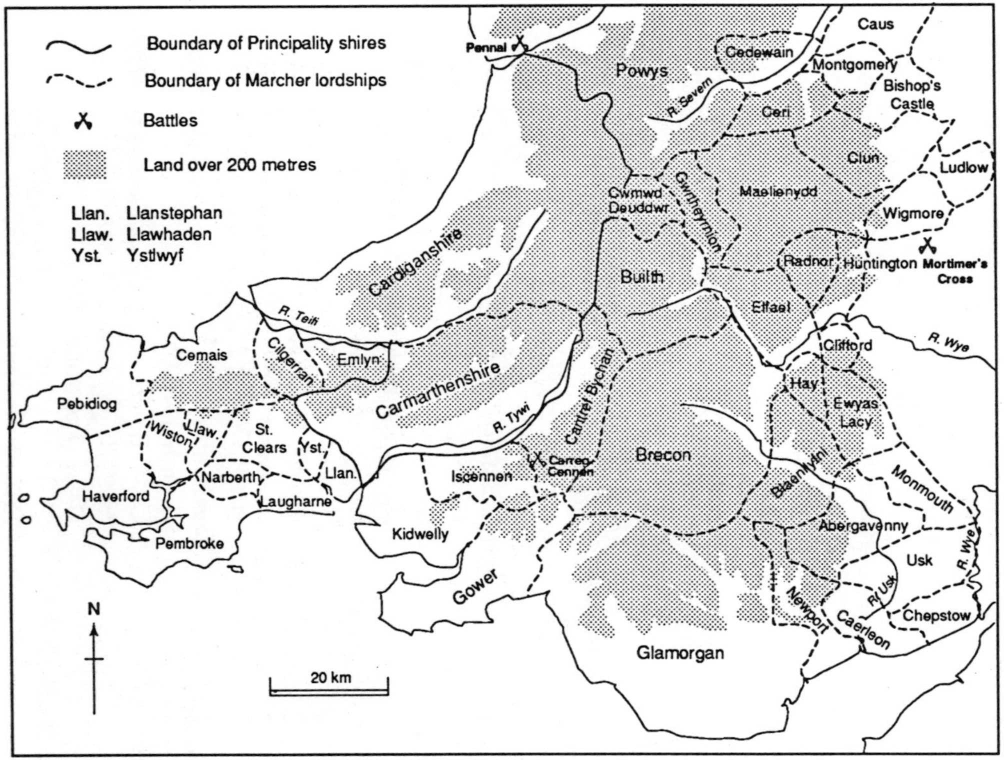

Map 1: Southern Wales *c.*1500

The boundaries are based on the administrative and lordship divisions shown in R. R. Davies, *Conquest, Coexistence and Change: Wales, 1063–1415* (Oxford, 1987), p. 393.

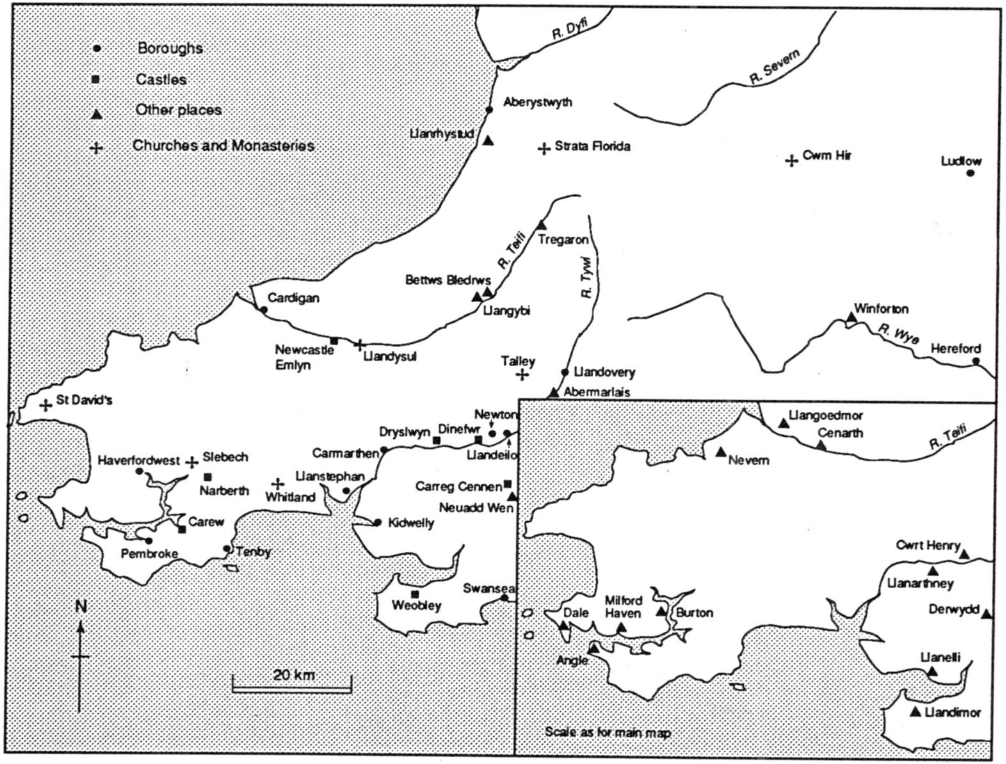

Map 2: Sir Rhys ap Thomas's interests in southern Wales

PART I

Servants and Victims of Lancastrian, Yorkist and Tudor Monarchs

Introduction

Wales could not fail to be profoundly affected by the Wars of the Roses and the establishment of Tudor rule. The dynastic disputes within the English royal family in the second half of the fifteenth century reverberated throughout Wales because the Crown and many of the leading protagonists in the civil wars had lordships and lands in the Marches and the Principality shires of Wales. Indeed, that most English of English historians, G. M. Trevelyan, concluded in his *History of England* (first published in 1926) that 'the Wars of the Roses were to a large extent a quarrel between Welsh Marcher lords, who were also great English nobles, closely related to the English throne'.[1] Few historians would now endorse Trevelyan's scale of priorities. But it is undeniable that in fifteenth-century Wales kings and Marcher lords enjoyed and exploited wide governmental authority – particularly to raise revenue and appoint local officials – as well as strategic aspects of lordship that enabled them to assemble armed retinues and fortify large castles.

This explains why Wales and its Marches were of critical importance in the civil wars. It is worth noting, by way of illustration, that the battle of Mortimer's Cross, near Wigmore, where the Lancastrian stalwart, Jasper Tudor, and his army from south-west Wales were scattered in February 1461, provided the momentum that took the young victor, Edward, earl of March, to the steps of the throne one month later. Thereafter, western Wales continued to be one of the most resistant regions to the consolidation of Yorkist power, and Harlech, the very last stronghold in England and Wales to be subdued, held out until 1468. The crucial battle of Tewkesbury, fought on the banks of the Severn on 4 May 1471, might well have turned out differently – and the fates of Lancaster and York might have been reversed – if the Lancastrian

[1] G. M. Trevelyan, *History of England* (3rd edn., London, 1945), p.259.

queen had been able to join with advancing forces from Wales before she
was confronted by Edward IV. And in August 1485, Henry Tudor won
his decisive engagement in the Leicestershire countryside after a long
march through west and central Wales, recruiting supporters as he went
in order to supplement the Franco-Scottish insurgents who had
accompanied him from France.

Furthermore, Welsh shires and lordships frequently changed hands
(and, consequently, political allegiance) between the 1450s and 1490s,
sometimes with bewildering speed. The lordship of Glamorgan, for
example, passed, not always easily or without dispute, from Beauchamp
to Neville in 1449, then, in *c*.1474, to Richard, duke of Gloucester (later
King Richard III), to Jasper Tudor, earl of Pembroke and duke of
Bedford, in 1486, and, following Jasper's death in December 1495, to his
young great-nephew, Henry, duke of York.[2] Lordship of the six counties
of the principality of Wales reflects even more sensitively the political
tergiversations of these years. They were ruled by Henry VI and, from
1456, by his only son, Edward of Lancaster, as prince of Wales, by
Edward IV (1461) and, from 1472, by his eldest son and prince, Edward
of Westminster. Then, soon after his accession in 1483, Richard III
endowed his only son, Edward of Middleham (died 1484), with the
principality of Wales; whilst in August 1485 Henry Tudor acquired the
principality along with the Crown, and he bestowed it on his first-born
son, Arthur, in 1489.[3]

Most Welsh subjects of kings, princes and lords were not directly or
actively involved in the hostilities of these decades. Yet with lordship so
direct and unstable, leading squires and landowners – some of them
knighted after the English fashion – generally proved loyal to their
current lord, under whom they might prosper, and were inclined to
embrace his causes and ambitions when called on to do so. As a result, at
Mortimer's Cross in February 1461, men from the lordships of the south-
east were as prominent on the Yorkist side as were others from the south-
west on the Lancastrian side.[4] Sometimes the royal feuds were
deepened and extended by family rivalries and local disputes that
already divided communities and were themselves perpetuated by more
distant events. The Vaughans of Tretower, in the Stafford lordship of
Brecon, adopted attitudes towards Richard III and the Tudors that
were partly dictated by their kinship with the Herberts of Raglan, but
more immediately by a bitter feud with Jasper Tudor that harked back
to Jasper's execution of Sir Roger Vaughan after the battle of

[2] T. B. Pugh (ed.), *Glamorgan County History*, Volume III: *The Middle Ages* (Cardiff, 1971), chs.IV,
XI.
[3] R. A. Griffiths, 'Royal government in the southern counties of the Principality of Wales, 1422–
1485' (unpublished University of Bristol Ph.D. thesis, 1962), pp.11–12. The six counties were those
of Cardigan and Carmarthen, Anglesey, Caernarfon and Merioneth, and Flint.
[4] H. T. Evans, *Wales and the Wars of the Roses* (Cambridge, 1915), pp.122–5.

Tewkesbury in 1471 – and that, in turn, was prompted by the accusation that Sir Roger had had a hand in the execution of Owen Tudor, Jasper's father, after Mortimer's Cross ten years before. Accordingly, in 1483 the Vaughans opposed their lord at Brecon, Henry Stafford, duke of Buckingham, when he rose in rebellion against Richard III. Two and a half years later, Sir Thomas Vaughan organized a rising thereabouts against Henry Tudor's insecure regime.[5] In the second half of the fifteenth century, the civil wars could be a potent influence on the social and political fortunes of leading figures and their lineages, in Wales as in England. Equally, some of Wales's most prominent families and their affinities had a significant impact on the stirring developments of the fifteenth and early sixteenth centuries.

Wales has always been assigned a distinctive part in the Wars of the Roses, not least because the first Tudor king, Henry VII, was part-Welsh by blood and landed in Pembrokeshire on his way to challenge Richard III for the Crown. It was, in truth, a different country from England and contemporaries recognized that this was so. Yet, Wales – its principality shires and its Marcher lordships – was a dominion of the English Crown, and its leading gentry and nobility, by marriage and mores, connection and travel, were increasingly absorbed into the king-centred society of court and country. In Wales such families were the backbone of society and the sinews of political life, and by the mid-fifteenth century their menfolk governed the country by virtue of the absence or indulgence of most Marcher lords and the Crown. They had successfully adjusted to the post-Glyndŵr world, and probably more quickly in the southern parts of Wales, which were not as closely identified with the great rebellion as were the north and north-west. Without noticeable difficulty, they attuned themselves to the polity and governance of the Marcher lordships and the principality shires; but as a corollary, they had to come to terms with the dynastic changes at Westminster in the second half of the century.

The most prominent gentry were often tempted to please themselves and avoid inconvenient obligations, and at the same time to exploit forcefully, and sometimes with violence, any opportunities that distant or enfeebled authorities allowed them. The prosperous lowlands and lively ports of the south, in touch as they were with Ireland, the Low Countries and France, as well as with Severnside's commercial culture, attracted the more ambitious of them. After all, the topography and sparse population of the hill country, and the frequency with which political frontiers there followed the larger rivers and bisected their fertile valleys – like those of Tywi and Teifi – meant that the cohesion of

[5] R. A. Griffiths and R. S. Thomas, *The Making of the Tudor Dynasty* (Gloucester, 1985), pp.52, 75–6, 99–100, 195. See below p.179 n.30 for a further reflection of the feud.

communities in individual shires and lordships was often less strong than in some of the counties of England. The leading gentry might array contingents from their localities for both foreign wars and domestic campaigns; and some of them did service, consonant with their allegiances, at the courts of Lancastrian, Yorkist and Tudor monarchs. The dynastic revolutions of the age had their victims, too, and attempts to reassert royal authority in Wales and the Marches in the late fifteenth and early sixteenth centuries threatened to cramp the independent style of leading gentry and to curb their power. Such families were the focus of lesser men's interests and loyalties: as owners of land, with dependent tenantry and neighbours (or affinities, if you will), and as protectors and patrons of churches, clerks and poets. To these more lowly folk, the political inclinations of their betters in a predominantly English context often seemed less important than their more immediate dominance of local society and their reputation more widely within Wales itself.

A small number of indigenous Welsh families, notably the Herberts, the Vaughans, the Griffiths of Penrhyn and the ancestors of the Rices of Newton and Dinefwr, and an equally small number that were part-Welsh in origin – the Stanleys, the Devereux, the Somersets and the Tudors spring to mind – helped to determine the course of the Wars of the Roses by their attitudes and allegiances. They may be considered to have replaced both the Welsh princes of the past and those English magnates who persisted in absenting themselves from their lordships and offices, and they were so regarded by their Welsh contemporaries. They made an essential contribution to the success of Henry Tudor in capturing the Crown in 1485, and in establishing his new dynasty in the decades that followed. Their subsequent rule and misrule in Wales had given way by the late 1520s and early 1530s to a new order which culminated in the Acts of Union. Yet until the middle of the twentieth century, little effort was made to assess Wales's experience and contribution during the civil wars. For a long time – indeed, from Henry VII's own day, when an Italian visitor to England in *c*.1498 observed that Welshmen 'may now, however, be said to have recovered their former independence, for the most wise and fortunate Henry the 7th is a Welshman'[6] – an apocalyptic interpretation of the Wars of the Roses held the field: the events of 1485 had seemingly been foretold by poets and seers during the two centuries following the death of Llywelyn ap Gruffydd, prince of Wales, in 1282.[7] In reality, Wales had a more complex part to play. The family of Sir Rhys ap Thomas seems, in

---

[6] C. A. Sneyd (ed.), *A Relation, or rather a True Account of the Island of England* (Camden Soc., 1st series, 37, 1847), p.19.
[7] Glanmor Williams, 'Prophecy, poetry and politics in medieval and Tudor Wales', in H. Hearder and H. R. Loyn (eds.), *British Government and Administration: Studies presented to S. B. Chrimes* (Cardiff, 1974), pp.69–86; G. A. Williams, 'The bardic road to Bosworth: a Welsh view of Henry Tudor', *THSC*, 1986, pp.7–31.

retrospect, to have taken a unique role in the century after 1430, particularly in south Wales. Moreover, its contribution to the establishment and sustaining of early Tudor rule was highly significant – until in 1531 Sir Rhys's grandson fell victim to the Crown as both were caught up in a distinctly changing world.

1

The Rise to Distinction

In Henry Rice's day, early in the seventeenth century, it was his family's tradition that his ancestors descended from Urien, the sixth-century king of Rheged, 'in a direct series and long concatenations of worthie progenitors'.[1] This tradition was formalized by heralds and genealogists in the late sixteenth and early seventeenth centuries, most notably by Lewys Dwnn (*fl.* 1568–1616), a deputy king of arms, who compiled his pedigree of Walter Rice, Henry's father, in 1596.[2] What amounts to the family's origin-story was current even earlier in the mid-fifteenth century, when praise poems in honour of Gruffydd ap Nicholas of Newton and Dinefwr alluded to the Urien descent.[3] Yet neither Henry Rice nor these poets offered any precise reference to generations earlier than Elidir Ddu in the early fourteenth century. Even the genealogists provided a lineal sequence of father and mother to son and wife only from Goronwy, the grandfather of Elidir Ddu, whom we may accordingly place in the first half of the thirteenth century. Lewys Dwnn contented himself with identifying Goronwy by a patronymic system that extended through twelve generations to 'Urien Rheged'.[4]

Incontrovertible contemporary evidence of Henry Rice's ancestors is available only at the beginning of the fourteenth century, and it must be said at once that later pedigrees and genealogies contain some suspicious features. The lapse of twelve generations between Urien Rheged and Goronwy would place the former in the ninth, rather than the sixth, century; and the marriages of Goronwy's son, Rhys ap Goronwy, and his grandson, Elidir ap Rhys, are linked with individuals who

---

[1] See below p.159.
[2] Dwnn, I, 210–11; *DWB*, pp.175–6. Cf. Bartrum, *300–1400*, I, 11, 51.
[3] Poems by Lewys Glyn Cothi (*fl.*1447–86) and Rhys Llwyd ap Rhys ap Rhiccert (*fl. c.*1450) noted in E. R. Ll. Davies, 'Noddwyr y beirdd yn Sir Gaerfyrddin' (unpublished University of Wales MA thesis, 1976), pp.65, 72.
[4] Dwnn, I, 210–11; CRO, Dynevor, Add. MS 73 (*c.*1600). Cf. NLW, Llanstephan 130 D f.5, *c.*1670.

apparently flourished in the mid-twelfth century, instead of in the mid-thirteenth.[5] It is possible, therefore, that the association of Henry Rice's family with putative descendants of Urien, king of Rheged, was created in the household of Gruffydd ap Nicholas in the fifteenth century, or else in that of Elidir Ddu a century earlier in order to mark Elidir Ddu's pilgrimage to the Holy Land. Certainly, it was later believed that 'Syr' Elidir Ddu was the first of his line to use the name 'Fitz Urien'.[6] It is all the more noteworthy, therefore, that the earliest known authentic documentary reference to a member of the family comes from 1302–3, when Elidir Ddu was fined for withdrawing from a suit laid before the hundred court of the new royal borough of Dinefwr.[7]

Described as a knight of the Holy Sepulchre and a knight of Rhodes by Lewys Dwnn, Elidir Ddu is recorded in the pedigrees as the son of Elidir ap Rhys, who testified in 1326 to the rights of the bishop of St David's in the *patria* of Llandeilo Fawr.[8] The journey to the Holy Land may have been inspired by the Knights Hospitaller of St John, whose Welsh commandery was situated at Slebech in Pembrokeshire.[9] In 1326 the family may already have been living at Crug, the house a short distance to the north of Llandeilo – and little more from the king's new borough – with which the family was later associated. It seems that Nicholas ap Philip ap Syr Elidir Ddu resided there when, in the last quarter of the fourteenth century, he married Sioned (or Jenet), the daughter of a neighbour, Gruffydd ap Llywelyn Foethus of Llangathen, which lies half-way between Dinefwr and Dryslwyn Castles. In 1355–8, Gruffydd was constable of Maenordeilo, the commote in which Crug stood.

> Nicholas ap Phe[lip] dwelled at Cryg, a simple howse in the parishe of Llandilo. He had issue one only soone called Griffith ap Nicholas which was begotten the very first night after his marriag, after a hurte which he received, of w[hi]ch after warde he died . . . There is a tradition of this Nicholas that having received a dangerous wound on his wedding day, being told by his physicians that in case he refrained from his wife's bed for

---

[5] Dwnn, I, 210–11; NLW, Llanstephan 130 D f.5; Bartrum, *300–1400*, III, 474. Suspicious, too, is the collateral appearance of 'Syr Elidir Marchog [the knight]' four generations earlier than Elidir Ddu, the knight of the Holy Sepulchre in the early fourteenth century, and of two daughters of Dafydd Fras three generations apart: Bartrum, *300–1400*, II, 324, 327, 330.

[6] NLW, Llanstephan 130 D f.5.

[7] PRO, SC2/215/17 m.2, calendared in E. A. Lewis, 'Materials illustrating the history of Dynevor and Newton from the earliest times to the close of the reign of Henry VIII', *WWHR*, I (1910–11), 184. See R. A. Griffiths, 'A tale of two towns: Llandeilo Fawr and Dinefwr in the Middle Ages', in H. James (ed.), *Sir Gâr: Studies in Carmarthenshire History* (Carmarthen, 1991), p.219.

[8] J. W. Willis-Bund (ed.), *The Black Book of St David's* (London, 1902), p.269; Dwnn, I, 210–11; F. Jones, 'Knights of the Holy Sepulchre', *JHSCW*, XXVI (1979), 23.

[9] W. Rees, *A History of the Order of St John of Jerusalem in Wales and the Welsh Border* (Cardiff, 1947), ch.III.

a few days, he should recover, or els assuredly dye: he however, would not refrain from his wife's society on his nuptiall night, thereby hastening his death, for soone after he dyed leaving his wife with child of a son.[10]

This tragi-romantic story of Gruffydd ap Nicholas's conception, with its implication that he never knew his father – just as Henry Tudor later on never knew his – may be part of family mythology. Later pedigrees concur in making Gruffydd an only child, yet Philip, John and David Nicholas were living at Newton in Henry V's reign, and John was still alive in Kidwelly in 1458–9.[11] Were they Gruffydd's brothers, outshone by his celebrity and obscured by his propagandists?

   Meanwhile, a family established at Llandeilo Fawr and Newton could readily exploit points of contact immediately across the Tywi in the commote of Iscennen in the lordship of Kidwelly (which from 1361 belonged to the king's son, John of Gaunt, duke of Lancaster) and in the Audleys' lordship of Llandovery. Philip ab Elidir Ddu was certainly prominent enough to be one of the local representatives who in 1362 formally witnessed the transfer of Iscennen and its impregnable fortress of Carreg Cennen to their new lord, John of Gaunt, into whose service Philip passed.[12] Of his son Nicholas, who allegedly died so soon after his wedding, we have no further knowledge, though his brother, Gwilym ap Philip, became influential in his own right south of the river. He may, for instance, be identified with John of Gaunt's receiver of the lordship of Kidwelly in 1387–8 and again by February 1400; and he was employed by Gaunt's son, King Henry IV, in collecting a general fine imposed on the community of Iscennen in 1408–9. His knowledge of the lordship of Llandovery was sought on 6 September 1391, when its descent was investigated at Carmarthen following the death of the last of the Audleys. In short, he may have been loyal to the Crown during Owain Glyndŵr's rebellion or, if his loyalties wavered at that time, was quickly reconciled to the king. He was later said to have died of wounds inflicted by one of his own kinsmen.[13]

   Thus, in the fourteenth century the ancestors of Henry Rice were well-to-do tenants living near Llandeilo Fawr, perhaps taking advantage of the creation of the new borough near Dinefwr Castle to become burgesses of Newton. Elidir Ddu distinguished himself by visiting the Holy Places, which made him one of the most noteworthy

---

[10] NLW MS 1602 D.f.204–5 (*c*.1609–30), partly printed in F. Jones, 'Sir Rhys ap Thomas: the blood of the raven', *TCASFC*, XXIX (1939), 29–30. See Dwnn, I, 210–11 (Sioned); NLW, Llanstephan 130 D f.5 (Jenet); Griffiths, *Principality of Wales*, p.386. Sir Rhys ap Thomas later associated the arms attributed to Llywelyn Foethus – on a cross, five crescents – with those of Newton and Dinefwr, a chevron sable between three ravens proper: M. P. Siddons, *The Development of Welsh Heraldry*, Vol.I (Aberystwyth, 1991), pp.26, 91, 130.
[11] R. A. Griffiths, 'Gruffydd ap Nicholas and the rise of the House of Dinefwr', *NLWJ*, XIII (1964), 257 and n.9.
[12] *CCR, 1360–4*, p.418; Griffiths, *NLWJ*, XIII (1964), 256–7.
[13] Ibid., p.257; NLW, Llanstephan 1602 D f.204 (Jones, *TCASFC*, XXIX (1939), 30).

figures in his lineage and the earliest member of his family to be identified by later poets as a historical figure. Henry Rice was, however, correct in regarding the career of Gruffydd ap Nicholas as the key phase in the substantial rise of the family's fortunes: posthumous child or no, Gruffydd's personality and qualities enabled him to exploit political, social and economic opportunities in south-west Wales in the aftermath of Glyndŵr's rebellion and in the decades prior to the outbreak of the Wars of the Roses.

Gruffydd ap Nicholas was well placed to lay his emphatic mark on the Tywi Valley once Henry V had initiated his policy of political reconciliation. From 1415 onwards, Gruffydd and his cousin, Rhys ap Gwilym ap Philip, shouldered various minor administrative respons-ibilities in the lordship of Kidwelly and across the River Tywi in the county of Carmarthen which doubtless gave them a certain position and influence. The Vale of Tywi was prosperous country, with small, scattered communities dominated by large royal castles and linked by modest market towns – apart from Carmarthen, almost certainly the largest borough in Wales at this time. By November 1424, Gruffydd had impressed sufficiently to be engaged by the steward of Kidwelly, Sir John Scudamore, as his deputy, a post which gave him judicial authority in the lordship. In the following year, he seemed the best available person to survey the king's castle, demesnes and boroughs of Dinefwr and Newton, which he knew intimately; and in October 1429 he joined Rhys ap Gwilym ap Philip in acting as deputy-constable of Dinefwr Castle in the continuing absence of Sir Roland Standish, the constable who was much occupied with warfare in France. In 1426 Gruffydd was sheriff of Carmarthenshire, the most prestigious of the offices he had so far filled; and in 1429 he began a three-year term (at least) as escheator of the county.[14] Such appointments gave Gruffydd and his cousin the opportunity to acquire property and modest wealth, albeit on a piecemeal basis – a lease here, agricultural profits there – so that by the mid-1430s Gruffydd had emerged not only as an important royal official in the lordship of Kidwelly and the principality county of Carmarthen, but also as the tenant of an expanding estate in the Tywi Valley, as far south as Llanelli and Llan-llwch, below Carmarthen, and as a burgess of both Dinefwr and Dryslwyn.[15]

This achievement was made possible in part by his ruthless ambition: he had, for example, taken advantage of the absence in France of his first wife's brother, Gruffydd Dwnn of Kidwelly, to eject him from the shrievalty of Carmarthen and briefly occupy it himself (as Dwnn

[14] Griffiths, *Principality of Wales*, pp.250–1, 271, 321.
[15] See Griffiths, *NLWJ*, XIII (1964), 256–68, and idem, 'Gruffydd ap Nicholas and the fall of the House of Lancaster', *WHR*, II (1965), 213–31, for full references.

reported to the king's Council on 13 January 1427).[16] More especially, it was facilitated by the patronage of greater men, not only Sir John Scudamore, the trusted Herefordshire knight whom the Lancastrian monarchy employed in Carmarthenshire as well as in Kidwelly, but also the king's kinsman, Edmund Beaufort, count of Mortain, who succeeded Scudamore as constable of Carmarthen Castle and steward of Kidwelly in 1433 and continued to employ Gruffydd as his deputy-steward. To Beaufort, who was mostly in France during the periods 1436–40 and 1448–50, he seemed a dependable local squire who could be relied on to oversee with vigour the count's interests and obligations throughout Carmarthenshire.[17] Gruffydd also moved in influential local circles. He took as his first wife Mabli, daughter of Maredudd ab Henry Dwnn, of a prominent Kidwelly family; his uncle, Gwilym ap Philip, was (presumably) already married to Mabli's sister, Gwalys. Gruffydd's second wife, Margaret, was the third daughter of Sir Thomas Perrot, and by 1434 Gruffydd was associated with the Pembrokeshire esquires, John Perrot and Richard Newton, the latter a distinguished lawyer.[18]

By the time Henry VI came of age in 1436–7, Gruffydd ap Nicholas seemed destined, given the right circumstances and his own skill to exploit them, for an even more prominent position in south Wales. As a caution, he could not have failed to note how Sir John Scudamore, the husband of Glyndŵr's daughter, had been deprived of all his public offices in August 1433, a victim of the penal legislation passed by Henry IV's Parliament in the midst of the Glyndŵr rebellion. Scudamore's misfortune did not adversely affect Gruffydd's position, but awareness of it may have prompted him in 1437 to seek formal letters of denizenship that would prevent a similar fate befalling him. The patronage of Edmund Beaufort is likely to have helped him to secure parliamentary approval of his petition, probably on 2 March 1437. The grant was well timed.

During Henry VI's reign, regional government in Wales was nominally in the hands of loyal peers; practical authority was exercised by lesser, frequently local, figures, among whom Gruffydd ap Nicholas is conspicuous. The growth of aristocratic faction by the 1450s simply accentuated these developments. In Carmarthenshire and Cardiganshire, the king's justiciars and chamberlains were invariably men of baronial rank who rarely visited south Wales. They perforce relied heavily on lieutenants. In the lordship of Kidwelly, the steward between 1433 and 1455 was Edmund Beaufort. Regardless of their personal allegiances at Westminster and the king's court, such officers as these

[16] Griffiths, *Principality of Wales*, p.271.

[17] Griffiths, *Principality of Wales*, pp.139–41, 201, 237, 265, 271, 281, 397, 410–12; M. K. Jones, 'The Beaufort family and the war in France, 1421–50' (unpublished University of Bristol Ph.D. thesis, 1982), pp.89–148 and ch.V.

[18] Griffiths, *Principality of Wales*, pp.201–2, 271 (Gruffydd Dwnn, Mabli's brother), 147 (Newton).

could hardly avoid depending on Gruffydd ap Nicholas as one of the most experienced, effective and influential of the Carmarthenshire gentry – to such an extent that during the 1440s he and his sons came to enjoy supreme political and administrative dominance in west and south-west Wales, except perhaps in parts of south Pembrokeshire. When many other Welsh gentry of their generation were fighting in France, Gruffydd and his sons advanced their careers by staying at home. On 2 August 1437, Gruffydd presided over the petty sessions at Carmarthen in place of Lord Audley, each of whose successors as justiciar allowed Gruffydd to deputize for him.[19] Thereafter, his role as deputy-justiciar is securely documented between 1444 and 1456. His activities as deputy-chamberlain are no less evident in the same period, when he was also acting for Edmund Beaufort in the lordship of Kidwelly.[20] This was as solid a foundation as any for governmental, political and social control of the entire Tywi Valley.

In a period of baronial faction and dynastic dispute, Gruffydd's associations with the great had their perils, but he generally avoided these by exploiting the great distance from Westminster and emphasizing the independent and self-contained jurisdiction of the principality of Wales and the lordship of Kidwelly. He was incautious enough to join the retinue of Humphrey, duke of Gloucester and justiciar of south Wales, on the duke's journey to Bury St Edmunds that ended in his imprisonment and sudden death in February 1447. Although Gruffydd and his company were hauled before the Court of King's Bench when Gloucester was arrested, Gruffydd was soon released and resumed his position in south Wales as if nothing untoward had happened.[21]

The Crown had already conferred on Gruffydd and his friends certain powers that enhanced his reputation and influence and presented opportunities to augment his wealth. The darker side of these powers was the temptation they offered to overcome rivals and oppress neighbours. On 2 December 1440 Gruffydd, his son John and his brother-in-law, John Perrot, secured a sixty-year lease of the castle, towns and demesnes of Dinefwr, his family's ancestral heath, in return for an annual rent of £5. There can be no doubt that Gruffydd was the leader of the trio.[22] In the years that followed, Gruffydd made his presence felt in the provincial capital, Carmarthen, where he was a burgess and lessee of mills and had a business relationship with one of the most notable of burghal families, the Redes. On 6 October 1449, Gruffydd, Thomas Rede and another influential burgess-lawyer, Lewys

[19] Ibid., p.143.
[20] Ibid., pp.151, 153, 185; R. Somerville, *History of the Duchy of Lancaster*, I (London, 1953), pp.639–40; PRO, DL29/574/9079 m.3*d*, 5.
[21] R. A. Griffiths, *The Reign of King Henry VI* (London, 1981), pp.496–8; idem, thesis cited, pp.507–16.
[22] Griffiths, *Principality of Wales*, pp.251–3.

ap Rhys Gethin, who happened to be mayor of Carmarthen in 1448–50, were allowed to farm the revenue of the entire town for twenty years at £20 per annum – a grant of considerable potential in the exploitation of Carmarthen's wealth to their collective profit.[23] The length of these leases gave a certain degree of permanence to ambitions that were partly founded on them.

On an even broader front, Gruffydd's position as escheator of Carmarthenshire from 1449 onwards meant that when, also on 6 October 1449, he, Thomas Rede and Lewys ap Rhys Gethin were granted the profits from all forfeitures in the county for twenty years, it was Gruffydd who was able to exploit them most effectively for his enrichment and, it may be thought, with deepening unpopularity.[24] As the years passed, Gruffydd had less and less to fear from other royal officers in the shire: from Carmarthen Castle, whose constable was his patron, Edmund Beaufort; from his cousin and collaborator, Rhys ap Gwilym ap Philip, who was so well regarded by the absentee sheriff of Carmarthen, James Butler, earl of Ormond, as to be used as his deputy (*c.*1443–4); or from the local landowners like Jankyn ab Owain, Maurice Bwl and Richard Rede who held the office of escheator of Carmarthenshire in the 1430s and 1440s when Gruffydd ap Nicholas happened not to hold the post and who in reality were his agents.[25]

The tentacles of Gruffydd's power gradually extended further afield in south Wales, with his sons filling the role of willing lieutenants. It was perhaps to be expected that he should turn his gaze at a relatively early stage towards Cardiganshire, the northern part of the principality of south Wales. Between 1436 and 1441 a succession of deaths among the younger members of the Clement family enabled him to establish his control over a substantial portion of that family's estates in the commotes of Pennardd and Genau'r Glyn in the northern half of the shire. The right to determine whom Philip Clement should marry was granted to him in 1435–6, and when Philip was succeeded by his brother soon afterwards, two-thirds of the family property was placed in the custody of Gruffydd and his patron, Edmund Beaufort. Some six years later, in July 1443, Gruffydd again acquired two-thirds of the estate when William Clement died, leaving a young daughter, Matilda, as his heiress.[26] This was the prelude to a more concerted advance through the Carmarthenshire hills to the Teifi Valley – and a violent one at that, spearheaded by Gruffydd's personal retinue. It was led by Thomas ap Gruffydd ap Nicholas and two confederates from the lower Teifi Valley – Einion ap Jankyn ap Rhys ap Dafydd, whose father had served with

[23] Ibid., pp.203–4, 312, 338–9, 350, 556.
[24] Ibid., pp.322–3.
[25] Ibid., pp.322–3.
[26] Griffiths, *NLWJ*, XIII (1964), 258–9, 262 and n.41.

Henry V in France, and Gruffydd ap Dafydd ap Thomas, an experienced official from the area.[27] In the course of the disorder that followed, Einion was accused of breaking into Llandysul Church and making off with £89 embezzled from the parson; given his influential protectors, efforts to apprehend him came to nothing. Thomas ap Gruffydd ap Nicholas and his confederates were opposed by two landowners of an older generation, Maredudd ab Owain and John (or Jankyn) ap Rhys ap Dafydd, who had been out with Glyndŵr and whose interests lay further north in the county. The signs are that victory went to the younger men, and to Gruffydd ap Nicholas whose towering figure stood behind them. Both Maredudd ab Owain and John ap Rhys ap Dafydd seem to have retired from public life soon after the confrontation, though not before an appeal had been lodged with the king's Council to secure the countermanding of Gruffydd's authority in south Wales. On 14 June 1439, Gruffydd, his son Thomas and their accomplices were accordingly summoned to Westminster. Gruffydd pleaded that he 'was so sike that he might nat wolle ride ne goo', and it is doubtful whether any of the other defendants made the journey.[28] Gruffydd even challenged, somewhat disingenuously, the propriety of summoning such a case to Westminster, in view of the fact that Carmarthenshire and Cardiganshire 'have a Justice and Chamberleyne and Chauncerie with fulle power for to trie and determine alle manere maters doon there'. Yet the ensuing inquiry at Carmarthen in September 1439 was inconclusive (as might have been expected), and the matter was postponed until the next meeting of the great sessions. Meanwhile, efforts to remedy the lawlessness in the principality counties foundered because of Gruffydd ap Nicholas's personal hold on the justiciarship, the chamberlainship and other agencies of law enforcement. He also seized the opportunity to extend his interests in the county town of Cardigan. When John Dier died about September 1441, his heiress was conveniently found guilty of felony and Gruffydd was able to lease the Dier lands and tenements in the borough of Cardigan.

The violent events of 1439 are the likely context of the commission of inquiry which is described in the Life of Sir Rhys ap Thomas and which, probably under the leadership of Sir Robert Whitney, received a humiliating reception from Gruffydd ap Nicholas and his sons.[29] Other, seemingly impressive, assertions of royal authority followed, including the dispatch of a commission of inquiry under Edmund Beaufort and Lord Audley, chamberlain of south Wales and lord of Llandovery; there was even a visit by Humphrey, duke of Gloucester himself to hold sessions at Carmarthen in September 1442. The outcome showed

---

[27] Griffiths, *Principality of Wales*, pp.323, 326–7, 184–5.
[28] PRO, E28/70; Griffiths, *Principality of Wales*, pp.273–5, 326–7.
[29] See below p.166.

Gruffydd ap Nicholas's remarkable skill in parrying temporary inter-
ference from on high whilst at the same time preserving his dominance
on the ground. Einion ap Jankyn's £10 fine was a small price to pay for
his violations of the law; in any case, his sister became Gruffydd ap
Nicholas's third wife at about this time. Gruffydd ap Dafydd ap
Thomas, on the other hand, seems to have been treated as a scapegoat.
An exceptionally heavy fine of 1,000 marks was imposed on him at the
sessions presided over by Duke Humphrey, and his public career
virtually came to an end. On 20 November, he was incarcerated in the
Fleet Prison in London pending payment of his enormous fine; in May
he was transferred under guard to Carmarthen. His brother Rhys, who
was a prominent figure in the Teifi Valley in the 1420s and 1430s, also
had a fine (100 marks) imposed on him at the same sessions, despite the
fact that he was married to Gruffydd ap Nicholas's sister-in-law.[30]
Gloucester's robust presidency of the great sessions of 1442 resulted in a
large number of fines being imposed at Carmarthen, many of them
surely connected with the recent disorders. But not even Gloucester's
energy could place a permanent check on Gruffydd ap Nicholas. At
Cardigan, a suspiciously large number of accused felons failed to turn up
at that county's great sessions; others escaped from custody – largely, it
seems, as a result of Thomas ap Gruffydd ap Nicholas's studied
negligence, for he was acting as sheriff of Cardiganshire in 1442 in the
absence of the earl of Ormond.

The violence in Cardiganshire in 1439 was part of a determined
attempt by Gruffydd ap Nicholas and his family to extend their influence
north of the Teifi. More subtle than armed confrontation with the ruling
establishment – though intimately connected with it – was the creation
of a social connection by careful deployment in marriage of Gruffydd ap
Nicholas's crop of children.[31] Angharad, who may have been the eldest,
married Jankyn (or John) Clement, whose death in 1435–6 left his
young son and heir in Gruffydd's eager care. Her sister Gwenllian
married none other than Gruffydd ap Dafydd ap Thomas; in 1439 he
rode with his brother-in-law, Thomas ap Gruffydd ap Nicholas, though
soon afterwards their paths separated. And Margaret married Jankyn,
the son of Rhys ap Dafydd ap Thomas, one of the rioters of 1439 whose
wife was the sister of another of Thomas ap Gruffydd ap Nicholas's
confederates, Einion ap Jankyn. Above all, it was the marriage of
Thomas ap Gruffydd ap Nicholas himself to Elizabeth, daughter of Sir
John Gruffydd of Abermarlais and Llansadwrn (Carmarthenshire) and
of Llangybi, Bettws Bledrws and Llanrhystud (Cardiganshire), that
cemented the position that Gruffydd ap Nicholas's family had won in
the northern county.

[30] Griffiths, *Principality of Wales*, pp.306–7.
[31] Bartrum, *300–1400*, II, 330.

Gruffydd's other sons were also supportive of their father's ambitions. John was associated with him in leasing Dinefwr from Michaelmas 1439; yet the pedigrees ignore him, and it is possible that he did not marry or produce an heir. Owain, by contrast, was cast in his father's image and bore the family's banner southwards to Pembrokeshire. The fear and distrust which his father inspired there were already evident in June 1438, when Margaret, the pregnant widow of Sir Thomas Malefant of Upton, Pembrokeshire, contemplated the long journey to join her mother in London. She was so frightened by stories of Gruffydd ap Nicholas and 'dyverse oyer of hur Enmyes to lye yn wayte for hur' that she placed herself in the charge of a Glamorgan man, Lewys Leyshon (or Gethin), one of her husband's servants; yet he, along with Gilbert Turberville of Tythegston (Glam.), abducted her during the journey through upland Gower.[32] As far as Owain ap Gruffydd ap Nicholas is concerned, the poet Lewys Glyn Cothi testifies to Gruffydd's full support of his son:

> Gruffydd gives three ravens of the same hue;
> And a white lion to Owain.
> Many a young man under the sun
> Wears linen bearing these.[33]

The activities of Owain and his retinue were causing the government concern by March 1443, and since the abbot of Whitland, as well as Gruffydd ap Nicholas, was summoned before the king's Council on 14 March to explain the young man's behaviour, it is possible that he had already made his presence felt in the lowlands bordering Pembroke-shire. Owain's arrest was ordered that same day, though with Gruffydd ap Nicholas in virtual charge of the government of the principality it may be doubted whether anything effective was done.

Towards the end of the decade, Gruffydd's interests in both north and south Pembrokeshire were considerably advanced when, first, in May 1449 Richard, duke of York, made his lordship of Narberth over to Gruffydd and the bishop of St David's, John de la Bere, perhaps in order to raise a mortgage on the eve of his departure for Ireland. Two years later, on 18 April 1451, Gruffydd intruded himself into a grant of the lordships of Cilgerran, Emlyn Is Cuch and Dyffryn Breuan that had previously been made to Gruffydd ap Dafydd ap Thomas and William ap John. This gave Gruffydd ap Nicholas a significant foothold in north Pembrokeshire, bordering the Teifi Valley which his supporters had

---

[32] *RP*, V, 14–16; Bartrum, *1400–1500*, VIII, 1256. It is worth noting that Owain ap Gruffydd ap Nicholas married at an unknown date Alison, the daughter of Sir Thomas Malefant's brother, Henry: ibid., IV, 649.

[33] E. D. Jones (ed.), *Lewys Glyn Cothi (Detholiad)* (Cardiff, 1984), p.6, translated in Siddons, *Welsh Heraldry*, I, 117.

invaded in 1439.[34]. Nor did the estates of Bishop de la Bere escape his attention for, as a noted absentee from his see (1447–60), the bishop committed them to Gruffydd's care. Since the bishop's estates were scattered over all the counties of the west and south-west, and elsewhere, such authority gave Gruffydd a roving commission in even larger parts of south and mid-Wales.

Meanwhile, in Pembrokeshire, Owain ap Gruffydd ap Nicholas continued his wayward career, installing himself in the thriving port of Tenby. Early in the 1450s, he was living in the town, even sitting in its courts alongside the mayor and bailiffs. Men from Carmarthenshire followed him, robbing, assaulting and holding Pembrokeshire men to ransom. Efforts to arrest him were ignored and by July 1452 the government was seriously concerned at the inability of its senior officials in the principality and at Pembroke to curb his rumbustious activities – indeed, the receiver of Pembroke was none other than John Perrot, Owain's uncle. It seems hardly surprising that on 30 September 1452 Owain and the parson of Carew, Philip ap Rhys, who had presumably been implicated in the disorders, should have secured a pardon for a wide range of serious offences, including armed uprisings and the deployment of liveried retainers.

Carmarthen was the centre of the ungovernable connection which Gruffydd ap Nicholas had constructed. Gruffydd's house at Crug and the house which he built in the borough of Newton are likely to have been inadequate for his needs by the middle decades of the century. Instead, he appropriated the royal castle at Carmarthen and converted it into a fortified residence for himself.[35] Its constable was his absent patron, Edmund Beaufort. Using the Crown's financial resources at the disposal of the chamberlain of south Wales, Gruffydd spent lavishly on the fortress – to the tune of about £64 in 1452–3 alone – in order to make it a comfortable residence defended by artillery. In the course of using Carmarthen as the focus of his dominion, he ignored constitutional proprieties, requiring the inhabitants of Iscennen, in the lordship of Kidwelly, to travel across the river 'to take justice at Cairmardine and nat at Kidwelly'.[36]

It was at Carmarthen, on New Year's Day 1448, that he adapted the somewhat antiquated procedure of the judicial duel as a piece of morbid theatre: two contestants were kitted out in white leather jackets; the accused was slain in the ensuing fight; the vindicated accuser, who had been entertained in Gruffydd's home for two months, even at his own

---

[34] P. A. Johnson, *Duke Richard of York, 1411–1460* (Oxford, 1988), pp.62–3. The intrusion into Emlyn Uwch Cuch was at the expense of Thomas Hopton, who was forcibly dispossessed. J. E. Lloyd, *History of Carmarthenshire* (2 vols., Cardiff, 1935–9), I, 240.
[35] NLW MS 1602 D f.205 (b); Llanstephan 130 D f.21; Jones, *TCASFC*, XXIX (1939), 30; see below p.23.
[36] Griffiths, *NLWJ*, XIII (1964), 161.

table, was beheaded and the head sold to the victim's friends for £40; and the scene was decorated (at a cost of 24s.) for the entertainment of the assembled company. It was evidently at Carmarthen, too, that Gruffydd presided in about 1451–3 over the celebrated 'eisteddfod' of poets, which not only proved a landmark in the development of the poetic metres but enhanced Gruffydd's reputation among contemporary poets and publicists. His ancestry, his commanding and widespread influence, and his powerful retinue were lauded by this group of poets. To Lewys Glyn Cothi (*fl.*1447–86), a Carmarthenshire man himself, he was 'the eagle of Carmarthen', where his paid retainers supported his pretensions.[37] Gwilym ab Ieuan Hen (*fl.*1440–80) lauded him for his learning and talent as a distinguished judge, and expressed satisfaction at the failure to remove him from office.[38] More extravagantly, Rhys Llwyd ap Rhys ap Rhiccert (*fl.*1450) thought him a second Alexander, the bearer of King Henry's standard and worthy to be compared with the outstanding Welsh captain of the Hundred Years War, Matthew Gough (or Goch), who was slain defending London against John Cade's rebels in 1450. A contemporary English writer assembled the vocabulary of chivalry to describe Matthew Goch as 'surpassing all the other esquires in war at that time in bravery, hardihood, loyalty and liberality'; to Rhys Llwyd, Gruffydd ap Nicholas's stature seemed no less.[39] The ascendancy which Gruffydd's sons won for him further north and south – Thomas in Cardiganshire, from Teifi to Dyfi, as the poets sweepingly recalled, Owain in Iscennen, from Tywi to Tawe – was admired by Hywel ap Dafydd ab Ieuan ap Rhys (*fl.*1450–80), a poet from Raglan in Gwent. And at the other end of Wales, Dafydd Llwyd of Mathafarn (*c.*1420–*c.*1500) regarded him graphically and longingly in a traditional prophetic light as 'Carmarthen's Constantine the Great' – which is not, however, likely to have appealed to Gruffydd in his practical mood:

> Lead the van, party of Urien,
> We are waiting for leaders;
> Raise your splendid ancient banner,
> Your ravens, and rout the Saxons;
> Lead, man, in one course,
> With the tamed ravens of the son of Urien of old.[40]

[37] E. R. Ll. Davies, thesis cited, pp.65–78; J. Jones and W. Davies (eds.), *The Poetical Works of Lewis Glyn Cothi* (Oxford, 1837), pp.131–7; Jones, *Lewys Glyn Cothi*, pp.116–20.

[38] H. W. Lloyd, 'Sir Rhys ap Thomas and his family, illustrated by the poems of contemporary bards', *Arch. Camb.*, 4th series, IX (1878), 211–12.

[39] Griffiths, *Henry VI*, pp.499–504, 521, 615, 627.

[40] W. L. Richards (ed.), *Gwaith Dafydd Llwyd o Fathafarn* (Cardiff, 1964), no.46; E. R. Ll. Davies, thesis cited, pp.74–6, translated in Siddons, *Welsh Heraldry*, I, 130; Lloyd, *Arch. Camb.*, 4th series, IX (1878), 202–6.

When the distinguished Flintshire poet, Dafydd ab Edmwnd (*fl.*1450–97), carried off the silver chair at Gruffydd's eisteddfod, he too expressed respect for Gruffydd ap Nicholas.[41] A few poems have even been attributed to Gruffydd himself; whether or not this is well founded, we may fairly concede to the Carmarthenshire tyro an interest in the Welsh literary scene that transcended the merely utilitarian.

Gruffydd's eisteddfod may be the general context of an intriguing episode apparently related by Sir Walter Scott (1771– 1832), who drew on it (from a source unknown) when composing his *Lay of the Last Minstrel*, published in 1805. During a family gathering at Dinefwr Castle in *c.*1450, a wandering minstrel arrived at the gate, unslung his harp and proceeded to sing an ancient lay in English. Gruffydd went out and commanded him to sing it in Welsh. The story seems to have been transmitted to John Williams (1792–1858), the distinguished philologist and classical scholar who established a school at Lampeter that was attended by Scott's son, Charles. In 1824 Scott, who valued Williams's 'extensive information, learning and lively talent' as 'the best school-master in Europe', was instrumental in appointing John Williams as rector of the new Edinburgh Academy, where he served until 1847 (apart from a brief interlude as professor of Latin in London University). Williams seems to have shared with Scott an interest in itinerant minstrels (or *vagarii*), or so Owen ('Morien') Morgan, the journalist and indifferent local historian, later claimed.[42]

Gruffydd ap Nicholas was a remarkable and extraordinary phenomenon. His ruthless behaviour and prodigious achievement may be explained by his singular character. Admiring poets naturally described a welcome patron of their art, and 200 years later Henry Rice saw him much as a product of his peculiarly disturbed times. Yet what can be deduced about Gruffydd from his deeds and misdeeds fits reasonably comfortably with the assessment in the Life of Sir Rhys ap Thomas:

> . . . a man of a hott, firie and cholerrick spiritt; one whos counsells weare all *in turbido*, and therefore naturallie fitlie composed and framed for the times; verie wise he was, and infinitlie subtile and craftie, ambitiouse beyond measure, of a busie stirring braine . . .[43]

Other factors are equally crucial to an explanation of his career. A number of developments intertwined in the early decades of the fifteenth century to paralyse the Crown's ability to impose its will and insist on observance of the law. The withdrawal of personal aristocratic lordship

[41] T. Roberts (ed.), *Gwaith Dafydd ab Edmwnd* (Bangor, 1914), pp.62, 107, 127–9; see below p.168.

[42] W. E. K. Anderson (ed.), *The Journals of Sir Walter Scott* (Oxford, 1972), pp.252 n.5, 322, 434, 395; *DWB*, pp.1051, 1142; O. M. Morgan, *A History of Wales* (Liverpool, 1911), pp.430–1; M. Magnusson, *The Clacken and the Slate* (London, 1974), pp.70–138 (brought to my attention by Dr J. E. Law).

[43] See below p.161.

from Wales had been a feature of the fourteenth century; the seizure of the English Crown by the house of Lancaster accentuated it. Mistrust, suspicion and fear of the Welsh were of long standing; the rebellion of Owain Glyndŵr gave them sharper point, and after the rebellion's end there was a recognition of the difficulty of governing Wales according to Henry IV's penal laws. After 1415, moreover, Henry V and his brothers were preoccupied with the French war. Under the young Henry VI, aristocratic faction was unavoidable during the 1420s and 1430s, and when the king came of age he focused most of his attention on his household and court. These features of royal rule tended to confer local power in Wales on local men, enabling them to use it for their own as well as the Crown's purposes, to a degree that rendered the Crown powerless by the 1440s to reassert its authority should circumstances demand it. Confronted by a fervently ambitious and determined Gruffydd ap Nicholas, and shackled by the Crown's own regime of absent officials, Henry VI and his ministers found themselves severely handicapped. Gruffydd also exploited English feudal and land law in his own interest in town and countryside, leasing or mortgaging lordships, accumulating wardships and marriages, and carefully deploying his own offspring. What brought him up short towards the end of his life was the urgent need of both the Crown and its Yorkist rivals to breathe new life into territorial lordship in Wales, albeit for temporary military and financial reasons.

On occasion Gruffydd was demonstrably eager to display his devotion to Henry VI, whose abdication of effective authority in south Wales was the foundation of Gruffydd's power. He alerted the king in April 1448 and again in June 1450 to threats to the coasts and shipping of south Wales. In May and September 1450, months of near-revolution in England, he assured Henry of the region's loyalty. He offered support to the apprehensive monarch when news arrived of the duke of York's sudden return from Ireland, and he produced 300 marks in Carmarthenshire, Cardiganshire and Kidwelly as a royal aid. When Henry's health collapsed and his regime was badly paralysed from 1453 onwards, Gruffydd found himself in an exposed position, vulnerable to those influential magnates whose own interests in southern and eastern Wales assumed more immediate and practical significance as the realm descended into civil war.

The Life of Sir Rhys ap Thomas notes that Gruffydd experienced particular difficulty with three magnates of the first rank: Richard, duke of York (died 1460), Jasper Tudor, earl of Pembroke (died 1495), and Humphrey Stafford, duke of Buckingham (died 1460), each of them lord of Marcher lordships close to Gruffydd's sphere of interest. On 23 November 1452 Jasper Tudor was created earl of Pembroke; in March 1453 Gruffydd was instructed to surrender to him the Pembrokeshire lordships of Cilgerran, Emlyn Is Cuch and Dyffryn Breuan. When Richard, duke of York became protector and defender of the realm on 27 March 1454, during Henry VI's incapacity, he too encountered Gruffydd at close quarters. On 25 May, the Council over which the duke presided reproved Gruffydd and his sons, Thomas and Owain, and their kinsman, Rhydderch ap Rhys, for abusing office and oppressing fellow subjects.[44] They were reminded of Henry IV's laws relating to Welshmen aspiring to office in Wales, and the Council made sure that the principal absentee officials in the principality of south Wales and the lordship of Kidwelly, the lords of Llandovery, Gower and Laugharne, and the bishop of St David's, were fully aware of them. After all, most – if not all – of these men had employed members of Gruffydd ap Nicholas's family in official positions in recent years; such Welshmen were now to be discharged. This seemingly fearless and direct action struck at one of the most potent sources of Gruffydd's power. It was ultimately of little avail, although Gruffydd himself may have been forced momentarily to seek refuge in the duke of Buckingham's lordship of Brecon in 1454; in August he was certainly at Hereford, where he fell foul of the escheator of Herefordshire after aiding a felon, Philip ab Hywel ap Rhys, of Knucklas in Maelienydd, one of York's lordships. After Gruffydd's arrest, he was found to have as much as 500 marks in his pocket. According to the Life of Sir Rhys ap Thomas, he was rescued from Hereford by the timely intervention of his son-in-law, Sir John Scudamore.[45]

About the same time, the Exchequer's auditors called a halt to Gruffydd's unauthorized expenditure on Carmarthen Castle, and the Council of the protectorate decided to review some of his judicial decisions. Gruffydd ap Dafydd ap Thomas, the erstwhile associate of Thomas ap Gruffydd ap Nicholas in 1439, and two of his servants had been placed in custody in Carmarthen Castle; now, in July 1454, the Council gave them a safe conduct 'out of tho parties whereas the said Gruffuth ap Nicholas hath any power or reule'. Despite this, they were assaulted by the brothers Thomas, Rhys and Dafydd ap Morgan ap Dafydd Fychan, three prominent Carmarthenshire officials who, we may safely assume, were in Gruffydd ap Nicholas's retinue.[46] After the duke of

[44] PRO, E28/83/63, 64, 37; Griffiths, *WHR*, II (1965), 218–19. Rhydderch is probably to be identified with Rhydderch ap Rhys ap Llywelyn Foethus, the cousin of Gruffydd ap Nicholas's mother, Jenet, daughter of Gruffydd ap Llywelyn Foethus: Griffiths, *Principality of Wales*, pp.153, 272, 321, 540, 548.

[45] See below p.168. Gruffydd may still have had the custody of the lands of Maud Clement (born *c*.1441) in 1454, including the manor of Llanfihangel Tal-y-llyn in the duke of York's lordship of Blaenllyfni (or Dinas), and half the manor of Yazor (Herefs.) which was held of York's retainer, Sir Walter Devereux. This may help to explain Gruffydd's presence in the eastern borderland in that year. See above p.14; D. E. Lowe, 'The Council of the Prince of Wales and the decline of the Herbert family during the reign of Edward IV', *BBCS*, XXVII, part 2 (1977), 278–82.

[46] Griffiths, *Principality of Wales*, pp.302, 303, 369, 384, 391, 301, 369, 383.

York's victory at the battle of St Albans, Gruffydd ap Dafydd ap Thomas again appealed to the royal Council, claiming that Gruffydd ap Nicholas had denounced him as one of York's servants and had threatened him with even worse treatment than before. By this stage, York had replaced Edmund Beaufort as constable of Carmarthen and Aberystwyth Castles, and at Kidwelly the steward was now Edward, the son of York's brother-in-law, Viscount Bourgchier. Gruffydd ap Dafydd ap Thomas, however, was not released from Carmarthen Castle and by the end of 1455 he was complaining once more, this time to Parliament, that the castles of Carmarthen, Cardigan, Aberystwyth, Kidwelly and Carreg Cennen were still in the hands of Gruffydd ap Nicholas and his sons and Rhydderch ap Rhys.[47] The severest of sanctions was threatened against Gruffydd ap Nicholas and his confederates if they did not vacate the fortresses: Gruffydd was required to give recognizances to the value of £3,000 for his good behaviour and his appearance before the king, and anyone who in future occupied the castles without authorization would be attainted of treason. Furthermore, the act of resumption of January–February 1456 deprived Gruffydd ap Nicholas of one of his most cherished grants, that of the castle, town and demesnes of Dinefwr, which were transferred on a twenty-year lease to Sir William Herbert of Raglan, one of York's most prominent tenants and councillors.

Within a few more months, Gruffydd had to contend with another rival, Jasper Tudor's elder brother Edmund, earl of Richmond, who was dispatched to south Wales to reassert the authority of the Lancastrian king against the growing power of the duke of York. Gruffydd and south Wales were thereby drawn irresistibly into the dynastic maelstrom that overwhelmed the Lancastrian monarchy and soon compromised Gruffydd's personal dominion. On 7 June 1456, Edmund was described as being 'at werre gretely in Wales' with Gruffydd, for the earl had taken control of Carmarthen Castle and had probably established himself in Pembrokeshire in place of his brother Jasper, the earl; in Kidwelly, his confrontation with Gruffydd caused uproar. There ensued two months later a veritable war between Earl Edmund and the duke of York's retainers from the eastern Marches, led by Sir William Herbert and Sir Walter Devereux, during which Edmund was made prisoner and Carmarthen and Aberystwyth Castles were recovered for York. This test of strength may have convinced Gruffydd that he had better come to terms with either the royalist party or the duke of York. He seems to have sought, first, 'the gode wille of Sir William Herbert yf he wold', but later in 1456 he came to an accommodation with Edmund Tudor.[48] A full pardon of treasons, rebellions and other offences was issued to

[47] Griffiths, *WHR*, II (1965), 223 and n.45.
[48] Westminster Abbey MS 5479* dorse.

Gruffydd and his sons Thomas and Owain on 26 October, and in 1456–7 Gruffydd was able to serve as mayor of the borough of Carmarthen. His choice of side proved a wise one, for after Earl Edmund died at Carmarthen in November 1456, it was his brother Jasper, acting on behalf of the Lancastrian king, who eventually triumphed in south Wales. On 21 April 1457 York formally surrendered the castles at Aberystwyth, Carmarthen and Carreg Cennen to Earl Jasper in return for £40 per annum, and Jasper installed himself at Tenby, where he proceeded to construct formidable fortifications that still largely stand today. As far as we know, Gruffydd ap Nicholas and his family were reconciled with him and henceforward supported his position in the west. Gruffydd's last known act – a significant one – was to make over to his son Owain (20 February 1460) the castle and lordship of Narberth and the lordship of Efelffre which he had acquired from York in 1449. At the same time, he retained control of Emlyn Uwch Cuch and denied the claims of Thomas Hopton's heir, Walter, who was steward of several Marcher lordships belonging to the duke of York.[49]

Gruffydd ap Nicholas, by this time an old man, is likely to have died soon afterwards. His son Thomas is recorded as farming the castle and borough of Dinefwr in 1460–1.[50] By then, Gruffydd's dominance in south-west Wales had been somewhat undermined by the intrusion of dynastic politics. The claim in the Life of Sir Rhys ap Thomas that he died at the battle of Mortimer's Cross on 2 February 1461, fighting beside York's heir, Edward, earl of March (soon to be King Edward IV), is likely to have been inserted as a satisfying fiction, designed to restore Gruffydd to centre-stage and on the winning side. There is no independent evidence that he lived so long, and no poet commemorated a heroic death in battle to complete the poetic tributes to him. Yet for a decade and more in the 1440s and early 1450s, he had wielded unchallenged power in much of west and south-west Wales, and not always with due regard for the law or the interests of the king and his subjects. With few effective mechanisms available to monitor and correct his actions, he enjoyed a dominance unequalled even by that of his grandson, Sir Rhys ap Thomas, after 1485. When his great-great-grandson, Rhys ap Gruffydd, acted in a similarly arbitrary fashion in Henry VIII's reign, he discovered that times had changed and so had the nature of provincial government. Rhys ap Gruffydd was led to the scaffold, whilst Gruffydd ap Nicholas probably died in his bed. His body was laid in an alabaster tomb which was accorded a place of honour before St Francis's image in the Grey Friars' Church, Carmarthen. The

---

[49] NLW, Slebech 279; Griffiths, *WHR*, II (1965), 228; Lloyd, *History of Carmarthenshire*, I, 240; *CPR, 1452–61*, p.552; Johnson, *Duke Richard of York*, p.233.
[50] Griffiths, *Principality of Wales*, p.253.

body and the tomb disappeared after the friary was dissolved by Henry VIII.[51]

[51] College of Arms H.8 f.25 (1530).

Elidir ap Rhys

Elidir Ddu

Philip

Gwilym

Rhys

Nicholas = Jenet (or Sioned), dau. of Gruffydd ap Llewelyn Foethus

Gruffydd = (1) Mabli, dau. of Maredudd ab Henry Dwnn, (2) Margaret, dau. of Sir Thomas Perrot, (3) Jane, dau. of Jankyn ap Rhys

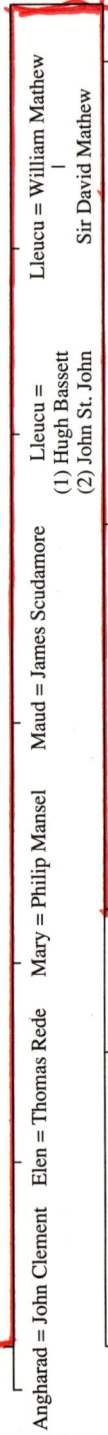

Angharad = John Clement   Elen = Thomas Rede   Mary = Philip Mansel   Maud = James Scudamore   Lleucu =   Lleucu = William Mathew
                                                                                                    (1) Hugh Bassett   Sir David Mathew
                                                                                                    (2) John St. John

Margaret = Jankyn ap Rhys   Rhys   Owain = Alison, dau. of Henry Malefant   Thomas = (1) Elizabeth, dau. of Sir John Gruffydd   John
                                              Morris   (2) Jenet, dau. of Henry Malefant

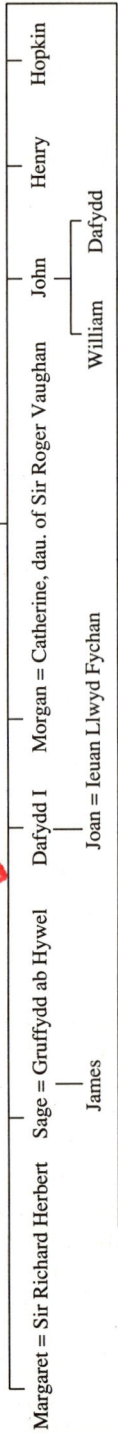

Margaret = Sir Richard Herbert   Sage = Gruffydd ab Hywel   Dafydd I   Morgan = Catherine, dau. of Sir Roger Vaughan   John   Henry   Hopkin
                                        James   Joan = Ieuan Llwyd Fychan   William   Dafydd

Sir Rhys ap Thomas   John   John = Elizabeth, dau. of Sir Thomas Vaughan
(d.1525)

Sir Thomas Jones

Select Pedigree of the Family of Sir Rhys ap Thomas

2

A Family of Renegades

The decades of Yorkist rule were a period of relative eclipse for the sons and grandsons of Gruffydd ap Nicholas. We cannot be certain of their detailed fortunes in these years, or of social developments in south-west Wales more generally. It is true that the royal administration in Carmarthenshire, Cardiganshire and Kidwelly was sustained by locally appointed officials in commote and cantref, lordship and shire, even in the most disturbed years. But behind the common phrases and bland statements of account rolls were communities – especially in Cardiganshire – that were reluctant to pay rents, courts that were often suspended and records that were occasionally destroyed.[1] It is true that the government of the principality and of Kidwelly was committed to staunch Yorkists like Sir William Herbert of Raglan, who was appointed justiciar and chamberlain of south Wales for life on 8 May 1461; John Dwnn of Kidwelly, appointed steward of Kidwelly for life from 14 August 1461 and constable of Carmarthen and Aberystwyth Castles for life from 9 September; Henry Dwnn, who became receiver of Kidwelly and constable of Kidwelly Castle for life on 21 November 1461; and William Herbert, the justiciar's bastard brother, who was appointed constable of Cardigan Castle from 2 August 1461. Yet in the confusion of these years, the sons of Gruffydd ap Nicholas avoided arrest (or worse).[2]

The eldest, Rhys, may have predeceased his father, since there is no reference to him after 1450 and no poem appears to have been addressed to him; but his family continued to live at the old family home at Crug until the mid-seventeenth century.[3] Owain, the second son, lived at

[1] Griffiths, thesis cited, pp.552–7.
[2] Somerville, *Duchy of Lancaster*, I, 640–2; Griffiths, *Principality of Wales*, pp.155–6, 186, 203, 219, 238, 277, 282, 287.
[3] NLW MS 1602 D f.204–5 (Jones, *TCASFC*, XXIX [1939], 30); F. Jones, *Historic Carmarthenshire Homes and Their Families* (Carmarthen, 1987), p.44.

Bryn-y-Beirdd, a substantial house opposite Carreg Cennen Castle on the northern bank of the Cennen River; he married Alison, daughter of the Pembrokeshire squire, Henry Malefant, presumably after he had begun to extend the family's influence southwards in the 1440s. The third son, Thomas, 'was owner of Neewtowne, built by Gr. ap Nicholas, for he was the youngest sonne. He attayned [through his wife, Elizabeth Gruffydd,] to the lordshipp of Llansadwrn and buylt Abermarlesse . . .'[4]

Political power was concentrated in the hands of the Herbert-Dwnn oligarchy, but sustained social control demanded constant attention to military security and local administration. Thomas and Owain ap Gruffydd ap Nicholas fought beside Jasper Tudor on the losing side at the battle of Mortimer's Cross on 2 February 1461, and in the months that followed resistance to the Yorkist regime in west Wales crystallized around them.[5] Sir William Herbert was commanded to pacify the region: on 24 and 28 September, he took oaths of loyalty from the communities of Carmarthenshire and Cardiganshire, which conceded 800 marks and 600 marks respectively, ostensibly to mark Edward IV's accession. Herbert and his retinue went further and successfully expelled the rebels from most of the king's castles during the winter of 1461–2 (for which the justiciar-chamberlain was paid £137. 6s. 8d. on 8 January) and Carmarthen's fortress was extensively repaired.[6] Carreg Cennen Castle proved a harder nut to crack. Thomas and Owain held out in this fortress, which commanded countryside especially familiar to them; it required a 200-strong force from Raglan, commanded by the justiciar-chamberlain's younger brother, Sir Richard Herbert, and their step-brother, Sir Roger Vaughan, to negotiate its submission. By 1 May 1462, Thomas and Owain had surrendered, and firm measures were taken, first, to install a garrison of eighteen soldiers and, then, to engage a large work-force of 500 engineers and labourers, armed with bars, picks and crowbars, to dismantle the castle's fortifications during the following three months.[7] It was never occupied again.

The government was determined to deny Thomas and Owain a focus for their resistance after the justiciar's men had withdrawn, though the price of Carreg Cennen's submission may have been their continued freedom. To root the brothers out of the countryside and fasten Yorkist

[4] NLW, Llanstephan 130 D f.21 (the quotation, 1 March 1595, correcting Jones, *TCASFC*, XXIX (1939), 30); NLW MS 1602 D f.205 (*c*.1609–30). See Jones, *Historic Homes*, p.17; Bartrum, *300–1400*, II, 330; *1400–1500*, VIII, 1256. After Elizabeth Gruffydd died, Thomas married Alison's sister, Jenet.

[5] H. T. Evans, *Wales and the Wars of the Roses* (Cambridge, 1915), p.124; J. H. Harvey (ed.), *William Worcestre: Itineraries* (Oxford, 1969), pp.202–3.

[6] PRO, SC6/1224/6 m.6–8.

[7] Ibid., 1224/7 m.6; H. M. Colvin *et al.*, *The History of the King's Works: The Middle Ages* (3 vols., London, 1963), II, 602; J. M. Lewis, *Carreg Cennen Castle* (new edn., Cardiff, 1990). The fine imposed on Owain and Thomas at the Carmarthenshire great sessions in 1463 was presumably related to this incident: PRO, SC6/1169/1 m.7.

rule upon it was much more difficult. Throughout the 1460s the local population seems to have been divided in its loyalties; the execution of justice was disorganized, and the collection of revenue often disrupted. At Dryslwyn in 1464 an uprising took place. We know very little about it and still less about who was behind it, though one of the ringleaders was Philip Mansel of Oxwich in Gower, who was attainted for his treason. He was married to Thomas's sister, Mary, and had accompanied Thomas and his brother at Mortimer's Cross in 1461.[8] The rising may have been part – perhaps even the origin – of the feud between Thomas ap Gruffydd ap Nicholas and Henry ap Gwilym, of Cwrt Henry in the commote of Catheiniog, which the poet Lewys Glyn Cothi and the author of the Life of Sir Rhys ap Thomas described, for both men are recorded as farming the castle and borough of Dryslwyn in 1464–5.[9] Nothing further is heard of Thomas in south Wales for almost a decade thereafter.

This may have been the moment when (as the Life again records) Thomas and one of his younger sons, Rhys, decided to escape to Burgundy, joining other Lancastrian exiles there. If family tradition and sixteenth-century pedigrees are to be trusted, this visit was a significant episode in Thomas's career, during which he entered the service of Philip the Good (died 1467) and Charles the Rash (died 1477), successively dukes of Burgundy. It is said that he formed a liaison with a high-born Burgundian lady of the ducal line, and that both he and Rhys (born about 1449) attended the rich and cultivated ducal court.[10] It is interesting to note that a kinsman of Thomas on his mother's side was John Dwnn of Kidwelly. A Yorkist supporter and one of Edward IV's lieutenants in south Wales, he knew Burgundy well in the 1460s and 1470s, and he accompanied Margaret of York to Bruges for her wedding with Charles the Rash in 1468. Is it fanciful to suppose that, despite their differing political allegiances, he eased his cousin's reception in Burgundy, which welcomed a number of Lancastrian exiles and Yorkist envoys and exiles in these years, and secured for him and Rhys ap Thomas an honourable entreé to the ducal service?[11]

[8] Evans, *Wales and the Wars of the Roses*, pp.151–2; *William Worcestre: Itineraries*, pp.202–3; Bartrum, *300–1400*, II, 330; *RP*, V, 511–12.

[9] Griffiths, *Principality of Wales*, p.266; see below p.174.

[10] See below p.172; Bartrum, *1400–1500*, IV, 643 and note f.

[11] M. Ballard, 'An expedition of English archers to Liège in 1467, and the Anglo-Burgundian marriage alliance', *Nottingham Medieval Studies*, XXXIV (1990), 157, 167–8, 172–4, notes the presence of Lancastrian exiles in Burgundy, including in 1467–70 'Jehan Auwain', who is plausibly identified with John ab Owain, escheator of Carmarthenshire in 1432–5 and 1457–61 (Griffiths, *Principality of Wales*, pp.322, 324). The escheator was associated with Gruffydd ap Nicholas on one occasion (1433) and he benefited from the attainder of Richard, duke of York in 1459 by securing the chief offices in the lordship of Narberth (29 May 1460). I am grateful to Mr Ballard for his advice.

In Wales, Thomas's elder sons, especially Morgan and Henry, continued to be thorns in the side of the Yorkist king, though Harlech Castle in Merioneth was the main focus of resistance. Several of Lewys Glyn Cothi's poems, lauding the fortitude and prowess of Morgan, Dafydd, Henry and Jankyn ap Thomas, may have been composed in the years following the departure of their father and brother to Burgundy. Morgan especially was commended as his family's champion, and he was counselled to cherish the support of his brothers and of south Wales more generally. An allusion to areas of conflict that included Dublin, Kent and the country between Alnwick Castle and Berwick-on-Tweed suggests a political context of Lancastrian plottings after 1461. Reference to Morgan sweeping the enemy from western Pembrokeshire, and to the prospect of north and south Wales rallying behind his ravens, may reflect Sir William Herbert's tightening grip on south-west Wales during the 1460s.[12] During Herbert's campaign in July and August 1468, culminating in the capture of the last major Lancastrian outpost, Harlech Castle, on 14 August, Morgan and his brother Henry, and their uncle Owain ap Gruffydd ap Nicholas and Owain's son, Maurice, were singled out as renegade leaders. On 14 July they were specifically excluded from a general pardon issued by King Edward as an enticement to surrender.[13]

Taking advantage of the temporary collapse of Herbert hegemony following the death of Sir William (since 1468 earl of Pembroke) after the battle of Edgecote on 26 July 1469, the brothers Morgan and Henry seized Carmarthen and Cardigan Castles. On 16 December, the king's brother, Richard, duke of Gloucester (born 1452), was empowered to recover them; that he was also authorized to offer a pardon is a measure of the regime's feeble hold on a region in which the family of Thomas ap Gruffydd ap Nicholas was still a force to be reckoned with, even though it was denied administrative authority by the Yorkists.[14] On 6 January 1470 a powerful commission headed by Gloucester was issued for south Wales; on 7 February the duke was appointed justiciar and chamberlain during the minority of the new earl of Pembroke, William Herbert II; on 18 June he was certainly at Carmarthen holding a meeting of the great sessions.[15] This visit may be the occasion when, according to Lewys Glyn Cothi, the king's brother, accompanied by 'a duke' from the borders of Gwent (perhaps the young duke of Buckingham, Henry Stafford), had an encounter with four of Thomas's sons, Morgan,

[12] E. R. Ll. Davies, thesis cited, pp.92–6; *Poetical Works of Lewis Glyn Cothi*, pp.145–50. See C. D. Ross, *Edward IV* (London, 1974), pp.45–63, and N. Davis (ed.), *Paston Letters and Papers of the Fifteenth Century* (2 vols., Oxford, 1971–6), II, 287.
[13] PRO, C67/46 m.38; Evans, *Wales and the Wars of the Roses*, pp.168–9.
[14] *CPR, 1467–77*, pp.180–1.
[15] Ibid., p.198; Griffiths, *Principality of Wales*, pp.158, 186; NLW MS 11723 E m.1; R. Horrox, *Richard III: A Study of Service* (Cambridge, 1989), pp.33–6.

Dafydd, Henry and Hopkin, together with their Basset, Rede and Mansel kinsmen, at Glasfryn, a location that can be identified with Cefnglasfryn, near Abermarlais. That Rhys ap Thomas is not mentioned may reflect his and his father's continuing absence in Burgundy.[16] Gloucester's intervention represented an assertion of Yorkist authority at the highest level, though it may be doubted whether it achieved much beyond discouraging another uprising.

The Readeption of King Henry VI (from 3 October 1470 to 11 April 1471) is likely to have been welcomed by Thomas's sons; indeed, Morgan and Henry, and their uncle, Owain, and his son, Maurice, who had all been denied a pardon by Edward IV in July 1468, received full pardon for their activities from Henry VI on 23 March 1471. Yet when Henry VI's regime finally collapsed, Morgan ap Thomas's loyalties were tested once too often: he was now prepared to obey Edward IV's commission to lay siege to Jasper Tudor and his nephew, Henry Tudor, earl of Richmond, in Pembroke Castle, to which they had fled. Tudor chroniclers from Polydore Vergil onwards (as well as the Life of Sir Rhys ap Thomas) record Morgan's siege by ditch and trench. But after eight days, his brother Dafydd arrived to help Jasper and Henry Tudor escape to Tenby and the open sea. To quote Polydore Vergil,

> Therle departyd from thence to Pembrowghe, whom incontinent Morgan Thomas, sent by king Edward, besegyd, and kept in with diche and trenche that he might not escape; but the viijth day folowing he was delyveryd from that distres by Davyd, broother to the sayd Morgan, hys assuryd faythfull frind, and departyd furthwith to a towne by the sea syde caulyd Tynby . . .[17]

Loyalty to the Lancastrian monarchy did not command family solidarity. Not unlike his grandfather, Morgan ap Thomas placed his own survival and future career in the forefront of his calculations, at least in the immediate aftermath of Lancaster's fall. Expectations of victory in poems addressed by Lewys Glyn Cothi to Thomas ap Gruffydd's sons, Dafydd and Henry, may date from the months of Lancastrian hope in 1470–1. After having played a part in the civil tumult for several years – for eight summers in Henry's case – success seemed within their grasp, and Lewys expected to hear soon that

[16] *Poetical Works of Lewis Glyn Cothi*, pp.167–9; Bartrum, *300–1400*, II, 330. Alternatively, the 'duke' may be an inaccurate reference to William Herbert II, earl of Pembroke, whose position in south Wales was effectively assumed by Gloucester during the earl's minority.

[17] PRO, C67/47 m.7; H. Ellis (ed.), *Three Books of Polydore Vergil's English History* (Camden Society, 1884), p.155; H. Ellis (ed.), *Hall's Chronicle of the Union of the Two Noble and Illustre Famelies of Lancastre and York, 1548* (London, 1809), pp.302–3; H. Ellis (ed.), *Holinshed's Chronicles*, III (London, 1808), 328; see below p.179.

Dafydd had been knighted and awarded the Lancastrian SS collar. Such hopes were dashed by the flight of Jasper and Henry Tudor; at least Dafydd, at Pembroke, maintained his loyalty to them.[18]

If, as seems likely, Thomas ap Gruffydd ap Nicholas and his son Rhys returned from Burgundy at about this time, in the hope of finding Henry VI still on the English throne (the Life claims that 'an accident' also led Thomas to return to Wales), they would surely have been bitterly disappointed to discover that Edward IV ruled again and that south-west Wales was more quiescent after the collapse of the brief Lancastrian restoration.[19] Thomas, according to tradition, had his own passage of arms with the forces of the new justiciar-chamberlain, William Herbert II, earl of Pembroke, who succeeded to these offices as his father's heir on 29 August 1471 at the age of about sixteen. Pembroke is known to have visited west Wales in May 1471 and again in September 1480, and he is likely to have accompanied Anthony Wydeville, Earl Rivers, the prince of Wales's chief counsellor, when he visited Carmarthen and Cardigan for the great sessions in 1474. The encounter between Pembroke's men and Thomas ap Gruffydd ap Nicholas may have occurred during this latter visit. In an engagement at Pennal in southern Merioneth, Thomas was killed. Certain pedigree compilers have left an interesting account of his end. One of the earliest, writing on 1 March 1595, noted Thomas's antagonism towards 'lorde Herbert', presumably William Herbert, the first earl who died in 1469; how the 'Erle of Pembrooke', probably the second earl, seized his house at Abermarlais and goaded Thomas into retaliating from his refuge at Harlech; and how Thomas died before the earl could track him down, and was secretly buried.

> Thomas ap gr proved a valiant man and fell out with the lorde Herbert and fled to Harlegh Castle, and there Died . . . The Erle of Pembrooke seised Abermarles, and as his steward was keping Coorte at Maes gwdyn, sodainlye Thomas ap Gr Came from Harlech with 40 horse, and tooke the Stewarde and hanged him there in a wch whereof the place tooke the name [The noose's field]. Whereupon the Erle sware he wold see Thomas ap Gr hanged, and therefore when he came to Harlech and laide seige to the Castle; and heeringe that Thomas ap Gr was dead, he made inquisition where his bodie was buried, meaninge to hange his bodie to save his oath. But Thomas ap Gr his ffriendes having intelligence of the Erles meaning, stale awaie his bodie out of the grave, and conveyed yt XXX miles of and buryd yt secretly.

[18] For another reason for Morgan's attitude, see above p.5.

[19] It may be significant that John ab Owain (if he is identifiable with Jehan Auwain in Burgundian service) seems to have returned to south Wales by 27 August 1471, when (as a gentleman) he was exempted from the pardon offered to other Lancastrian fugitives there. Ballard, *Nottingham Med. Stud.*, XXX (1990), cited above n.11.

Another writer shortly afterwards was a little more precise and added that the secret burial took place among the fabled army of saints on Bardsey Island.[20]

'The History of the Gwydir Family', written by Sir John Wynn between 1580 and 1616, records the particular circumstances of Thomas's death at Pennal, a good distance south of Harlech and just across the River Dyfi from Cardiganshire:

> Some affirme John ap medyth [a kinsman of Sir John Wynn's forebears] to have bene at a fielde in Penyal for Tho' Gruffith, which field was fought betweene Thomas gruffith ap Nicolas and Henry ap gwilim; and the earle of Pembrookes captaynes where Thomas ap gruffith gott the field, but received there his deathes wounde.[21]

This account suggests that the encounter was part of the feud between Thomas and Henry ap Gwilym, who evidently embraced the Yorkist regime in Carmarthenshire and was farming Dryslwyn Castle and borough in the 1470s. According to the Life, Thomas was severely wounded at Pennal by Dafydd Goch, whom he killed, and was finally dispatched by 'some base fellow (a servant noe doubt, or friend of the others)'. Dafydd Goch appears to have been a Yorkist servant, who had been rewarded by Edward IV with Stapleton, in the lordship of Maelienydd, in January 1462.[22] In a poem written soon afterwards, Dafydd Llwyd, who lived at nearby Mathafarn, added that Thomas died on Good Friday; but he triumphantly proclaimed that the noble oak of Thomas's family was not uprooted by his slaying, implying that some of its branches survived.[23]

The date of the encounter at Pennal is not certainly known, but it is likely to have occurred between 1472 and 1474. On 5 November 1472, Rhys ap Thomas, as one of his father's heirs, received a general pardon for offences, and for entering his inheritance without a licence, and for all monies owed to the king prior to 30 October.[24] This suggests that Thomas ap Gruffydd ap Nicholas was either dead – perhaps fairly recently – or had been deprived of his possessions, and that more than one of his sons were still living. The escheator of Carmarthenshire had custody of Thomas's property as 'new escheat' in 1473–4, prior to its passing to his heirs. This would indicate that Thomas died in 1473 or

[20] Griffiths, *Principality of Wales*, pp.158, 187; NLW, Llanstephan 130 D f.21; NLW MS 1602 D f.204 (*c.*1609–30) (the version in Jones, *TCASFC*, XXIX (1939), 30, needs correction); F. Devon (ed.), *Issues of the Exchequer, Henry III–Henry VI* (Record Commission, 1837), p.495.
[21] J. Ballinger (ed.), *The History of the Gwydir Family* (Cardiff, 1927), p.27, whose punctuation is preferred to that of J. G. Jones, *The History of the Gwydir Family and Memoirs* (Llandysul, 1990), p.27.
[22] See below p.177; Griffiths, *Principality of Wales*, pp.265–6; Evans, *Wales and the Wars of the Roses*, pp.147–8. For two poems to Dafydd, see Jones, *Lewys Glyn Cothi*, pp.39–40; *Poetical Works of Lewis Glyn Cothi*, pp.141–4.
[23] Richards, *Gwaith Dafydd Llwyd*, pp.132–4; Bartrum, *1400–1500*, IV, 643–4.
[24] *CPR, 1467–77*, p.360; PRO, PSO 1/36/1891.

1474, though the administrative procedures of shire government may have been less than swift and efficient in these uncertain times.[25]

Circumstances intensified the isolation of Gruffydd ap Nicholas's sons and grandsons from official sources of power in west Wales during the 1470s. On 20 November 1472 the two-year-old prince of Wales, Edward of Westminster, was formally granted the revenues of the principality of Wales, including Carmarthenshire and Cardiganshire. During the next four years, and by stages in response to political circumstances rather than any long-term plan, the prince's Council gradually grew in size and was entrusted with more extensive powers of governmental oversight – and not simply in the principality – than had been commonly exercised by the councils of princes in the past.[26] These developments did not involve major structural changes in the principality, but the prince's advisers did seek to make his control of the western shires more effective. His Council remained a somewhat distant authority, usually operating from Ludlow Castle, but some of the councillors and trusted administrators, including several of high rank, regularly made the journey to Carmarthen and Cardigan in most years, both to hold meetings of the great sessions and to demonstrate more generally the reality of regal authority. Among them were Anthony Wydeville, Earl Rivers, the prince's uncle and most senior counsellor; Hugh Huntley, a highly experienced administrator, especially in the duchy of Lancaster's Welsh lordships, who presided at the Carmarthenshire and Cardiganshire sessions in 1475 and 1477; and John Herbert, an illegitimate kinsman of the second earl of Pembroke. At the same time, efficient administrators loyal to the Yorkist regime were acting in the earl's place as deputy-chamberlain of south Wales: these men included Huntley and John Herbert and, in 1476–7, Richard Mynors, an usher of Prince Edward's chamber; Sir John Dwnn, the steward of Kidwelly and constable of Kidwelly and Carmarthen Castles; and Sir John Morgan, of Tredegar in the Stafford lordship of Newport, who was acting as chamberlain in 1473–5.[27] William Herbert II, earl of Pembroke, might be the justiciar-chamberlain and steward of Cantrefmawr and Cardiganshire, but the prince's Council directed affairs and its authority extended into a number of the Pembrokeshire lordships, not least because the earl was young and of lesser calibre than his vigorous father.

[25] PRO, SC6/1169/6 m.9.

[26] Griffiths, 'Wales and the March', pp.159–62; Lowe, *BBCS*, XXVI, part 2 (1977), 278–97; idem, 'Patronage and politics: Edward IV, the Wydevills and the Council of the Prince of Wales, 1471–83', ibid., XXIX, part 3 (1981), 545–73.

[27] Griffiths, *Principality of Wales*, pp.158–62, 186–9, 203, 277. Sir John Dwnn's eldest brother, Robert, became constable of Cardigan Castle on 27 June 1471, following the execution of Sir Roger Vaughan by Jasper Tudor at Chepstow (ibid., pp.219–21).

This conciliar dominance was intensified in 1479, partly in response to the damaging dispute between Herberts and Vaughans which had divided Pembrokeshire since the winter of 1473–4 and enabled rebels to seize Pembroke Castle in 1478. Riots further east in Cantrefmawr before and during 1479 were a reminder of the region's instability, and at Aberystwyth Castle to the north, where the staunch Yorkist, Sir Walter Devereux, was constable from 1463 until 1483, a new prison was constructed in May 1479.[28] Later in the year, a bold attempt was made to bring reconciliation and peace to Pembroke. Efforts had been made to end the disputes among prominent Yorkists since January–February 1476; but the undertaking of 21 March 1479, whereby the earl of Pembroke and Sir Walter Herbert were forbidden to cross the River Severn into Wales for one year, was the prelude to the earl's removal from the justiciarship and chamberlainship of south Wales and to his exchange of the earldom of Pembroke for that of Huntingdon by 4 July 1479.[29] At the queen's request, Edward IV was eventually persuaded to pardon all the contestants on 18 November 1479.[30] In that year, too, a conscious effort was made to commend the regime to the local populace of Carmarthenshire and Cardiganshire, by offering for the first time to pay officers of the commotes an annual fee.[31]

Not only was the county of Pembroke (with the title of earl) transferred to the prince 'for the reformation of the wele publique, restful governaunce and mynystration of justice in the said parties of South Wales', but the partnership in government of Huntley and Mynors had been formalized a few months earlier when the former replaced Pembroke as justiciar of south Wales and as steward of Cantrefmawr and the lordship of Llanstephan on 16 April 1479, and the latter was appointed chamberlain of south Wales and steward of Cardiganshire the following day.[32] Henceforward, and for the next four years at least, they governed the principality shires with growing confidence, aided from time to time (especially at the first great sessions to follow, in June 1479) by others of the prince's commissioners, including Bishop Robert Tully of St David's, Sir William Young of Shropshire (who was also steward of Haverford from 1479 and of Pembroke from 1480), Thomas Limerick and John Twyneowe, two

[28] Ibid., pp.238–9; PRO, SC6/1225/7 m.6; 1210/6.
[29] P. M. Barnes, 'The Chancery *Corpus Cum Causa* file, 10–11 Edward IV', in R. F. Hunnisett and J. B. Post (eds.), *Medieval Legal Records* (London, 1978), pp.439–40. Dr Lowe (*BBCS*, XXVII, part 2 (1977), 293–5) made the important point that although the act of resumption of 1473 did not result in Herbert's being deprived of the justiciarship and chamberlainship, its provisions were a reminder of his vulnerability until his actual removal from west Wales in 1479.
[30] PRO, PSO 1/46/2359 B and C, 2384, 2386; *CPR, 1467–77*, p.429; Lowe, *BBCS*, XXIX, part 3 (1981), 562–3.
[31] PRO, SC6/1169/9; 1163/9 (1478–9).
[32] Lowe, *BBCS*, XXVII, part 2 (1977), 293–5; Griffiths, *Principality of Wales*, pp.159–61, 283, 189, 287.

Gloucestershire lawyers who were connected with the household of John
Alcock, bishop of Worcester from 1476 and president of the prince's
Council, and John ap Rhys, the prince's attorney-general in all his
lordships and counties in the south-west of Wales. Huntley and Mynors
also had authority in the lordships of Pembroke and Haverford from
about 1477 onwards. Despite the extraordinarily wide-ranging powers
conceded by Richard, duke of Gloucester who was Protector of the
realm following the death of Edward IV, to his collaborator, Henry
Stafford, duke of Buckingham, on 16 May 1483, it is possible that
Mynors continued in effective charge of the financial management of
Carmarthenshire and Cardiganshire until the accession of Henry Tudor.

This reorganization of Yorkist government in the western parts of
Wales allowed no place for Gruffydd ap Nicholas's family in the 1470s
and early 1480s. They had every justification for resenting their
treatment and, in retrospect, it may seem short-sighted to have excluded
from the greater administrative, political and financial offices the élite of
local society. The justiciars, the chamberlains and the constables of the
three major castles of the principality – Carmarthen, Cardigan and
Aberystwyth – were rarely in the hands of local men at all during these
years. At Dinefwr, with which Gruffydd ap Nicholas's family had special
ties, one of the Herbert circle, John Vaughan, was in charge in the mid-
1470s. For the remainder of the period 1465–76, Henry ap Gwilym's
brother, Lewis (or Llywelyn) ap Gwilym ap Thomas, and their nephew,
Morgan ap Rhys ap Gwilym, were farming the borough, castle and
royal demesnes at Dinefwr.[33] The replacement of Thomas ap Gruffydd
ap Nicholas and his sons at both Dryslwyn and Dinefwr by Henry ap
Gwilym and his kinsmen was a particular irritant, doubtless turned into
a fierce feud that culminated in Thomas's slaying.

The family seems to have been further crippled by personal
misfortune. Not too long after Thomas ap Gruffydd ap Nicholas's death,
his sons Morgan and Dafydd followed him to the grave, neither leaving
a male heir. According to Lewys Glyn Cothi, in a poem which amounts
to an elegant request to Jankyn ap Thomas for a brigandine for
Gruffydd Basset, a kinsman of Jankyn's and the poet's friend, Jankyn
was a staunch defender of the Vale of Tywi who kept a veritable arsenal
of weapons at his home; but he too had no children and seems to have
disappeared from the scene. Their brother John I may not have left any
legitimate heirs either, and his illegitimate brother, also called John
(II), seems to have settled in Gower. Another bastard son named John
(III), whom the pedigrees cite as having been born to Thomas ap
Gruffydd's Burgundian paramour, was doubtless too young to take an
active role in affairs before 1485; at some stage, he married a daughter of
Sir Thomas Vaughan of Bredwardine (Herefs.), where he and his family

[33] Ibid., pp.252–4.

resided until his son, Sir Thomas Jones, returned to claim part of the patrimonial inheritance after the attainder of Rhys ap Gruffydd in 1531. Of Thomas ap Gruffydd ap Nicholas's legitimate sons, only Rhys (born about 1449), who probably returned from Burgundy with his father early in the 1470s, seems to have been capable of heading the family and bearing the banner of three ravens.[34] Thus, in the decade before 1483, Yorkist rule was imposed on Carmarthenshire and Cardiganshire by the prince's Council with reasonable effectiveness. The threat from Gruffydd ap Nicholas's family had been curbed and its position in the community neutralized.

The duke of Buckingham received extraordinary powers throughout Wales on 16 May 1483, including the custody of all royal castles and uninhibited powers of appointing local officials. He even had considerable latitude in disposing of the royal revenues: auditors were instructed to approve whatever expenditure he might incur.[35] A week later, he received complementary authority to 'supervise all our subjects' and to array them armed whenever the king should require them.[36] During Buckingham's five months of supreme power, there was no opportunity for Rhys ap Thomas and his relatives to recover the family's earlier position. Buckingham's treason and rebellion in October 1483 caused Richard III to review his policy towards Wales. His delicate position dictated that he enlist only those on whom he could safely rely, but such servants were not easy to find in west Wales. Sir John Dwnn was retained in Kidwelly, and Richard Mynors seems to have resumed his duties as chamberlain of south Wales. Otherwise, King Richard chose to reinstate William Herbert II, earl of Huntingdon (and soon to marry the king's bastard daughter Catherine) as justiciar of south Wales on 15 November 1483. Richard further dispatched his henchman, Sir James Tyrell, of Gipping in Suffolk, with a retinue at least 140 strong. Their expenses were to be paid by Richard Mynors, which suggests that Tyrell was destined for the west; on 6 March 1484 Mynors was required to pay him £113. 14s. 6d. for fortifying Pembroke Castle.[37]

Practically the only source that reveals the attitude of Rhys ap Thomas towards Buckingham and Richard III is the later Life. It states that Rhys declined to involve himself in Buckingham's rebellion because of the animosity between the duke and Rhys's family.[38] If this were so, it

[34] *Poetical Works of Lewis Glyn Cothi*, pp.151–60; E. R. Ll. Davies, thesis cited, pp.100–4; Bartrum, *1400–1500*, IV, 643.

[35] PRO, PSO 1/56/2840, 2844; R. Horrox and P. W. Hammond (ed.), *British Library, Harleian Manuscript 433* (4 vols., London, 1979–83), I, 28–30; *CPR, 1476–85*, p.349; Somerville, *Duchy of Lancaster*, I, 640–2, 648.

[36] PRO, PSO 1/56/2841, 2843.

[37] Horrox, *Richard III*, p.209; *Harleian 433*, II, 114; Griffiths, *Principality of Wales*, pp.162, 189, 283, 287.

[38] See below p.195.

would have been an animosity shared by many prominent Welsh landowners in south-east Wales. Richard III, on the other hand, seems to have appreciated the wisdom of attracting local grandees to his side after his seizure of the throne, for on 4 February 1484 Rhys was granted for life an annuity of 40 marks by the king – apparently the first mark of Yorkist favour to any member of the family since 1465.[39] The absence of all records relating to the principality of south Wales during Richard's short reign may indicate that he was unsuccessful in his bid to impose his rule on Carmarthenshire and Cardiganshire.

By this stage, Henry Tudor was 'the central figure in the opposition to the new king'.[40] He, too, may have sought the support of Rhys's family, by attracting their erstwhile Lancastrian sympathies to the Tudor cause. According to the Life, Trahaearn ap Morgan of Kidwelly, a lawyer who was employed by those conspiring in Henry Tudor's interest, set out to persuade his friend Rhys ap Thomas to join them. Trahaearn, whose family hailed from the dead Buckingham's lordship of Newport, was usually referred to as Morgan of Kidwelly: he had married Jenet, the daughter of Henry Dwnn of Kidwelly (died 1469), though his family had had earlier connections thereabouts.[41]

Trahaearn sent word to France that both Rhys ap Thomas and John Savage, who may have been a Cheshireman and one of Lord Stanley's kinsmen, were willing to support another insurrection against King Richard, this time avowedly in Henry Tudor's favour.[42] Such a mission is borne out by Edward Hall in his chronicles completed in 1532 (and echoed by Raphael Holinshed). In this instance, Hall's testimony seems preferable in one respect to that of Polydore Vergil (followed by Richard Grafton), who names the emissary as John Morgan:

> But a better messenger came from John Morgan, a lawyer, who signyfyed the seme tyme that Richerd, by surname Thomas, a man of great service and valyant, and John Savage, were wholy geaven to erle Henryes affayres . . . (Polydore Vergil)

> But in the meane ceason, ther came to the Earle a more ioyfuller message from Morgan Kydwelly learned in the temporall lawe, whiche declared that Ryce ap Thomas, a man of no lesse valyauntnes then actyuitee, and Ihon Savage an approued capteyne, woulde with all their powre be partakers of his quarell.[43] (Edward Hall)

[39] *CPR, 1476–85*, p.406; *Harleian 433*, I, 112.

[40] Evans, *Wales and the Wars of the Roses*, pp.204–5.

[41] See below p.197. Trahaearn should be distinguished from Richard III's servant, Morgan Kidwelly, and from Trahaearn's own brother John, later bishop of St David's, and from his kinsman, John Morgan, who aided Henry when he landed in 1485. Horrox, *Richard III*, pp.86–7, 286–7; Evans, *Wales and the Wars of the Roses*, pp.216–18; Bartrum, *300–1400*, I, 200–1; *1400–1500*, III, 391, 394, 396; F. Jones, 'The Annals of Muddlescwm', *Carms. Antiquary*, XXI (1985), 11–26.

[42] Vergil, *English History*, p.215; *Hall's Chronicle*, p.410; see below p.198.

[43] Vergil, *English History*, p.217; H. Ellis (ed.), *John Hardyng's Chronicle . . . with the continuation by Richard Grafton* (London, 1812), p.541; *Hall's Chronicle*, p.410; *Holinshed's Chronicles*, III, 434.

According to the *Life*, Richard III took what may be thought a characteristic precaution, requiring Rhys to swear an oath of fidelity to the king and to hand over his only legitimate son, Gruffydd ap Rhys, as a hostage. These plausible demands rest squarely on the testimony of Rhys's descendant, Henry Rice, and some may be inclined to object that they were invented later to explain Rhys ap Thomas's delay in declaring publicly for Henry Tudor in 1485. Rhys's alleged response to the king is in the form of a letter, written from Carmarthen by the abbot of Talley on Rhys's behalf in 1484; the only version of it appears in the *Life*. Yet it is worth noting that Henry Rice claimed to have seen the letter himself before it was destroyed in the Whitehall fire of 1619, and in general his credentials as an archival historian are impressive. In his response, Rhys assured Richard III that he would guard Milford Haven as instructed, and he agreed to swear the required oath. But as for his son, who was between the ages of four and five, he begged the king to reconsider his demand. High-handed actions of this kind, which in Rhys's case threatened the integrity of a prominent Welsh family, may easily have inclined Rhys ap Thomas to be even more receptive to Morgan of Kidwelly's persuasions.[44]

From one point of view, the projected invasion of Henry Tudor was akin to earlier ventures during the past thirty years when generations of Rhys's family were urged to support one side or the other in the English dynastic quarrels. From another point of view, the circumstances of 1484–5 offered an opportunity for the family to repair its depressed fortunes and recover the social and political dominance it had once enjoyed in west Wales: that required the adaptation of earlier Lancastrian loyalties – and not a little courage.

The *Life of Sir Rhys ap Thomas* seeks to glorify its central character to the point of eulogy. At crucial points in its narrative, such as during 1483–5, its author inserted certain details relating to Rhys's career into a general narrative of his times of a sort that was available in sixteenth-century histories like those of Polydore Vergil and Edward Hall. And yet, Rhys's refusal to join the duke of Buckingham's rebellion against Richard III in October 1483 because (as the *Life* asserts) he resented Buckingham's ambition to dominate Carmarthenshire parallels the reaction of other Welshmen to the duke and their reluctance to join his rising.[45] Likewise, the claim that Henry Tudor sent appeals from Brittany to various people in England and Wales, including Rhys, is likely to be true, for it is hinted at in sources other than the *Life*. Such a letter was seen by one of Henry Rice's acquaintances, Sir Thomas Lake, James I's attorney-general, among the confiscated archives of

[44] See below p.199. For Richard's demand that Thomas, Lord Stanley place his son George, Lord Strange in the king's custody in July 1485, see Horrox, *Richard III*, p.323.
[45] Griffiths and Thomas, *The Making of the Tudor Dynasty*, pp.99–100; T. B. Pugh, *The Marcher Lordships of South Wales, 1415–1536: Select Documents* (Cardiff, 1963), pp.240–1.

Rhys's grandson in the basement of the Banqueting Hall of the Palace of Whitehall; when the building went up in flames in 1619, the letter was destroyed. The British Library, moreover, contains several copies of a similar letter, which is the only known communication from Henry Tudor to his friends in England and Wales before he landed in Milford Sound in August 1485.[46]

According to later writers, Trahaearn ap Morgan advised Henry Tudor to make straight for Wales as soon as possible in expectation of support. Such plans were jeopardized early in May 1485 when Savage was arrested at Pembroke, where he had been intriguing on Henry's behalf.[47] Polydore Vergil had opportunity to discuss the events of August 1485 with survivors of the Bosworth campaign who were still at Henry VII's court, including Christopher Urswick, Vergil's friend and one of Henry's intimates since the days of exile, and even with the king himself. But his description of the landing in Milford Sound and the march through Wales to Shrewsbury does not seem to have been based on the recollections of Welshmen who welcomed the pretender ashore. Rather does Vergil re-create the rumour-ridden atmosphere of un-certainty and apprehension that was bound to grip a small force of invaders unsure of their reception. Certain of the rumours concerned Rhys ap Thomas, who had seemingly signified to Henry his willingness to join the insurgents. Polydore Vergil does not record that Rhys met Henry near Dale on 7 August, or that he publicly welcomed him with a fine speech and placed his retinue at Henry's disposal (as the later Life asserts). It may be doubted whether that was logistically possible if Rhys were based in the Tywi Valley. Rather, in the first days of the enterprise in Wales, rumours were rife in Henry's camp that Rhys was cautious and his attitude ambivalent. At Haverford on 8 August, Henry 'understandeth that Rycherd Thomas and John Savage, with all ther force and frindes, dyd help king Richerd to thuttermost of ther power, clene contrary to that he was certyfyed of in Normandy'.[48]

The reality of the situation was rather different, for

> thinhabytants of Pembrough at the same very time comfortyd all ther dysmayed myndes, for they gave intelligence, by Arnold Butler, a valyant man, demanding forgeavene of ther former offences, that they wer ready to serve Jaspar ther erle.[49]

Rhys ap Thomas may have been cautious, reluctant to renounce openly his allegiance to Richard III; indeed, he may not have done so until just

---

[46] Griffiths and Thomas, *Tudor Dynasty*, p.115; see below p.212 n.8.

[47] Griffiths and Thomas, *Tudor Dynasty*, p.143; *Harleian 433*, III, 172–3; J. M. Williams, 'The Stanley Family of Lathom, *c.*1450–1504: a political study' (unpublished University of Manchester MA thesis, 1979), pp.237–9.

[48] Vergil, *English History*, p.216; D. Hay, *Polydore Vergil* (Oxford, 1952), p.207. Hall, Grafton and Holinshed note no significant differences.

[49] Vergil, *English History*, p.216.

a few days before Henry reached Shrewsbury. But this is not to deny the possibility that privately he resolved to join the insurgents as soon as he judged it wise to do so, and he may have communicated precisely that to Henry Tudor after his landing. It is even possible that this strategy was deliberately designed to deceive and confuse King Richard and his advisers, who were 250 miles away. Rhys and John Savage had good cause to fear Richard and his long arm in south Wales, where Richard Williams and Sir James Tyrell, his servants, were powerful.[50]

When Henry and his men approached Cardigan, worse rumours 'suddeynly spred throwgh the whole camp, thautor wherof was uncertayne': Sir Walter Herbert (*c*.1463–1507), the earl of Huntingdon's younger brother, was said to be at Carmarthen with a large army. Only when Henry's scouts returned did it become clear that 'ther was no hinderance to ther voyage immynent'.[51] If an army were assembled at Carmarthen, it was by no means certain to be overtly hostile to the pretender. In fact, 'a man of highe parentage', Richard Griffith, who may be identified with Richard ap Gruffydd ap John of upland Gower, arrived at Henry's encampment with his modest company. He had recently been with Sir Walter Herbert and Rhys ap Thomas, and his appearance among Henry's force 'did above the rest make them all mery'. Later that same day, John Morgan of Tredegar arrived, perhaps also from Herbert's and Rhys's army further east. He had been a royal official in Carmarthenshire and Cardiganshire during the 1470s and may have been in contact with Rhys at that time.[52] According to the Life, Rhys was friendly with both Richard Griffith and John Morgan, and their appearance in Henry's camp may have enabled Rhys to keep in touch with the pretender and negotiate the timing and terms of his own public desertion of the king.[53]

Rhys continued to shadow Henry's march, not without causing further apprehension among parts of Henry's army: 'he understoode by the scowtts that Harbert and Rycherd [ap Thomas] wer before him in armes.' Henry concluded that the time for Herbert and Rhys to declare their hand had come. At this point, Henry dispatched 'certane of his most faythfull servants with secrete messages' to those whom he considered his friends and supporters, to inform them of the route he intended to follow to 'passe over Severn, and throwgh Shropshire to go to London, and therfor desyryd them to mete him, with whom in place

---

[50] Griffiths and Thomas, *Tudor Dynasty*, p.143; Horrox, *Richard III*, pp.209–11. In a poem, Huw Pennant (*fl*.1465–1514) assumed that Rhys ap Thomas would support Henry once he landed in Wales, but we do not know whether or not he was writing with hindsight. E. P. Roberts, *Dafydd Llwyd o Fathafarn* (Caernarfon, 1981), p.30.

[51] Vergil, *English History*, pp.216–17. For Herbert's communication with Henry before the landing, see Griffiths and Thomas, *Tudor Dynasty*, pp.128–9.

[52] Vergil, *English History*, p.217; Grafton, p.541; *Hall's Chronicle*, p.410; *Holinshed's Chronicles*, III, 434–5; Bartrum, *1400–1500*, I, 200–1; II, 250; III, 391, 394.

[53] See below p.209.

and time convenyent he wold impart more of his intent'. That done, he
set off for Shrewsbury. Of Henry's servants, Christopher Urswick was
sent to Henry's mother (Lady Margaret Beaufort), the Stanleys and Sir
Gilbert Talbot; another messenger is likely to have sought out Sir
Walter Herbert and Rhys ap Thomas.[54] Always prudent and cautious,
Henry 'resolvyd to go agaynst them, and whan he had ether put them to
flight or receavyd them into his obedience to make haste against king
Richard'.[55] Edward Hall's chronicle goes further: according to Henry's
scouts, Sir Walter and Rhys intended 'to encountre wyth hys [Henry's]
armye and to stoppe their passage'. Grafton went further still: they were
'in a redynes to geue hym battail . . . he determyned to set vpon theim,
and either to put theim to flight, or els to make theim sweare homage and
feaultee unto hym, and to take theim with hym in his hoste against kyng
Richard'.[56]

   The routes which Henry and Rhys followed independently towards
Shrewsbury, where they met, can hardly have been chosen without a
measure of co-ordination. According to the Life, whose circumstantial
detail encourages belief, Rhys marched up the Tywi Valley to
Llandovery, then east to Brecon in the Usk Valley, and then northwards
to the neighbourhood of Welshpool. The eventual meeting between
Henry and Rhys is traditionally said to have taken place on Long
Mountain, the high ridge overlooking Welshpool from the east. There
both forces are thought to have spent the night, probably of 16 August.
The Tudor chroniclers are imprecise about the location of their meeting,
but the outcome is not in doubt. Take Polydore Vergil (and his
informants):

> whom Richerd Thomas met by the way [toward Shrewsbury] with a gret
> bande of soldiers, and with assuryd promysse of loyaltie yealdyd himself to
> his protection.[57]

This meeting had been preceded two days earlier by one or more
contacts between Henry and Rhys, presumably when Henry was
between Machynlleth, where he signed and dated a letter on 14 August,
and Welshpool.[58] This was a critical contact for both Henry and Rhys,
and for the future government of Wales.

> Two days before Henry had promyssyd to Richerd Thomas the
> perpetuall lyvetenantship of Wales, so that he wold coome under his

[54] Vergil, *English History*, p.217; Hay, *Polydore Vergil*, p.207; Griffiths and Thomas, *Tudor Dynasty*, pp.93, 101, 108–9, 112, 114–15, 119, 129, 172.
[55] Vergil, *English History*, p.217.
[56] *Hall's Chronicle*, p.411; *Holinshed's Chronicles*, III, 435; Grafton, p.542.
[57] Vergil, *English History*, p.217; *Hall's Chronicle*, p.411; Grafton, p.542; *Holinshed's Chronicles*, III, 435.
[58] Griffiths and Thomas, *Tudor Dynasty*, p.147.

obedience, which afterward when he had obtanyd the kingdom he geve lyberally.[59]

The exchange presumably took place by means of a messenger. Henry Tudor was nothing if not a political realist, but the extent of the royal favours bestowed on Rhys ap Thomas after Bosworth and the intimacy of the relationship between the two men do not suggest that Rhys's ultimate support for Henry was founded on naked ambition or plain bribery.

At Bosworth on 22 August, Rhys's aid was significant, presumably as one of Henry's leading commanders. Family tradition put his force at between 1,800 and 2,000 men, and they included a number of landowners and officials from Carmarthenshire and Cardiganshire, serving alongside the French and Scots who made up the bulk of Henry's army. A number of these Welshmen were rewarded with offices in the principality or the lordship of Kidwelly after the battle was over.[60] According to the 'Song of Lady Bessy', one of the Stanley family poem-sagas composed at the beginning of the sixteenth century, he had brought 8,000 'spears' with him – a likely exaggeration. Richard's battle-line began to break under pressure from Rhys ap Thomas and the 10,000 whom (the poem claims) he commanded – another exaggeration. This was the first and most graphic indication which Henry had yet received of the military abilities of his Welsh commander.[61] The supreme accolade of striking the blow that killed Richard III has been claimed for several in Henry's army. Guto'r Glyn, in his praise-poem addressed to Rhys after the battle was over, may be taken as implying that it was delivered by Rhys himself – 'killed the boar, destroyed his head'. This might be thought an excess of flattery on the part of an obsequious poet were it not for the fact that the Burgundian writer, Jean Molinet, noted that a Welshman delivered the final stroke with a halberd when Richard's horse was stuck in the marsh of the battlefield.[62] But one can go no further than that.

[59] Vergil, *English History*, p.217; *Hall's Chronicle*, p.411; *Holinshed's Chronicles*, III, 435; Grafton, p.542.

[60] Griffiths, *Principality of Wales*, pp.189–90, 203–4, 221, 276, 287–8, 308, 411, 494, 500–1, 516, 541, 552; Evans, *Wales and the Wars of the Roses*, pp.223–4; Somerville, *Duchy of Lancaster*, I, 640; Griffiths and Thomas, *Tudor Dynasty*, chs. 10–11.

[61] J. O. Halliwell (ed.), *Percy Soc. Publ.*, XX (1847), 33–42; J. W. Hales and F. J. Furnivall (eds.), *Bishop Percy's Folio Manuscript* (London, 1868), III, 259; Griffiths and Thomas, *Tudor Dynasty*, p.224.

[62] I. and J. Ll. Williams (eds.), *Gwaith Guto'r Glyn* (Cardiff, 1939), pp.263–4; E. W. Jones, 'Wales and Bosworth Field: selective historiography', *NLWJ*, XXI (1979), 51–2; J. A. Buchon (ed.), *Chroniques de Jean Molinet*, II (Paris, 1828), 409.

3

Sir Rhys ap Thomas

The accession of Henry Tudor heralded a revolution in Rhys ap Thomas's fortunes in Wales and offered him a prominent role on an even broader front in Tudor service. It is sometimes said that Henry VII failed to fulfil the promise made to Rhys before Bosworth that the Welshman would become 'chief gouernour of Wales' and enjoy its 'perpetuall lyvetenantship'. Yet apart from the king's own uncle, Jasper Tudor, no one received such commanding authority in large parts of Wales as Rhys did, and he, unlike Jasper, normally resided in south Wales and therefore took full opportunity to exercise his new powers. The chroniclers who recorded the king's promise also acknowledged this reality when they noted that Henry 'afterward when he had obtanyd the kingdom he gave lyberally to Rhys'.[1] Throughout his reign, Henry VII appreciated unswerving loyalty and he retained a particularly strong attachment to those who had sustained him in or before 1485. To expect a king who shrank from creating new peers to have ennobled his steadfast Welsh squire on Bosworth Field is unrealistic. To expect him to have conferred on Rhys the kind of all-embracing power in Wales and the English borderland that Henry Stafford, duke of Buckingham, enjoyed briefly under Richard III is to ignore the obligations which Henry owed to others with interests in Wales – his uncle Jasper and his stepfather, Thomas, Lord Stanley, amongst them – as well as the reluctance of a circumspect new king to follow the precedent of Buckingham's extraordinary commission. In these contexts, it would seem that Rhys ap Thomas had good reason to be content with his treatment after 1485.[2]

[1] Vergil, *English History*, p.217; *Hall's Chronicle*, p.410; Grafton, p.542; *Holinshed's Chronicles*, III, 435; see below p.46; W. Ll. Williams, 'A Welsh insurrection', *Y Cymmrodor*, XVI (1902), 6.

[2] J. M. Lloyd, 'The rise and fall of the House of Dinefwr (the Rhys family), 1430–1530' (University of Wales MA thesis, 1963), pp.18, 22–3. In other respects, this thesis is a valuable study of Sir Rhys ap Thomas, though it excludes an assessment of the Life and of contemporary poetry.

What Henry VII recognized in Rhys ap Thomas was that combination of military prowess, influence in south and west Wales, and personal loyalty in a crisis which had been crucial to Henry's seizure of the throne in August 1485. It underpins the testimonial in the *Anglica Historia* of Polydore Vergil, who could easily have encountered Rhys face to face at the court of the first two Tudor monarchs: to the Italian historian employed by Henry VII, Rhys seemed 'a man noted for strength of will and military experience', 'an excellent leader in war'. A little later, Richard Grafton ranked him as one of Henry's counsellors 'as well circumspecte as wise'.[3] His motto, 'Secret et Hardy', still to be seen on his Garter plate in St George's Chapel, Windsor, seems particularly apt. The tradition, repeated by the author of the Life, that Henry Tudor looked on this Welshman, only seven or eight years his senior, as 'Father Rice' may seem an exaggeration; but there can be no doubt that the king held him in the highest esteem for qualities that were of enduring value throughout the reign.[4]

Rhys ap Thomas was dubbed a knight bachelor three days after Bosworth, on 25 August 1485, by a grateful king who was probably still at or near Leicester.

> And today is declared a knight.
> And his raven and his shield – line by line –
> To Harry the king power is long given.[5]

He attended Henry's coronation in Westminster Abbey on 30 October.[6] Thereafter, on those occasions when he was in the king's company rather than in Wales, his views were sought on matters military, political and judicial as a royal councillor.[7] When another of the major regal festivities of the reign, Queen Elizabeth's coronation, took place on 25 November 1487, Sir Rhys was in attendance; and within a couple more years, he had become a knight of the body in the king's household.[8]

From Henry VII's point of view, Sir Rhys's greatest assets were his standing and power in Wales, particularly in the Tywi Valley in the west. The king had eventually benefited from this position during the march to Bosworth. Accordingly, in the autumn of 1485, Henry took decisive steps to enhance Sir Rhys's public authority in the entire region

[3] Hay, *Polydore Vergil*, pp.52, 97; Grafton, p.550.
[4] Plate 5.
[5] W. A. Shaw, *The Knights of England* (2 vols., London, 1906), II, 23; Siddons, *Welsh Heraldry*, I, 113 (from NLW, Llanstephan 7, p.308).
[6] BL, Egerton MS 985 f.24b–26b.
[7] Hay, *Polydore Vergil*, p.6; PRO, E30/612; C. G. Bayne (ed.), *Select Cases in the Council of Henry VII* (Selden Soc., 1958), pp.30, 32.
[8] J. Leland, *De Rebus Britannicis Collectanea* (6 vols., London, 1715), IV, 231; NLW, Dynevor, A 93 (e).

between the Herefordshire border and St George's Channel, comple-
menting that wielded by Jasper Tudor in Pembrokeshire, Glamorgan
and south-east Wales. With the Marcher lordships of Edward Stafford,
duke of Buckingham (born in 1478), at the king's disposal during the
duke's minority, on 3 November 1485 Sir Rhys was given supreme
authority in Brecon as the king's lieutenant and steward of the lordship
and constable of Brecon Castle; and he was given these offices for life,
which may justifiably be regarded as an unusual boon in lordships that
were only temporarily in the king's custody.[9] Three days later, one of
the two most senior offices in the royal shires of Carmarthen and
Cardigan came Sir Rhys's way: on 6 November, he was appointed
chamberlain of south Wales. This appointment, again made for life,
gave him control of the wealth and resources of the two shires, and since
Jasper Tudor was appointed justiciar of south Wales a month later there
can be little doubt that it was Sir Rhys who had effective overall charge
of the southern part of the principality of Wales. Lewys Glyn Cothi
advised as much when he urged Jasper Tudor to take Rhys into his
confidence, in the interests of the new dynasty:

> Take, Wales knows well your lineage,
> The raven into your secrets;
> The fitting swallow [Henry VII] and ravens
> Will bring splendour to London.[10]

It is true that Rhys did not, at the same time, secure the constableships of
the king's castles at Carmarthen and Cardigan, but at least in
Carmarthen, arguably the largest town in Wales at this time and the
headquarters of the king's administration in the south, his dominance
was such that he was chosen mayor of the borough on at least four
separate occasions after 1485 – in 1488, 1494, 1500 and 1516.[11] By the
same royal patent of 6 November, Sir Rhys became steward – for life, of
course – of the lordship of Builth, which bordered both Carmarthenshire
and Brecon.[12] South and south-central Wales were evidently to be Sir
Rhys ap Thomas's bailiwick, under the general supervision of the king
himself and, shortly, of Prince Arthur's Council in the Marches (or of
Jasper Tudor in its absence). As steward of Brecon and Builth, on 1
March 1490 Sir Rhys concluded with the king an indenture that was
designed to ensure orderly government in the two lordships; in 1495 he
joined the president of Prince Arthur's Council in holding sessions at
Brecon. Elsewhere in the south and south-east, he was to be found acting

---

[9] Ibid., A 93 (a); *CPR, 1485–94*, p.24; PRO, SC6/Henry VII/1652 m.2*d*. On 9 March 1490, the
king granted Sir Rhys an annuity of 100 marks from the lordship's resources, also for life: NLW,
Dynevor, A 93 (e).
[10] *CPR, 1485–94*, p.65; Griffiths, *Principality of Wales*, pp.162, 189; Siddons, *Welsh Heraldry*, I, 118.
[11] Griffiths, *Principality of Wales*, pp.351–2; CCL MS 4.30 (*c*.1726).
[12] *CPR, 1485–94*, p.65.

as an itinerant justice in the king's duchy of Lancaster estates in 1493 (and probably at other times too).[13]

Sir Rhys's military talents were enlisted by the king on several occasions in the first dozen years of the reign, against both rebels at home and enemies abroad. Some eight months after Bosworth, there were riots and risings in several places where the king had not yet stamped his authority: in Yorkshire, the west Midlands – particularly at Warwick, Birmingham and Worcester – and even in London in April and May 1486.[14] When Sir Thomas Vaughan of Tretower raised the standard of revolt at Brecon, Hay and Tretower itself in mid-April, Sir Rhys ap Thomas was on hand to resist; he may have returned towards Wales with the king's uncle, Jasper Tudor, a while before. With a substantial force of 140 men, Sir Rhys defended Brecon Castle for seven weeks, later drawing £48 to cover expenses; 'gounepouder' bought for the castle's protection against further attack cost 10s.[15] Sir Rhys's prompt intervention in the Welsh Marches contributed materially to the rapid collapse of these early risings against Henry VII.

Lambert Simnel's rebellion in 1487 brought Sir Rhys and his retinue into the field (in June) in the company of the king himself.[16] If Lewys Glyn Cothi is to be believed, they were accompanied by Rhys's bastard brother, John, an experienced soldier:

> When in the battle attacks were made
> On the ravens, and them and the king,
> John the steel-breasted was not
> Idle there at the fight.

Then, when war with France became unavoidable in 1492, Sir Rhys was among the first to assemble at Winchester, with a retinue of Welshmen 590 strong, ready to cross the Channel from Portsmouth to besiege Boulogne (from 22 October). His contract, which was probably concluded in May 1492, provided for a force of six men-at-arms (with pages), 250 demi-lances and 260 infantry, who were to serve overseas for one year in the first instance, muster at Winchester on 6 June, and receive expenses from their homes and a month's wages in advance before embarking at Portsmouth. In the event, the retinue consisted of twelve lances, 286 demi-lances and 292 archers, who were paid wages for one month from 20 October. Sir Rhys was also one of the senior captains whom the king consulted before quickly coming to an

[13] K. Williams-Jones, 'Another "Indenture of the Marches", 1 March 1490', *BBCS*, XXIV, part 1 (1970), 93–4; PRO, DL37/62 m.33; E101/414/6 f.103*v*, 124*v*.

[14] C. H. Williams, 'The rebellion of Humphrey Stafford in 1486', *EHR*, XLIII (1928), 181–9; Thomas, thesis cited, pp.334–42.

[15] PRO, SC6/Henry VII/1651 m.6; 1652 m.2*d*; BL, Egerton Roll 2192 m.5.

[16] M. Bennett, *Lambert Simnel and the Battle of Stoke* (Gloucester, 1987), pp.75, 83; Jones, *Lewys Glyn Cothi*, pp.67–8, 163–4; Siddons, *Welsh Heraldry*, I, 118.

agreement with King Charles VIII at Etaples on 3 November that
enabled the English and Welsh army·to withdraw on advantageous
terms.[17]

Even more crucial was Sir Rhys's contribution to the suppression of
the Cornishmen's rising in 1497. He and his retinue were recruited in the
spring as part of an army intended to repel a Scottish invasion in support
of the next pretender, Perkin Warbeck. At forty-one lances and 696
demi-lances, one tenth of the entire vanguard under the command of
Giles, Lord Daubeney, Sir Rhys's retinue was the backbone of the king's
forces and received a total payment of £382. 16s. 0d. for its pains.[18] In
the event, it was not needed in the north; but some weeks later the
soldiers were diverted to confront the rebels from Cornwall, who were
massing on Blackheath and threatening London. There, on 17 June,
alongside the earls of Essex and Suffolk, Sir Rhys played a vital role,
deploying his archers and cavalry to outflank the rebels and put them to
flight; his retinue was duly paid £239. 8s. 4d. for its service.[19] A later
family claim that Sir Rhys personally apprehended the rebel leader,
James Tuchet, Lord Audley, one of his own neighbours as lord of
Llandovery, cannot be substantiated; but that he was instrumental in
Audley's capture is undeniable – and a fellow Welsh esquire from
Carmarthenshire, William Thomas of Aberglasney, did indeed seize
Audley's brother at Blackheath.[20]

Sir Rhys was again at the king's side a few months later when, in
September, Henry marched against Perkin Warbeck in the west
country. At Taunton, in the first days of October, the rebel forces were
put to flight by the royal vanguard under Lord Daubeney, Robert, Lord
Willoughby, and Sir Rhys ap Thomas. Later family tradition proudly
remembered the pursuit and Sir Rhys's part in it.[21] His bravery and
notable military successes in 1497 raised his reputation even higher in
the eyes of the king, who showed his regard by creating him a knight
banneret after Blackheath.[22]

The death of Jasper Tudor on 21 December 1495 paved the way for
an enhancement of Sir Rhys's influence in Wales. A fortnight afterwards

[17] Hay, *Polydore Vergil*, p.52; PRO, E30/612; M. Condon, 'An anachronism with intent? Henry VII's Council Ordinance of 1491/2', in R. A. Griffiths and J. Sherborne (eds.), *Kings and Nobles in the Later Middle Ages* (Gloucester, 1986), pp.242–3; PRO, E36/285 f.8v, 15v, 16, 35; E101/76/6, transcribed in Lloyd, thesis cited, appendix pp.120–4.
[18] I. Arthurson, ' The King's voyage into Scotland: the war that never was', in D. Williams (ed.), *England in the Fifteenth Century* (Woodbridge, 1987), p.20; PRO, E405/79 f.36v.
[19] Hay, *Polydore Vergil*, pp.94, 96–7; cf. *Hall's Chronicle*, p.479; *Holinshed's Chronicles*, III, 515; PRO, E101/414/6 f.68v, 70v. See I. Arthurson, 'The rising of 1497: a revolt of the peasantry?', in J. Rosenthal and C. Richmond (eds.), *People, Politics and Community in the Later Middle Ages* (Gloucester, 1987), pp.1–18.
[20] See below p.244; PRO, E405/79 f.40r; Griffiths, *Principality of Wales*, pp.205–6.
[21] See below p.244; Hay, *Polydore Vergil*, p.107; *Hall's Chronicle*, p.485; *Holinshed's Chronicles*, III, 518–19; PRO, E101/414/6 f.85r, 87v.
[22] Shaw, *Knights*, II, 29.

(4 January 1496), he was appointed justiciar of south Wales in Jasper's place, thereby giving him formally the authority which he had most likely enjoyed in practice for a decade past.[23] Then, after William Devereux died, on 1 April 1502 Sir Rhys secured for life the constableship of Aberystwyth Castle, whose garrison numbered twelve archers; this appointment was made by Prince Arthur only a day before the prince's death.[24] Marcher lords also had confidence in him, among them the duke of Buckingham who, newly come of age, in 1500 nominated Sir Rhys to be a commissioner to ensure law and order in his lordships of Hay and Huntington.[25]

The king's trust in – and, indeed, affection for – Sir Rhys scarcely dimmed as the years passed. It is nicely reflected on a private level in the responsibility which the king laid on his Welsh knight to oversee the building of a new tomb for the body of Henry's father, Edmund Tudor, earl of Richmond. Sometime after the fortieth anniversary of the earl's death at Carmarthen in November 1456, Henry VII assigned £43. 10s. 0d. from the clerical subsidy of 1496–7, collected in the archdeaconries of St David's and Cardigan, for 'the making of a newe tombe for our most dere fadre', and part of an annual gift of alms to the Grey Friars' Church in Carmarthen where Edmund had been buried. Sir Rhys received the money and was presumably responsible for commissioning the fine tomb-chest in Purbeck marble which survived the dissolution of the friary, when it was removed to St David's Cathedral where it may still be seen.[26] More personal still was Sir Rhys's dispatch to the king of quantities of metheglin, the spiced mead that was a speciality of Wales, and for which Henry developed a taste in the latter years of his life. On 21 June 1505, a servant of Sir Rhys was rewarded for taking a hawk to the king; in the years that followed both Sir Rhys and his son sent hawks and falcons to enliven King Henry's hunt.[27]

The most public sign of the esteem in which Henry VII held this Welsh subject, who neither by lineage, marriage nor wealth merited a peerage, was election to the Order of the Garter.[28] Within eighteen months of the rout of Warbeck's forces, he was nominated on St George's Day 1499 to fill the vacancy caused by the recent death of the king's

---

[23] PRO, SC6/Henry VIII/1862 m.6; Griffiths, *Principality of Wales*, p.162. For Sir Rhys holding great sessions in south Wales, see PRO, E36/214 f.616 (1505).

[24] Griffiths, *Principality of Wales*, p.239; NLW, Duchy of Cornwall, Welsh Box 1 m.2.

[25] Pugh, *Marcher Lordships*, pp.257, 274. Mr W. R. B. Robinson tells me that he was mistaken in asserting (*Glamorgan County History*, III, 272) that Sir Charles Somerset did the same in Gower in 1500, when Sir Rhys was merely prominent at the sessions meeting.

[26] PRO, E404/84, unsorted, 18 Henry VII (16 May 1503); Westminster Abbey MS 28018 (25 September 1517). The nineteenth-century brass on the tomb-chest replaces one presumably put there in Sir Rhys's day and removed in the seventeenth century: E. Allen, 'The tomb of the earl of Richmond in St David's Cathedral', *Arch. Camb.*, 5th series, XIII (1896), 315–20.

[27] BL, Add. MS 59,899 f.79v, 89v (1505); PRO, E36/214 f.46, 217, 268, 282 (1506–8).

[28] J. Anstis, *The Register of the Most Noble Order of the Garter* (2 vols., London, 1724), II, 237–9, 247–9; *CP*, II, 546; VII, 168; XII, part 2, 738.

uncle, Viscount Welles. His sponsors were Prince Arthur himself and
some of the king's closest advisers who had also fought against the rebels:
the earl of Shrewsbury, Lords Cobham and Daubeney, and Sir Edward
Poynings. On that occasion, Henry VII felt it more appropriate to
choose the queen's cousin, Richard de la Pole, as the new knight.
However, in due time, on 22 April 1505, Sir Rhys, who was by then in
his mid-fifties, became one of the Garter knights, in the company of
scions of two distinguished noble families with Welsh connections,
Henry Stafford (born *c*.1479 and later to be earl of Wiltshire), and
Richard Grey of Ruthin, earl of Kent (born *c*.1478). The Life describes
with enthusiasm the festivities which were organized at Carew Castle to
celebrate the first anniversary of Rhys's election. The nature and
circumstantial detail of this account strongly suggest that it is based, at
least in part, on a herald's record of an event which mirrored the Garter
celebrations that customarily took place at Windsor on the same day.[29]
Few such grandiose events are otherwise known to have been organized
outside the court circle in the early decades of the sixteenth century, but
in 1522 Henry VIII authorized each Garter knight who was absent from
the king's annual celebrations at Windsor to hold a religious ceremony
and 'grand feast' wherever he might be. The king's order is likely to have
formalized what was already taking place, and Sir Rhys ap Thomas and
his son (who took a prominent role in the jousts at Carew in 1506)
probably attended the Garter celebrations arranged by Prince Arthur
and his entourage at Hereford in April 1500. These may have inspired
Sir Rhys to organize his own commemorative celebration six years later.
To mark the signal honour in 1505, two sturdy oak chairs were made
and decorated with his arms enclosed within the Garter and its famous
motto, *Honi soit quy mal y pense*. Although the chairs are usually dated to
c.1520, it is not fanciful to suggest that they were carved locally in south-
west Wales as part of a set designed for the notable celebrations at Carew
Castle in 1506.[30]

   In 1509 Sir Rhys ap Thomas could hardly have expected to cultivate
the same kind of intimate relationship with the eighteen-year-old Henry
VIII that he appears to have had with Henry VII. On the other hand,
he had no reason to fear the consequences of the change of monarch.
Indeed, despite his age, and Sir Rhys was about sixty in 1509, his
soldier's reputation and his standing as a loyal Welsh governor were
fully appreciated by the new king and his advisers. Furthermore, a
valuable link between the younger generations of the two families had
been forged by Sir Rhys's eldest son and heir, Gruffydd ap Rhys, and

---

[29] See below pp.246ff; S. J. Gunn, 'Chivalry and the politics of the early Tudor court', in S. Anglo
(ed.), *Chivalry in the Renaissance* (Woodbridge, 1990), p.125; E. Ashmole, *The Institutions, Laws and
Ceremonies of the Most Noble Order of the Garter* (2 vols., London, 1672; 1 vol., Baltimore, 1971), esp.
pp.614–17.
[30] Plate 4b.

Prince Arthur. Gruffydd was a member of Arthur's household by the time the prince married Catherine of Aragon, the ill-fated princess of Spain, on 14 November 1501. Catherine was sixteen, her husband one year younger. On 17 November, during the wedding festivities, Gruffydd was one of those created knights of the Bath.[31] When, in 1529, it became crucial to Henry VIII and his plans to divorce Catherine (whom he had married after his elder brother's death) to establish whether the marriage of 1501 had ever been consummated, Sir Gruffydd ap Rhys's recollection of Arthur's boast to his friends of what happened on the wedding night was repeated at court. According to Sir Arthur Willoughby, who as a young man was also in Arthur's service, Gruffydd had heard the young prince's triumphant words as he emerged from his chamber in the bishop of London's palace:

> Willoughby, bring me a cup of ale, for I have been this night in the midst of Spain. Masters, it is good pastime to have a wife.

Conveniently for the protagonists of 1529, Sir Gruffydd had been dead for eight years and was in no position to deny or corroborate Willoughby's testimony.[32]

When Prince Arthur died, less than five months after his wedding, Sir Gruffydd seems to have been with him at Ludlow. He took a prominent part in the doleful funeral procession that made its way through the border countryside to the prince's final resting place before the high altar in Worcester Cathedral. According to a herald's account of the procession, Sir Gruffydd, with an officer of arms at either side, 'in morning abitt rode on a courser trappid with blak, with a litill scochyn on the coursers forhed', bearing Arthur's banner embroidered with the prince's arms immediately in front of the coffin. Towards the end of the funeral service in the cathedral, at the point when St John's Gospel was being sung, Sir Gruffydd offered the banner to the dean.[33] His master's premature death seems to have had an unusually deep effect on his household knight, for when Sir Gruffydd ap Rhys himself died long afterwards, in 1521, he too was buried (doubtless as he had wished) in the monastic cathedral at Worcester. Sir Gruffydd's imposing tomb-chest, which his father probably commissioned, stands today in the eastern transept, close to the elaborate chantry chapel which Henry VII erected to commemorate his dead son. Of Purbeck marble, Sir Gruffydd's tomb has affinities with Edmund Tudor's tomb-chest, whose

---

[31] CRO, Dynevor, Add. MS 112; G. Kipling (ed.), *The Receyt of the Ladie Kateryne* (EETS, 296, 1990), pp.50–1; 'The epytaphye of Sir Gryffyth Apryse' refers to 'all of my feloys that was with Prince Arthur, in seruice with me full dyllygente': *Anglia*, XXXI, 349; see below p.86.

[32] *LP, Henry VIII*, IV, part 3, 2577; J. J. Scarisbrick, *Henry VIII* (London, 1968), pp.188–9. Like Sir Gruffydd, Master Arthur Willoughby was present at Prince Arthur's funeral in 1502: Kipling, *The Receyt of the Ladie Kateryne*, p.82.

[33] Ibid., pp.83, 86, 92; Leland, *Collectanea*, V, 375, 377, 380.

placing in Carmarthen's friary had been supervised by Sir Rhys ap Thomas two decades before.[34]

Although Arthur's death may have been a shock for Sir Gruffydd, it did not adversely affect his material fortunes, still less those of his father. Like the sons of other ambitious landowners, Sir Gruffydd entered Lincoln's Inn to learn the law on 26 February 1509. In the decade that followed, he joined his father in both war and administration, and spent a good deal of time at Henry VIII's court. At the outset of the new reign, on 4 May 1509, both Sir Rhys and Sir Gruffydd received a general pardon from Henry VIII in expectation of future service.[35] With no one of Jasper Tudor's stature to lord it in Pembrokeshire, Sir Rhys was able to extend his authority from Carmarthenshire and Cardiganshire southwards – and evidently with the notion that his son should inherit this dominion. By August 1509 Sir Rhys was acting as steward in the lordship of Pembroke, and his son had become steward of the small lordship in south Cardiganshire that encompassed the eastern half of the commote of Iscoed (Uwch Hirwern) and the western part of Gwynionydd (Is Cerdyn).[36] Meanwhile, on 11 May, Sir Rhys had been authorized to continue as justiciar of south Wales during the new king's pleasure, and on 6 November arrangements were formally made for Sir Gruffydd to succeed him as chamberlain whenever Sir Rhys should die.[37] Eighteen months later still, on 8 April 1511, a similar arrangement allowed Sir Rhys's hold on the stewardship of Builth eventually to pass to his son, whose own service to the Crown was already attracting appreciative comment.[38]

Sir Rhys may have over-reached himself in one respect, and a dangerous one at that. Although a dominant figure in the borough of Carmarthen, he had not so far been able to secure control of the royal castle there. Since June 1498, the constable had been Gruffydd Rede, whose family had been prominent in the town for generations. Rede stood by Henry Tudor in the difficult days of 1485 and was rewarded accordingly in the lordship of Kidwelly and, later, as steward of Pembroke.[39] When Henry VIII appointed him his steward, receiver, approver and chancellor of the lordships of Pembroke and Haverford and of the barony of Cemais on 18 May 1509, Sir Rhys may have felt affronted. Within a few weeks – certainly by 9 July when his will was

---

[34] See above p.49.

[35] *The Records of the Honourable Society of Lincoln's Inn* (2 vols., London, 1896), I, 34; *LP, Henry VIII*, I, part 1, 255.

[36] Ibid., Addenda, I, part 1, 22; Lloyd, thesis cited, p.56; Griffiths, *Principality of Wales*, pp.9, 345, 541.

[37] *LP, Henry VIII*, I, part 1, 122, 404; Griffiths, *Principality of Wales*, p.190; see above p.49; Lloyd thesis cited, pp.41–2.

[38] PRO, C66/614 m.9; PRO, E36/215 f.15, 79, 114; T. D. Lloyd (ed.), *Baronia de Kemeys* (Cambrian Arch. Soc., 1861), pp.107–8.

[39] PRO, SC6/Henry VII/1862 m.4d; Griffiths, *Principality of Wales*, pp.203–4.

being administered – Gruffydd Rede had been murdered. Sir Rhys was not among those named in May 1511 as having been present at the constable's slaying, but the poet and herald, Gruffydd Hiraethog (died 1564), later recorded his belief that Sir Rhys was ultimately responsible.[40] Such a crime might explain one of the alarming rumours circulating in London a few months after Henry VIII's accession. Thomas, Lord Darcy reported to the keeper of the privy seal, Richard Fox, that he had been informed 'that Sir Risse ap Thomas has gone to the sea, fled forth of his country'.[41] Darcy was decidedly sceptical about this story; and in any case, Sir Rhys quickly recovered his composure and retained his position. He acquired the stewardship of Pembroke following Gruffydd Rede's death, though it may be significant that another Carmarthenshire squire who had served Prince Arthur, William Thomas, was preferred as constable of Carmarthen Castle.[42] The outbreak of hostilities with France in 1512 was a forcible reminder to Henry VIII that he needed Sir Rhys's notable fighting skills.

Sir Gruffydd's earliest known experience of the warfare which his father relished was not auspicious. Early in 1512, he and his retinue of 500 joined the substantial army of the marquess of Dorset that was being sent to aid King Ferdinand of Spain in his invasion of Gascony, the duchy held by English kings until 1453. On 1 February Sir Gruffydd was assigned a loan of £333. 6s. 8d. by the king's cofferer to help finance his retinue, as well as conduct money of £266. 13s. 4d. for his men. The army set sail from Southampton early in June, Sir Gruffydd being engaged as Dorset's 'counsaillor'. His father was asked to contribute some men to the enterprise, but he did not join it in person. Sir Rhys was fortunate, for the expedition was a calamity. After weeks spent inactively at Fuenterrabia in northern Spain, in deteriorating conditions, the army from England abandoned its position at the end of August and returned home.[43]

Sir Gruffydd was less prominent the following year, when Sir Rhys took pride of place, along with the earl of Shrewsbury and Sir Charles Somerset, in command of the vanguard of the king's army that invaded northern France. On this occasion, things went much better, especially for the Welsh contingent. By 15 May 1513, Sir Rhys had raised a large retinue of almost 3,000 infantry and light cavalry, his speciality. A

---

[40] *LP, Henry VIII*, II, part 2, 1450; NLW, Peniarth MS 136 B, p.391, noted in F. Jones, 'Annals of an old manor house: Green Castle', *Carms. Antiquary*, XXVII (1991), 7; *Companion to Welsh Lit.*, p.230.

[41] *LP, Henry VIII*, I, part 1, 75; P. S. and H. M. Allen (eds.), *Letters of Richard Fox, 1456–1527* (Oxford, 1929), p.44.

[42] Griffiths, *Principality of Wales*, pp.205–6; see above p.48.

[43] *Hall's Chronicle*, p.527; PRO, SP1/7 f.44; *LP, Henry VIII*, I, part 1, 255, 671, 690; II, part 2, 1454, 1481; Scarisbrick, *Henry VIII*, pp.29–30. The loan was due for repayment by 31 May 1515: PRO, E36/215 f.596, 600. PRO, E101/417/7 no. 54 and 417/2/2 no. 141 are receipts signed by Sir Gruffydd for 500 marks each, dated 4 March and 13 May 1512.

month later, it crossed to Calais where, on 13 June, Sir Rhys and his son left with Sir Gilbert Talbot, the deputy-lieutenant of Calais, £3,000-worth of gold, silver and plate for safe keeping; perhaps it was intended as security should extra funds be needed. The personal expenses of war were high, and it seems likely that Sir Rhys and his son had to purchase from the king clothing and war harness worth £900, a sum which they optimistically arranged to repay by Whitsun 1515.[44]

According to the chronicler, Raphael Holinshed, Shrewsbury, Somerset and Sir Rhys, 'a gentleman of such spirit and hardiness, that he is named the floure of the Welshmen, as the poet saith: Ricius Thomas flos Cambrobritannum', moved out from Calais on 13 June, marching for three days past Sangatte towards Marquise, as if heading for Boulogne. In fact, their objective was the town of Thérouanne further inland, which was reached on 22 June, when the English vanguard pitched tents a mile off in preparation for a siege.[45] Sir Rhys was one of the king's chief military advisers on this campaign, and he took an active role as a cavalry trouble-shooter. To begin with, he and his horsemen deterred French probings of the vanguard's position around Thérouanne:

> [they] daily skowered the country, and many tymes encountered with the Frenchmen, and slewe and toke diuerse prisoners, so that the Frenchmen drewe not toward the siege, but turned another waie.

Another opportunity to show his mettle came on 27 June, when supplies from Guines for the besiegers at Thérouanne were intercepted by a French force under the duc de Vendôme. When this news reached the besiegers,

> sir Rise ap Thomas caused his Trompet to blowe to the stirroppe, and he with his horsemen sought the Duke of Vandosme all the country, whiche hearyng of the commyng of sir Rise, with greate hast retreted backe to Bangey [i.e. Blangy] Abbey, where the Frenche kynges greate army laie. Sir Rise herying that he was returned came the next daye agayn to the sege.[46]

The king arrived at Calais on 30 June with the bulk of his army, though it was another three weeks before they all set off in the direction of Thérouanne, which they had reached by 1 August.[47] In the meantime, on 16 July, a substantial French force, 6,000 strong, appeared on a hill a

[44] *LP, Henry VIII*, I, part 2, 902, 924, 1062; PRO, E101/62/14; J. G. Nichols (ed.), *The Chronicle of Calais* (Camden Society, 35, 1846), p.10; *HMC, Various Collections*, II (1903), 308; PRO, C1/513/26 (*c.*1525); see below p.60. For a repayment for 'harness', see PRO, E36/215 f.681; *LP, Henry VIII*, II, part 2, 1489.

[45] *Holinshed's Chronicles*, III, 576; Nichols, *Chronicle of Calais*, p.11; *Hall's Chronicle*, pp.537–8; C. G. Cruickshank, *Army Royal: Henry VIII's Invasion of France, 1513* (Oxford, 1969).

[46] Hay, *Polydore Vergil*, pp.208–9; *Hall's Chronicle*, pp.538–9.

[47] Scarisbrick, *Henry VIII*, pp.35–7.

mile away to the north-west of the town, threatening the English and Welsh besiegers. This was the signal for one of those daring and successful forays by Sir Rhys ap Thomas which caught the imagination of observers and chroniclers alike. With a detachment of pikemen, he put the French to flight, capturing four and leaving five of their number dead on the field.[48]

As the king and his grand army approached, a more serious crisis arose which Sir Rhys was again instrumental in resolving. During the night of 26–7 July, two or three of the larger English guns were abandoned while a river was being negotiated. Next day, the earl of Essex and Sir Rhys, with a detachment of 300 English cavalry, some Burgundian horse, and English and German infantry, were sent to recover the guns which the French were intent on capturing. Sir Rhys retrieved one of the largest, but the French then attacked in considerable force.

> Sir Rice ap Thomas beyng a man of great experience, sagely perceyued in what case the matter stode, saide to therle of Essex, sir we be not vii.C. horsemen, let us not be to folysh hardy, our comission was to sette the gonne and none other, let vs folowe the same, therle agreed therto and so softly and not flyeng maner retreted and folowed the gonne.[49]

The French mistook this tactic for flight, discovering their error when they pursued Essex and the English forces:

> sodainly apered in sight a great company of horsmen and the kynge knewe not what thei were: but at the last it was preceyued that it was the valiant knyght Sir Rice ap Thomas with his retinue whiche came to the kyng aboute none: which gentilly receyued hym and sent hym to therle of Essex, which incontinently departed and compassed the hill and ranne to therle and when they were ioyned, they drewe them about the hyll accompaignyed with sir Thomas Gylforde capitayne of ii.C. archers on horsbache to thentent to have set on the Frenchmen,

who were forced to retire.[50] In this engagement, Sir Rhys lost one of his own men, but twenty of the French were left for dead.[51]

The main engagement at Thérouanne took place on 16 August. A large French army approached bent on raising the English siege. The rout of the French led English commentators to christen this the Battle of

[48] *HMC*, X, appendix 4 (1885), pp.446–7; *LP, Henry VIII*, I, part 2, 954.
[49] *Hall's Chronicle*, pp.542–3.
[50] Ibid., p.541; *Holinshed's Chronicles*, III, 578; Cruickshank, *Army Royal*, p.39.
[51] *LP, Henry VIII*, I, part 2, 998–1000, 1057–62 (from BL, Cotton, Cleopatra C V f.64ff.); W. C. Trevelyan, 'Account of Henry the Eighth's expedition into France, AD 1513', *Archaeologia*, XXVI (1836), 475–8. It was alleged, following this engagement, that Sir Rhys renounced an arrangement to exchange two prisoners rather than one for his servant, David 'de Pouel' (*LP, Henry VIII*, I, part 2, 1002). 'Davy Appowell', of the English guard left at Tournai in 1513, led a revolt against English authority in 1515: W. E. Hampton, 'The White Rose under the first Tudors: Part 3, Richard de la Pole, "The king's dreaded enemy"', *Ricardian*, VII, no. 99 (December 1987), 527.

the Spurs, and again Sir Rhys was prominent. He lost two of his men in the action, but took three French prisoners. Among the captives that day were the duc de Longueville, who was seized by Sir Rhys himself, according to the Life and Rice family tradition. In view of the fact that Sir Rhys and the lord steward of Henry VIII's household, the earl of Shrewsbury, secured four French standards during the battle, there may be some truth in the claim. When the action was over, it was Sir Rhys who described events to the king – and his own role in them. The duc de Longueville and six other prisoners were consigned to the Tower of London.[52]

We may presume that Sir Rhys and his men remained with King Henry and assisted in the capture of the city of Tournai on 24 September. When the king and his commanders returned to Calais, Sir Rhys received a handsome reward of 500 marks from Henry himself on 20 October, perhaps in particular recognition of de Longueville's capture.[53] Sir Rhys's men were soon back at Calais, somewhat depleted in numbers – by about 520 – and ready to be transported to Dover during the days that followed, *en route* for Carew, which was presumably their original assembly-point.[54] Among the captains of Sir Rhys's retinue who survived the campaign were Sir John Wogan and Sir Owen Perrot from Pembrokeshire, Henry ap John from Carmarthenshire, and several younger members of his own family, including his son Owain, his grandson, Owain Gwyn ap Dafydd, his nephew, Dafydd ap John ap Thomas, his son-in-law, Henry Wyriot of Orielton in Pembrokeshire, and Thomas ab Owain, a kinsman and one of the 'graundes capitaynes' in 1513 who was later to transfer his loyalties to Sir Rhys's grandson, Rhys ap Gruffydd.[55]

If Henry VIII at his accession had entertained any doubts about Sir Rhys ap Thomas's loyalty or his usefulness, even when in his mid-sixties, the campaign of 1513 banished them. Father and son returned to Wales with undiminished influence. Neither the burgeoning power in south-east Wales of Charles Somerset, created earl of Worcester in February 1514, nor the influence of Charles Brandon, created duke of Suffolk at the same time, in the north and north-east significantly prejudiced Sir Rhys's position in the south-west of Wales.[56] Indeed, his dominion was strengthened when, on 4 June 1515, he was confirmed in his possession of

---

[52] See below p.263; *LP, Henry VIII*, I, part 2, 998, 1057–62; *Archaeologia*, XXXVI (1836), 475–8; *Holinshed's Chronicles*, III, 585–7; *Hall's Chronicle*, pp.549–51; PRO, E36/215 f.273.

[53] *Hall's Chronicle*, p.551; BL, Stowe MS 146 f.105.

[54] *LP, Henry VIII*, I, part 2, 1098; PRO, E101/61/2; E101/56/19; 60/30.

[55] *LP, Henry VIII*, I, part 2, 1055, 1098, 1101; Bartrum, *1400–1500*, X, 1754; IV, 645, 644, 646; Griffiths, *Principality of Wales*, pp.266, 344–6, 385; see below p.96.

[56] W. R. B. Robinson, 'Early Tudor policy towards Wales: the acquisition of lands and offices in Wales by Charles Somerset, earl of Worcester', *BBCS*, XX, part 4 (1964), 427–36; S. J. Gunn, 'The régime of Charles, duke of Suffolk, in north Wales and the "reform of Welsh government", 1509–25', *WHR*, XII, no. 4 (1985), 461–94.

the castle and lordship of Narberth, and over the next five years he was authorized by Sir William Parr, steward of Pembroke, to act as steward and receiver of that lordship.[57] In the lordships of Haverford and Rhos, the interests of Sir Gruffydd ap Rhys were promoted when Sir Rhys and his son were granted the offices of steward, receiver, approver and chancellor there on 16 May 1517, for life and in survivorship, in explicit recognition of their services overseas and at home on many occasions. Between 1515 and 1519 – and probably at other times too – Sir Rhys served as a judicial commissioner in the lordships of Pembroke, Haverford and Cilgerran.[58] Sir Gruffydd, on his own account, was mayor of Carmarthen in 1513–14 (an office he had held twice before, in 1504–6 and 1511–12), and he also became mayor of Kidwelly in 1514.[59] Otherwise, his activities were more often directed towards the eastern Marches and the English border shires, with which he was familiar from his days in Prince Arthur's service. On 25 September 1514, he became steward and receiver of the lordship of Dinas for life, but here he was quickly – and perhaps jealously – superseded in both offices by Charles Somerset, earl of Worcester.[60] This did not prevent Sir Gruffydd, more so than his father, from playing a part in maintaining the supervisory control of the Council in the Marches and the border shires following Henry VIII's accession: by means of periodic commissions of the peace and of *oyer* and *terminer*, and by the indentures for good order which Edward IV and Henry VII had concluded in the past with Marcher lords and their chief officials. He regularly served on such commissions in Gloucestershire, Herefordshire, Shropshire and Worcestershire after his return from France in November 1513 until his death in 1521. From time to time, wider-ranging commissions which encompassed Wales and the Marcher lordships and enabled the commissioners to muster security forces if need be included Sir Gruffydd, and occasionally his father too.[61]

One of Sir Rhys's important duties in the south-west was to guard the extensive waterways of Milford Sound, whose labyrinthine creeks and rivers snaked their way into several lordships in which he (and his son) had power – Haverford, Rhos, Pembroke and Narberth. The flourishing

---

[57] NLW, Slebech Papers 3273; PRO, SC6/Henry VIII/5573–6; Henry VIII/345 m.120. Henry VII seems to have asserted his rights in Narberth; hence the desirability of the 1515 patent in Sir Rhys's favour. R. F. Isaacson (ed.), *Episcopal Registers of the Diocese of St David's, 1397–1518* (2 vols., London, 1917–20), II, 534–7, 576–7, 696–7, 722–3, 786–7; see below p.61.

[58] PRO, C66/630 m.15; *LP, Henry VIII*, II, part 2, 1043; PRO, SC6/Henry VIII/345 m.112, 114, 117, 121, 123.

[59] Griffiths, *Principality of Wales*, p.352; PRO, DL5/5 f.23.

[60] PRO, C266/25 no. 29; NLW, Dynevor A60; *LP, Henry VIII*, I, part 2, 1400, 1467; II, part 1, 81; Robinson, *BBCS*, XX, part 4 (1964), 427–36.

[61] *LP, Henry VIII*, I, part 1, 933, 1537–46; II, part 1, 70, 189–91, 193, 318, 327; II, part 2, 1282, 1387; III, part 1, 396, 445; III, part 2, 592, 915; PRO, Stac 2/28/76/IV; Gunn, *WHR*, XII, no. 4 (1985), 474–6; CRO, Dynevor A73.

commercial connection between the ports of south-west Wales and
Ireland was threatened with disruption from time to time by disorder in
Ireland. On two occasions in the early 1520s, Sir Rhys was required to
take measures on the government's behalf. Early in June 1520, King
Henry requested him to send a small cavalry contingent, fifty-strong, to
Ireland in August to support the efforts of the new chief governor,
Thomas Howard, earl of Surrey, to suppress rebellion there and assert
royal power. Three years later, when the French were dabbling in the
violent politics of Ireland, and rumours were abroad of an impending
descent from Ireland by Richard de la Pole, the pretender to King
Henry's throne, Sir Rhys helped assemble a fleet of ships to protect the
seas between Wales and Ireland.[62]

Military capacity, counsel and a congenial presence were what
commended Sir Rhys and Sir Gruffydd, in their differing ways, to Henry
VIII. The younger man was one of the king's intimate body-servants in
his household by 1518, and probably long before that.[63] As such, he was
nominated by George Talbot, earl of Shrewsbury, and Thomas
Howard, earl of Surrey, two highly placed fellow soldiers, for election to
the Order of the Garter which his father had long graced; although he
was not successful in 1518, it is tolerably certain that had he lived the
honour would eventually have been his.[64] As it was, later in the year he
was in the company (which also included Edward IV's bastard son, Sir
Arthur Plantagenet, and two Welsh knights, Sir Henry Owen and Sir
Gruffydd Dwnn) that entertained Cardinal Campeggio and his fellow
legate from the Pope on their visit to England in September 1518 to
discuss an anti-French alliance.[65]

Gruffydd's father, meanwhile, had been summoned to court for a
more important and more ceremonious occasion. He attended at
Greenwich on 5 July when Henry VIII discussed a proposed league
with the Emperor Maximilian and his son, the Archduke Charles, and
he stayed on at the palace for the extraordinarily lavish and theatrical
banquet two days later. Sir Gruffydd was also present, and had the
ceremonial duty of bearing a towel and basin for the king.[66] Father and
son were invited to join the king and Queen Catherine on the vast
cavalcade to the Field of Cloth of Gold between Guines and Ardres, not
far from Calais, in June 1520. Dame Jenet, Sir Rhys's wife, accompanied
them in the queen's entourage on the long journey to France. It was Sir

[62] *LP, Henry VIII*, III, part 1, 301; part 2, 1396, 1439. See A. Cosgrove (ed.), *A New History of Ireland*, II: *Medieval Ireland, 1169–1534* (Oxford, 1987), pp.662–73; Hampton, *Ricardian*, VII, no. 99 (December 1987), 535.
[63] *LP, Henry VIII*, II, part 2, 1357; PRO, E36/215 f.262, 270, 278, 301, 336, 370, 403.
[64] Anstis, *Garter Register*, II, 284; *CP*, XI, 706–9; IX, 615–20.
[65] *Harleian 433*, III, 167; Scarisbrick, *Henry VIII*, pp.69–71.
[66] *LP, Henry VIII*, II, part 2, 1095, 1097; Scarisbrick, *Henry VIII*, pp.67–8; College of Arms MS M.8 f.61ff.; BL, Add. MS 21116 f.40.

Gruffydd who, with a detachment of 100 light cavalry, replaced his aged father in charge of security for the climax of the expedition, the meeting between King Henry and King Francis I of France. He was commissioned to survey places suitable for ambushes, and to report to Henry VIII in person every morning.[67] When Francis had departed and Henry turned to meet Charles, now the emperor, at Gravelines on 10 July, Sir Gruffydd was again in attendance. From the standpoint of security, everything went well. From Sir Gruffydd's point of view, it may have been a costly commission, but at least Henry VIII rewarded him with a grey horse 'with cut year' which cost the king £37. 6s. 8d.[68] Within a year, Sir Gruffydd was dead.

Sir Rhys was to respond once again – for the last time – to a summons to give advice and lend distinction at a diplomatic meeting and accompanying festivities for a foreign potentate, this time on the Downs between Dover and Canterbury with the Emperor Charles V in the early summer of 1522. Otherwise, he seems to have been preoccupied in his last years with his estates, the inheritance of his young grandson, Rhys ap Gruffydd (born *c*.1508), and with making provision for the three ladies of the family should they outlive the old warrior himself.[69] His reputation was that of an immensely distinguished and influential Welsh knight widely admired for his chivalric style and military experience.

It is not possible to form more than a shadowy and partial impression of the considerable wealth and extensive estates of Sir Rhys ap Thomas. Hardly any of the documents that once lay in his muniment chests appear to have survived, most likely because they were seized by the commissioners appointed on 12 December 1531 after the attainder of his grandson for treason, and then perished when the banqueting hall of Whitehall burnt down in 1619. If the grants, leases and accounts relating to the estates were stored at Westminster, they have yet to come to light.[70] The commissioners were hindered in their task at Carew Castle by at least one of the chaplains of Rhys ap Gruffydd's widow, Catherine Howard, who was found to have hidden as many as four boxes of documents relating to estates in Narberth, Kidwelly and Carew itself.[71]

[67] College of Arms MS M.6 *bis* f.67, 67*v*; *LP, Henry VIII*, III, part 1, 239, 243; Scarisbrick, *Henry VIII*, pp.76–9; J. G. Russell, *The Field of Cloth of Gold* (London, 1969), pp.56, 63–4, 198; *Foedera*, VI, 182.

[68] PRO, E326/B8102; *LP, Henry VIII*, III, part 1, 326, 410.

[69] Ibid., part 2, 967; Scarisbrick, *Henry VIII*, p.95.

[70] An enfeoffment to Sir Rhys, dated 31 July 1510, of land at Redberth, in the parish of Carew (*CAD*, V, 540; *LP, Henry VIII*, I, part 1, 315), is endorsed 'Redbarh', which may indicate a simple archival filing system; cf. R. A. Griffiths, 'The Cartulary and Muniments of the Fort family of Llanstephan', *BBCS*, XXIV, part 3 (1971), 313 n.2, 335ff. A release of land at Lilston (Pembs.) to Sir Rhys, dated 27 May 1524, is *CAD*, V, 270. And a copy of an indenture, dated at Carmarthen on 23 January 1515, whereby Sir Rhys leased to William (or Gwilym) ap Gwilym Wehydd, a former mayor of Carmarthen, and his wife a building plot in New Carmarthen, is PRO, LR1/229 f.90; Griffiths, *Principality of Wales*, p.352.

[71] *LP, Henry VIII*, V, 285, 301; PRO, SP1/53 f.148; below p.114.

According to Rhys ap Gruffydd, his grandfather had kept a large hoard of gold and silver coin, worth £10,000–12,000 by the time of his death, and Dame Jenet revealed that the quantity of gold and silver which her husband had taken to France in 1513 (and which was deposited with the deputy-lieutenant of Calais) was worth £3,000, of which only £300 was spent on the wars. Sir Rhys's annual income from rents and other sources in the last dozen years of his life was put at 1,000 marks (£666. 13s. 4d.).[72] Rhys ap Gruffydd further claimed that most of Sir Rhys's land purchases took place before 1513, but regrettably their details remain elusive. The survey (or *valor*) of the forfeited properties of Rhys ap Gruffydd, and jointures safeguarded to the three surviving widows of Sir Rhys, Sir Gruffydd and Rhys himself, which was compiled by the king's commissioners in 1532, may confidently be regarded as a survey of estates held by Sir Rhys at the time of his death in 1525.[73] The net recorded value (including the jointure estates) amounts to £638. 18s. 1½d., which accords closely with Rhys ap Gruffydd's estimate a few years before.

Sir Rhys could expect a further income in his latter years from annuities and fees from offices that exceeded £400 a year. Three-

	£	s.	d.
From 3 November 1485:			
Brecon lordship, offices	40	0	0
From 6 November 1485:			
South Wales, chamberlain	60	0	0
Builth lordship, offices	24	4	0
From 9 March 1490:			
Brecon lordship, annuity	66	13	4
From 4 January 1496:			
South Wales, justiciar	53	6	8
From 1 April 1502:			
Aberystwyth Castle, office	91	5	0
By August 1509:			
Pembroke lordship, offices	?		
From 16 May 1517:			
Haverford and Rhos lordships, offices	40	0	0
(with Sir Gruffydd ap Rhys)			
Total at least	375	9	0

Sources: PRO, E36/151 f.55–6; SC6/Henry VII/1652 m.2d; Henry VIII/345 m.75, 92, 97, 123.

[72] PRO, C1/513/26; below p.90.
[73] PRO, SC12/23/43. Cf. PRO, SC6/Henry VIII/4882–3, royal accounts for 1531–3 of Rhys ap Gruffydd's forfeited estates in the lordship of Kidwelly. A rental of the lordship of Kidwelly from Sir Rhys ap Thomas's day is PRO, DL43/12/14 (*c*.1498–1503), part of which is edited by W. H. Morris, 'A Kidwelly town rental of the early 16th century (*temp.* Henry VII)', *Carms. Antiquary*, XI (1975), 55–87.

quarters of this, the handsome endowment that accompanied political power, had been conferred on him by Henry VII. Here lay the wherewithal for sustaining and extending his social, landed and administrative influence in south Wales.

This degree of wealth must be regarded as a minimum, for we no longer have more than a hint of additional income from royal gifts, military expeditions and wars, the marriages and wardships which Sir Rhys negotiated, and his (and his son's) relationships at court and with the nobility. Sir Rhys, in sum, was as wealthy as a modest English lord.

It is reasonably clear that Sir Rhys acquired much of his landed estate by means of inheritance from his father and grandfather, by marriage diplomacy and the exploitation of mortgages. The inheritance from the predatory Gruffydd ap Nicholas was considerable and central to the family's fortunes. Apart from scattered properties throughout the lordship of Kidwelly, in the borough of Carmarthen and the Tywi Valley, the lordship of Emlyn Uwch Cuch was worth about £64 a year in 1532 and the lordship of Narberth (to which the Crown still had claims) was worth about £125 a year.[74] These holdings enabled Sir Rhys to exercise rights as patron in the churches of Llanedi in the lordship of Kidwelly; Pen-boyr, Llangeler and Cilrhedyn in the lordship of Emlyn Uwch Cuch; and Narberth, Llanddewi Felffre, Llanbedr Felffre (Lampeter Velfrey), Cilymaenllwyd and Castelldwyran in the lordship of Narberth.[75]

From his mother, Elizabeth, daughter of Sir John Gruffydd (died 1471), Sir Rhys apparently inherited the Gruffydd family estate in Cardiganshire (especially at Llangybi and Llanrhystud, together worth £20. 10s. 0d. in 1532) and in Carmarthenshire, where the house and manor at Abermarlais, near Llansadwrn, were worth £27. 7s. 0½d. in 1532.[76] But how and when Sir Rhys acquired the substantial estate in Gower, centred on the manors of Weobley and especially Landimôr (and worth in all £48. 12s. 1½d. in 1532), is not certainly known; in 1507, by which time his eldest son, Gruffydd ap Rhys, had married Catherine St John, they could be assigned to her as her jointure.[77] Sir Rhys certainly had personal contacts with landowners in Gower by about 1487, when he stood as godfather to Rice Mansel of Oxwich. This at

[74] See above p.24; Lloyd, *History of Carmarthenshire*, I, 240. That the jointure assigned to Dame Jenet included income from Emlyn Uwch Cuch as well as much of Narberth's profit, and £36. 16s. 10d. from Carmarthen, suggests that these estates were in Sir Rhys's hands before 1485.

[75] Isaacson, *Episcopal Registers*, II, *passim*; PRO, E36/151 f.37–8.

[76] These estates may have been Elizabeth's dower; on the other hand, Sir Rhys may have acquired them by dubious means, since in 1485–9 he was farming them during the minority of Walter Gruffydd (born 1473), his mother's nephew: Griffiths, *Principality of Wales*, pp.10, 146, 160, 274–5; Isaacson, *Episcopal Registers*, II, *passim*.

[77] PRO, SC12/23/43; W. de Gray Birch, *A Descriptive Catalogue of the Penrice and Margam Manuscripts*, 4th series, part 2 (London, 1904), pp.125–6, 130. See D. Rees, 'The Gower estates of Sir Rhys ap Thomas', *Gower*, XLIII (1992), 31–41.

```
                    Sir John de la Bere (d.1388) = Agnes Turberville of Coity
      ┌──────────────────────┬──────────────────────────────────────────┐
  John de            Elizabeth = Sir Oliver St John of Fonmon     Margaret = Sir Elias Basset
  la Bere                           │                                         │
  (d.1403)                    John St John                                    │
     │                          (d.1424)                                      │
  Thomas                           │                               John Basset
     │              Alexander St John of Weobley                              │
     ?                        (fl.1449)                                       │
     │                           │                                           │
   John          (2) John St John  =  Lleucu, dau. of Gruffydd  =  (1) Hugh Basset
  (fl.1432)                              ap Nicholas
```

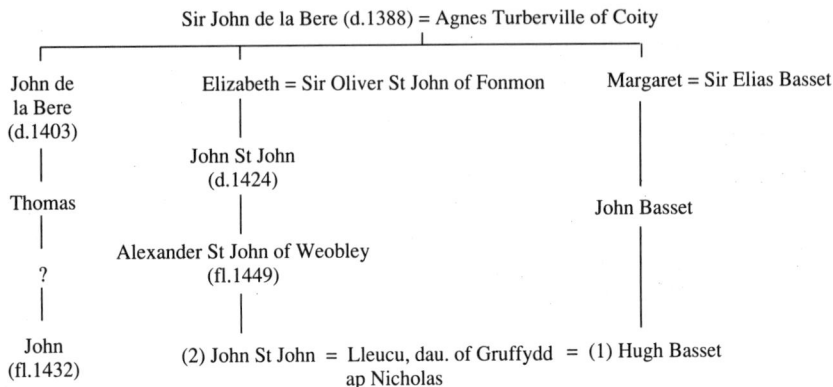

The descent of Weobley

least is likely to be the implication of a later report that Rice had been christened by a 'Wealsh man who was acquainted with the name of Rice, and such a Wealsh man as was not ashamed of the same name but bore it himself, viz., Sir Rice ap Thomas, who christened the said Sir Rice Mansell at the ffonte'. Moreover, Philip Mansel had married Mary, daughter of Gruffydd ap Nicholas, and Jenkin Mansel, Rice's father, seems to have been a close friend of Sir Rhys ap Thomas, who invited him to the Garter festivities at Carew in 1506.[78] Yet earlier links between Sir Rhys ap Thomas's family and Gower, especially with the St John family that once held the manor of Weobley, are murky. It is worth noting that Gruffydd ap Nicholas's daughter, Lleucu, married, as her second husband, John St John of Gower, who may have acquired Weobley, Landimôr and Rhosili when the de la Beres, to whom they were related at the beginning of the fifteenth century, died out.[79] The estates which Sir Rhys inherited could have reached him from Aunt Lleucu.

Like many a landowner of the period, Sir Rhys was a past master at marital diplomacy. Although his own marriages were strangely unproductive, he took half a dozen or more mistresses, and produced a goodly clutch of illegitimate offspring – perhaps as many as a dozen who lived to adulthood. Most of his children figured in the marriage stakes. Sir Gruffydd was his only legitimate child by his first wife, Efa, daughter

---

[78] *Catalogue of the Penrice and Margam Manuscripts*, 4th series, part 2, p.131 (no. 3767); G. Williams, 'Rice Mansell of Oxwich and Margam (1487–1559)', *Morgannwg*, VI (1962), 34–7; see below p.253.
[79] W. G. Thomas, *Weobley Castle* (London, 1971), pp.9–11; *Limbus*, p.480; Bartrum, *300–1400*, II, 330; *1400–1500*, IX, 1567–8; cf. 'Parochialia . . . by Edward Lhuyd', *Arch. Camb.*, suppl. vol.III (1911), 78, 144. If the Bassets of Beaupré (Glam.) acquired Gower land from the marriage of Sir Elias Basset with Margaret, daughter of Sir John de la Bere of Weobley, it may have been inherited by their descendant, Hugh Basset, whose wife was Lleucu, Gruffydd ap Nicholas's daughter. Bartrum, *1400–1500*, I, 57.

of the prominent Carmarthenshire gentleman, Henry ap Gwilym (died after 1493) of Catheiniog, the builder of Cwrt Henry, near Llangathen, and once the bitterest foe of Thomas ap Gruffydd ap Nicholas. Efa and her sister were Henry's coheiresses and, the two families having sunk their differences, Sir Rhys acquired lands on the eastern side of the River Cothi (valued at £13. 12s. 0d. in 1532) which he later assigned as part of the jointure of his son's wife, Catherine St John.[80] Efa's younger sister, Jenet, was married to Sir William Mathew of Radyr in Glamorgan who presumably also enjoyed some of his father-in-law's Carmarthenshire properties. When Efa died and Sir Rhys sought consolation elsewhere, he lighted on Sir William's sister, Jenet Mathew; not only might she one day help him to secure more of Henry ap Gwilym's estate (should Sir William and his wife have no heirs), but she was also the young widow of Thomas Stradling (died 1480) of St Donat's and had custody of her son Edward (born 1472), heir to the substantial Stradling estates in south Wales and the west of England. Young Edward and his inheritance were at first placed in the care of Sir James Tyrell, Richard, duke of Gloucester's agent in Glamorgan, but by 1485 the heir was in Sir Rhys's charge, seemingly without authorization but probably following his mother's re-marriage.[81] This astute union, then, though it provided Sir Rhys with no children, gave him additional resources and social influence beyond his habitual haunts further west.

The marriage of Jenet Mathew lasted until Sir Rhys died in 1525, and Dame Jenet was often at court beside her husband. As for Sir Rhys's children, they were conceived in others' beds. His extramarital relationships were pursued on at least two complementary fronts. Three of his mistresses lived reasonably close at hand in west Wales. Gwenllian, who may have been the first in a long line, was the sister of the abbot of Talley, the Premonstratensian house situated not far from Sir Rhys's family home at Newton, near Llandeilo Fawr. Jenet Fychan was a local girl, too, the daughter of Gruffydd ap Dafydd Goch of Catheiniog, the commote in which lay some of Sir Rhys's estates, including his first wife's family home at Cwrt Henry. And so was the daughter, also named Jenet, of Maredudd ap Dafydd Fychan ap Henry Gwyn of Talley.[82] In the vicinity of his estates in Cardiganshire, he evidently struck up a relationship with Elizabeth, daughter of Richard Mortimer of Coedmor, which was situated near the borough of Cardigan where Richard was mayor in 1480–1 and again in 1514–15.[83] When he

---

[80] PRO, SC12/23/43; Jones, *Historic Homes*, pp.42–3; see above p.29; Griffiths, *Principality of Wales*, pp.265–6.

[81] R. A. Griffiths, 'The rise of the Stradlings of St Donat's', *Morgannwg*, VII (1963), 29–30; W. Campbell (ed.), *Materials for a History of the Reign of Henry VII* (2 vols., RS, 1877), II, 253; *CPR, 1485–94*, p.217.

[82] Bartrum, *1400–1500*, IV, 645; VII, 1202.

[83] Griffiths, *Principality of Wales*, p.430; Bartrum, *1400–1500*, VIII, 1407.

travelled further afield, additional liaisons were formed: with Mary, the daughter of Sir Roger Kynaston, whose estates lay at Knockin and Middle (Salop), not far from Oswestry, whereabouts Alice Kyffin, another inamorata, may have lived.[84] Each of these women was the mother of one or more of Sir Rhys's children who survived to adulthood; of other relationships, in Wales, at court or on campaign, we know nothing.

Sir Rhys owed it to his bastards to arrange marriages for them and to settle them as securely as possible; with his ambitions and instincts, he is certain to have regarded them also as instruments of family policy. None of the arrangements made compares with the marriage of his legitimate son, Gruffydd, to Catherine, daughter of Sir John St John of Bletsoe in Bedfordshire, but they are significant none the less for their indications of Sir Rhys's social horizons. Two words of caution are needed: not all the partners of Sir Rhys's bastards can be identified, and of course it is impossible to say exactly when each marriage was contracted. Nevertheless, it may be noted – without surprise – that three of his offspring found partners in the Tywi Valley. Margaret, Gwenllian's daughter, married Henry ap John, mayor of Carmarthen in 1502, constable of Dryslwyn Castle in 1514–20, and a captain in Sir Rhys's retinue in France in 1513. The couple settled at Rhydarwen, near Llanarthne, where doorways in their early-sixteenth-century home still bear carved shields, one of which supports the arms of Sir Rhys ap Thomas as a knight of the Garter.[85] Gwenllian, whose mother is unknown, married Gwilym ap Thomas, who may well have been the squire for the body in Henry VIII's household who lived at Llangathen.[86] Of Sir Rhys's two sons named Dafydd, the younger married Anne, daughter of John ap Rhys, mayor of Carmarthen in 1498–9; they settled near Llansawel.[87]

Two other matches reflect Sir Rhys's expanding interests in Pembrokeshire after 1485, and his efforts to forge links with the leading gentry there. The older Dafydd married Alison, daughter of Arnold Martin, and settled at Treicert, near Nevern in the lordship of Cemais; Mary Kynaston's daughter Margaret took as her husband Harry ap Thomas Wyriot of Orielton, whose family had long been prominent in the shire; and another son, William, settled at Sandyhaven, not far from Dale on the northern shore of the Haven.[88] Finally, in Cardiganshire, Jane, daughter of Elizabeth Mortimer, married Dafydd Llwyd ab

---

[84] Griffiths and Thomas, *Tudor Dynasty*, pp.146–7; Bartrum, *1400–1500*, I, 138.

[85] Griffiths, *Principality of Wales*, pp.266, 344; Jones *Historic Homes*, pp.171, 200; *RCAHM, Carmarthenshire*, pp.69–70; *TCASFC*, XI (1916–17), 38, 54, 58.

[86] Jones, *Historic Homes*, p.109, though his wife is here given as Gwenllian, daughter of Llywelyn ap Gwilym of Bryn Hafod, not far from Llangathen.

[87] Griffiths, *Principality of Wales*, p.344; Jones, *Historic Homes*, p.113.

[88] B. E. Howells, 'Studies in the social and agrarian history of medieval and early modern Pembrokeshire' (University of Wales MA thesis, 2 vols., 1956), p.125; Bartrum, *1400–1500*, X, 1754; Griffiths, *Principality of Wales*, pp.267, 270, 375.

Ieuan, who hailed from the northern commote of Creuddyn, where he was reeve in 1516–17.[89] Her sister, also called Jane, married Dafydd Llwyd ap Thomas ab Owain, who was from the Llangeitho area of the Cardiganshire commote of Pennardd.[90] Only Gwenllian, Jenet Fychan's daughter, found a husband at a considerable distance, though Lewis Sutton, from Haydock in Cheshire, may have encountered her when he was escheator of Carmarthenshire and Cardiganshire between 1502 and 1506.[91] Her second husband, however, was Hywel Gwyn ap Rhydderch, a native of Llanfair-ar-y-bryn in the commote of Hirfryn, part of the lordship of Llandovery.[92]

Sir Rhys's most notable coup was the marriage of his son and heir to Catherine St John, daughter of Sir John St John (died 1525) of Bletsoe in Bedfordshire and of Fonmon and Pen-marc in Glamorgan. We do not know when the marriage contract was negotiated by the two fathers, but it is likely to have had the personal approval of Henry VII, for Catherine was the king's kinswoman. She was the great-granddaughter of the long-lived Margaret Beauchamp, heiress of Bletsoe, whose first husband was Sir Oliver St John; her second was John Beaufort, duke of Somerset (died 1444), the father of King Henry's mother, Margaret Beaufort; for her third she took Leo, Lord Welles (died 1461), the father of Henry VII's step-uncle, John, Viscount Welles (died 1499). Sir Gruffydd's marriage to Catherine St John may have taken place while he was in the service of Prince Arthur (died 1502); it had certainly taken place by *c.*1507, for his son, Rhys, was born *c.*1508 and pedigrees indicate that a daughter, Elizabeth, was Sir Gruffydd's first-born.[93] By marrying her, Sir Gruffydd ap Rhys was entering that small, self-conscious family circle on which Henry relied heavily and which he enlarged only with the utmost circumspection.[94] In the years up to 1497, Sir Rhys ap Thomas had won the king's regard and trust to such a degree that his heir was received into Prince Arthur's household and in due course was given a bride with royal lineage, if of the half-blood. It is worth noting, too, that Viscount Welles was granted the Welsh lordships of Caerleon and Usk in August 1490, and that he and Sir Rhys served together on the king's expedition to France in 1492.[95]

Nor should the role of Margaret Beaufort, countess of Richmond, in promoting this union be discounted. She and her third husband,

[89] Griffiths, *Principality of Wales*, p.467; Bartrum, *1400–1500*, III, 358.

[90] Bartrum, *1400–1500*, III, 367.

[91] Griffiths, *Principality of Wales*, p.328. They settled at Spittal, in north Pembrokeshire, Bartrum, *1400–1500*, X, 1624; IV, 645; *DNB, s.n.* Sir Richard Sutton.

[92] Bartrum, *1400–1500*, X, 1644.

[93] *CP*, II, 45; XII, part 1, 47–8; XII, part 2, 444–50; J. S. Leadam (ed.), *Select Cases before the King's Council in the Court of Star Chamber*, II (1509–44) (Selden Soc., 1963), p.25 n.3; Bindoff, *HP*, III, 255–8; Bartrum, *1400–1500*, IX, 1567–8; IV, 645.

[94] Griffiths and Thomas, *Tudor Dynasty*, ch.13.

[95] *CP*, XII, part 2, 448.

Thomas, Lord Stanley, had custody of Margaret Beauchamp's estates (including Bletsoe) when she died in 1482 and before Bletsoe passed to the St Johns.[96] The monumental inscription on the tomb of Sir John St John (died 1558) says that he was brought up by Lady Margaret, his grandfather's half-sister, and it may be that his sister, Catherine St John, also grew up in Lady Margaret's household. Their father, Sir John St John, was Lady Margaret's chamberlain and an executor of her will.[97] Moreover, the St Johns were already connected with Sir Rhys ap Thomas's family, for Dame Jenet, Sir Rhys's second wife, was the first cousin of Catherine's grandmother, Elizabeth Mathew, and so Jenet, too, may have encouraged the match. Sir Rhys himself was a more distant cousin of Elizabeth Mathew, whose grandmother was a daughter of none other than Gruffydd ap Nicholas.[98] The circumstances were set fair for a marriage between Gruffydd and Catherine St John to be approved at court and sanctioned by two influential matriarchs, the countess of Richmond and Dame Jenet. It may not be a coincidence that about this time Sir Rhys ap Thomas was given responsibility for building the new tomb at Carmarthen's friary for the body of the countess's first husband, Edmund Tudor.[99]

The marriages of Sir Gruffydd's children merited equally careful thought, and his father was seemingly ready with useful advice. Without doubt, their greatest achievement was to secure Catherine Howard, one of the daughters of Thomas Howard, earl of Surrey and (from 1514) duke of Norfolk (1443–1524), and his second wife, Agnes, for Sir Gruffydd's son and heir, Rhys ap Gruffydd. Despite having fought for Richard III at Bosworth, Howard was reconciled to Henry Tudor and had become lord treasurer by 1501, a position he continued to hold under Henry VIII (until 1522). He took part in the negotiations leading to the marriage of Prince Arthur with Catherine of Aragon; and if the presence of the Countess Agnes at Arthur's wedding in 1501 reflects her own association with the royal couple's household (and Agnes herself was then only about twenty-four), then she could easily have met Sir Gruffydd ap Rhys and his family in the prince's service. Furthermore, Norfolk's eldest son, Thomas Howard, earl of Surrey (1473–1554), served with Sir Gruffydd on the disappointing campaign to Spain in 1512 and, as admiral, had responsibility for conveying the king's army to France in 1513, the retinue of Sir Rhys and his son included. Sir Rhys

---

[96] Ibid., p.444.

[97] Bindoff, *HP*, III, 255–8.

[98] N. H. Nicolas (ed.), *Testamenta Vetusta* (2 vols., London, 1826), II, 524; Bartrum, *1400–1500*, VI, 873; IX, 1567–8; III, 473.

[99] See above p.49; M. K. Jones and M. G. Underwood, *The King's Mother* (Cambridge, 1991), pp.32–3, 112–14, 125–6.

John Beauchamp of Bletsoe (d.*c*.1412)

John (d. unm.)

Margaret = (1) Sir Oliver St John, (2) *c*.1442, John Beaufort, (3) 1447, Leo, Lord Welles
duke of Somerset (d.1461)
(d.1444)

Margaret Beaufort (d.1509)

John, Viscount Welles (d.1499)

Henry VII (d.1509)

Sir David Matthew = Lleucu, dau. of Gruffydd ap Nicholas

William

Thomas

Sir John St John = (2) Elizabeth

Jenet = (2) Sir Rhys ap Thomas (d.1525)

Sir John St John (d.1525) = Margaret, dau. of Morgan ap Jankyn

Sir John St John (*c*.1495–1558)

Catherine (d.1553) = Sir Gruffydd ap Rhys (d.1521)

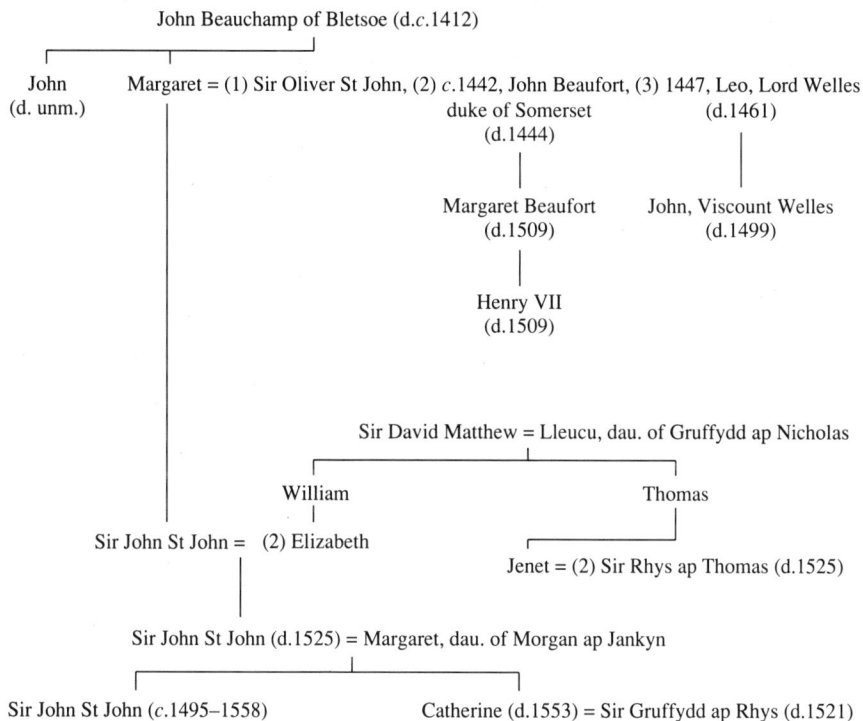

The St John connection

returned from this latter expedition with his and his family's reputations at their highest.[100]

The marriage negotiations are likely to have been initiated by Sir Rhys and Sir Gruffydd, whose interests coincided with those of the Howards at this juncture. Sir Rhys especially could hardly have failed to be apprehensive at the growing power of Charles Brandon, Henry VIII's friend and companion, in north and north-east Wales. Of even

[100] *CP*, IX, 612–16; M. J. Tucker, *The Life of Thomas Howard, Earl of Surrey and Second Duke of Norfolk, 1443–1524* (The Hague, 1964); S. E. Vokes, 'The early career of Thomas Howard, earl of Surrey and third duke of Norfolk, 1474–*c*.1525' (unpublished University of Hull Ph.D. thesis, 1988).

more direct concern was Brandon's purchase, early in 1514, of the wardship of Roger Corbet, who had a claim to lands in Emlyn Uwch Cuch which Sir Rhys and his family had long occupied; the Corbets were related to another of Brandon's friends, Walter Devereux, Lord Ferrers. Already, in January 1513, Brandon had used his influence to secure for his uncle, Sir Robert Brandon, the wardship of John Carew of Haccombe, and Sir Rhys may have felt that such wealthy and influential connections of the rising courtier might place in jeopardy even his hold on Carew Castle. By 1513, the Howards had their own difficulties with Brandon, over military policy and over the estates of John, Viscount Lisle (died 1504), whose wife (died 1512) was a daughter of Thomas Howard, earl of Surrey. Custody of these estates, situated mainly in the western counties, was transferred from the Howards to Brandon in 1513, when the latter was created Viscount Lisle by Henry VIII and contracted to marry Elizabeth, the child-heiress of the Lisles. Many were shocked when, on 1 February 1514, Brandon was further elevated to the dukedom of Suffolk, on the very day that the dukedom of Norfolk was restored to Thomas Howard and his eldest son succeeded to Thomas's title of earl of Surrey. If the Howards cast round for allies to curb Brandon's burgeoning power in Wales and the west, Sir Rhys ap Thomas's family was among the most influential available. Less than six weeks after the ceremonies of creation in Parliament, the bargain between them had been struck.[101] On 12 March 1514, an agreement was made between the duke and Sir Rhys and his son, Sir Gruffydd, for the marriage of Catherine Howard and Rhys ap Gruffydd.[102] The clauses of this agreement show all the hard-headed business sense of landowners who were prepared to conclude an alliance but, in the case of Sir Rhys and Sir Gruffydd, were anxious to protect their own inheritance. It was accordingly provided that Rhys ap Gruffydd, who was born about 1508, should marry Catherine by the time he was fourteen, when the couple's trustees would receive from Rhys's father and grandfather an estate worth 100 marks; a further 100 marks' worth would be assigned but be retained for Sir Rhys's use during his lifetime; and the same arrangement was made in Sir Gruffydd's favour. The careful Welshmen also agreed to give Rhys ap Gruffydd a further 300 marks after the death of Sir Rhys and his wife and Sir Gruffydd and his wife, and another 100 marks' worth of property, which Rhys's mother, Catherine St John, presently held in jointure (mainly in the Gower peninsula), once she was dead. It amounted to fat promises, to be fulfilled in the future. In return,

[101] S. J. Gunn, *Charles Brandon, Duke of Suffolk, c.1484–1545* (Oxford, 1988), pp.5, 14–15, 19, 21, 22–7; idem, *WHR*, XII (1985), 461–94; Vokes, thesis cited, pp.125–51.

[102] NLW, Dynevor, A 59, transcribed in Appendix II of Lloyd, thesis cited, pp.125–34. Provision was made for Norfolk to cease payments arising from the contract if his daughter died before Rhys ap Gruffydd was sixteen and left no heir, and also for any daughters of Sir Rhys and Sir Gruffydd left unmarried at the knights' deaths.

the duke of Norfolk promised to pay Sir Rhys and Sir Gruffydd £200 in cash at the time of the marriage, another £200 one year later, and a further £200 one year after that. The marriage contract offered imminent benefits to the Welshmen. Half of the trustees were drawn from East Anglia and the duke of Norfolk's household, among them Sir Philip Tilney (whose sister the duke had married in 1497), Sir Richard Wentworth, Sir Thomas Blennerhassett, Sir Nicholas Appleyard, Sir Philip Calthorp and Amery Berwick. On the Welsh side, Sir Thomas Cornwall and his son Richard were Shropshire companions in arms of Sir Rhys and Sir Gruffydd, Sir James ab Owain was a Pembrokeshire knight, William ap John ap Thomas was Sir Rhys's cousin, and Dafydd ap Llywelyn ap Gwilym (possibly of Castell Hywel in south Cardiganshire) and Gruffydd ap Maredudd Fychan may have been their personal servants.[103] When Sir Gruffydd died prematurely in 1521, it was in the interest of both families to arrange the wedding as soon as possible, if it had not recently already taken place: after all, a further estate of 100 marks was now due to the couple's trustees under the terms of the contract, and for Sir Rhys ap Thomas the need to fortify his line had become urgent. The marriage had certainly taken place by 20 August 1522, and when Thomas Howard, duke of Norfolk, died at Framlingham Castle (Suffolk) on 21 May 1524, Sir Rhys ap Thomas's young heir was summoned to take his place alongside other chief mourners of the close family in the procession that accompanied the body to Thetford Priory for burial. On 22 June Rhys ap Gruffydd knelt before the hearse during a solemn dirge in Diss Church on the way, and at Thetford on 24 June he led the duke's horse into the priory church at the funeral service itself.[104]

Apart from his son, Sir Gruffydd had three daughters. All three married well, if in rather less exalted circles than their brother – testimony to the position which their father held at court during Henry VIII's first decade as king. The husband of the eldest, Elizabeth, was Charles (later Sir Charles) Herbert of Troy, near Monmouth, whose father, Sir William (died 1524), administered the lordships of Kidwelly, Monmouth and the Three Castles (Skenfrith, Grosmont and White Castle) for Henry VII and Henry VIII, and was an illegitimate son of William Herbert, earl of Pembroke (died 1469), 'King Edward's master-lock' in Wales during the 1460s.[105] Of the other daughters, Mary

---

[103] Bindoff, *HP*, III, 583; I, 443, 421–2, 705–7, 325–6; Isaacson, *Episcopal Registers*, II, 811; see below p.80; Griffiths, *Principality of Wales*, p.522; R. Virgoe, 'The recovery of the Howards in East Anglia, 1485–1509', in E. W. Ives, R. J. Knecht and J. J. Scarisbrick (eds.), *Wealth and Power in Tudor England* (London, 1978), pp.11, 14; Nicolas, *Testamenta Vetusta*, II, 604.

[104] A. Leigh Hunt, *The Capital of the Ancient Kingdom of East Anglia* (London, 1870), pp.367–78. Two sons, Thomas and Gruffydd, were evidently born in 1524 and 1526 respectively (NLW, Dynevor A 61; see below p.117). Yet Catherine was able to visit her sister-in-law, the countess of Surrey, at Norfolk's house at Stoke-by-Nayland in Suffolk in 1523 (Vokes, thesis cited, pp.310–11).

[105] Bartrum, *1400–1500*, IV, 645; V, 780, 783; Somerville, *Duchy of Lancaster*, I, 648, 651–2; Bindoff,

did not marry until after the death of her father and when her mother
had moved to Cornwall as the wife of Sir Piers Edgecombe (by 1525).
She then married John Luttrell, the heir of the Luttrell estates at
Dunster and elsewhere in Somerset.[106] At the time of her husband's
death from sweating sickness in 1551, Mary (who died in 1588) was
facing charges of adultery; she later married James Godolphin of
Gwinear in Cornwall.[107] The third sister married into the Whites of
Hampshire, though it is not easy to identify her husband. He may have
been a son of Robert White of South Wanborough (died 1521) and his
wife Elizabeth, daughter of Sir Thomas Englefield. Like Sir Gruffydd ap
Rhys, Englefield (died 1514) had been in Prince Arthur's service,
notably in Wales; he later became a councillor of both Henry VII and
Henry VIII, and was an executor of the former's will in 1509.[108] By such
social, personal and public contacts were influential marriages made in
the fifteenth and sixteenth centuries.

A man who could show such circumspection and imagination in his
marriage policy is likely to have exploited other means to extend his
estate and augment his wealth, especially by securing wardships in
prominent families and negotiating mortgages and land purchases.
Sadly, little of Sir Rhys's personal archive survives to give more than a
glimpse of his intentions and successes in these directions. Presumably as
a result of his marriage to Jenet Mathew, widow of Thomas Stradling, it
was claimed in February 1488 that Sir Rhys had assumed, without
authority, the wardship of young Edward Stradling, pocketing £208 in
three years as a consequence. Sir Rhys transferred the Stradling estates
to Edward, 'my son', on 6 August 1494, after he had come of age.[109] He
was very likely the guardian of other heirs and heiresses, though we can
only be certain of Jenet Wogan, his ward in 1518. As the daughter of
Henry Wogan, one of the sons of Sir John Wogan of Wiston, not far from
Haverfordwest, and Henry's wife, Catherine Mathew, Jenet was the
niece of Sir Rhys's wife, who presumably took an interest in the girl from

HP, II, 336–7; Griffiths, 'Wales and the March', p.159.

[106] Bartrum, *1400–1500*, IV, 645; Wedgwood, *HP*, p.735; H. Maxwell-Lyte (ed.), *Documents and Extracts illustrating the History of the Honour of Dunster* (Somerset Record Soc., 33, 1918), pp.289–90; Bindoff, *HP*, III, 254–5. The Somerset manor of East Quantoxhead was settled on the newly wed couple (H. Maxwell-Lyte, *A History of Dunster*, I [1909], 142).

[107] J. Strype, *Ecclesiastical Memorials*, II, part 2 (Oxford, 1822), 204; Maxwell-Lyte, *History of Dunster*, I, 161–2. Mary had some of her father's household goods at Dunster in 1553; for a picture which includes portraits of her daughter, Catherine Luttrell, and her husband, Sir Thomas Copley, ibid., p.164.

[108] Wedgwood, *HP*, p.301; Bindoff, *HP*, III, 607; J. S. Roskell, *The Commons and their Speakers in English Parliaments, 1376–1523* (Manchester, 1965), pp.305–6, 310–11. An early seventeenth-century note in CRO, Dynevor, Add. MS 73, records that a daughter called Dorothy married Humphrey White. 'The epytaphye of Sir Gryffyth Apryse' implies that Catherine St John lost a young child shortly before Sir Gruffydd's death in 1521: *Anglia*, XXXI, 248 ('The late losse of your chylde was a grete greuance').

[109] *CPR, 1485–94*, p.217; Campbell, *Materials*, II, 253; G. E. Evans, 'The seal of Sir Rhys ap Thomas, 1494', *TCASFC*, XXVI (1936), 15–17.

Radyr in Glamorgan.[110] When Jenet Wogan married, on 15 August 1523, her partner might seem to have been a surprising choice, Richard Cornwall (died 1569), the son of Sir Thomas Cornwall (died 1537) of Burford in Shropshire. But the connections were there, forged in royal and military service: Sir Thomas was at Blackheath and in France with Sir Rhys ap Thomas, and at Prince Arthur's funeral and in Spain with Sir Gruffydd ap Rhys; he was a prominent figure in the Marches, and when trustees were nominated in 1514 to supervise Sir Gruffydd's marriage contract both Sir Thomas and Richard Cornwall were numbered among them.[111]

The movements, interests and relationships of these Anglo-Welsh gentry were finely enmeshed. In the case of Sir Rhys ap Thomas and his progeny, the horizons were geographical, social and political. If, as seems likely, Sir Rhys's was the guiding hand, he looked beyond the Vale of Tywi to south Cardiganshire, eastern Pembrokeshire and to the rich lowlands of Glamorgan to establish liaisons with Welsh *uchelwyr* and Anglo-Welsh knights and esquires – and, in his heir's generation, to associations fostered at court, in camp and in the English borderland. The ties and relationships criss-crossed the pedigrees in ways that on the surface may seem fortuitous, though if the messages between relatives had survived, or messengers had left a record of their missions, what might we not learn of proposals, suggestions and information to compare with the marital manœuvres and investigations of the Pastons of East Anglia? 'Since the kin formed a community, marriage meant not so much intimate association with an individual as entry into a new world of the spouse's relatives, uncles, nephews and distant cousins.'[112]

Sir Rhys and his family acquired rights and profits from property wherever the condition of lordship allowed, and this included the ecclesiastical sphere. Before 1519, Sir Gruffydd ap Rhys had been allowed to lease the considerable Slebech estates of the Knights of the Hospital of St John of Jerusalem. But according to Clement West, the local commander of the Order, the arrangement turned sour, even though West was a knight of the king's body. Sir Gruffydd abused his position by cutting down more than 2,000 oaks without licence, failing to keep buildings in a proper state of repair, and demanding extortionate sums from the tenantry. When payment of the rent fell into arrears, West retaliated, only to precipitate (he claimed) a vicious attack on his house at Slebech in August 1519, whilst Sir Gruffydd continued to exploit the estate as before. Sir Rhys ap Thomas's promises of remedy degenerated into further violence the following year, and the king's absence at the Field of Cloth of Gold impeded West's campaign for

---

[110] *LP, Henry VIII*, II, part 2, 1490; Bartrum, *1400–1500*, II, 166; VI, 873.

[111] Bindoff, *HP*, I, 204–7; NLW, Dynevor, A 59; Gunn, *WHR*, XII, no. 4 (1985), 478–9.

[112] L. Stone, *The Family, Sex and Marriage in England, 1500–1800* (London, 1977), p.86.

redress. A desperate plea to Cardinal Wolsey in the Court of Requests is unlikely to have seriously inconvenienced the two indomitable and ruthless knights.[113]

Mortgages, especially when unredeemed, could be even more lucrative. It is often claimed that in order to finance his retinue in the king's expedition to France in 1513, Sir Edmund Carew (1464–1513) mortgaged his rich estates, including Carew Castle, to Sir Rhys ap Thomas, and that after Sir Edmund was fatally shot while sitting in his tent outside Thérouanne at the outset of the siege, the estate passed to Sir Rhys.[114] It is tolerably clear, however, that Rhys was already lord of Carew before he and Sir Edmund set out for France: according to the Life, Sir Rhys's Garter celebrations were held at Carew in 1506, and as early as 1497 he was acting as patron of St Mary's parish church there. The mortgage may have been arranged even earlier, for in 1493 Sir Edmund Carew assigned his rights of patronage in St Mary's Church, Carew, to Richard Newton, esquire; he may have been ready to dispose of his properties and rights, but may not yet have done so to Sir Rhys. On the other hand, early in the seventeenth century, it was believed that Sir Edmund's grandfather, Thomas Carew, the son (probably the eldest) of Nicholas Carew (died 1470), had been responsible for mortgaging the estate, and this, too, seems plausible.[115] Sir Edmund's death may have finalized its transfer to Sir Rhys.

Having obtained the major prize, on 29 July 1510 Sir Rhys granted a 20-mark mortgage on two further tenements at Redberth, some three miles north-east of Carew Castle.[116] There is no hint in this transaction – and Sir Rhys bound himself in the sum of 100 marks to observe the mortgage's terms – of the unscrupulous acquisition of properties of which Elis Gruffydd, the Flintshire chronicler, accused him:

> And indeed many men regarded his death [i.e. the execution of Rhys, grandson of Sir Rhys, in 1531] as Divine retribution for the falsehoods of his ancestors, his grandfather and great-grandfather, and for their oppression and wrongs. They had many a deep curse from the poor people who were neighbours, for depriving them of their houses, lands and riches. For I heard the conversation of folk from that part of the country who said that no common people owned land within twenty miles from the dwelling of old Sir Rhys son of Thomas, that if he desired such lands he would appropriate them without payment or thanks, and the

---

[113] E. A. Lewis, *An Inventory of the Early Chancery Proceedings concerning Wales* (Cardiff, 1937), p.291; PRO, Req. 2/10/76; F. Jones, 'Sir Rhys ap Thomas and the Knights of St John', *Carms. Antiquary*, II (1945–57), 70–4.

[114] *Hall's Chronicle*, p.538; *LP, Henry VIII*, I, part 2, 1057–62.

[115] See below p.247; Isaacson, *Episcopal Registers*, II, 668–9, 718–19; NLW, Llanstephan 130 D f.4; H. Owen, *Old Pembrokeshire Families* (London, 1902), p.16; W. G. Spurrell, *The History of Carew* (Carmarthen, 1921), pp.28–9; Lewis, *WWHR*, II (1911–12), 71 and n.3.

[116] *CAD*, V, 540; *LP, Henry VIII*, I, 315.

disinherited doubtless cursed him, his children and his grandchildren, which curses in the opinion of many men fell on the family, according to the old proverb which says – the children of Lies are uprooted, and after oppression comes a long death to the oppressors.[117]

This stern, apocalyptic verdict is surely exaggerated, but to any who suffered from Sir Rhys's creation of parks near his residences it might not have seemed unjustified. And he certainly set out to augment the Carew estate by further acquisitions within two or three miles of it, at Sageston, Cresselly, Snelston, Yerbeston, Pincheston, Milton and Crickchurch, on the eastern side of the meandering River Cleddau. Sir Rhys's appetite for acres, his passion for parks and hunting, and his high reputation as a captain of light cavalry may explain the arrangements, described in the later Life from a 'traditional report', whereby he ensured a supply of horses and horsemen, and at the same time acquired 'certain patches of land within their estates' from tenants who were prepared, and expected, to turn out, when needed, in the knight's service. The campaigns of the Wars of the Roses seem to have witnessed a revival in the use of cavalry in England, especially of light cavalry and scouts (or 'scourers'), and at the same time tournaments gained renewed popularity in royal and noble households. And Sir Rhys may have been particularly struck, during his years in exile, by the organization of the Burgundian armies, which assigned greater prominence to light and heavy cavalry, and by the methods used to raise such retinues.[118]

In the years up to the departure for France in 1513, Sir Rhys spent considerably on buildings and parkland.[119] His house at Newton, the minuscule borough in the lee of Dinefwr Castle, was built by his ancestors and was no longer large or splendid enough for Sir Rhys's taste, or to serve as his chief residence. Nevertheless, it seems to have sprawled over a number of burgages at Newton, with the result that the place was seriously depopulated by the early decades of the sixteenth century. The inventory of Rhys ap Gruffydd's possessions made in 1532 noted that the house had its own hall, 33 feet by 20 feet, paved with Flanders tiles, roofed with slate and entered up a flight of twelve steps. A chamber at each of its western and eastern ends, paved with tiles, was complemented by a small chamber, 12 feet square, on the north side, and one of two inner rooms served as a study. On the south side of the hall was a tower which housed a chapel above and a low-vaulted chamber below. On this side, too, there was a kitchen, larder and buttery, and beneath the hall a wine cellar. The approach to the house

---

[117] Jones, *TCASFC*, XXIX (1939), 31–2; *MSS in the Welsh Language*, I, x. Sir Rhys's further acquisitions, which were annexed to Carew, are noted in *CPR, 1580–2*, p.26.

[118] See below p.191; A. E. Goodman, *The Wars of the Roses* (London, 1981), pp.175–81; R. Vaughan, *Charles the Bold* (London, 1973), pp.197–222.

[119] PRO, C1/513/26.

on the north side was flanked by a single-storey lodge, and a 'backhouse', brewery and corn store stood nearby; other outbuildings included stables and a barn, which were dilapidated by 1532.[120] When John Leland, the tireless Tudor traveller, visited Newton in the mid-1530s, he found the little town 'sumtime a long streat nowe ruinus'.[121]

Things seemed happier at Sir Rhys's mother's house up river at Abermarlais, though the park may well have been laid out at the expense of tenantry. 'The parke there is paled, and in cumpas .ii. miles and a half and well wooded.' Inside Leland found a 'welle favorid stone place motid, now mended and augmentid by Sir Rhese ap Thomas', and the survey of Rhys ap Gruffydd's property in 1532 confirms this impression: 'The seid manor place stondeth within a parke and is moted and cumpassed with water round aboute.'[122] The main part of the house, 136 feet by 33 feet, on the east side contained a hall, a study and domestic offices and apartments. The gateway, facing south, was flanked by a prison tower. Extensive stables, one of the buildings as much as 100 feet long by 24 feet in breadth, lay to the west and north of the main house, and on the north side, too, was the chapel with a cellar, all of 36 feet by 23 feet.

Even more imposing was Sir Rhys's newly acquired residence of Carew Castle, where he lived in the finest opulence.[123] The Garter festivities were held in 1506 in an imposing fortress which Leland learned had been 'repairid and magnificently buildid by Syr Rhese ap Thomas'. In the vicinity were extensive parks which he had created and which Leland visited:

> Cumming from [Lamphey] towarde Tinbighe I rode by a ruinus waulle of a parke sumtime longging to Syr Rhese, now voide of dere. In the parke is veri litle or no hye woode, but shrubbis and fyrris, like as is in the .ii. parkes about Carew, waullid with stones.[124]

At the castle itself, Sir Rhys reconstructed the medieval hall (some 81 feet long) on the western side of the large court, as well as the eastern range, with its grand stairway to a lesser hall, and, probably, the entrance and outer gatehouse beyond. Several ornamental features and fireplaces from Sir Rhys's day still survive; so do the great oriel window of the main hall, and the porch with its shields of the royal arms of England, and of Prince Arthur and Catherine of Aragon. The

[120] Griffiths 'A tale of two towns', in James, *Studies in Carms. History*, p.220 and nn.87–9; PRO, E315/151; Lewis, *WWHR*, II (1912), 115–17.

[121] L. T. Smith (ed.), *The Itinerary in Wales of John Leland* (London, 1906), p.57.

[122] See above p.61; Leland, *Itinerary*, p.52; *RCAHM, Carmarthenshire*, p.182; PRO, E315/151; Jones, *Historic Homes*, pp.3–4. The old house was demolished early in the nineteenth century.

[123] Sir Rhys's war retinue seems to have assembled at Carew in 1513 and returned there afterwards: see above p.56.

[124] Leland, *Itinerary*, pp.115–16. For the two parks, enclosures and columbarium in 1555, see PRO, LR1/229 f.18–19.

battlements and turrets were altered for visual effect ('to view the country') rather than with military purposes in mind, and two stable blocks, one near the river all of 128 feet in length, and a substantial smith's forge catered for Sir Rhys's horses. All this rebuilding to create an imposing residence was more than likely complete by 1506.[125]

Newcastle Emlyn, which was renovated by Sir Rhys and augmented with a large gatehouse, is best regarded as a defensive and administrative headquarters and a hunting box. As the 1532 survey said of one of the smaller towers of this fortress, originally built in the thirteenth century, it was admirably positioned 'to view and see the cuntre'. It had few of the comforts and embellishments of Abermarlais or Carew. Its most notable feature was the large stable block, 120 feet long and in a state of good repair, which stood outside the castle walls close to the river, 'within which stable baith rowme with particions for .xxii. horses. And over the same a fayre galery selyd with a chamber with .x. glasse wyndoes in the same and covered with sklate'. Nearby was a 36-foot-long slaughter house to which was brought the game from Sir Rhys's hunting parties in his forest barely a mile away, 'which is well woddeed with a certein red dere therein'.[126] Hunting seems to have been a passion with Sir Rhys and his family. In the manor of Cae Gurwen in upland Gower, close to the forests of the Black Mountains, was a house called Neuadd Wen. The estate had probably been inherited from Sir Rhys's mother, but the house was 'as fame remaineth [according to the antiquary, Rice Merrick, later in the sixteenth century] built by Sir Rhys ap Thomas knight for a lodge when he came to that part to hunt'.[127]

We know less about Sir Rhys's smaller castle in Gower, Weobley, overlooking the River Llwchwr and south Carmarthenshire beyond, because in 1532 it was held by his daughter-in-law, Catherine Edgecombe, and was not forfeited to the Crown when her son was attainted. But there, too, Sir Rhys ap Thomas (or his son, Sir Gruffydd, who seems to have held it after his marriage) undertook some residential building, most notably a fine two-storey porch block that provided 'a more stately entrance to the [lofty] hall and private quarters, as befitted even this minor residence of one of the most important Welshmen of his day'. This porch is reminiscent of Sir Rhys's ceremonial works at Carew that were designed to reflect the dignity of a Garter knight. As for Narberth Castle in Pembrokeshire, its value to Sir Rhys ap Thomas

[125] R. F. Walker, 'Carew Castle', *Arch. Camb.*, CV (1956), 81–95; D. J. C. King and J. C. Perks, 'Carew Castle, Pembs.', *Archaeological Jnl.*, CXIX (1962), 270–307; PRO, E315/151/7; Owen, *Public Records relating to Pembs.*, III, 68–71; and *RCAHM, Pembrokeshire*, pp.51–2.

[126] *RCAHM, Carmarthenshire*, pp.220–1; Leland, *Itinerary*, p.57; C. Parry, 'Survey and Excavation at Newcastle Emlyn Castle', *Carms. Antiquary*, 23 (1987), 11–27.

[127] D. Rees, 'Neuadd Wen: changing patterns of tenure', in James, *Studies in Carms. History*, p.48 and n.16; 'Parochialia . . . Edward Lhuyd', *Arch. Camb.*, suppl. vol. III (1911), p.146.

appears to have been limited, for in 1532 it was described as 'greatly in decay'; and though Leland found it 'a little preati pile of old Syr Rheses', the adjacent borough amounted to nothing more than 'a poore village'. As a fortress, its quadrangular courtyard was well defended with five drum towers, and against the west wall a gallery had been built, 76 feet by 10 feet, 'with three chambers or lodgings under the same'; but in 1532 no mention was made of deer or other game in the forest associated with the castle.[128]

With a substantial estate and a sizeable income from his offices, Sir Rhys also had an heir, Gruffydd, who was at least as well connected at court and in gentle society. He had made provision for Sir Gruffydd and his wife to enjoy jointly an estate in the Tywi Valley and, especially, in Gower that was worth about £72 per annum, aside from property that Sir Gruffydd acquired on his own account. For example, Sir Gruffydd was leasing land in Kingswood and Gawdon (now, extraordinarily, Golden Hill!) in St Mary's parish, Pembroke, in 1519–20; he also secured lands and tenants in Winforton, in the Vale of Wye, by offering a mortgage of £40 to one of his own cousins and servants, James ap Meurig, in about 1512.[129] And in 1514, of course, advantageous financial arrangements were made for Sir Gruffydd's young son when he should marry Catherine Howard. These prudent provisions were seriously jeopardized when Sir Gruffydd died, sometime between July and October 1521. Moreover, he died intestate and in debt, partly because of the costs of war incurred in 1512–13 and, doubtless, the heavy expenses of court life.[130]

Sir Rhys ap Thomas spent his last few years repairing the damage caused to his plans by his son's early death. In July and August 1522, those lands which Sir Gruffydd had held (apart from the jointure lands which passed to his widow), and those, worth 100 marks, which the marriage contract had assigned to trustees for the use of Sir Gruffydd

[128] Thomas, *Weobley Castle*, pp.14, 19–25; *RCAHM, Pembrokeshire*, pp.246–7; Leland, *Itinerary*, p.62.
[129] PRO, SC6/Henry VIII/345 m.118; B. G. Charles, *Non-Celtic Place Names in Wales* (London, 1935), pp.22–4. James's father was Sir Rhys ap Thomas's brother, John ap Thomas, and Sir Gruffydd was seemingly concerned lest the lands pass from his family. Half the mortgage was unpaid at the time of Sir Gruffydd's death; his father absolved James from paying the remainder when Edward Hopton fraudulently claimed that Sir Gruffydd had granted the lands to him. See CRO, Dynevor A 73, enclosing copies of Sir Rhys's letters and certificates to the Council in the Marches which dealt with the Hopton suit against James ap Meurig's heiress, Marjorie Meurig, in 1524–5. These copies seem to have been made about the time, c.1630s, when a large pedigree was constructed whose initial purpose was to detail the descent of the Winforton lands. The copy-letters and -certificates, and copies of depositions of witnesses during the case (1525–36), were incorporated in the pedigree, NLW, Pedigree Box 13 (drawn to my attention by Dr R. K. Turvey).
[130] *LP, Henry VIII*, III, part 2, 592, 779, 1528. His debt to the Crown still amounted to £420 in 1523; in 1532 it had grown to £506. 13s. 4d., aside from whatever Sir Piers Edgecombe, the husband of Sir Gruffydd's widow, had repaid from his wife's inherited goods (ibid., V, 716; PRO, KB27/1075 m.61). The inscription on his restored tomb in Worcester Cathedral mistakenly places his death on 29 September 1522 (*sic*). V. Green, *The History and Antiquities of the City and Suburbs of Worcester* (2 vols., London, 1796), I, 154.

during his lifetime, were formally assigned to the use of Sir Rhys ap Thomas and his wife, Dame Jenet, with every expectation that they would eventually pass to Rhys ap Gruffydd and his heirs.[131] Determined to reassert his own control, and with his grandson still a minor, on 30 April 1522 Sir Rhys concluded a thirty-year lease of all the lands settled on Catherine Howard at the time of her marriage to Rhys ap Gruffydd, in return for 200 marks per annum, their precise value according to the marriage contract. This was control enough, for in 1552 Sir Rhys would be well beyond the age of one hundred![132]

Death came too soon for Sir Rhys ap Thomas himself. He was already ailing when he made his will, 'Syke in body', on 3 February 1524. His last known communication was to the Council in the Marches on behalf of James ap Meurig's sister on 4 April 1524 from Carmarthen. There he died in the summer of 1525, at the age of about seventy-six.[133] His will directed that he be buried in the Greyfriars' Church, Carmarthen, where his mother, Elizabeth Gruffydd, lay; and he made arrangements that his widow, Dame Jenet, should in due time be buried beside him. In the friary, too, was the tomb, whose construction he had supervised, of Edmund Tudor, earl of Richmond, the father of Sir Rhys's greatest benefactor. By the time that William Fellows, Lancaster Herald, reached Carmarthen in 1530, on his visitation of churches in south Wales, a 'goodly tomb' had been erected for Sir Rhys on the north side of the choir, close to the high altar.[134]

In his will, Sir Rhys made substantial bequests to churches with which he had been associated during his lifetime, several of them situated on or near his scattered estates. Apart from £20 to St David's Cathedral, he was most generous to the churches in Carmarthen itself: the Greyfriars received £20 in cash and £5 in land to establish a perpetual chantry with two priests to pray for his and his wife's souls; St John's Priory received £6. 13s. 4d.; the Rood Church and St Catherine's Hermitage each had a vestment worth £2. 13s. 4d., St Peter's Church a vestment and a chalice together worth £5, and St John's and St Barbara's Chapels each a vestment worth rather less at £2. A little way outside the borough, the church at Llan-llwch was given a vestment, also worth £2. Elsewhere, Aberystwyth Church was bequeathed a

---

[131] PRO, SC2/215/31; NLW, Dynevor A 61, A 44 m.6d.

[132] NLW, Dynevor A 61. Cf. the value of Catherine Howard's estate *c.*1525 at £203. 18s. 0d., just about 300 marks' worth, in PRO, SC12/25/53.

[133] PRO, PROB, Bodfeld, XXXV (proved on 5 December 1525), imperfectly published in D. Jones, 'Sir Rhys ap Thomas: a study in family history and Tudor politics', *Arch. Camb.*, 5th series, IX (1892), 90–1; CRO, Dynevor, Add. MS 73.

[134] College of Arms MS H.8. Fellows noted that it was 'in the place where laye Sir Rice app Griffeth greate uncle to Sir Ryce app Thomas'. He may have meant Sir Rhys ap Gruffydd of Abermarlais (died 1356), Sir Rhys ap Thomas's great-great-great-uncle; his son, also named Sir Rhys ap Gruffydd, died in London in 1380 and was presumably buried there. Griffiths, *Principality of Wales*, pp.99–102, 262–3.

vestment worth £2. 13s. 4d. Further south, St Hilary's Church in Uwch Aeron and Llanrhystud Church were each left a vestment worth £2, and so was the tiny church dedicated to Our Lady at Llandyfeisant, near the ancestral home of Newton, and the chapel at Pontargothi, not far from his first wife's home of Cwrt Henry. Carew was singled out for special favour: Dame Jenet was charged with commissioning a special silver cross for the parish church, and no limit was placed on its cost. As for the religious orders, Sir Rhys left £8 in cash for a pair of organs for the Cistercian abbey church at Cwm-hir in mid-Wales, where the famous picture of Jesus may have attracted his devotion.[135] The current popularity of the friars in England and Wales prompted him to think of the Dominicans of Brecon and Haverfordwest, who received £2. 13s. 4d. for new vestments for their churches. The Franciscans at Carmarthen, of course, attracted particularly handsome bequests, and their house in Hereford, where Henry VII's grandfather, Owen Tudor, had been buried after Mortimer's Cross in 1461, also received a vestment valued at £2. 13s. 4d.

Sir Rhys made careful, though simple, provision for several of his family. Dame Jenet had pride of place, receiving for her life almost all Sir Rhys's holdings in the borough of Carmarthen (which appear to have formed her jointure), £100 in cash, a quantity of linen and bedding, and all the plate which was in the care of Sir Rhys's clerk and chaplain, Master John Gruffydd, who seems to have acted as his treasurer.[136] She was also assigned for life the income from one-third of his estates, except those lands which he had set aside for the jointure of Catherine Howard, his grandson's wife.

As for Sir Rhys's 'Baase sons', at least four of them, they were left his herds of cattle, oxen and rothers (young oxen), and his flocks of sheep, those sons who were not married receiving more than those who were.[137] Sir Rhys's illegitimate daughters are not mentioned in the will, presumably because they were already provided for in marriage. His heir was, of course, his young grandson, Rhys ap Gruffydd, who was nominated executor of the will, receiving advice in this regard from his maternal grandfather, the elderly duke of Norfolk. The only specific condition was that Rhys should use any remaining plate to negotiate the marriage of his sister, Elizabeth, who would soon wed Sir Charles Herbert.[138] Sir Gruffydd ap Rhys's widow, Catherine St John, did not rate a mention. This may be because she had married Sir Piers

---

[135] Williams, *The Welsh Church*, p.356. The abbey was also the burial place of Llywelyn ap Gruffydd, prince of Wales, in 1282: D. H. Williams, 'The White Monks in Powys I', *Cistercian Studies*, XI (1976), 73–101.

[136] Master John Gruffydd had custody of the vast quantity of plate belonging to Sir Rhys and his son in 1513, *HMC, Various Collections*, II (1903), 308.

[137] See above p.64.

[138] See above p.69.

Edgecombe of Cornwall a short while before Sir Rhys died and had already moved to Cotehele, her new home on the River Tamar, north of Plymouth. The Edgecombes' 'first homecoming' took place during 1524–5, when the town of Plymouth sent the couple three gallons of wine to mark the occasion. We can only speculate as to how they met, though it may be noted that Sir Piers, like Sir Gruffydd ap Rhys, had been knighted at the marriage of Prince Arthur, and in 1513 joined the expeditionary force to Tournai and Thérouanne. Catherine took with her to Cotehele 'all the plate in her keeping which was Sir Griffin Rice's, her late husband, with all her apparel and stuff of household left by him'.[139] Among these possessions were, presumably, the pair of Welsh chairs and the 'Cotehele Tester', an oak cupboard front of eight carved panels of pastoral and Tudor heraldic designs, which may still be seen in the mansion.

During his long life, Sir Rhys had formed a large circle of friends and servants, officials, councillors and retinue captains. They were drawn from those parts of west Wales where he had estates, particularly Carmarthenshire and the lordship of Kidwelly, and they were inter-leaved with the establishments of Church and state, and the local administrations of the region. As such they helped to extend Sir Rhys's network of influence and control, by the way providing the individuals themselves with opportunities for advancement under his special patronage. What particular evidence we have suggests that some of them at least were well treated by Sir Rhys, but three of them, Thomas Brein (or Bryne) of Pen-boyr, one of his clerks, John ap Dafydd ap Rhydderch from south Cardiganshire, a servant in his chamber, and Lewys ap Thomas ap John, one of his councillors from the Carmarthen area and overseer of his will, proved less than loyal at the time of Sir Rhys's death – or so Rhys ap Gruffydd later claimed.[140]

Aside from Lewys ap Thomas ap John and Thomas Brein, Sir Rhys's councillors included Master John Gruffydd, who did duty as his treasurer. We may suppose, too, that he relied from time to time on those local laymen and clerics who witnessed his will in 1524: Dr Dafydd Mothvey (or Myddfai, in Carmarthenshire), warden of the Franciscan

---

[139] Nicolas, *Testamenta Vetusta*, II, 647–50, 739; Bindoff, *HP*, II, 82. Catherine Edgecombe's name is inscribed on f.1 of the mid-fifteenth-century illuminated manuscript of John Lydgate's Troy Book and the Story of Thebes which was made for William Herbert, earl of Pembroke (died 1469). It passed into the family of the Percy earls of Northumberland after 1476, and Catherine may have had access to it through the widow of the earl who died in 1527; she (died 1542) was a daughter of Sir Robert Spencer of Devon. See G. F. Warner and J. P. Gilson, *Catalogue of the Western Manuscripts in the Old Royal and King's Collections* (4 vols., London, 1921), II, 308–10. For Cotehele, see J. Lees-Milne and C. Brocklehurst, *Cotehele House, Cornwall* (revised edn. M. Trinick, National Trust, 1979); D. R. Saer, *The Harp in Wales in Pictures* (Cardiff, 1991), no. 7, illustrating a Welsh crowther and harpist from the cupboard, which is here dated *c*.1550–70.

[140] PRO, C1/513/26; see below p.90; Griffiths, *Principality of Wales*, pp.295, 346, 404, 409; *LP, Henry VIII*, I, 924, 1002, 1062; Bartrum, *1400–1500*, III, 344; IX, 1498; PRO, LR1/229 f.125–6*v*.

Friary at Carmarthen; Master John Lewis (1478–1541), treasurer of St David's Cathedral, who had served Sir Gruffydd ap Rhys in 1512 and was still helping Sir Gruffydd's widow to sort out his affairs in 1530; Ieuan Llwyd Fychan, who was married to Rhys's niece Joan, daughter of Dafydd ap Thomas, and was receiver of Kidwelly from 1505 to 1514; Gruffydd Higon, an influential burgess of Carmarthen who was mayor of the borough in 1522–3; and Philip Davy (ap Maredudd ap Rhys), one of Sir Rhys's more distant kinsmen.[141] The overseers of the will seem closer to him: William ap John ap Thomas and Thomas Jones were his first cousins, and in 1514 William had been nominated as a trustee in the marriage agreement with the duke of Norfolk.[142] Dafydd Llwyd may have been the reeve of Creuddyn in Cardiganshire, where Sir Rhys had lands, and Lewys ap Thomas ap John was bailiff itinerant of Carmarthen from about 1506.[143] There were five clerics among the overseers, prominent men either at Carmarthen or the episcopal city. They included the prior of Carmarthen, Dr John Vaughan (died in 1527/8), archdeacon of St David's by 1518; Thomas Llwyd, precentor or 'chantor' of St David's; Master William Stradling, chancellor of St David's by 1512; and Master Lewis Gruffydd, probably the vicar of Llangadog Fawr in the lordship of Kidwelly.[144] Sir Rhys's connection with St David's is reflected by the presence of his arms within the Garter among the roof-bosses of the ante-chapel of the cathedral's Lady Chapel which were carved early in the sixteenth century.[145]

Sir Rhys's loyalty to at least one of his servants is known to have extended to the manipulation of mortgage law, which he otherwise commonly used to his own advantage:

> Wilcock ap Mores Castle was the yongest of Mores Castle sonnes, for the howse of Trebethod being Mores Castles Chief house, was his; and John Wilcock was Wilcocks yongest soone, for he, after his fathers decease had trebethod, which John had two sonnes William and John. This William served Sir Rees ap Thomas, Knight. in howse. He had trebethod by the Counten[an]ce of his master, but his brother John entred into the howse and expulsed his brother William. Whereupon Sir Rees ap Thomas coming to Llanelly, beinge a greate Commaunder and Chief ruler in those Cuntreys took his mans parte and thrust out John Wilcock, threatening that if the said John wold presume to plaie such a part again, he wolde hange him by the next tree he showld finde. And, to bridle the said Johns attempts, Sir Rees ap Thomas gave unto his man five poundes in morgag upon the landes, in presence of the people; but Imediatlye upon the

[141] *Le Neve*, XI, 59; NLW, Pedigree Box 13; Somerville, *Duchy of Lancaster*, I, 643; Griffiths, *Principality of Wales*, pp.345, 352–3; Bartrum, *300–1400*, II, 332; *1400–1500*, III, 372; IV, 655.

[142] Bartrum, *1400–1500*, IV, 643, 647; Griffiths, *Principality of Wales*, p.295; see above p.69.

[143] Griffiths, *Principality of Wales*, pp.339, 467, 295, 346, 404, 409.

[144] *Le Neve*, XI, 61, 68, 57 and n.2; Bartrum, *1400–1500*, III, 385.

[145] E. Allen, 'The arms of Sir Rhys ap Thomas, KG', *Arch. Camb.*, 5th series, XIV (1897), 80.

Departure of the people, receaved his money back again. And so the lande contynued without any rent paide to Sir Rees ap Thomas, Sir Griffith Rees, or Mr Rees Griffith all theire liefe tymes; untill that long after the Attainder of Mr Rees Griffith, John Vaughan of Golden Grove, understandinge of this, bought it of the Kinge. But hearinge that Ellen William, wife to Mores Dd. Mores, was daughter and heire to the foresaid William, and by reason that he had knowledg that the moneye so geeven upon the lands by Sir Rees was but a collowr, as well appeered by reason that Sr Rees nor any of his posteritie received no profit therebye, he gave the said Ellen William abowt a bushell of pilcornne or some small trifle, and had a release from her, and so his issue now enioythe the same to this daie.[146]

His hospitality, especially to his kinsmen, was equally well remembered in anecdote:

Sir Rhys ap Thomas was entertaining a friend to dinner when the brother-in-law of Sir Rhys called at the house. As the door was not opened to his first knock, he immediately left. The knight, hearing this, directed that his brother-in-law be brought back to the table board, saying 'Bring him back without fail, for he will be deeply offended at having had a locked door at my house'. His servants brought him back and Sir Rhys at once saw that food was placed before him. The knight apologised for the poorness of the fare, saying, 'I am sorry you did not come earlier since there is now very little except bones and sinews. But cheer up, we'll make up for it at supper!'. The brother-in-law shrewdly replied, 'What can one expect but bones and sinews where ravens and dogs are found so often!' For Sir Rhys's guest bore *dogs* and Sir Rhys *ravens*, as arms.[147]

Sir Rhys's household acted as a magnet for a large and talented group of Welsh poets who were attracted especially by the reputation of the knight himself. Rhisiart ap Rhys Brydydd, himself a distinguished versifier, was accused by a fellow Glamorgan poet, Iorwerth Fynglwyd (*fl.*1485–1527), of spending far too much time in Sir Rhys's service. Yet Iorwerth himself was unable to resist the attractions of Sir Rhys, and both poets secured an entrée to his household following his marriage to the Glamorgan widow, Jenet Mathew, in the early 1480s; in 1525 Iorwerth penned a moving elegy on the old knight's death.[148] Also from Glamorgan was Ieuan Rudd, who sang one of his poems at the wedding of Sir Rhys and Jenet, though we do not know where their marriage took place.[149]

---

[146] NLW MS 1602 D f.153, in Jones, *TCASFC*, XXIX (1939), 31 (*c.*1609–30). For another household servant, Thomas ap Gruffydd, who was at Carew and Carmarthen in 1519–22 and was living in the lordship of Elfael by 1529, see NLW, Pedigree Box 13.

[147] NLW MS 6499 B f.26, translated in Jones, *TCASFC*, XXIX (1939), 32–3.

[148] H. Ll. Jones and E. I. Rowlands (eds.), *Gwaith Iorwerth Fynglwyd* (Cardiff, 1975), pp.43–6; C. Lewis, 'The literary tradition of Morgannwg', in Pugh, *Glamorgan County History*, III, 511–15; *Companion to Welsh Lit.* s.n., and *DWB*, s.n.

[149] Lewis, 'Literary tradition', p.457.

Many other poets gravitated to one or other of Sir Rhys's residences at Carmarthen, Newton, Newcastle Emlyn, Narberth and, especially, Carew, which was compared by a frequent literary visitor, Rhys Nanmor, to King Arthur's palace.[150] We cannot know precisely what their motives were. Some, like Rhys Nanmor (*fl.*1485–1513), who may have lived at St David's, were doubtless members of his household circle. Others, like the Anglesey poet, Lewys Môn (died 1527), whose patron, Sir William Gruffydd of Penrhyn, fought in France with Sir Rhys ap Thomas in 1513 and married Sir Rhys's step-daughter, Siân Stradling, were welcomed when they were on tour.[151] So too were Siancyn Fynglwyd (*fl. c.*1470) when Sir Rhys was a young man; Guto'r Glyn (*c.*1435– *c.*1493), who, though mostly active in north-east Wales, visited Abermarlais; Ieuan ap Rhys ap Llywelyn, a guest of Sir Rhys and Dame Jenet early in the sixteenth century; Ieuan Deulwyn, from Kidwelly, who certainly knew Newton; and, above all, Tudur Aled (died *c.*1525), one of the most highly esteemed of contemporary Welsh poets who, though a north Walian, knew Narberth, Abermarlais, Carew and Newcastle Emlyn well. Tudur seems to have died while visiting Sir Rhys, probably early in 1525, and, like Sir Rhys himself, he was buried in the Greyfriars' Church at Carmarthen, having first assumed the habit of a Franciscan.[152]

If some of these poets were not fortunate enough to receive an invitation to Sir Rhys's hall, they sought to attract his attention (and patronage) with a praise-poem or two, very likely vying with each other to secure his favour.[153] Others lauded the accomplishments of the most renowned Welshman of his day (short of the royal family) – as did Dafydd Llwyd (*c.*1395–*c.*1486) of Mathafarn, who addressed poems to a number of prominent figures whom he admired or who were famous in his time. Later, Lewys Morgannwg (*fl.*1520–65), a notable Glamorgan poet who was especially attracted to Welsh gentlemen whose families prospered under Tudor rule, met Tudur Aled in Sir Rhys's household and seemed as a result to have established an intimate relationship with him.[154]

[150] M. G. Headley, 'Barddoniaeth Llawdden a Rhys Nanmor' (unpublished University of Wales MA thesis, 1938), pp.183, 372; E. R. Ll. Davies, thesis cited, p.127.

[151] E. I. Rowlands (ed.), *Gwaith Lewys Môn* (Cardiff, 1975), pp.115–24, 133–5, 144–7, 203–7; T. G. Jones (ed.), *Gwaith Tudur Aled* (2 vols., Cardiff, 1926), I, 145–9. Siân Stradling was the daughter of Thomas Stradling (died 1480) and Jenet Mathew: Bartrum, *1400–1500*, X, 1622.

[152] Williams, *Guto'r Glyn*, pp.263–4; E. R. Ll. Davies, thesis cited, pp.125ff.; E. I. Rowlands, 'Tudur Aled' in A. O. H. Jarman and G. R. Hughes, *A Guide to Welsh Literature*, II (Swansea, 1979), 323–5.

[153] E. I. Rowlands, 'The continuing tradition', in Jarman and Hughes, *Welsh Literature*, II, 317–18; E. Ll. Davies, thesis cited, p.126; Lewis, 'The literary tradition', p.510. See J. M. Williams and E. I. Rowlands (eds.), *Gwaith Rhys Brydydd a Rhisiart ap Rhys* (Cardiff, 1976), pp.19–23; one of Rhisiart's poems addresses St David, Henry Tudor and Sir Rhys jointly.

[154] Richards, *Dafydd Llwyd*, pp.25–6, 35–7, 71–2, 113–15; Lewis, 'The literary tradition', p.512.

What their audience heard were poetic illustrations of themes that pandered to the self-regarding pride of Sir Rhys and his family: the intoning of his descent, on his father's side, from Nicholas and Elidir in the fourteenth century, and, on his mother's, from the yet more distinguished line of Ednyfed Fychan, seneschal of princes in the mid-thirteenth century and the progenitor in Cardiganshire of the servant and commander of English kings, Sir Rhys ap Gruffydd (died 1356), a century later. This link with Ednyfed Fychan enabled poets such as Lewys Glyn Cothi, Siancyn Fynglwyd and Rhys Nanmor, writing after 1485, to publicize the blood connection between the royal house of Tudor and the family of Sir Rhys ap Thomas, both of which could claim Ednyfed as an ancestor.[155]

As past masters of myth and tradition, the poets traced the line of Sir Rhys's blood to the shadowy sixth-century king of the northern British, Urien of Rheged. This was a theme echoed by Huw Cae Llwyd (*fl.*1431–1505) in his elegy to Sir Rhys; by Lewys Glyn Cothi (*c.*1420–89), to whom genealogy, heraldry and local traditions of the Tywi Valley were the very stuff of his upbringing and writings; and by Siancyn Fynglwyd, Rhys Nanmor, Tudur Aled and Ieuan Deulwyn.[156] Dafydd Llwyd, with his penchant for prophecy and ultimate British salvation, in the tradition of Merlin, triumphantly prepared to make a link even with the legendary Arthur.[157]

More immediate was the stress which they laid on Sir Rhys's own accomplishments and generosity, his feats in battle from Bosworth onwards, and especially on his election to the Order of the Garter in 1505. Dafydd Llwyd was among the first to acknowledge his key role in the downfall of Richard III, and others, including Guto'r Glyn, echoed such praise.[158] One of Rhys Nanmor's most notable poems, written by someone who has been described as Sir Rhys's household poet for the entertainment and self-esteem of his patron and his son, celebrated the knight's role against the rebels at Blackheath in 1497, and in the costly expeditions to Boulogne in 1492 and to Calais and Thérouanne in 1513.[159] Tudur Aled, who may have died under Sir Rhys's roof in 1525, also lauded the knight's interventions against the Cornishmen and in France. As for others of his fraternity, it was the renovated castle at Carew which epitomized the knightly qualities revealed in these exploits, and to be invested with the Garter symbolized the 'golden

[155] E. R. Ll. Davies, thesis cited, p.109; *Poetical Works of Lewis Glyn Cothi*, pp.163–6.

[156] L. Harries (ed.), *Gwaith Huw Cae Llwyd ac Eraill* (Cardiff, 1953), pp.89–90; Williams, *Guto'r Glyn*, pp.263–4; Jones, *Tudur Aled*, I, 69–80; II, 383–6; Jones, *Lewys Glyn Cothi*, pp.67–8, 163–4.

[157] Richards, *Dafydd Llwyd*, pp.113–15; Roberts, *Dafydd Llwyd, passim*; E. R. Ll. Davies, thesis cited, pp.106–16, 127, 131, 140.

[158] Ibid., p.122.

[159] Ibid., pp.116–19; Headley, thesis cited, pp.132, 137–43; Williams and Rowlands, *Rhisiart ap Rhys*, pp.20–1; E. I. Rowlands, 'Terwyn a Thwrnai', *NLWJ*, IX (1955–6), 295–300.

Ednyfed Fychan
(d.1246)

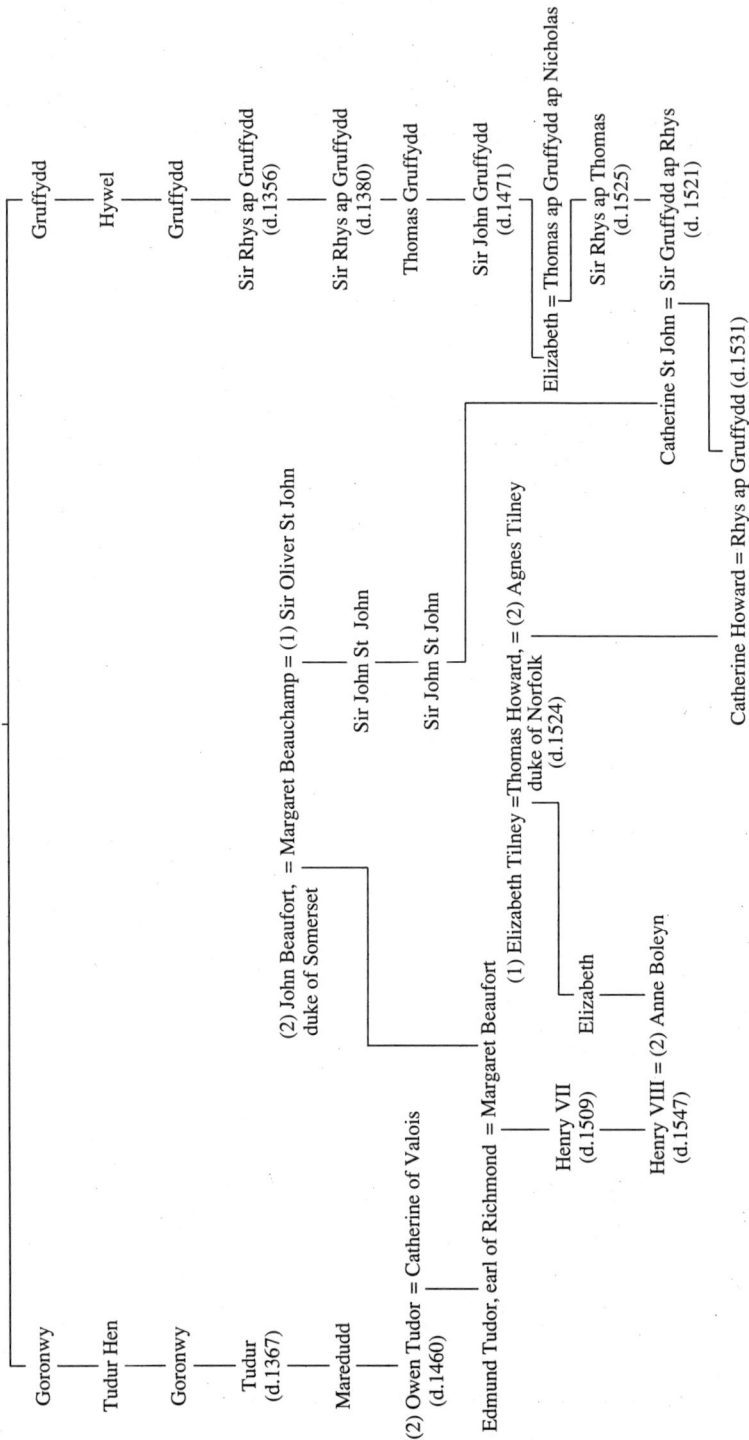

Goronwy

Tudur Hen

Goronwy

Tudur
(d.1367)

Maredudd

(2) Owen Tudor = Catherine of Valois
(d.1460)

Edmund Tudor, earl of Richmond = Margaret Beaufort

Henry VII
(d.1509)

Henry VIII = (2) Anne Boleyn
(d.1547)

Elizabeth

(2) John Beaufort, = Margaret Beauchamp = (1) Sir Oliver St John
duke of Somerset

Sir John St John

Sir John St John

(1) Elizabeth Tilney = Thomas Howard, = (2) Agnes Tilney
duke of Norfolk
(d.1524)

Gruffydd

Hywel

Gruffydd

Sir Rhys ap Gruffydd
(d.1356)

Sir Rhys ap Gruffydd
(d.1380)

Thomas Gruffydd

Sir John Gruffydd
(d.1471)

Elizabeth = Thomas ap Gruffydd ap Nicholas

Sir Rhys ap Thomas
(d.1525)

Catherine St John = Sir Gruffydd ap Rhys
(d. 1521)

Catherine Howard = Rhys ap Gruffydd (d.1531)

Sir Rhys ap Thomas's Family and the Royal House of Tudor

treasure' (*aur*) that was Rhys himself.[160] Iorwerth Fynglwyd (*fl.*1485–
1525) marked the imposing figure which he cut among the knights at
court, at Henry VII's palace of Sheen (to be replaced by the grander
palace of Richmond after the disastrous fire in December 1497):

> It is unlikely that nine Saxons would give in Sheen
> A challenge to the Raven of Harry the King.[161]

Henceforth, in outbursts of chivalric admiration, he could be compared
with Hector, Arthur, Launcelot and Roland, heroes of romance, and
with slightly lesser chivalric figures such as Sir John Mandeville,
Godfrey de Bouillon and Guy of Warwick; and his opulent residence at
Carew seemed akin to Arthur's palace.[162] For all the trumpeted links
with Arthurian tradition and British myths, Sir Rhys's career and his
feats were placed squarely in the context of service to the Tudor
monarchs, his kinsmen.[163]

A rare insight into the cast of Sir Rhys's mind – confirming the
plaudits of the poets – is afforded by the few, but striking, surviving
personal possessions of his family. The two oak Garter chairs; the fine
oak tester valances from Sir Rhys's bed, depicting scenes of siege and
war against the French; and the remnant of an oak cupboard at
Cotehele House in Cornwall, carved by a Welsh craftsman, Harri ap
Gruffydd, and portraying harpists and the pleasures of the chase – each
illustrates the pride, self-confidence and sense of honour which also won
the regard of his contemporaries. Above all, Sir Rhys's life was
conceived in a chivalric mould. This is what inspired his commissioning
of a copy of the Welsh prose translation of 'La queste del Saint Graal',
the noblest of all the adventures of King Arthur's Knights of the Round
Table, who in turn were the inspiration of the chivalric order Sir Rhys
had joined in 1505.[164]

His household was 'one of the most important cultural centres in
Wales' (concludes Ceri Lewis), and an anonymous English lament
portrays Sir Gruffydd ap Rhys as loath to leave its precincts in death in
1521:

> Farewell! knyghthode, farewell! chyualrye;
> Of the curteys courte, farewell! good cumpanye.[165]

---

[160] Jones, *Tudur Aled*, I, 38–44; E. R. Ll. Davies, thesis cited, p.122; Headley, thesis cited,
pp.220–5.
[161] Jones and Rowlands, *Iorwerth Fynglwyd*, no. 17; Siddons, *Welsh Heraldry*, I, 131.
[162] E. R. Ll. Davies, thesis cited, pp.123, 139; Jones, *Tudur Aled*, I, 41; Headley, thesis cited, pp.142,
145. Sir Gruffydd ap Rhys, 'prince of Carew', was also compared to Hector: Jones, *Tudur Aled*, I,
159–61.
[163] E. R. Ll. Davies, thesis cited, p.120.
[164] NLW, Mostyn 184 (written in Glamorgan), in T. Jones (ed.), *Ystoryaeu Seint Greal*: Rhan I, *Y
Keis* (Cardiff, 1992), p.xvii.
[165] Bodleian, Rawlinson C 813, printed in *Anglia*, XXXI (1908), 347–50; D. J. Bowen, 'Marwnad Syr

This epitaph, and the associated 'Lamentatyon of the Ladye Gryffythe', are the only poems in English known to have been addressed to a member of Sir Rhys's family in the fifteenth and sixteenth centuries, though their author may have been from south-west Wales and in Sir Gruffydd's entourage at the Field of Cloth of Gold in 1520. Composed in English soon after Sir Gruffydd's burial in 1521, the epitaph may be taken to imply that he was fatally wounded, perhaps in one of those vigorous tournaments that sometimes claimed unintentioned victims in the later Middle Ages:

> Be-warre! dethe cummeth soden and not aspyed;
> when ye thynke lest, he wyll doo vyllanye,
> O that I hade nott forcast his slyghtye sottelte!
> Now ye be warnyd, ye may take better nede;
> of his soden darte ye shall haue lesse drede . . .
> Farewell! England, farewell! Walys;
> I take my leve now att thys tyde.
> Farewell! Cales and Englyshe pales.
> Fare-well! King Henry, I may nott abyde,
> dethe hathe me lancyde in-to the syde.

There had been jousts and passages of arms at the Field of Cloth of Gold the previous year, but in view of the poem's *envoi* to Calais it might be more plausible to suggest that Sir Gruffydd came unexpectedly to grief during Cardinal Wolsey's mission to Calais (2 August to 27 November 1521) to negotiate a peace between France and the Emperor Charles V.[166]

The poet dwelt on the appropriateness of his interment at Worcester, close to the chantry recently erected to commemorate his early friend and master, Prince Arthur:

> To my olde master now wyll I be gone,
> Prince Arture, with hym styll to abyde.
> Ytt slaketh my sorowes to thynke vpon
> My chance ys to lye soo nye to his syde.
> What shulde I more wyshe yn thys worlde wyde
> butt yn reste perpetuell to make merye
> with that noble Prynce in eternall glorye?

Gruffudd ap Rhys', *BBCS*, XXV (1972), 31; R. Garlick and R. Mathias (eds.), *Anglo-Welsh Poetry, 1480–1980* (Bridgend, 1984), pp.49–51.

[166] P. Gwyn, *The King's Cardinal* (London, 1990), ch.5; Russell, *Field of Cloth of Gold*, ch.5 ('The Feat of Arms').

Henry ap Gwilym

Morris

Sir Rhys ap Thomas = (1) Efa, (2) Jenet (d.1535), dau. of Thomas Mathew
(d.1525)

(1) Sir Gruffydd = Catherine, dau. of Sir John St. John = (2) Sir Piers Edgecombe   Owain

Jane I =
Dafydd Llwyd ab Ieuan

Jane II =
Dafydd Llwyd ap
Thomas ab Owain

Dafydd I =
Alison, dau.
of Arnold Martin

(d.1521)   (d.1553)

Dafydd II= Anne, dau. of John ap Rhys   Margaret I = Henry ap John

Margaret II = Henry Wyriot

Elizabeth = Jankyn Llwyd

Owain Gwyn

William

Gwenllian II = (1) Lewis Sutton, (2) Hywel Gwyn ap Rhydderch

Gwenllian I = Gwilym ap Thomas

Mary = John Luttrell

Dorothy = ? Humphrey White

Elizabeth = Sir Charles Herbert   (1) Rhys = Catherine (d.1554) = (2) Henry Daubeney, earl of Bridgwater
dau. of Thomas
Howard duke of
Norfolk

Gruffydd [Rice] = Elinor, dau. of Sir Thomas Jones

Thomas
(d.1544)

Sir Walter (d.1636) = Elizabeth Mansel

Henry Rice (d.1651)

Select Pedigree of the Descendants of Sir Rhys ap Thomas

4

Crisis and Catastrophe: Rhys ap Gruffydd

In 1525 the fortunes of one of Wales's most influential and illustrious families passed into the hands of a young man of about seventeen years of age.[1] To judge by Rhys ap Gruffydd's personal relationships and actions, he was vigorous and determined, but without the circumspection that often comes with maturity; and he cherished expectations that, not unreasonably, were cast high. He quickly became aware that Henry VIII's regime offered no guarantees of continued favour following the death of his grandfather, even though his family had been a stout pillar of early Tudor rule. When that rule was beset by diplomatic and dynastic dilemmas which had serious security implications, Rhys ap Gruffydd became one of its earliest and most spectacular victims.

Within weeks of Sir Rhys ap Thomas's death in the summer of 1525, the supreme royal office in south Wales, that of justiciar of the counties of Carmarthen and Cardigan, was assumed on 22 August by Walter Devereux, Lord Ferrers; it was an appointment made for life. At the same time, Ferrers succeeded Sir Rhys as steward and receiver of the lordship of Builth and constable of Builth Castle, again for life.[2] These patents were a severe blow to the young Rhys ap Gruffydd. His youth doubtless told against him at Westminster, but the granting of appointments for life to the 36-year-old Ferrers (who lived until 1558) gave a clear signal that Sir Rhys ap Thomas's heir was not regarded in high places as a suitable inheritor of Sir Rhys's provincial power. This rebuff was compounded within a year when, on 25 May 1526, Ferrers also became chamberlain of south Wales, the senior financial official in the southern counties of the principality.[3] In some ways, he was not an

[1] He was born c.1508: NLW, Dynevor A 96 (e); CCL MS 4.20; W. Ll. Williams, 'A Welsh insurrection', *Y Cymmrodor*, XVI (1902), 2 n.l.
[2] Griffiths, *Principality of Wales*, pp.162–3.
[3] Ibid., p.192.

inappropriate choice as the king's governor in south-west Wales, for he was a major landowner in Herefordshire and Gloucestershire and the Welsh Marches. Moreover, his family had acquired estates in Pembrokeshire in the mid-fifteenth century, and his grandfather had been a prominent Yorkist agent in Wales.[4] Furthermore, two years before Sir Rhys's death, when Welshmen from south Wales were recruited for the duke of Suffolk's expedition to France, they served under the command of Ferrers, rather than of Sir Rhys the septuagenarian.[5] And yet, not many years before, reservations had been expressed about his abilities when a successor to the earl of Surrey as chief governor of Ireland was being sought. Cardinal Wolsey objected to the king's suggestion of Ferrers (in October 1521) as 'wanting experience in such weighty matters'.[6] On balance, he does not seem the sort of person calculated to smooth Rhys ap Gruffydd's ruffled feathers or sustain the young man's loyalty and self-esteem.

The shift of authority in south Wales may have been in prospect as early as the death of Sir Gruffydd ap Rhys in 1521, for a circumspect government would have considered the consequences of old Sir Rhys ap Thomas's demise. Already, on 11 December 1521, the reversionary rights which Sir Gruffydd enjoyed in the offices of constable of Aberystwyth Castle and as steward, chancellor, receiver and surveyor of the lordship of Haverford were conveyed to Sir William Thomas of Aberglasney; and James ap Jankyn, a yeoman of the Crown, replaced him as constable (or *rhaglaw*) of the commotes of Cardiganshire on 13 November 1521.[7] More fundamental changes that affected the whole of Wales were made in 1525 by Cardinal Wolsey, probably in part-response to the death of Sir Rhys. The commissioners in the Marches were re-organized as a council of appeal interposed between the Welsh localities and Westminster, and henceforward under the nominal headship of the nine-year-old Princess Mary. Before the year was out, she had been installed at Ludlow. Membership of the princess's household and the council was deliberately and closely linked with the new regime in south Wales. Lord Ferrers, the new justiciar, was steward of Mary's household and a councillor in the Marches. The new chamberlain was, albeit briefly, Sir Giles Greville, appointed on 14 August 1525: he was controller of Mary's household and another of her councillors. The treasurer of the princess's household, Sir Ralph Egerton, became steward, receiver, chancellor and surveyor of the lordships of Haverford and Rhos in place of Sir William Thomas, who had secured the reversionary interest in 1521. Just as Rhys ap Gruffydd

[4] *CP*, V, 321–8; B. E. Howells, 'Studies in the social and agrarian history of medieval and early modern Pembrokeshire' (unpublished University of Wales MA thesis, 2 vols., 1956), p.129.
[5] M. B. Davies, *Bull. Faculty of Arts, Fouad I University, Cairo*, VII (1944), 35–6.
[6] *LP, Henry VIII*, III, part 2, 697.
[7] Griffiths, *Principality of Wales*, pp.239, 541–2; *LP, Henry VIII*, III, part 2, p.779.

was barred from gathering the south Wales offices into his hands, so he was excluded from Mary's council. It was manifestly intended that the influence of Rhys's father and grandfather should not be perpetuated. On one level, to prefer Lord Ferrers to Rhys ap Gruffydd simply meant the substitution of one satrap for another. But in other respects, the government is certain to have seen political and financial merit in weakening that intimate relationship between social and economic dominance and governmental authority in south-west Wales which Sir Rhys ap Thomas had forged – as, indeed, had Gruffydd ap Nicholas in the previous century. In the process, however, conditions were being created for the emergence of personal resentments and public disorder in the region. Later in the year, opportunity was taken to bring the overpowering regime of Charles Brandon, duke of Suffolk, to an end in north Wales, but there the dangers were fewer, for Suffolk had manifold interests elsewhere.[8]

The way the wind was blowing was appreciated by at least three of Sir Rhys ap Thomas's intimate servants: Thomas Brein, Sir Rhys's clerk, John ap Dafydd ap Rhydderch, a servant of his chamber, and Lewys ap Thomas ap John, a prominent gentleman from the Carmarthen area who was of his 'counsaill' and an executor of his will.[9] They deftly moved into Ferrers's service, much to the fury of Rhys ap Gruffydd, who later charged them with grossly and criminally abusing their position as Sir Rhys's servants, taking advantage of his grandfather's inability to read and write, in order to feather their own nests and embezzle some of Sir Rhys's wealth 'by craftie and untrue meanes'. Sir Rhys's alleged illiteracy is difficult to credit, unless it reflects the infirmities of old age which might well have made him vulnerable to unscrupulous servants. According to Rhys ap Gruffydd, there should have been between £10,000 and £12,000 in Sir Rhys's coffers at the time of his death, but only 1,000 marks were found. John ap Dafydd ap Rhydderch was known to have purloined clothes and silks from Sir Rhys's wardrobe (worth more than 100 marks), and the trio was further accused of making off with some of the family muniments. Brein was said to have sealed blank pieces of parchment with Sir Rhys's seal of arms in the days prior to the knight's death, in order later to issue acquittances and impose fines for his own enrichment, thereby defrauding Rhys ap Gruffydd of part of his inheritance. That it was their more recent connection with Ferrers that particularly rankled is indicated by Rhys's pleas to Cardinal Wolsey to entertain his charges in the Court of Chancery, so as to avoid the sessions in south Wales over which Ferrers

---

[8] P. Williams, *The Council in the Marches of Wales under Elizabeth I* (Cardiff, 1958), pp.11–13; Lloyd, thesis cited, pp.61–2; Gunn, *WHR*, XII, part 4 (1985), 477–8, 488–9; D. Starkey, *The Reign of Henry VIII: Personalities and Politics* (London, 1985), pp.86ff.; Griffiths, *Principality of Wales*, p.191; *LP, Henry VIII*, IV, part 1, 1872.

[9] Griffiths, *Principality of Wales*, p.295; Lloyd, thesis cited, pp.76–7; see above p.79.

presided. This constitutional point drew a protest from Ferrers, for in 1525 the Council in the Marches had been envisaged as the appeal court for Wales.[10]

Rhys appears to have cultivated Wolsey and, as he reminded the cardinal in 1529, gave him loyal service, no doubt in the expectation of receiving sympathetic treatment from the king's minister.[11] The nature of his relationship with Wolsey is not precisely known; he may have been introduced to the cardinal by the Howards. Be that as it may, when Wolsey journeyed to Calais in July 1527 to meet Francis I, Rhys was in his entourage, as was his uncle, Sir John St John. Indeed, according to the recollections (*c*.1554–8) of Wolsey's gentleman usher and later biographer, George Cavendish, the king's great minister treated Rhys with good-humoured familiarity. In the course of instructing his 'noblemen and gentilmen' to act as befitted servants of Henry VIII's lieutenant and ambassador, he reminded them that the French king's retinue

> wylbe at the first metyng as ffamylier with you as they had byn acquayntyd with you long byfore and commyn with you in the frenche tong as thoughe ye vnderstode euery word they spoke; therefore in lyke maner, and be ye as famylier with them agayn as they be with you; yf they speke to you in the ffrenche tong speke you to them in the Englysshe tong for if you vnderstand not them, they shall no more vnderstand you. And my lord spekyng merely to oon of the gentilmen there (beyng a .welsheman) sayd Rice, quod he, speke thou welshe to hyme. And I ame well assured that thy welshe shall be more defuse to hyme, than his frenche shall be to the.[12]

There can be no doubt about the hostility which Rhys ap Gruffydd felt for Lord Ferrers. The new justiciar disdained even to call on Rhys's services in the years following his appointment; instead, he engaged in the south Wales administration certain border gentry who were known to him or were already in Devereux service.[13] Tension 'hathe ben a doyng ever sythe'. The justiciar's high-handedness was further interpreted by Rhys's wife, Catherine Howard, as sinister, with Ferrers ostensibly claiming the protection of the law whether 'hit be right or wrong'. The unhappy relationship between Rhys ap Gruffydd and Lord Ferrers was widely advertised, which may account for a curious incident which took place at Oxford about 20 June 1528. As Rhys (it must surely be the Carmarthenshire gentleman) and two of his servants, Hugh and

---

[10] PRO, C1/513/26; Lloyd, thesis cited, pp.78–80; *LP, Henry VIII*, IV, part 1, 1872; see above p.89.

[11] PRO, SP1/53 f.112; *MSS in the Welsh Language*, I, ix (from NLW, Mostyn MS 158).

[12] Nichols, *The Chronicle of Calais*, p.439; R. S. Sylvester (ed.), *The Life and Death of Cardinal Wolsey*, by George Cavendish (EETS, 243, 1959 for 1957), pp.47–8, 82, 212–13, 227; *LP, Henry VIII*, IV, intro., p.cclxiii. Both versions of Cavendish's Life mis-identify Rhys ap Gruffydd.

[13] E.g., Griffiths, *Principality of Wales*, pp.162–6, 192.

William Morus, were making their way to London, they were attacked 'aboute the universite of Oxford' and detained in Oxford Castle by the sheriff of Oxfordshire. The unfortunate trio strove to gain their release, eventually appealing to Cardinal Wolsey, presumably with success.[14] Meanwhile, the president of Princess Mary's Council in the Marches, John Veysey, bishop of Exeter, reported optimistically to Wolsey on 5 July 1528 that 'the matter between Lord Ferrers and young Mr Risse is pacified'; yet it cannot have helped matters that the king, on 12 December 1528, authorized both Ferrers and Rhys to enlist cohorts of retainers beyond what the law allowed.[15]

By March 1529 Rhys was driven to petition Wolsey again, this time to urge that he be appointed deputy-justiciar and deputy-chamberlain of south Wales, over the head of Lord Ferrers, to whom Rhys promised to pay any sum of money that Wolsey considered appropriate. At the same time, he denounced Ferrers's present deputies for oppressing his servants and tenants.[16] It was a desperate offer without result. As for the justiciar's attitude to Rhys, Elis Gruffudd, a chronicler who was no admirer of Rhys or his family, commented that Ferrers was jealous of the Welshman's popularity in south Wales:

> When Rhys went to Wales the whole country turned out to welcome him, and this made Lord Ferrers envious and jealous.[17]

There may be some truth in this. Ferrers is certain to have distrusted the young man and resented his complaints and manœuvres. Cardinal Wolsey viewed their mutual accusations as a complete breakdown in personal and public relationships. By 1529 the two men were almost literally at one another's throats.

In his actions in south Wales, using what authority he retained in the region, especially in Pembroke where he acted as both steward and receiver by leave of Sir William Parr, Rhys ap Gruffydd showed himself to be energetic and high-handed by turns.[18] Often his peremptoriness served the interests of the local gentry; at other times it did not. When, in the first part of 1528, there was a major descent on south Pembrokeshire by Irishmen from the territories of the rebel Irish earl of Desmond, James Fitz Maurice (died 1529), who had been intriguing with France and the emperor, Rhys responded with deportations and expulsions, authorized from Pembroke Castle in the absence of Sir William Parr, who spent most of his time from 1525 on the duke of Richmond's council

[14] PRO, SP1/54 f.212–13; C1/561/24; for Moruses of Llanelli, Griffiths, *Principality of Wales*, pp.343, 352; Bartrum, *1400–1500*, VIII, 1409.
[15] *LP, Henry VIII*, IV, part 2, 1957; Lloyd, thesis cited, p.76; PRO, C54/397 m.39.
[16] *LP, Henry VIII*, IV, part 3, 2356; Williams, *Y Cymmrodor*, XVI (1902), 8.
[17] From NLW, Mostyn MS 158, in Williams, *Y Cymmrodor*, XVI (1902), 11; *MSS in the Welsh Language*, I, ix.
[18] Bindoff, *HC*, III, 60–2; NLW, Bronwydd Deed 1286.

in northern England. When Rhys encountered resistance to his tactics from the mayor and burgesses of Tenby, he appealed to Wolsey and sought extra powers to prevent the Pembrokeshire gentry from harbouring Irishmen and taking them into their service.[19]

Rhys's handling of a case of piracy off south Pembrokeshire in the spring of 1529 was more pragmatic. According to the merchants of Pembroke and Tenby, freebooters operating from a Bristol ship were deterring Breton and Portuguese merchants from trading with their towns. When the pirates entered Milford Haven to offer a cargo of salt for sale to the people of Pembrokeshire, Rhys failed to persuade the captain to answer the complaints in the king's court, presumably at Pembroke. He also resisted the local clamour to seize the salt ship in reprisal. Instead, he agreed to the merchants' suggestions that he should buy the salt ship with its cargo of thirty tons of salt, arm it and use it against the freebooters, who had meanwhile intercepted, seized and robbed another Bristol ship bound for Ireland. Offering to take the side of their captain, William Hughes, before the king and Wolsey, he even persuaded Hughes to take command of the salt ship, now armed with twelve cannon and 200 men, along with another vessel, the *Matthew* of Bristol, and three large coastal barges (or picards) – a veritable fleet – in order to apprehend the pirates. The freebooters continued their activities, even pursuing ten picards from Ireland into Milford Sound. Rhys's improvised fleet under Hughes's command attempted to surround the renegade Bristol ship in order to delay the rovers' departure. As the vessel tried to leave the Sound and Rhys's men assembled on both sides of the Haven, the wind fell and the ship struck a rock, leaving it with no alternative but to surrender. Rhys sent the rovers captive to Pembroke Castle and so avoided violence. He claimed half the value of the ship and its tackle as a prize, and he asked Wolsey that he be allowed to keep the vessel for coastal defence. As for William Hughes and the pirates, Rhys was commissioned to try them for felony. The chief appellant on 10 July was John Salman, a shipowner from Southampton who was probably the owner of the salt ship. The defendants were William Hughes and his men, who were declared guilty but kept in prison pending the finding of sureties for their good behaviour. Each member of the jury was also obligated in the sum of £100 to provide further evidence if need be. It seems a surprising verdict. The outcome was less than satisfactory for John Salman, scarcely just towards the pirates who were freed, and distinctly advantageous for Rhys ap Gruffydd, who seems to have profited from the incident and at the same

---

[19] *LP, Henry VIII*, III, part 2, 1584; IV, part 2, 1962, printed in H. Ellis (ed.), *Original Letters illustrative of English History*, Ist series, 1 (1825), 191–5; *Arch. Camb.*, 2nd series, iv (1853), 123; E. Laws, *Little England beyond Wales* (1880), p.236, and Owen, *Calendar of MSS relating to Pembs.*, I, 33. See Lloyd, thesis cited, pp.66–7; *CP*, IV, 32; Cosgrove, *Medieval Ireland*, pp.672–3, 677.

time had posed as the guardian of the king's coast. Rhys wrote to Wolsey on several occasions during these months, from 'my power [poor] house at Carew', which his grandfather had so extensively modernized.[20]

Later in 1529, further actions of Rhys's at Tenby were even more questionable. A Spanish ship, the *Mary* of Bilbao, put into the port to trade on or about 3 November. An armed galleon, captained by Nicholas Quayle of Morlaix in Brittany, arrived soon afterwards and claimed that the *Mary* had originally belonged to Quayle and John Legett, and that it had been wrongfully captured by the forces of the emperor in time of peace. The Spanish captain of the *Mary*, Melchior de Loriaga, flatly denied this, asserting that the incident mentioned had occurred off the Ile de Ré in mid-February 1528, three weeks after the declaration of war between the emperor and the French king on 22 January. Melchior sought the help of the chancellor of England, Sir Thomas More, to have the ship restored to him, along with its tackle and ordnance (worth £100), which had been taken to Carmarthen. Rhys ap Gruffydd intervened, in collusion with Quayle. He announced himself to be a 'judge of the admiralty' and in this capacity ordered the arrest of the *Mary*, which he promptly purchased from Quayle. He then expelled the Spanish sailors, prepared the vessel for sea with Loriaga's rigging, and proceeded to deploy it (according to Loriaga) with artillery and men on freebooting exploits out of Milford Haven. Loriaga had to make his own arrangements, at his own cost, to house his Spanish sailors in Tenby for two months before securing passage home for some of them on three English ships sailing from Tenby. Rhys again intervened and forbade their departure. Meanwhile, in a court held at Tenby, the mayor bound Quayle and his sureties to prove by 24 June his ownership of the vessel and his version of events – or else to compensate Loriaga. But they made off to Brittany and the mayor was so cowed by Rhys ap Gruffydd that he felt unable to pursue the matter.[21]

Not that Rhys was unaware of the risks of incurring the government's displeasure by his manipulation of the law and his oppression of the king's subjects and foreigners alike in south Wales. On 20 January 1529 he eagerly reported to Wolsey from Carew an incident which he may have hoped would enhance his standing at court. He had apprehended John Sant, who early in 1528 slew a servant of William Brereton, a prominent Cheshire gentleman who was also a member of the king's privy chamber and a victim, perhaps, of its internecine rivalries towards the end of Wolsey's period of dominance. Sant was responsible for spreading rumours around Ludlow, where the Council in the Marches

[20] *LP, Henry VIII*, IV, part 3, 2363, 2572; PRO, SP1/53 f.112–14; 54 f.268; Lloyd, thesis cited, pp.68–70; T. B. James (ed.), *The Port Book of Southampton, 1509–10*, vol. 2 (Southampton Record Soc., 33, 1990), p.186.

[21] PRO, C1/651/19–22, petitions scheduled for presentation in the Chancery on 18 November. See Lloyd, thesis cited, pp.71–4; R. J. Knecht, *Francis I* (London, 1982), p.216.

usually met, that King Henry VIII was dead. Sant was arrested in one of Lord Audley's lordships – perhaps Llandovery – and confined in a neighbouring castle, from which he escaped. Rhys proudly reported that he had recaptured him.[22]

This piece of drama aside, the problems which Rhys ap Gruffydd caused in south Wales were of far greater interest to the government. Complaints against him were variously lodged in the Chancery, the Council in the Marches, and before Cardinal Wolsey in Star Chamber. Matters were already close to crisis-point in June 1529 when arrangements were being made for the holding of the annual great sessions at Carmarthen by Lord Ferrers. In preparation for his arrival in Carmarthen, Ferrers instructed his lieutenant, James Leche, who was also bailiff of the borough, to request the mayor for lodgings for the justiciar's entourage when it should arrive on 5 June. Apparently the mayor authorized his serjeants to assign certain houses to Ferrers's servants. Rhys ap Gruffydd, who was bent on a show of strength at the sessions – 'apon a wytfull mynde and malicyously disposed to mak quarrels', his enemies later claimed – made similar arrangements to lodge his retinue in the town.[23] When Leche arrived with the mayor's mandate, he discovered that most of the available lodgings had been commandeered by Rhys's men. Thomas ap Morgan, one of Rhys's servants, fixed his lord's 'bayges upon papers paynted' to the doors of the houses assigned to Ferrers's men to prevent them from lodging there. Much of this circumstantial detail was provided by Ferrers about ten days later, and there is no reason to doubt its essential accuracy.

Rhys's wife, Catherine Howard, saw the situation somewhat differently. According to her testimony, Ferrers's servants removed Rhys's badges and appropriated the lodgings already claimed for him and his men. On 6 June, therefore, Rhys alerted his 'friends and adherents', 'kinsmen, lovers and friends', who were nearest to hand in Carmarthenshire, Cardiganshire and the lordship of Kidwelly. To make his appeal as effective as possible, he used proclamations in country churches to rouse them to come armed to Carmarthen the next day. Precise evidence on this point was later offered on Ferrers's behalf: Dafydd ap Rhys Baas, a bastard son of Sir Rhys ap Thomas, admitted issuing such proclamations in the churches of Llansadwrn and Llanwrda, midway between Llandovery and Llandeilo, whilst the curate of Llanwrda confessed that he too had been involved. The immediate outcome is unknown, though the threat to public order is

[22] *LP, Henry VIII*, IV, part 3, 2281–2; E. W. Ives (ed.), *Letters and Accounts of William Brereton of Malpas* (Lancashire and Cheshire RS, 1976); idem, 'Court and county palatine in the reign of Henry VIII: the case of Sir William Brereton of Malpas', *THSLC*, CXXIII (1972), 1–38.

[23] Rhys was joint bailiff of Carmarthen in 1529–30, but it is not known (ct. Williams, *Y Cymmrodor*, XVI (1902), 11) whether he held the office in the previous year. Griffiths, *Principality of Wales*, p.346; Lloyd, thesis cited, p.82.

plain.[24] Nevertheless, as Ferrers was able to report to the Council in the Marches on 16 June, he managed to dissolve the meeting of the great sessions 'to the kynges profit and advauntaige according to the olde custom therine usid'.[25]

A week later, on 15 June, an even more serious incident occurred in Carmarthen Castle itself. Two of Rhys's servants, including his kinsman, Thomas ab Owain, a veteran of the French campaign of 1513 and, since 1516, the king's attorney in the lordship of Haverford where Sir Rhys ap Thomas had been powerful, had been arrested by Ferrers for the earlier violence, and were being held in the castle. Thomas accordingly forfeited a recognizance of 650 marks imposed in the Carmarthen chancery to ensure his peaceable behaviour.[26] At about seven o'clock in the evening of 15 June, Rhys ap Gruffydd and more than forty of his well-armed men burst into the fortress and made for Ferrers's chamber, where the justiciar was conferring with local gentlemen. An argument about Thomas ab Owain's arrest led Rhys and Ferrers to draw their daggers and make as if to set on one another. Ferrers angrily sent his chaplain to report the incident to Wolsey that same evening and to the president of the Council in the Marches the next day. He explained that his men had disarmed Rhys and put him in custody without bail under a bond of £1,000 – though only with difficulty. Indeed, Lewys ap Thomas ap John, one of the gentlemen present, was wounded in the head; formerly one of Sir Rhys ap Thomas's servants who had joined forces with Lord Ferrers, he was now described as one of the king's 'sworn servants'.[27] We can easily imagine Rhys ap Gruffydd's particular distaste for Lewys.

Next day, Catherine Howard, not hesitating to act in her husband's name now that he was in custody, again shifted the emphasis when she wrote to Cardinal Wolsey in 'rewde wrytting for hit is in hast'. She indignantly reported that her husband had been wounded in the arm during the fracas, and claimed that Thomas ab Owain, a loyal king's servant, had been falsely arrested for trying to release from Carmarthen Castle another of Rhys's servants called Jankyn. She gave a warning about the inflammatory effect which Ferrers's actions would have on the locality and she sought the cardinal's sympathy, capitalizing on Wolsey's relationship with Catherine's half-brother, the duke of Norfolk. Catherine and Rhys kept in close touch with the Howards: she had visited the countess of Surrey in 1523, and Rhys had attended the

[24] PRO, SP1/54 f.109–10, 112–13, 119–20; Stac. 2/18/234 m.1–2, printed in Jones, _Arch. Camb._, 5th series, IX (1892); WRO, 705: 24/3 (vi). Apart from the last, these documents were noted by Williams, _Y Cymmrodor_, XVI (1902), 12ff., and Lloyd, thesis cited, pp.82ff.

[25] WRO, 705: 24/3 (vi); Griffiths, _Principality of Wales_, pp.27–30.

[26] WRO, 705: 24/3 (vi); PRO, Stac. 2/18/234; _LP, Henry VIII_, Addenda, I, part 1, 177; II, part 1, 518; I, part 2, 1101; Griffiths, _Principality of Wales_, pp.345–6, 352.

[27] _LP, Henry VIII_, IV, part 3, 2511–2; PRO, SP1/54 f.109–10; Stac. 2/18/234 m.2.

second duke's funeral at Thetford Priory (Suffolk) in June 1524 as an honoured relative. As to the link with Wolsey, Rhys took the precaution of giving a 40s. annuity to one of his household servants, Thomas Alvard (died 1535), who moved into the king's household in 1529 as a gentleman usher of the Chamber, and was keeper of York Place, Wolsey's former home, from 1530.[28]

Catherine set about assembling more of Rhys's friends and retainers in Carmarthenshire, Cardiganshire and Pembrokeshire, and from the countryside between Builth and St David's, in order to rescue Rhys. That night, a force of about 140 penetrated the western outskirts of Carmarthen and made their way to the Dark (or Wynveth) Gate. They sent messages to Ferrers, ordering him to release Rhys, or at least to refrain from sending him to Westminster; if he refused, they would burn the castle gate and release him themselves. By the following day, 17 June, even larger numbers of insurrectionists had arrived in the town, from further afield in Pembrokeshire, the lordships of Narberth, Emlyn and Kidwelly, and from Carmarthenshire north of the River Cothi; some tenants of the abbot of Talley and the bishop of St David's were persuaded to join them. Rhys ap Gruffydd and 120 ringleaders would shortly be indicted as rebels in the county court of Carmarthen, presumably at Ferrers's direction.[29] The report to Star Chamber enables us to analyse Rhys's following in some depth.

This was no undisciplined rabble. Rather was it a significant lordly retinue that bespeaks Rhys's substantial influence in the region. The leaders whose names we know were well-to-do esquires, clerks or gentlemen who presumably still valued a connection with Rhys ap Gruffydd's family. From south Carmarthenshire, Rhys Rede was a member of the long-established Rede family of Carmarthen, whilst Lewys ap Hywel ap Philip married Gwenllian, daughter of Sir Thomas Phillips.[30] Those from upland Carmarthenshire were of similar ilk, including a nephew of Bishop John Morgan (died 1504), William ap John Ddu and his son Philip from the Llandeilo area, and John ap Llywelyn Ddu, who was bailiff of Gwidigada in 1514–23.[31] Several of the Pembrokeshire ringleaders had even closer links with Rhys or his grandfather, for John Wogan and William ab Owain (1486–1574) had presided at the Pembrokeshire county court in 1526 in place of Rhys: William, described in the indictment as a lawyer, hailed from Nevern and married Elizabeth, daughter of Sir George Herbert of Swansea. Henry Wyriot of Orielton married Sir Rhys ap Thomas's daughter,

[28] *LP, Henry VIII*, IV, part 3, 2512; PRO, Stac. 2/18/234; SP1/54 f.112–13; Gwyn, *King's Cardinal*, pp.178–9, 565–70; Vokes, thesis cited, pp.297, 310–11; *LP, Henry VIII*, V, 559; H. M. Colvin *et al.*, *The History of the King's Works*, vol. IV, part 2 (London, 1982), 306.
[29] PRO, Stac. 2/18/234.
[30] PRO, E315/364 f.44*v*; Bartrum, *1400–1500*, IX, 1463; VI, 933 (for another, Owain ap Morgan).
[31] Griffiths, *Principality of Wales*, p.404; Bartrum, *1400–1500*, IX, 1510, 1511; V, 730; IV, 573.

whilst William ap Dafydd ap William married his granddaughter.[32] In the lordship of Kidwelly, David, Roger and Morgan Vaughan were brothers, the sons of Hywel Vaughan, and Thomas Vaughan may have been another (though the pedigrees are silent about him).[33] William ap Thomas Goch, who assembled tenants from the bishop's lands in support of Rhys, was from Ystrad-ffin in the lordship of Llandovery and was usefully married to a daughter of Richard, abbot of Strata Florida in Cardiganshire.[34]

Ferrers could pose as a bulwark against 'the greate Rebell and Insurreccion of the people': 'ther was not such insurreccion in Walys at any tyme a man can remembre'.[35] He exaggerated, but in re-establishing order and dispersing the rioters, his achievement appeared to be commendable. The upshot was that Rhys ap Gruffydd was placed under a bond of £1,000 to keep the peace and remain in Carmarthen Castle until instructions arrived from the Council in the Marches, which had been kept abreast of events.[36] But until this issue was resolved and either Rhys or Ferrers (or both) had been reproved, the confrontation between the rivals would not end. Indeed, prior to a hearing in Star Chamber later in the year, two of Rhys's servants – Gruffydd ap Morgan, an usher of his hall, and Gruffydd ap John, his falconer – ambushed and killed Ferrers's lieutenant as justiciar, the lawyer Reynold ap Morgan, on 6 August.[37] Some reported that the two murderers were later to be seen in Tenby in Rhys's company. Eventually, on the king's instructions, Rhys ap Gruffydd and Lord Ferrers were given an opportunity to lay their charges against one another before the Council in the Marches, as the designated court of appeal from the Welsh shires and lordships. Each was bound in an obligation of £1,000 to keep the peace until the Michaelmas term, when the entire matter would be referred to Star Chamber at Westminster. Rhys and Ferrers duly appeared before this tribunal. Elis Gruffudd, the chronicler, who attended the hearing at Westminster, was not impressed by Wolsey, still less by Ferrers and Rhys ap Gruffydd:

> and it chanced that I was present on that day with many others from all parts of the kingdom, when and where I heard the ugliest accusations and charges that two gentlemen could bring each against other – charges and accusations which thousands of poor men would not for any amount of

[32] Howells, thesis cited, p.138; Bartrum, *1400–1500*, X, 1754; III, 450; VI, 1199; B. G. Charles, *George Owen of Henllys* (Aberystwyth, 1973), pp.7–22.

[33] Bartrum, *1400–1500*, VII, 1198. They were of Trimsaran, near Llanelli, and Llandyfaelog, not far from Kidwelly.

[34] Ibid., X, 1615.

[35] PRO, SP1/54 f.119–20.

[36] WRO, 705: 24/3 (vi).

[37] PRO, Stac. 2/18/234; Williams, *Y Cymmrodor*, XVI (1902), 20–1; Griffiths, *Principality of Wales*, p.346.

wealth have had brought against them by word of mouth, much less in writing . . . And notwithstanding the numerous threats of the Cardinal against them I never once heard a word from him in defence of the poor whom both had grievously wronged according to the written statements of each about the other . . . each of them made the most serious complaints and allegations against the other that was possible, not only about the affray that had been between them, but in respect of the oppression of the people and the bribery of which each said the other was guilty. And when the Court had listened to their mutual accusations for some time, the Cardinal summoned the case before him into the Star Chamber.[38]

Wolsey, realizing the extreme delicacy of the situation, censured both men, Ferrers especially for intemperately over-reacting towards an impetuous youth. They were then commended to go about their lawful business in peace.

This was, in fact, no solution at all, merely a postponement of further trouble between them. In retrospect, it may be said that Rhys had shown no respect for the king's justiciar and at times scant regard for the king's authority. Ferrers, for his part, had displayed no subtlety in his dealings with Rhys and an alarming lack of understanding of the consequences of his robust actions. Wolsey the politician read the storm-signals for what they were and temporized. In any case, by the beginning of October 1529 he was no longer the king's chief minister.

Some months later, Catherine Howard may have taken up the cudgels once again on behalf of her husband. The reason may lie in an assault on Rhys's position in Pembrokeshire, where he held Sir William Parr's commission as steward and receiver. As we have seen, Rhys's behaviour towards the mayor of Tenby and his partisan judgements in the case of the Spanish captain, Melchior de Loriaga, led to petitions to the Chancery in the winter of 1529–30. The intervention of Sir Thomas More, who succeeded Wolsey as chancellor on 26 October, may have been decisive. On 22 January, Sir William Parr's rights in the two Pembroke offices were reaffirmed, but since he was still occupied in the north he was associated in the offices with John Docwray, a Hertford-shire gentleman to whom the Crown gave other commissions. Rhys ap Gruffydd's earlier compact with Parr seemed at an end.[39] Sometime later, Catherine Howard laid siege to Ferrers and killed some of his men. This may have been the time when James ap Gruffydd ap Hywel installed himself in Rhys's castle at Newcastle Emlyn with a strong force. James was the son of Sir Rhys ap Thomas's sister, Sage; he lived at

[38] Williams, *Y Cymmrodor*, XVI (1902), 22–3; *MSS in the Welsh Language*, I, ix–x; M. B. Davies, 'The "Enterprize" of Paris and Boulogne, 1544', *Bull. Faculty of Arts, Fouad I University, Cairo*, XI, part 1 (May 1949), 39; PRO, Stac. 2/18/234.
[39] See above p.94; *LP, Henry VIII*, IV, part 3, 2772, 2931; Lloyd, thesis cited, pp.64–5; Hasler, *HC*, II, 42.

Castell Maelgwyn, an estate not far from Cilgerran in north Pembroke-shire.[40] Attempts to arrest him following the issue of a royal warrant to Ferrers on 7 October 1530 seem to have resulted in the wounding of William Vaughan of Cilgerran (1496–1549), another of Rhys ap Gruffydd's adherents. But James was eventually apprehended by Ferrers's retainer, James Leche, and packed off to the Tower of London.[41] Such surges of lawlessness are likely to have been the cause of Rhys ap Gruffydd's own arrest shortly before 15 October. The imperial ambassador, Eustace Chapuys, was told that 'he himself has threatened to finish what his wife had begun'. Rhys accordingly found himself in the Tower, too, until he was released on bail on grounds of ill health about June 1531.[42] This most recent outbreak of violence in south Wales intensified distrust of Rhys ap Gruffydd at Westminster, and underlined the difficulty of subjecting him and his wife to the king's authority. But it was the interposition of other, external circumstances which in November 1531 cast Rhys into the abyss.

On 21 September 1531, some three months after his release, Rhys was re-arrested. By 26 September, Chapuys had heard that he planned to escape to either Scotland or the imperial court in order to plot against Henry VIII.[43] When his trial opened in King's Bench on 22 November, an indictment of treason was framed by a Middlesex jury of present-ment. There can be no reasonable doubt that it was officially inspired. The charges arose from events that allegedly took place in the capital, so there was no question of the Council in the Marches entertaining the case. Rhys was found guilty five days later, and attainted and executed. The official record of the trial ignores lawlessness in south-west Wales, which would have been the proper concern of the Council in the Marches or, perhaps, the court of Chancery. It concentrates instead on accusations of recent plots in London since the summer of 1531.[44] Efforts had been made to gather information from Rhys's servants. William Wolf, one of his chaplains and evidently from Haverford, was sum-moned to the Star Chamber 'for certayne causes to him to be obiecte on the kinges behaulf', but Thomas Cromwell, whose influence in the government was growing daily, discharged him from appearing (so

---

[40] *CSP, Span.*, IV, part 1, 762 (though Williams, *Y Cymmrodor*, XVI (1902), 17–18, regards this as referring to the events of June 1529); *Acts PC*, II, 224. According to Gruffydd Rice half a century later, five or six of Ferrers's servants were slain in this or related encounters between the justiciar and Catherine Howard, as well as three or four of Rhys's own men: see below p.291; Bartrum, *1400–1500*, V, 726; Fenton, *Historical Tour*, p.500.

[41] *LP, Henry VIII*, V, 209; PRO, C82/634/10; Griffiths, *Principality of Wales*, pp.221–2; Bartrum, *1400–1500*, IX, 1415.

[42] *CSP, Span.*, IV, part 1, 762; part 2, 248; Williams, *Y Cymmrodor*, XVI (1902), 29–31.

[43] *CSP, Span.*, IV, part 2, 248.

[44] PRO, KB9/517/3; KB27/1081 *rex* m.6, printed in Williams, *Y Cymmrodor*, XVI (1902), 33–9. One of the justices of King's Bench present was the recently appointed (July 1531) John Spelman, who kept his own record of the trial: J. H. Baker (ed.), *The Reports of John Spelman*, vol. 1 (Selden Soc., 93, 1977 for 1976), pp.xiii, 47–8.

Cromwell notified the mayor of Haverford on 19 June 1532).[45] Whatever the sources of information available to the accusers, it was claimed that on 28 August 1531, at Rhys's lodgings in Islington, near London, he and William Hughes, a gentleman from Carew who may be identified with the pirate captain protected by Rhys in 1529, and Edward Llwyd, a yeoman from Carew, plotted the deposition and death of the king. They allegedly discussed the implications of the prophecy that James, along with the Red Hand and the Ravens, would conquer England. It was further alleged that Rhys tried to raise £2,000 by mortgaging certain of his lands, notably the lordships of Narberth and Carew, to Robert White, a London citizen and clothier, so that he could make his way to the Isle of Man and Ireland, en route to Scotland, in order to rouse allies in the cause. King James V of Scotland was expected to lead an army against England and in the course of sweeping Henry VIII from his throne would install Rhys in the principality of Wales.

The indictment further maintained that a few days after the Islington meeting, on 1 September, not only did Rhys send Edward Llwyd to the Tower to persuade his kinsman, James ap Gruffydd ap Hywel, to join the plot, but he adopted the style and honour of Rhys ap Gruffydd 'FitzUrien' to strengthen his claims to lordship in the principality of Wales. Edward Llwyd told James that if William Hughes came, he should give him credence too. Messages were said to have passed to and from Rhys, to the Tower and back again. On 3 September, James allegedly negotiated on Rhys's behalf with one of James's creditors, a London merchant called John Hughes, to raise money by selling or mortgaging land, both to pay off James's debts and to acquire a substantial sum of cash. Next day, William Hughes entered the Tower with a priest whose mission was to seal the arrangements by administering the sacrament to James. According to Justice Spelman's notes of the case, James refused the sacrament but fell in with the rest of the plans. Between 4 September and 21 September two developments occurred, though the precise link between them is not certainly known. James ap Gruffydd ap Hywel escaped from the Tower and sought sanctuary in Westminster Abbey, and the decision was taken to re-arrest Rhys ap Gruffydd and lodge him once more in the Tower.

Certain additional information about Rhys's downfall is contained in the dispatches of the imperial ambassador, Chapuys, to his master, Emperor Charles V, who was watching affairs in England intently, not least because of his concern for the position of his aunt, Queen Catherine. These letters, still preserved among the imperial archives in Vienna, are a pot-pourri of fact and fancy, rumour and speculation, as well as of evidence gleaned from such political trials as Rhys's. They help

[45] R. B. Merriman (ed.), *Life and Letters of Thomas Cromwell* (2 vols., Oxford, 1902), I, 345; *LP, Henry VIII*, V, 497; Bartrum, *1400–1500*, X, 1756.

us towards an understanding of the circumstances in which Rhys ap Gruffydd found himself in the autumn of 1531 and provide strong hints as to why he met the fate he did.[46]

By 1527, Henry VIII was deeply worried about the failure of Queen Catherine to produce a male heir to sustain the dynasty. The king's suspicion of anyone who might challenge his Crown explains his harsh treatment of, for example, Edward Stafford, duke of Buckingham, whose royal blood and unwise pretensions resulted in his execution in 1521 under the veil of a plot to kill the king. The behaviour of Rhys ap Gruffydd later in the decade could have been construed in a similar light in view of the common heritage of the Tudors and the family of Sir Rhys ap Thomas which Welsh poets popularized. and Rhys ap Gruffydd's own links with the king through his mother, Catherine St John, and his wife, who was the aunt of Henry's intended consort, Anne Boleyn. At the very least, here was another brash and over-mighty subject, presuming on his regal connections at an awkward time for His Majesty.[47]

Chapuys was alert to the similarities between the cases of Rhys ap Gruffydd and Buckingham, and he pointedly noted that both were executed on the same spot on Tower Hill. Henry's continuing apprehensiveness about a dynastic threat after 1521 tallies with a story which Henry Rice related early in the seventeenth century. Charles Howard, the earl of Nottingham, who died in December 1625 at the ripe old age of about eighty-eight, was a nephew of Rhys's wife, Catherine Howard. There was a tradition in his family that one day when Henry VIII was out hawking at Wandsworth, his falcon seized a fowl, but a raven swooped down and separated the falcon from its prey. One of the king's companions wryly – perhaps slyly – commented on the presumption of the raven, which deserved to be pulled down from its perch 'to secure your majesty'. True or not as a hunting anecdote with political overtones, it illustrates what some believed to be the king's dynastic anxieties in the Rhys ap Gruffydd affair.[48]

At least one Welsh poet, Lewys Morgannwg, in addressing Rhys ap Gruffydd, repeated allusions to his family's descent from Arthur and ancient British kings that were commonplace in earlier decades. It was a theme which could have struck a jarring chord with the king's advisers for in 1530–1, at the height of the discussions about Henry's divorce from Queen Catherine, the king's own Arthurian and British heritage was enlisted in the campaign to assert his imperial status.[49] One of the

---

[46] *CSP, Span.*, IV, part 1, 762; part 2, 248, 323; V, part 1, 235.

[47] B. J. Harris, *Edward Stafford, Third Duke of Buckingham, 1478–1521* (Stanford, Calif., 1986), chs. 7, 8; above p.83; M. Levine, *Tudor Dynastic Problems, 1460–1571* (London, 1973), pp.48–60.

[48] *CSP, Span.*, IV, part 2, 323; see below p.287.

[49] Lewis, 'The literary tradition', in Pugh, *Glamorgan County History*, III, 510–11, 512–13; see above p.82; Scarisbrick, *Henry VIII*, pp.272–3. The duke of Norfolk stressed these British associations; he doubtless heard much about them in relation to Rhys ap Gruffydd during his

charges against Rhys in November 1531 was that he had adopted the name of 'FitzUrien', which had venerable associations with the British kings of Rheged. The charge was true enough, but seventeenth-century pedigrees record that a number of his forebears had used 'FitzUrien', the first being Syr Elidir Ddu, knight of the Holy Sepulchre, in the fourteenth century; and it is indisputable that poets had been alluding to Urien for generations past.[50] Nevertheless, as circumstantial evidence of regal presumption, not unlike the Staffords' use of the royal arms of England and Buckingham's interest in his royal pedigree, Rhys's British associations might have appeared to detract from the imperial dignity of the Tudor king at a particularly delicate moment.

Popular prognostications of a conspiracy between James V of Scotland, the son of Henry VIII's sister Margaret; the so-called 'Red Hand', which may have been an allusion to Owain Lawgoch (died 1378), the elusive Welsh rebel who was the last direct male descendant of the princes of Gwynedd and had made at least two descents on Wales with French and Spanish aid; and Rhys ap Gruffydd, whose badge bore three ravens, would have seemed no less alarming than other prophecies in vogue in Henrician England and Wales. There was a centuries-old tradition of political prophecy, even older in Wales than in England, that gained widespread currency from time to time, and foresaw assaults on England and its kings from the north and the west, from Wales, Ireland and Scotland. It was even predicted that the English realm would be dismembered once victory had been achieved. It seems that such utterances were experiencing a revived popularity by the 1530s, and those associated with the hapless Rhys ap Gruffydd were an example of the *genre*. There is, however, no independent evidence that this particular prophecy was current in 1531, or had ever been current. It is true that William Neville, when he made his rich and miscellaneous confessions on 30 December 1532, said that both Buckingham and 'Young Rise' (among others) 'had cast themselves away by too much trust in prophecies'; but he was speaking a year after this particular prophecy had been well publicized at Rhys's trial. If it had a currency in some quarters, its elements may have seemed a heady brew to a king whose father had enlisted similar vaticinatory musings in his own interest after 1485.

A century later, Henry Rice rightly pointed out that England and Scotland were enjoying a period of truce in 1531, and that James V was preoccupied with establishing his authority in his own realm. But there was at least one cause of tension between the two kings and that concerned James's search for a bride. In foiling his proposed marriage to

---

father's marriage negotiations with Sir Rhys ap Thomas and Sir Gruffydd ap Rhys in 1514.
[50] NLW, Llanstephan 130 D f.5; see above p.9.

Catherine de Medici, the Pope's kinswoman, Henry VIII was responsible for turning James's thoughts to the earlier idea of an imperial match. Both emperor and Pope were cultivating the Scots at the very time when they were locked in the divorce dispute with Henry. Stories of a treasonable plot involving a Scottish invasion were not, therefore, entirely implausible in a time of truce.[51] An apocalyptic Welsh dimension was quite another matter in early Tudor England. Yet for those who believed in 'rumour, magic and prophecy' – and there were many such in England and Wales in the early sixteenth century – a highborn (and disenchanted) personage like Rhys was inspiring (and fearful) material.[52]

The king's determination to divorce Queen Catherine in order to marry Anne Boleyn was much more real. This determination had already led him into a confrontation with Catherine's nephew, Emperor Charles V, and with the Pope who declined to grant an annulment. On 18 June 1529, the same day that Carmarthen was in uproar, a special court convened to pass judgement on the king's marriage opened at last at Blackfriars. Two years later, the king's 'great matter', with its ever widening implications, had made only desultory progress, and in the summer of 1531 Henry banished Queen Catherine from the court and never saw her again. Meanwhile, the English clergy were brought to acknowledge the king's supremacy 'as far as the law of Christ allows', and later in 1531 Henry planned further measures to resolve the great question of the day.[53] At this very juncture, Rhys ap Gruffydd found himself on the wrong side of the law as a result of his own behaviour, and an embarrassment to the monarch because of his associations. Eventually, on 21 September 1531 he was re-arrested.

According to Chapuys, at the time of Rhys's execution on 4 December, the Welshman and his wife were accused of speaking disparagingly of Anne Boleyn:

> there is a rumour about town that had it not been for the Lady, who hated him because he and his wife had spoken disparagingly of her, he would have been pardoned and escaped his miserable fate.[54]

Anne's mother was none other than Catherine Howard's half-sister; their brother was the duke of Norfolk. But opinion in the Howard family was sharply divided on the subject of Anne's liaison with the king and

---

[51] A. D. Carr, *Owen of Wales* (Cardiff, 1991); G. R. Elton, *Policy and Police* (Cambridge, 1972), ch.2; G. Donaldson, *Scotland, James V to James VII* (Edinburgh and London, 1965), pp.45–6; see below p.284. See T. M. Smallwood, '*The Prophecy of the Six Kings*', *Speculum*, 60 (1985), 586–92; S. L. Jansen, *Political Protest and Propaganda under Henry VIII* (Woodbridge, 1991), pp.28–9, 110, 168.

[52] The phrase is the title of ch.2 of Elton, *Policy and Police*. As Henry Rice pointed out, attempts to moderate the wilder effects of prophecies led to the 1542 statute against the judicial use of prophecy: *SR, III, 850*; see below p.287.

[53] Scarisbrick, *Henry VIII*, pp.147–62.

[54] *CSP, Span.*, IV, part 2, 323.

the propriety of Queen Catherine's divorce. At least her relatives were in the best possible position to know Anne's character. Duke Thomas was exasperated by her sharp-tongued haughtiness by 1531, as he sought with increasing desperation to preserve his position of power by maintaining his loyalty to Henry VIII – alternating 'between vindictive fright and sycophantic self-preservation', as E. W. Ives put it. The duchess, Elizabeth Stafford, daughter of the duke of Buckingham executed in 1521, was openly sympathetic towards the queen.[55] Rhys ap Gruffydd's relationship with Catherine of Aragon is hard to divine. Long before, his father was in Prince Arthur's household at the time the prince died in 1502. He may have continued in the service of Arthur's widow thereafter, like his kinsman, Thomas ab Owain.[56] Whether or not Rhys and his wife had made incautious remarks about the king's paramour, rumours that they had done so may well have been sufficient. If Cardinal Wolsey had been able to moderate the impact of the law on Rhys in the past, the downfall of the king's minister by October 1529 removed that protection. Thereafter, Rhys's brother-in-law Norfolk, who was facing the prospect of a second close relative in ten years going to the block for treason, did nothing to help him. Indeed, Rhys's trial may have fortified the duke's instinct for survival; in the somewhat obscure factionalism of Henry VIII's court in the latter part of 1531, that may have been one of its purposes. Years later, at the end of 1546, when Norfolk was arrested and placed in the Tower, he told the king's Council that both Buckingham and Rhys ap Gruffydd – their association in his mind is striking – had hated him, and that Rhys had 'wished he had found means to thrust his dagger in me'.[57]

By September 1531, therefore, Rhys ap Gruffydd was in a vulnerable position of triple jeopardy. The decision was taken to return him to prison and try him for treason. Almost immediately, rumours started to circulate that the evidence against him was contrived, and belief in his essential innocence persisted in the decades that followed. Writing to Charles V on the morning of the execution, Chapuys reported that one of Rhys's servants had tried to entice him into a conspiracy to induce the Scots to invade England with Welsh aid. Rhys was believed to have rejected the suggestion but refused to tell the authorities the name of the person who had approached him. Despite his apologies, he was condemned to death.[58] In May 1534, John Hale, vicar of Isleworth, was

[55] F. R. Grace, 'The life and career of Thomas Howard, third duke of Norfolk (1473–1554)' (unpublished University of Nottingham MA thesis, 1961), pp.112ff.; J. Guy, *Tudor England* (Oxford, 1988), p.130; R. M. Warnicke, *The Rise and Fall of Anne Boleyn* (Cambridge, 1989), pp.116, 145–6; E. W. Ives, *Anne Boleyn* (Oxford, 1986), pp.157, 159, 173. Relations between the duchess and the duke were themselves strained.
[56] See above p.51; T. Jones, 'A Welsh chronicler in Tudor England', *WHR*, I, no.1 (1960), 3.
[57] *LP, Henry VIII*, XXI, part 2, 283.
[58] *CSP, Span.*, IV, part 2, 323.

told by one of the Scudamores (presumably from Herefordshire) that following Rhys's execution, Welshmen and priests were 'sore disdained nowadays':

> And what think ye of Wales? – Their noble and gentle Ap Ryce so cruelly put to death, and he innocent, as they say, in the cause.[59]

Members of Rhys's blighted family, particularly (it seems) Catherine Howard, were able to clothe these rumours with plausible detail. By Elizabeth's reign, it was believed in the family circle that James ap Gruffydd ap Hywel, 'whoe was corrupted by th'adversaries of the said Ryse Griffithe', had confessed that he had persuaded Rhys to sign a blank letter 'wherein the said James procured suche matters to be wrytten as conteyned tresone'. Following the accession of James I, Sir Walter Rice returned to this theme, informing the new king that Rhys 'was by direct meanes and practizes attainted of treason for conspiringe (as it was falsly proved)' with his grandfather, James V. The witnesses against Rhys, he said, were 'two meane men of noe reputacion credit or worth, whereof thone beinge James Griffith', who acted partly 'by the persuasion of the great and heavy adversaries of the saide Rice Griffith'. The other was Edward Llwyd, who 'by persuasion and reward' of 500 marks also affirmed Rhys's guilt. This latter piece of intelligence had allegedly been uncovered by Catherine Howard and others.[60] The family testimony may, of course, be tainted, for during the remainder of the Tudor century and in the early decades of the seventeenth century, determined efforts were made to re-gild Rhys ap Gruffydd's reputation and recover the estates forfeited in 1531. Nevertheless, there are weighty hints that suggest that the story is well founded. Justice Spelman's surviving notes of the trial are revealing.[61] They show that whereas the jury of presentment indicted Rhys and several companions – William Hughes, Edward Llwyd and James ap Gruffydd ap Hywel – and that they were in custody in the Tower (apart, perhaps, from James who may already have escaped), only Rhys and one companion, William Hughes, were arraigned in King's Bench on 24 November. The charges against Edward Llwyd and James ap Gruffydd ap Hywel were evidently not pursued. In fact, on 27 November, when the trial jury assembled to consider the indictment, James was brought from sanctuary, in the company of the abbot of Westminster, the elderly John Islip (died 1532), who was trusted by Henry VIII, in order to give evidence.[62] He substantiated the charges face to face (*facie ad faciem*) with Rhys and William Hughes. Of Edward Llwyd we learn little more, though he is

[59] *LP, Henry VIII*, VIII, 215, 230.
[60] See below pp.124, 127.
[61] *Spelman's Reports*, I, 47–8.
[62] M. D. Knowles, *The Religious Orders in England*, Vol. III (Cambridge, 1959), 96–9.

likely to have been the servant who, contemporaries believed, had provided the information on which the case could be built at the outset.

That same day, Rhys and William Hughes were swiftly found guilty and James ap Gruffydd ap Hywel and Edward Llwyd were acquitted.[63] On 13 June 1532, Thomas Cromwell had still not concluded what he described as James's 'matyer', but he hoped to speak to the treasurer of the king's household very shortly.[64] This matter probably related to the pardon which James had been promised soon after the execution, in return for £526. 13s. 4d., an obligation for 400 marks of which was handed over to the king. When financial arrangements for its full repayment had been completed, James, who seems still to have been in sanctuary at Westminster, was formally granted his pardon on 20 June 1532.[65] Moreover, by 1533 he appears to have been awarded a lease of two weirs at Cenarth, near Castell Maelgwyn.[66] Yet later that summer, James and his family suddenly fled abroad, taking ship from Kidwelly. Thereafter, he travelled western Europe, from Ireland to Scotland, the Low Countries, Germany, even, by 1538, to Italy, making known his commitment to Queen Catherine's cause and the old faith, offering his services, seeking funds and proclaiming his distinguished ancestry and position in Wales. Henry VIII's agents were never quite able to get their hands on him, though reports of his movements were carefully filed at Westminster. He may eventually have returned, perhaps at the time of Queen Mary's accession in 1553. According to Henry Rice, who obtained his information from those who knew his grandfather, whilst he was abroad James confessed to his deceptions in 1531, 'and being sore troubled in conscience he returned home with intent to acknowledge his offence and to submitt himself' to Gruffydd Rice. Gruffydd spurned him and, as far as Henry Rice knew, James retired to Cardiganshire to die.[67] As for Edward Llwyd, Henry Rice understood that he, 'being ashamed of his villaine, fled his Country, and was never hard off after-wardes'.[68]

Why should James ap Gruffydd ap Hywel have turned on his kinsman, and Edward Llwyd have deserted his master, in this way? James had been incarcerated in the Tower since October 1530 for seizing the castle at Newcastle Emlyn, where William Vaughan and

---

[63] PRO, KB27/1081 *rex* m.6.

[64] Merriman, *Cromwell*, I, 344–5. James had been awarded £3. 6s. 8d. 'by the king's command' on 3 October 1531, while preparations for the trial were in train: N. H. Nicolas (ed.), *Privy Purse Expenses of King Henry the Eighth* (London, 1827), p.167.

[65] *LP, Henry VIII*, V, 508; PRO, SP1/68 f.158–9; Williams, *Y Cymmrodor*, XVI (1902), 54–9. It seems that John ab Owain, 'who sometime was towards Rice Griffith' and was also put in the Tower, was released for a fine of £26. 13s. 4d.; he may be identified with the bailiff of Carmarthen in 1516–17. Griffiths, *Principality of Wales*, p.345.

[66] PRO, E315/12/19 f.197.

[67] CCL MS 4.20; Williams, *Y Cymmrodor*, XVI (1902), 47, 59–93; NLW, Dynevor A 94b (iii). He may still have been alive in 1555, when his Cenarth lands were said to be in the queen's hands for debt: PRO, LR1/229 f.125–6v.

[68] NLW, Dynevor A 94b (iii); CCL MS 4.20.

others had been wounded or killed. To avoid prolonged captivity, or worse, and in view of the deteriorating position of Queen Catherine, to whom he later claimed he was devoted, James may have been prepared to turn appellor in September 1531 and accuse Rhys ap Gruffydd of treason. A few years later, James Leche, Lord Ferrers's lieutenant in south Wales, recalled that he had arrested James ap Gruffydd ap Hywel, who 'appeched Sir Rice Griffith, attainted for treason'.[69]

Certain particulars of the indictment of 1531 suggest how a charge of treason could have been contrived. After his release from the Tower about June 1531, Rhys ap Gruffydd might well have tried to raise cash on the security of his estates from merchant-financiers like Robert White and John Hughes. Along with a clerk named William Jenkins, Rhys had certainly been indebted to a Thomas White, a merchant tailor of London, to the tune of £160 since 5 July 1527. In the court of King's Bench on 28 May 1530, Rhys reported the arrangements he had made to repay the sum, namely, the sale of four mills at Luggbridge (Herefordshire), which he had inherited, to another London tailor for £141. This transaction was carefully recorded on the plea roll and was easily traceable. Equally, Rhys might have wished to keep in touch, through Edward Llwyd and William Hughes, with his kinsman, James ap Gruffydd ap Hywel, whom he had left in the Tower, perhaps even offering to pay James's debts to John Hughes. James and Edward Llwyd concluded that the best way to win their freedom was by providing king's evidence, exploiting the testimony of Robert White and John Hughes to corroborate the discussions about money.[70] One interested observer, Elis Gruffudd, who was not particularly well disposed towards Rhys ap Gruffydd, found it difficult to accept the charges. Hearing of the alleged plot while he was in Calais, he concluded that 'it is likely that Syr Rhys was not so foolish as to believe in his heart that the king of the Scots would in any way make him prince of Wales if he succeeded in winning the crown of the kingdom'.[71]

Later in the century, family tradition had it that Catherine Howard discovered that her husband's enemies had bribed James and Edward Llwyd to fabricate the charges of treason.[72] Those 'great and heavy adversaries' (to use Sir Walter Rice's words) were at the heart of Henry VIII's government. Here, Justice Spelman's personal record of the trial he probably witnessed is decisive.[73] It demonstrates how carefully and swiftly conducted the trial was – and at the highest level. On 22 January the Middlesex jury of presentment was assembled in Westminster Hall before the justices of King's Bench, who sent them

[69] *Acts PC*, II, 244; Williams, *Y Cymmrodor*, XVI (1902), 47.
[70] PRO, KB9/517/3; KB27/1075 m.40r and *v*.
[71] NLW, Mostyn MS 158; Jones, *WHR*, I (1960), 11.
[72] See below p.128.
[73] *Spelman's Reports*, I, 47–8.

into the exchequer chamber nearby where the king's attorney and others of the king's advisers (*auterz de counsel de roy*) provided the evidence on which to indict Rhys and his companions. Two days later, Rhys and William Hughes were brought from custody to be arraigned on the indictment. A trial jury had been assembled by the sheriff of Middlesex by 27 January, when Rhys and William Hughes heard the indictment and James ap Gruffydd ap Hywel's personal evidence. Both prisoners were examined by none other than leading members of the king's Council (*lez seniorz de le counsell le roy*), who (using methods unknown to us) elicited and recorded their statements. After his evidence was completed, James was allowed to return with Abbot Islip to sanctuary, while the chief justice, Sir John FitzJames, who had signed the articles of impeachment of Cardinal Wolsey in 1529, 'summed up the effect of the evidence and charged the jury upon it'.[74] The justices waited, 'without rising for their ease'. Within two hours the jury returned with what must surely have been the anticipated verdict: guilty as charged. The second justice, Sir Humphrey Coningsby, who had been one of Henry VII's legal counsel, condemned them to the traitor's death of hanging, drawing and quartering.[75]

In fact, as befitted his station, Rhys ap Gruffydd was beheaded, on Tower Hill on the morning of 4 December. William Hughes was drawn to Tyburn the same day, and hanged and quartered. The king gave the final authorization for their execution, but the details were arranged by two of his and Anne Boleyn's intimates, Christopher Hales, the attorney-general, and Thomas Cromwell. Others, such as Ferrers and members of Princess Mary's Council in the Marches, would not have been sorry to hear the news. Rhys's body was taken the short distance from the Tower to be interred in the Holy Cross Friary in Hart Street.[76]

The significance of Rhys ap Gruffydd's trial is many-layered. He suffered disproportionately harshly for his youthful arrogance and demonstrable misdeeds in south Wales. As far as his family is concerned, it seemed rank ingratitude, as Chapuys realized:

> [Rhys's] father was formerly Governor of Wales, and his grandfather also, and one of those who did great service to Henry VII in his early necessities and the conquest of this kingdom.[77]

Not everyone was convinced that to treat such a prominent Welshman in this way, with its lingering suspicions of a contrived condemnation,

---

[74] *DNB, s.n.* FitzJames. He jibbed at presiding over further political trials: Ives, *Anne Boleyn*, p.383.
[75] *DNB, s.n.*; Guy, *Tudor England*, p.67.
[76] *LP, Henry VIII*, V, 259; *LP, Henry VIII*, Addenda, I, part 1, 250; W. D. Hamilton (ed.), *A Chronicle of England . . . by Charles Wriothesley*, I (Camden Soc., 1875), 17; J. Stow, *A Survey of London*, ed. C. L. Kingsford (2 vols., Oxford, 1908; repr. 1971), I, 147; *Holinshed's Chronicles*, III, 775. The friary was dissolved in 1539 and afterwards demolished. For Hales, who was close to Cromwell, see Ives, *Anne Boleyn*, p.261; Warnicke, *Anne Boleyn*, pp.105, 117.
[77] *LP, Henry VIII*, V, 259; *CSP, Span.*, IV, part 2, 323.

was likely to achieve the king's ends in Wales. John Hale, the vicar of Isleworth, had dark forebodings in May 1534, arising from Rhys's execution:

> I think not contrary but they [the Welsh] will join and take part with the Irish, and so invade our realm. If they do so, doubt ye not but they shall have aid and strength enough in England . . .[78]

Rhys was not, in truth, the stuff of which inspiring national leaders were made, in life or in death, though such expressions of opinion were placed before the king's Council and doubtless influenced its thinking about the major administrative, judicial and constitutional changes that soon followed.

Rhys's execution, like that of the duke of Buckingham ten years before, was an act of judicial murder, based on charges devised to suit the prevailing political and dynastic situation. Not only was Rhys a troublesome relative of the king, but his Howard kinsmen may have needed to be taught a lesson and brought to heel. In planning his exemplary downfall, efforts were made to meet the demands of English legal procedure, but hardly those of any concept of unimpeachable evidence. In the nature of the case, decisions were made and plans laid behind closed doors, confidentially, even secretly. His accusers were able to take advantage of circumstances and attitudes in the sixteenth century that were inclined to accept rumour as fact and prophecy as plausible design.

Moreover, the charges of treason may be connected with proposals that were made during 1531, apparently by Thomas Cromwell and his (and Anne Boleyn's) ally, Thomas Audley, speaker of the Commons in Parliament, to extend the scope of England's treason laws in order to take account of opposition that might arise from Henry's treatment of Queen Catherine, the clergy and the Pope.[79] They conceived of treasonable offences that closely mirrored Rhys ap Gruffydd's alleged activities. Thus, when their discussions resumed in the last months of 1531, the king instructed Cromwell to insert a clause in the proposed bill to the effect 'that the first accused of any manner treason shall have his pardon and a certain sum for his labour for the detection of any such treason'. This provision would have been an encouragement to Edward Llwyd and James ap Gruffydd ap Hywel to turn on Rhys ap Gruffydd. Consider, too, another of the proposals: it would be treason to 'consent or agree, privily or openly, to contribute or pay any sums of money to any foreign prince or other estate, contrary to the prerogative royal or in

---

[78] *LP, Henry VIII*, VIII, 230; cf. *CSP, Span.*, V, part 1, 235.

[79] For Cromwell and for Audley, who acquired an unsavoury reputation as an expert in judicial murder, not least for his role in Queen Anne's execution, see Ives, *Anne Boleyn*, pp.187, 192–3, 203, 260, 362, 386, 409; *CP*, I, 348–50.

prejudice of the king's business and this his realm'. Even Rhys's execution in December 1531 may have had a bearing on this treason bill, for it seems to have been abandoned soon afterwards and was never presented to Parliament in 1532. Sir Geoffrey Elton has commented that:

> It rested on no coherent principle but from the first to last presented something of a collection of ideas, almost as they might have come into someone's head casually and in the passage of time.

Had the framers a specific purpose in mind at a particular juncture in the autumn of 1531, namely, to do away with a troublesome Welshman *pour décourager les autres*, and, once this was accomplished, was the draft bill abandoned?[80]

Although Justice Spelman regrettably did not record the names of the king's councillors who took an active part in prosecuting Rhys ap Gruffydd at his trial, it is tempting to suggest a key role in the affair – as in so much else from 1531 onwards – for Thomas Cromwell. The patronage and direct influence in south Wales which were made available as a result of Rhys's attainder may explain why it was Cromwell who kept Rhys's family archives in his possession.[81] Indeed, the minister's part in the destruction of Rhys ap Gruffydd may help to explain how, by the end of 1531, Cromwell was well on the way to becoming Henry VIII's pre-eminent adviser, and why the duke of Norfolk, who dominated the king's counsels earlier in the year, 'had no cause to encourage the rise of Cromwell'.[82]

In sum, Rhys ap Gruffydd was a victim of his times: of dynastic circumstances beyond his control, of personal relationships and political rivalries of the most intense sort, and of developments that in retrospect made him one of the earliest martyrs of the English Reformation.

---

[80] Elton, *Policy and Police*, pp.264–72.
[81] *LP, Henry VIII*, VI, 136, 139. The fine made for his pardon by James ap Gruffydd ap Hywel on the king's order was recorded by Cromwell himself: ibid., V, 295.
[82] G. R. Elton, *Reform and Dissent* (Cambridge, 1973), pp.42, 117 n.70.

5

Restoration and Rehabilitation

Gruffydd ap Rhys (*c*.1526–92), or Gruffydd Rice as he was commonly known in official circles, began his quest to rehabilitate his family's reputation and restore its landed wealth soon after Henry VIII died in 1547. Neither task was easy. To dispel the prevailing mistrust of this family of distinguished lineage and recent royal connection was unlikely to be accomplished swiftly during decades of dynastic uncertainty and turbulent religious and political change. To restore to the family its substantial forfeited estates would not be welcomed by those – including the king himself – who had acquired an interest in them since 1531.

According to the parliamentary act of attainder of November 1531, the lands and properties of Rhys ap Gruffydd were forfeited to the Crown. The act safeguarded the interests of the three widows of the family in respect of lands and possessions held by each of them (or by others for their use) for life or jointly with their late husbands. The act also protected the position of Roger Corbet, one of the Devereux's kinsmen who had inherited the Hoptons' claims in Emlyn Uwch Cuch denied by Gruffydd ap Nicholas and his successors.[1] In 1531 just about half the family estates were held by the three widows between them: Dame Jenet (died 1535), the widow of Sir Rhys ap Thomas; Dame Catherine (who died in December 1553), the widow of Sir Gruffydd ap Rhys and, since 1525, the second wife of Sir Piers Edgecombe of Cotehele in Cornwall; and Lady Catherine Howard (died in May 1554), the widow of Rhys ap Gruffydd who quickly married Henry, Lord Daubeney, created earl of Bridgwater in 1538.[2] According to a survey made of Rhys ap Gruffydd's forfeited estates, these widows

---

[1] *SR*, III, 415–16; see below p.123. Roger Corbet's grandfather, Sir Richard (died 1492), married Elizabeth Devereux, daughter of Walter Devereux, Lord Ferrers (died 1485). Roger's great-grandfather, Sir Roger Corbet (died 1467), married Elizabeth, sister and heiress of Walter Hopton (died 1461). See above p.24; Wedgwood, *HP*, pp.222–3; Johnson, *Duke Richard of York*, p.84 n.35; *LP, Henry VIII*, I, 277.
[2] Bindoff, *HC*, II, 81–3; *CP*, II, 311; Nicolas, *Testamenta Vetusta*, II, 739.

together enjoyed an annual disposable income of about £360. Dame Jenet's properties were mostly in the borough of Carmarthen, where she presumably continued to live, though she also received a substantial income from the lordship of Narberth which made her jointure worth about £91 per annum; on her death in 1535 all this reverted to the king.[3] The lands of Dame Catherine Edgecombe were situated mostly in the lordship of Gower. The manors of Landimôr and Weobley were the most valuable of them, and at Weobley Dame Catherine had a comfortable residence much enhanced during the early Tudor period. Along with lesser properties in the mid-Tywi Valley, not far from Newton, her holdings were worth in all about £72 per annum in 1532.[4] Catherine Howard was the wealthiest of the three in terms of their jointures. Her portion was heavily concentrated in Pembrokeshire, where she held the manors of Burton and Angle, and especially the castle and lordship of Carew, which had been a favourite family estate since Sir Rhys ap Thomas's day. In all she could expect an annual income of about £196 from these estates after 1531.[5] The rest of Rhys ap Gruffydd's lands reverted to the Crown. They were concentrated in Carmarthenshire, on both sides of the River Tywi with the manor of Newton at their centre, and in the lordships of Kidwelly and Narberth. There were more distant properties, namely, in the lordship of Emlyn to the north, others in Cardiganshire (most notably at Llangybi and, nearer the coast, at Cilcennin and Aberystwyth) and in south Pembrokeshire. In all, the Crown acquired a windfall worth about £334 per annum, more than 85 per cent of it in Carmarthenshire. It also acquired the advowsons of a number of churches in Pembrokeshire valued in total at £149. 6s. 8d.[6] This estate was augmented when each of the widows died, most handsomely of course in 1554–5.

In the years before the dissolution of the monasteries, this was a useful additional source of income for the Crown – the value of a substantial English abbey. Henry VIII could either retain the estates in his own hands or, like kings before him, use them to discharge his debts, dispense favours and make rewards. To begin with, the first and most prudent course was adopted. Thomas Cromwell, a rising member of the king's

---

[3] PRO, SC12/23/43; NLW, Dynevor A 45. Jenet's interests in Carmarthen were worth £36. 16s. 10d., the lordship of Emlyn £9, and Narberth £45. 11s. 1d., totalling £91. 7s. 11d.

[4] Gower £48. 12s. 1½d., Carmarthen £4. 3s. 4d., and the Tywi Valley £19. 10s. 2d., totalling £72. 5s. 7½d.

[5] Pembrokeshire £148. 4s. 8½d. (including Carew at £77. 18s. 5d. at least), Carmarthenshire £29. 0s. ½d., as well as £18. 18s. 4d. from Narberth, totalling £196. 3s. 1d. Cf. a valor of her lands after Sir Rhys's death (£203. 18s. 0d.) in PRO, SC12/25/53.

[6] Carmarthenshire £233. 11s. 8¼d., Pembrokeshire £13. 8s. 11½d., Cardiganshire £35. 11s. 10d., other 18s. 4d., and Narberth £60. 0s. 1½d., totalling £343. 10s. 11¼d. The advowsons were of Carew; Narberth, Llanddewi Felffre, Cilymaenllwyd and Castelldwyran in the lordship of Narberth; Llangeler, Pen-boyr and Cilrhedyn in the lordship of Emlyn; Henry's Moat in Cemais, and Hodgeston free chapel. PRO, E36/151 f.37–8.

inner Council, seems to have had a hand in formulating the instructions given to a commission on 12 December 1531 to investigate and secure the lands, household goods, horses and cattle, documents and arms, of Rhys ap Gruffydd. The five commissioners were effectively headed by Thomas Jones (died 1558–9) of Abermarlais, one of Rhys ap Gruffydd's own kinsmen and, what was equally to the point, a loyal member of the king's household who had fought in France in 1513.[7] Among his colleagues was Morris ap Harry (or Parry) of Carmarthen, who also had long-standing connections with Henry VIII's household. He was knowledgeable about Pembrokeshire, where he had been constable of Tenby Castle, and Cardiganshire, where he was constable of Cardigan Castle. If, as seems likely, he was the son of Henry ap Gwilym of Cwrt Henry in Carmarthenshire, he too was related to the family whose affairs he was now charged with investigating. William Brabazon and John Smith, on the other hand, were associated with Anne Boleyn as marchioness of Pembroke.[8] The commissioners set about their task in January 1532, visiting almost all the significant locations of Rhys ap Gruffydd's interests.[9] William Brabazon, assisted by Hugh Walley, was still at Carew Castle on 26 March 1532 when Lady Howard's chaplain came forward to claim her ladyship's jointure. When the chaplain sought permission to clean the castle's chambers, the commissioners became suspicious and a search revealed that he had hidden four boxes of documents relating to Rhys ap Gruffydd's lands in Narberth, Carew and Kidwelly, as well as fine linen and a quantity of silverware (including a sign of a raven, the family emblem) worth about £40, all of which now belonged to the king.[10] The commissioners' final instruction was to find suitable officials to administer the attainted lands on behalf of the Crown, and in the following months four such persons were appointed.

What commended this small group to the government was their local knowledge, proven loyalty, and their close connection with Henry VIII's household. In view of Thomas Cromwell's interest in the fate of Rhys's lands, we may reasonably suppose that he authorized their appointment. Between them, they were to administer those of Rhys's lands that had reverted to the king. Thomas Jones, a gentleman usher of the king's chamber, turned from investigating his kinsman's property to administering a large part of it: he became steward, surveyor and receiver of the lordship of Emlyn, and of the manor of Abermarlais (or

[7] *LP, Henry VIII*, V, 285, 301; Bindoff, *HC*, II, 453–4.
[8] Griffiths, *Principality of Wales*, pp.225–6, 265; see above p.63; *LP, Henry VIII*, V, 553. Brabazon was also a servant of Cromwell's (ibid., pp.537–8).
[9] PRO, E36/151 f.27–33. The Shropshire lawyer, George Bromley (died 1533), was also named but does not appear to have visited south-west Wales. *LP, Henry VIII*, V, 285; Somerville, *Duchy of Lancaster*, I, 409; Bindoff, *HC*, I, 508.
[10] PRO, SP1/53 f.148.

lordship of Llansadwrn, as it was sometimes called), with an annual fee of £6. 13s. 4d. His appointment on 3 April 1532 had been preceded, on 29 March, by that of Hugh Vaughan of Kidwelly, who became bailiff and rent collector of rather less valuable properties in the lordship of Kidwelly; he was a groom of the chamber and his wife was one of Sir Rhys ap Thomas's relatives.[11] Then, on 7 April, John Phillips, one of the stewards in the king's chamber, was appointed steward, surveyor and receiver of more scattered lands elsewhere in Carmarthenshire, and in Cardiganshire and south Pembrokeshire; his family had interests of their own in the region.[12] That leaves Sir William Thomas of Aberglasney (Carmarthenshire), who willingly took responsibility for the remaining lands in Cardiganshire, Carmarthenshire and the lordship of Builth; his loyalty and integrity were beyond question, for he had served both Arthur and Henry as princes of Wales, was well known at court, and had been knighted for his part in the French expedition of 1513.[13]

Although Hugh Vaughan handed £75. 16s. 4½d. to Cromwell's agents a little before July 1535, it gradually became clear that these royal officers were encountering difficulties in collecting rents and other payments that fell into arrears in all three counties.[14] This may have been one reason why Henry VIII's advisers soon took to negotiating leases of the properties – invariably for twenty-one years, as was the custom at that time – in return for an annual rent. This policy had certain merits: it ensured at least a steady return; the length of the leases enabled them to be reviewed every generation or less; and should a return of the lands to Rhys ap Gruffydd's descendants ever be contemplated, the government's hands would not be too tightly bound. Moreover, leases were a useful means of attracting loyalty from those eager for royal patronage. This process of leasing Rhys ap Gruffydd's lands was supervised by the general surveyors of Crown lands and, then, by the Court of Augmentations created in the wake of the dissolution of the monasteries in 1536. Properties in the lordship of Kidwelly occupied by members of Rhys ap Gruffydd's family seem to have remained in their possession, despite efforts to the contrary. Thomas John ap Morris ab Owain continued to live at the mansion of Bryn y Beirdd, near

---

[11] *LP, Henry VIII*, V, 456; Bindoff, *HC*, II, 453–4; III, 515–16; PRO, SC6/Henry VIII/4882, 4883 m.1d. In December 1535, Vaughan was succeeded by John Avery, yeoman of the king's bottles; when he died in 1546, his son Thomas, also a king's servant, was persuaded to take the job (*LP, Henry VIII*, VIII, 119; XXI, part 2, p.232). Both Vaughan and Avery were servants of Thomas Cromwell.

[12] *DWB*, pp.752–3; NLW, Slebech 23. He had difficulty in executing his commission for, as he reported to Cromwell on 21 September 1534, Lord Ferrers had taken to mustering the tenantry in Phillips's charge: *LP, Henry VIII*, VII, 458.

[13] Griffiths, *Principality of Wales*, pp.205–6; *LP, Henry VIII*, VI, 136.

[14] *LP, Henry VIII*, VIII, 446. Vaughan had left the money with Jankyn (or John) Llwyd, apparently his deputy and one of Cromwell's servants (below n.20). See PRO, E315/12 no.19 f.197–8; /364 f.42–5; /384.

Carreg Cennen, refused to pay rent to the king, and claimed the house and its park by right of inheritance.[15]

A handful of grants from Rhys ap Gruffydd's forfeited estate was made in the last two years of Henry VIII's reign. The recipients were either prominent Welsh figures with a claim on the king's patronage, or individuals with a special interest in south-west Wales. The most favoured treatment was accorded Thomas Jones (knighted in 1542), who obtained in fee the lands of Llansadwrn, Abermarlais and Maenordeilo which were worth about £40 in 1532 and which Jones purchased for £737. 9s. 10d. He thereby enlarged his own family's estate in the vicinity of Abermarlais, where he moved into Rhys ap Gruffydd's house. This unusual opportunity to purchase property outright may owe something to the advocacy of Sir William Herbert, later earl of Pembroke, who was close to the king and with whom Jones was allied.[16]

On 1 June 1545, Gruffydd Higon, a Carmarthen burgess whose family had shown impeccable loyalty to the Crown over 150 years and had been associated with Rhys ap Gruffydd's forebears for almost as long, received (along with his wife, Sage) properties, mostly in Carmarthen borough, for twenty-one years at an annual rent of £22. 9s. 3d. This was the bulk of the town property held by Dame Jenet at the time of her death ten years before.[17] In the following year, William Devereux, the younger son of Rhys ap Gruffydd's sworn enemy, Lord Ferrers, secured some of his rival's most cherished lands – at Newton, Llandeilo Fawr and Dryslwyn – as well as extensive lands on the eastern side of the River Tywi in the lordship of Llandovery, and others in north Cardiganshire, on a twenty-one-year lease at £9. 14s. 9d.[18] Then, on 22 December 1546, Roger Williams (died 1583), from Pen-rhos in Monmouthshire, received the remainder of the Cardiganshire lands at an annual rent of £27. 4s. 4d.[19] The other two lessees under Henry VIII were kinsmen-by-marriage of Rhys ap Gruffydd, and yet Carmarthenshire men who were also members of the king's household. John (or Jankyn) Llwyd had been escheator of Carmarthenshire and Cardiganshire since 1512 and a groom of the chamber since 1509; his wife was Elizabeth, one of Sir Rhys ap Thomas's illegitimate daughters. Now, in May 1546, as a sewer of the royal chamber, he concluded a lease for twenty-one years of the lands and mines in Carnwyllion and Kidwelly in the lordship of Kidwelly, for an increased rent of almost £54

[15] H. A. Lloyd, *The Gentry of South-West Wales, 1540–1640* (Cardiff, 1968), pp.64–9; PRO, E315/12 no.19 f.198; /364 f.43.
[16] *LP, Henry VIII*, XX, part 1, 519 (3 June 1545); PRO, SC12/23/43; *CP*, X, 704–9; see above n.3.
[17] PRO, LR1/229 f.30–2; *CPR, 1563–6*, p.436; Bindoff, *HC*, II, 431–2; Griffiths, *Principality of Wales*, pp.335–53.
[18] *LP, Henry VIII*, XXI, part 1, 688 (13 July); Bindoff, *HC*, II, 42; Hasler, *HC*, II, 35.
[19] *LP, Henry VIII*, XXI, part 2, 345; *DWB*, pp.1069, 1075.

per annum (the properties were valued at less than £53 in 1532).[20] Finally, John Vaughan (died 1574), eldest son of Hugh Vaughan who had administered the Kidwelly estates of Rhys ap Gruffydd from 1532, leased the lands in the commote of Iscennen.[21] Thus, by the time Henry VIII died on 28 January 1547, two-thirds of the Carmarthenshire estates, and all those in the lordship of Kidwelly and in Cardiganshire had been disposed of, partly to relatives of Rhys ap Gruffydd, a substantial portion in perpetuity to Sir Thomas Jones. The prospects of Rhys's son, Gruffydd, were dispiriting.

The death of the king who had contrived Rhys ap Gruffydd's condemnation for treason coincided with Gruffydd Rice's coming of age. Following his father's execution, Gruffydd and his older brother, Thomas Rice, had been placed in the charge of the highly respected bishop of Durham, Cuthbert Tunstall (died 1559); they do not seem to have been brought up by their mother or any other Howard. Although Tunstall sympathized with Catherine of Aragon's predicament and was outspoken to the king about the divorce and his treatment of the clergy, as the children's guardian he had the great merit of being head of the Council in the North, where he spent most of his time from the summer of 1530. Here the Rices could be kept out of harm's way, possibly at the episcopal palace of Auckland: there they may even have met their uncle, the duke of Norfolk, on his occasional visits to the Scottish border. According to Henry Rice, when Thomas was about seventeen or so, he 'gott a way privatly' from the bishop's household, crossed the northern border and found his way into the service of Mary, the baby queen of the Scots. This piece of family history was proudly noted in Henry Rice's petitions to Charles I: it would not have been well received if told earlier to Elizabeth I. Thomas was apparently given command of 200 men at the time of the insurrection of Donald Bubh, who had the support of Clanranald and other highlanders in his bid to become Lord of the Isles. Following an ambush of part of Queen Mary's army at Kinloch-lochy in July 1544, at the battle of Blar-na-leine (The Field of Shirts), fought in such fierce heat that the combatants discarded their coats and fought in their shirts, Thomas was slain in the queen's service.[22]

His brother Gruffydd, followed the less spectacular path – certain to be a long and difficult one – of restoring his family's fortunes in Wales.[23]

[20] *LP, Henry VIII*, XXI, part 1, 483; Griffiths, *Principality of Wales*, pp.329, 411; Bartrum, *1400–1500*, II, 20; IX, 1497–8; F. Jones, 'Lloyd and Mears of Plas Llanstephan', *Carms. Antiquary*, XIV (1978), 46–7; see above n.14.

[21] *LP, Henry VIII*, XXI, part 1, 248, 763; Bindoff, *HC*, III, 515–16; Hasler, *HC*, III, 549–50; Bartrum, *1400–1500*, I, 71; IV, 649.

[22] BL, Add. MS 23113 f.3; NLW, Dynevor A 97 (c); NLW MS 1602 D p.207. See C. Sturge, *Cuthbert Tunstal* (London, 1938), *passim*; D. Gregory, *The History of the Western Highlands and Isles of Scotland* (2nd edn., Edinburgh, 1881; repr. 1975), pp.154–63.

[23] In December 1541, Gruffydd seems to have been in the household of the duchess of Norfolk (who lived apart from the duke), perhaps after his brother had fled from Tunstall's care: *LP, Henry*

When the first parliament of Edward VI's reign opened at Westminster on 4 November 1547, it was Gruffydd who presented a petition on behalf of the Rices. This was the basis for an act in the Parliament's first session which removed the stain of treason from the family escutcheon. The price he paid was an admission of the justice of the original treason charge of 1531 and an acknowledgement that both Henry VIII and Edward VI were fully entitled to dispose of his father's estates. What Gruffydd sought in 1547 was the cleansing of his blood so that he could inherit and convey property in the future. This was duly granted by the new king.[24] The first step on the road to rehabilitation had been successfully negotiated. Despite Gruffydd's admission, it may also reflect a sceptical view in high places of the treason charge itself.

Recovery of the family's lands was much more difficult, mainly because it would entail reassembling properties that had already been granted to others. Not until 4 November 1552 was Gruffydd able to make any headway, and even then he received only a modest grant which enabled him and his male heirs to enjoy most of the family estates in the commote of Iscennen, in return for an annual rent of £7. 4s. 9d; lordship of the property was retained by the king.[25] It was a significant, but limited, concession. In the mean time, the consequences of attainder continued to gather. Modest grants from the attainted estates were granted to others by Edward VI on twenty-one-year leases. In 1549–50 John Powell, a Cardiganshire gentleman from King Edward's household whose own properties lay in Cardigan and Llangoedmor, leased mills at Cenarth, near Cardigan, for an annual rent of £6. 10s. 0d., which was close to the value assigned them in 1532.[26] And in 1551 Sir Thomas Jones secured an interest in Cardiganshire by acquiring a substantial tenement at Cenarth for a rent of £1. 6s. 8d.[27] These were small grants, and it is possible that with Gruffydd Rice seeking to restore the family fortunes, the Crown desisted from disposing of significant properties from the stock in its hands.

The accession of Queen Mary I on 19 July 1553 may have been even more welcome. At the time of his attainder in 1531, Rhys ap Gruffydd had been associated with the cause of Mary's mother, Catherine of Aragon, and it might therefore be expected that the new regime would look kindly on Rhys's son. It may have been an encouragement to Gruffydd that his uncle, the duke of Norfolk, who had been disgraced in Henry VIII's last months, was restored to his title and estates in August 1553. The death of Gruffydd's mother, Catherine, countess of Bridgwater, less than a year later, in May 1554, led to a marked improvement

VIII, XVI, 661, 683.
[24] NLW, Dynevor A 3; PRO, C65/155 no. 21 (26 January 1548); NLW, Dynevor A 62–3.
[25] CRO, Dynevor Box 338/1.
[26] *CPR, 1557–8*, pp.106–7; Bindoff, *HC*, III, 143.
[27] *CPR, 1557–8*, pp.106–7.

in his fortunes. Henry VIII had briefly enjoyed her estates following her arrest and attainder in January 1542 for misprision of treason for concealing the adultery of her kinswoman, Catherine Howard, Henry's fifth consort. But they were returned to her after she was pardoned on 5 February 1543. In return for what was described as Gruffydd's service, on 10 October 1554, he and his male heirs were granted the ultimate reversion of the manors of Angle and Burton in south Pembrokeshire which amounted to about half the estates that his mother held in jointure at the time of her death. The annual value was estimated to be £65. 19s. 5¾d., though Gruffydd could not occupy the manors immediately.[28] Towards the end of Queen Mary's reign, he appears to have been enjoying an annual income of about £82 from his lands.

Nevertheless, Mary appreciated present service as much as past loyalty, and she (and her husband, Philip of Spain) continued the policy of awarding leases for twenty-one years out of Rhys ap Gruffydd's forfeited lands. The recipients were as likely to be her servants with little or no connection with Wales as influential figures in the far south-west. William Clerke of Hertfordshire, who received a small property in Cardiganshire in April 1555, may have been recommended by his master, William Herbert, earl of Pembroke.[29] Thomas Myckelwright, who was granted the Carmarthenshire lands of Gruffydd's grandmother, Dame Catherine Edgecombe, was a servant of both Mary and her Spanish consort. At £25. 7s. 0d., Myckelwright's rent was a little higher than the valuation of 1532, and he also had to pay a substantial entry fine of £21; but he was encouraged to threaten his new tenants with dispossession if they refused to recompense him for his outlay. This was a good bargain for the Crown, even for Myckelwright, but for the tenantry of the Vale of Tywi it was downright oppressive.[30]

Unquestionably the most substantial of Mary's grants went to Sir John Perrot – and on terms similar to those negotiated with Sir Thomas Jones a decade before. In recognition of his services to the queen and King Philip and despite his turbulent relations with the earl of Pembroke, in May 1555 Perrot was granted in fee the castle and lordship of Carew and its associated lands, which until recently had been held as her jointure by the countess of Bridgwater.[31] This estate had been valued at £60 per annum in 1532 and its alienation in 1555 was bound to be a blow to Gruffydd Rice, demonstrating that even Mary's regime was not ready to restore the Rices to their main estates. In fact, Perrot was the stepson of Sir Thomas Jones, who had brought him up at

[28] NLW, Dynevor A 5; *CPR, 1554–8*, pp.27–8; see above p.113; *DNB*, IX, 618–19; NLW, Dynevor A 96 (b). For the countess's treason, see *LP, Henry VIII*, XVII, 13; XVIII, part 1, 123; Scarisbrick, *Henry VIII*, pp.431–3; PRO SC11/995.
[29] *CPR, 1554–8*, p.280; Bindoff, *HC*, I, 656–8; Hasler, *HC*, I, 614–15.
[30] PRO, LR1/229 f.65v–67; *CPR, 1555–7*, p.165. See also *CPR, 1554–7*, pp.333–4.
[31] *CPR, 1554–5*, p.299; PRO, LR1/229 f.18–19; Bindoff, *HC*, III, 86–8; Hasler, *HC*, III, 205–7.

Haroldston, the Perrots' seat in Pembrokeshire. Between them, Sir Thomas and Sir John dismembered Rhys ap Gruffydd's former estate, though they were the only ones thus far to be quite so favoured. For its part, the Crown had tightened its grip on the estate following the deaths of the two widows in 1554–5. As for Gruffydd Rice, he had secured something, but not much, before he courted his own disaster in the autumn of 1557.

On a visit to North Auckland, co. Durham (where he had spent his childhood in Bishop Tunstall's household), Gruffydd Rice was involved in murder. On 30 September 1557, at eight o'clock in the evening, Matthew Walshe was waylaid and killed by his wife Agnes, Gruffydd Rice, and a tailor called James Halle who was Gruffydd's servant.[32] We can only speculate as to the circumstances that took Gruffydd to co. Durham and led him to consort with Agnes in a conspiracy against her husband. To Bishop Tunstall, it was a 'shamefull murdre'. Gruffydd and his servant fled to Wales, and on 10 October Gruffydd's lands and goods were seized by the Council in the Marches. Soon afterwards the two culprits were apprehended. Gruffydd was attainted and forfeited the properties which he had been slowly reassembling over the past decade. It was a major setback in the campaign of rehabilitation and recovery.

Thereafter, it was inevitable that grants from the estate should continue to be made and of a more permanent sort. Thomas Heybourne, a yeoman attendant at the Tower of London who had served Henry VIII, Edward VI and Mary, and his wife received lands in St Florence for life in survivorship on 16 April 1558. Three months later, Thomas Borage, one of the queen's senior cooks, acquired the manor of Angle in tail male. Both properties had been recently forfeited by Gruffydd Rice. Weobley and the Gower property of Catherine Edgecombe, however, had been in the Crown's hands since Catherine's death in 1554. In the weeks following Queen Mary's death, efforts were made to sell them for twenty times their annual value of £49. 16s. 1d., and by 1560 they were in the possession of the earl of Pembroke.[33]

With the death of his father, Sir Thomas, in prospect, on 26 June 1558 Sir Henry Jones, who maintained a close connection with the Herberts, secured the reversion of earlier grants of property at Cenarth on the Teifi that had been made to John Powell and Sir Thomas Jones in 1549–51, as well as a much more valuable grant – albeit for twenty-one years only – of the lordship of Emlyn, which was worth about £55 per annum in 1532 and had been in the Crown's hands ever since.[34] The annual rent

---

[32] *CPR, 1558–60*, pp.113, 175; *Acts PC*, VI, 183, 201; BL, Add. MS 23113 f.3d; Durham University Library, Church Commission Deposit, Durham Bishopric Estate Papers, Miscellaneous 220736.A.1.

[33] *CPR, 1557–8*, pp.219, 310–11, 377; J. D. Davies, 'Weobley Castle', *Arch. Camb.*, 5th series, IV (1887), 20–1; Clark, *Cartae*, V, 2034–7.

[34] PRO, LR1/229 f.125–6v; *CPR, 1557–8*, pp.106–7; Bindoff, *HC*, II, 451–2; Hasler, *HC*, II, 383–4.

of these lands together was fixed at almost £59 for half a year – possibly as much as 60 per cent in excess of their recorded value. Perhaps Sir Henry hoped to convert his leases into outright possession now that Gruffydd Rice was a fugitive.

When Queen Mary died, Gruffydd's fortunes were at their lowest ebb. He could hardly expect much from Elizabeth I, the daughter of Anne Boleyn. Moreover, his most urgent priority was a pardon for the murder at North Auckland. At the beginning of Elizabeth's reign, he married Elinor, daughter of Sir Thomas Jones who controlled a number of Rhys ap Gruffydd's former estates and died at about this time. We do not know if the couple waited until the old man was dead before marrying.[35] Carefully calculated or not, this marriage proved of enormous benefit to Gruffydd Rice in one respect: in January 1559, Elinor was instrumental, along with certain 'magnates', in securing a pardon for the North Auckland murder for Gruffydd, who was said to be manifestly penitent. Moreover, he was anxious to play a public role in Carmarthenshire, just as his forebears had done. He was persistent and Elizabeth I relented to the extent of granting the pardon, but what of the estates? To begin with, she was understandably cautious in bestowing her favours. On 13 January 1560, the queen approved arrangements whereby Gruffydd could eventually recover much, if not all, of his mother's estates in south Pembrokeshire, apart from the substantial lordship of Carew. For the moment, this amounted to a grant of the reversion of the properties given to Queen Mary's servants in 1558, though Elizabeth added the manor of Burton which Gruffydd himself had forfeited in 1557, and some lands in Carmarthenshire which included the ancestral manor of Newton and property in Llandeilo. In all, these lands were worth about £100 a year. It was a not insignificant boon, though Queen Elizabeth was disinclined to go further.[36]

When it came to his grandmother's lands in Gower, Gruffydd was decidedly less fortunate. A few days earlier, these had been disposed of in fee simple to William Herbert, earl of Pembroke, at a valuation of £50 per annum, more or less the figure recorded in 1532.[37] This arrangement implied a permanent shift in the landed interest of the Rices, away from Carmarthenshire and towards south Pembrokeshire, though they retained the lands at Newton and Dinefwr with which the family had been associated since at least the beginning of the fourteenth century.

Gruffydd responded with a petition that acknowledged Elizabeth's generosity but requested the restoration of those of his father's lands that were still in Crown hands (which he claimed were worth between 700

---

[35] Bindoff, *HC*, II, 451–4; NLW, Dynevor A 6.

[36] PRO, C66/946 m.25–6; *CPR, 1558–60*, p.386; CRO, Dynevor, Box 338/2.

[37] *CPR, 1558–60*, p.385; Birch, *Penrice and Margam MSS*, 4th series, part 2 (1904), pp.125–6.

and 800 marks a year) or, failing that (and more realistically), a lease of these same estates in return for an annual rent. According to Gruffydd, he was finding it difficult to support his wife Elinor and their children on an annual income of less than £100.[38] For a gentleman of Gruffydd's lineage, poverty spelled disgrace, and the greater the gap between his resources and his pretensions, the more desperate his appeals. Early in Elizabeth's reign, he was nominated a JP in Carmarthenshire (serving from 1564 until his death in 1592) and was sheriff of the county during 1567–83. In 1571 he served as mayor of the borough of Carmarthen, and, as an alderman, in 1576 he joined the earl of Essex in forwarding a successful petition to the queen for a charter to found a free grammar school in the town.[39] Yet his financial situation remained parlous – or so he said.

The road back to respectability and wealth proved to be a long one, and when lands were returned to him they were more often than not conceded only on lease. On 14 October 1563, he secured a twenty-one-year lease of the Cardiganshire estates that had been leased to Roger Williams in 1546.[40] More frequently, Queen Elizabeth disposed of available portions of the estate elsewhere, albeit for rent rather than by outright grants in fee. Those who benefited were usually local landowners whose families had already exploited the Rices' misfortunes. In 1566 alone, Francis Lloyd negotiated a twenty-one-year lease of part of the Kidwelly lands which John Llwyd (presumably his father) had received in 1546; John Vaughan of Golden Grove had a forty-year lease – a particularly advantageous grant – of the town properties in Carmarthen granted to Gruffydd Higon and his wife in 1546; and Sir John Perrot, ever the voracious landowner, received by the queen's own warrant additional Pembrokeshire acres, formerly held by the countess of Bridgwater, in return for an annual rent of £12.[41]

Gruffydd's position was far from secure; and it was not helped by a suspicion that he was a Catholic at heart. In June 1571 a small part of the Cardiganshire property which he had leased in 1563 was made over in reversion and in fee simple to Henry, Lord Scrope of Bolton, who had loyally served against the Scots and helped to suppress the Northern Rebellion in 1569.[42] Most grants, however, were renewals of existing leases prior to their expiry. A few, again for twenty-one years, were concluded with local grandees: some of the countess of Bridgwater's

[38] NLW, Dynevor, A 15 (undated).
[39] *DWB*, p.847; Lloyd, *Gentry of South-West Wales*, p.199; PRO, C66/1209 m.13d; 1218 m. 2d, 3d, 4d; J. R. S. Phillips (ed.), *The Justices of the Peace in Wales and Monmouthshire, 1541 to 1689* (Cardiff, 1975), pp.157–9, 205 (Pembs., 1567).
[40] *CPR, 1560–3*, p.488; see above p.116. The rent was slightly reduced from £27. 4s. 4d. to £26. 14s. 2d., though Gruffydd had to pay a fine of £3 to the Exchequer.
[41] *CPR, 1563–6*, pp.515, 436; *1575–8*, p.193.
[42] *CPR, 1569–72*, p.310; *CP*, XI, 548–9; Lloyd, *Gentry of South-West Wales*, p.186.

south Pembrokeshire lands went (in 1575) to William Spencer and Henry Powell, the latter possibly the son of John Powell of Cardigan; and the Carmarthenshire lands formerly held by Dame Catherine Edgecombe, and later leased to Thomas Myckelwright, were acquired by Lady Joyce Gamage of Glamorgan.[43] There was no question of restoring them to Gruffydd Rice. Indeed, Queen Elizabeth turned a deaf ear to his further petitions. And £8-worth of lands slipped from his grasp by 1576 as a result of a lengthy and expensive suit before the Council in the Marches initiated by its vice-president, Sir Andrew Corbet, which may have been connected with the counter-claims of Corbet's and Gruffydd's ancestors in Emlyn Uwch Cuch.[44]

Soon after this, he addressed several new petitions to the queen and her lord chamberlain, Thomas Radcliffe, earl of Sussex. The reason is tolerably clear. Both Radcliffe's mother and Gruffydd's mother were daughters of Thomas Howard, duke of Norfolk (died 1524). Moreover, Sussex's grandfather, like Gruffydd's grandfather and great-grand-father, had been at the sieges of Tournai and Thérouanne in Henry VIII's reign, and all three had attended King Henry at the Field of Cloth of Gold in 1520. And, again like Gruffydd's grandfather, Sussex's grandfather had been in the service of Prince Arthur at the beginning of the century.[45] Gruffydd Rice may have anticipated his influential kinsman's aid. At the same time he resolved to confront head-on the root cause of his sad and deteriorating situation. In order to gild the shame of his father's attainder, he proceeded to detail his great-grandfather's unique service to the founder of the Tudor dynasty. This account of the main features of Sir Rhys ap Thomas's career laid the groundwork for the Life of Sir Rhys which Gruffydd's descendants were to sponsor half a century later. He went further and, for the first time in a public document, characterized his attainted father as the dupe of evil men:

> That whereas Sir Ryse ap Thomas, Kniyghte, great graundfather unto your sayd servaunte dyde in his lief tyme manye great and acceptable services to your Majesty's moste noble graundfather and father of worthie memories, especiallie withe the service of xviii hundred horsemenne at his owne charge at the landinge of your majesty's said moste noble graundfather at Mylforde Haven in Wales, and in the Battayle of Bossworthe, And afterwarde with xv^en hundred horsemenne at Blakhethe feeld where he tocke the Lord Awdley prisoner. And synce in the service of your moste noble father at Tyrwynne and Turney withe xv^en hundred horses where he also tucke prisoner the Ducke Longuvile. In recompence of whiche and other his many true and faythfull services yt pleased their Majesties graciouslie to advaunce him to the moste noble order of the

---

[43] For reissues of earlier leases, see *CPR, 1572–5*, pp.371–2, 496; *1575–8*, pp.193, 377, 392, 393, 471–2; *1580–2*, p.26. New leases are in *CPR, 1572–5*, p.493; *1575–8*, p.197; *1578–80*, p.222.

[44] Bindoff, *HC*, I, 697; see above p.112. The suit cost Gruffydd £400.

[45] NLW, Dynevor A 14, 95 (a and b); *CP*, XII, part 1, 522–5.

Gartere and to other great offices and lyvinges in Sowthe Wales where he then dwelled, After whose deathe Ryse Griffithe Esquier, heyre to the said Sir Ryse and father to your majesty's said servaunte, beinge a yonge gentlemanne of good hope and lyke credite was perswadyde by on James Griffith ap Howell his nere kynsmane (whoe was corrupted by th'adversaries of the said Ryse Griffithe) to put his hande to a blanke wherein the said James procured suche matters to be wrytten as conteyned tresone, as he the said James, beinge flede oute of the Realme fore dyverse tresons and excepted in dyverse pardones afterwarde confessed, fore whiche the said Ryse Griffithe was attaynted wherbye alle his lyvinge amountinge to the yerlie value of a thowsand poundes at the leaste came to the handes of your moste noble father.

Gruffydd concluded this litany of loyalty by asking the queen either for a part of his father's estates that were still in her hands (estimated in May 1576 to be worth £324. 5s. 4½d.) to be held in fee simple, or a lease of these same lands for an annual rent. Perhaps following advice from the earl of Sussex, he then submitted a specific request to lease his father's Carmarthenshire, Pembrokeshire, Cardiganshire and Breconshire lands, or as much of them as the queen could concede in fee simple.[46] And he larded this second petition with expressions of abject humility, underlining his 'meere necessitie and extreame povertie', prostrating himself 'in most humble manner . . . uppon his knees', and claiming that if he were denied 'he shall not be able to shewe his face in the world'.

There is no record that this desperate combination of family pride and personal abasement achieved anything before Gruffydd Rice died on 1 September 1592. It is true that in June 1581 Gruffydd's earlier lease (1563) of the Cardiganshire lands was renewed for another twenty-one years; but he was required to pay a substantial entry fine of £52. 2s. 0d., in addition to an annual rent, an indication of the inflation in land values that had taken place during the mid-sixteenth century, as well as of the determination of the queen's officials to exploit her resources to the full. Gruffydd's financial plight was made even worse at this juncture by a serious dispute with Sir John Perrot, as a result of which each of them entered into a £1,000 bond, on behalf of themselves, their friends and their servants, to keep the peace.[47] Gruffydd's son, Walter, later claimed that the earl of Sussex's death on 9 June 1583 dealt a body-blow to Gruffydd's suits, and although the good offices of Elizabeth's one-time favourite, Robert Dudley, earl of Leicester, were enlisted instead, Leicester's waning influence, his absence in the Low Countries and, ultimately, his death in 1588 dashed any real chance of reviving

---

[46] NLW, Dynevor, Á 14, 46–7, 95 (c and d); see below Appendix IV. Sussex may have claimed a reward for his son Henry: *HMC, Calendar of the Manuscripts of the Marquess of Salisbury*, part 13 (1915), p.117.

[47] *CPR, 1580–2*, p.60; PRO, C66/1204 m.7–8; BL, Add. Ch. 39986; *Acts PC, 1581–2*, p.88.

Gruffydd's campaign.[48] There had been, in truth, compelling forces working against his interests for nearly sixty years: the Crown had enjoyed the profit from many of Rhys ap Gruffydd's forfeited properties, and the title to some of them had been alienated. The family's hold on its erstwhile Carmarthenshire and Pembrokeshire estates had been especially weakened. Kinsmen, notably Perrot and the Joneses, had reaped most, but others from south Wales had secured profitable leases, as had loyal servants and supporters of the Tudor monarchs. The campaign of rehabilitation and recovery was far from successfully concluded when Gruffydd Rice died.

Gruffydd's eldest son and heir, Walter (born about 1562), continued his father's efforts. He seems to have been well placed to do so since he was in the queen's service. He began his campaign in the Court of Wards, which instituted an inquiry at Llandeilo Fawr on 12 June 1593 into the Rice estate. The outcome, early in February 1594, was the delivery to Walter of Angle and Burton manors in Pembrokeshire, Newton manor in Carmarthenshire, and lands in Iscennen, and also a reversionary grant, some months later, of other lands in Carmarthenshire and Pembrokeshire worth £47. 19s. 9½d.[49] Walter also made progress with the Cardiganshire properties which Gruffydd was leasing at the time of his death. On 23 December 1595 a new twenty-one-year lease was negotiated by Walter in return for £5. 2s. 8d. in annual rent.[50] Yet when he tried to go further, he encountered obstacles.

Probably soon after his father's death, he re-presented Gruffydd's petition for a grant in fee of that part of the forfeited inheritance that was still in royal hands or, failing that, anything that Queen Elizabeth thought appropriate. To strengthen his case, Walter repeated his father's allusions to Sir Rhys ap Thomas's 'diverse great and acceptable services' and to the malicious accusation of treason levelled against Rhys ap Gruffydd, 'a yonge gent of greate Towardnes'. The family's sad circumstances which Gruffydd had not been able to remedy were such that Walter could describe himself as 'a poore gent with wife and tenne children and in great debts and necessitie'.[51]

Elizabeth I was unmoved. Walter submitted a further petition about October 1597. Like his father before him, he concluded that this second approach was likely to be more successful if it were more specific. He accordingly pointed to the disadvantages of such reversionary grants as he and his father had received: the trouble with Elizabeth's grant in

---

[48] Gruffydd may have recovered lands in the parishes of Llanlluan and Llanarthne in Iscennen in his latter years: NLW, Dynevor, A 65 (25 March 1587).

[49] NLW, Dynevor A 11, 66; *CSP, Dom., 1591–4*, p.527; CRO, Dynevor, Box 283/1; PRO, C66/1420 m.20–2; 1410 m.25. Gruffydd's widow, Elinor, retained her dower lands valued at £23. 6s. 8d.

[50] CRO, Dynevor, Box 338/3.

[51] NLW, Dynevor, A 96 (b, c and d); CRO, Dynevor, Additional MS 112. NLW, MS 1602 D p.207 *r* and *v*, subsequently notes four sons and seven daughters.

1592 of the reversion of £40-worth of forfeited lands in the lordship of Narberth over a period of forty years was that existing tenants often had long leases still to run. As Walter ruefully explained, with some exaggeration, his expenses in maintaining the reversionary claim were disproportionate to the anticipated return. He reported that he had offered to dispose of his interest to the tenants concerned, but that they had offered either little or nothing in return. He therefore asked the queen for the fee farm of the lordship of Narberth, whose reversion he held, in return for £61 in rent. The queen (he said) would thereby lose little or nothing, and if it were granted to him he would trouble her no more.[52] Nothing transpired. Not even heroic sentiment represented by the role accorded Rhys ap Thomas 'and his Soldiers joining Henry and his companions' before Bosworth in a new play, *Henry Richmond, Part 2*, which was performed in 1599 by the company assembled by the Elizabethan impresario, Philip Henslowe, could overcome the realities and limitations of royal patronage.[53]

Walter was no less concerned to advance his reputation among Wales's gentry class. As far back as 1 May 1578, when Walter was sixteen, his father had made an agreement with Sir Edward Mansel, of Margam in Glamorgan, that Walter should marry Sir Edward's daughter, Elizabeth. This began a very close relationship between the two families, especially between Sir Robert Mansel, the admiral, and Walter's son Henry. As a young man, Walter took a prominent part in public life in Carmarthenshire, as a JP in 1583 (until 1615), MP in 1584 and sheriff the following year.[54] On 1 February 1601, Walter was described as 'one of her Majesty's servants, now in Court, an esquire of fair living in Carmarthenshire and Pembrokeshire', when his opinion was sought on the likely effect on west Wales of the abortive rising of Robert Devereux, earl of Essex, the great-grandson of Rhys ap Gruffydd's enemy. To move in such circles required a substantial income and a landed position. He may well have felt that the new Stuart king would be more sympathetic to his plight. Within months of Queen Elizabeth's death in March 1603, Walter had been knighted by James I. Moreover, as MP for Carmarthen Boroughs in Elizabeth's last Parliament (1601), he was re-elected to serve in James I's first Parliament, which assembled on 19 March 1604.[55] The corridors of influence and patronage were only steps away. At home, he cultivated an interest in family history with enthusiasm and dedication. He enlisted an

---

[52] NLW, Dynevor, A 96 (a), A 99 (b). Walter would have had to have waited between three and nineteen years before the majority of the leases would become available to him.

[53] R. A. Foakes and R. T. Rickert (eds.), *Henslowe's Diary* (Cambridge, 1961), pp.126, 287–8.

[54] NLW, Dynevor, 'B 316; Hasler, *HC*, III, 289–90; Phillips, *JPs*, pp.159–63. He was recommended for the commission of the peace by his father-in-law, Sir Edward Mansel: BL, Harleian MS 6993 f.64.

[55] *HMC, Salisbury MSS*, II (1906), 93; Hasler, *HC*, III, 289–90.

acquaintance, Thomas Jones (died 1609) of Fountain Gate, near Tregaron in Cardiganshire – the celebrated Twm Siôn Cati – who compiled pedigrees for a number of self-regarding Welsh families, especially in south Wales. His pedigree for Walter ap Gruffydd (or Walter Rice as he was known) was completed on 22 March 1605. Its purpose was to display Walter's descent from kings and English noblemen: 'discended from Seaven Kinges, Fyve Dukes, fyfteene Earles and twelve Barons; And but nyne discentes Between him and the farthest of them'. Walter also pursued his antiquarian interests at the College of Arms, where in 1600 York herald of arms, Ralph Brooke, provided him with a fine emblazoned pedigree-roll, all of ten feet long, which survives to this day in the Welsh National Folk Museum, duly signed by Brooke, whose own family was shown to be linked with Sir Walter's. The family's collateral links with the Tudors and the Howards were vividly displayed in its beautiful series of personal arms.[56]

Pinning his hopes of more material gain on the new king, Sir Walter turned to the courts, employing lawyers and seeking counsel's opinion on the terms by which he held his present properties and how he could recover others. In one other respect, circumstances may have seemed favourable for a renewed approach: in February 1601, Robert Devereux, earl of Essex, the great-grandson of Rhys ap Gruffydd's bitter antagonist, was executed for plotting against the old queen and some of her ministers. Some time before December 1607, therefore, Sir Walter even felt bold enough to ask King James to declare his grandfather, Rhys, innocent of treason and to restore his heirs to the family estates. Walter intended submitting this bold request to the Privy Council, with the support of Sir John Fortescue, chancellor of the duchy of Lancaster (of which Kidwelly was a part) and himself a privy councillor. He concentrated on showing how improbable it was that Rhys should have been guilty of treason, but he could not resist also listing (with some exaggeration) the devoted services of Sir Rhys ap Thomas. He added his own embroideries, asserting that Queen Elizabeth had promised to restore to Gruffydd Rice whatever of the family lands remained in her possession, but that she had been dissuaded from doing so by Gruffydd's enemies before her own death intervened. This is unlikely to be true.

> Rice Griffith beinge but three and twenty yeares of age in the three and
> twentieth yeare of the raigne of King Henrie the eight was by direct
> meanes and practizes attainted of treason for conspiringe (as it was falsly
> proved) with your noble grandfather James the fift kinge of Scottlande to
> conquerre Englande and Wales, that your famous auncester shoulde be

---

[56] CRO, Dynevor, Add. MS 111, 112; *DNB*, s.n.; *DWB*, s.n.; *Companion to Welsh Lit.*, s.n. The Dynevor pedigree book includes miscellaneous inserted leaves that contain various pedigree notes from *c*.1600, some based on pedigrees then at Dynevor, and all testifying to an absorbing interest in the Rice family descent.

kinge of Englande and the saide Rice Griffith by composition prince of Wales, moved thereunto as it was falsly pretended by a false prophesy that Kinge James of scottlande with the redde hande and the raven (beinge the cognizance of the saide Rice Griffith) shoulde conquerre all Englande by reason of which attainder not only the goodes and chattelles but alsoe the landes of the saide Rice Griffith then worth per annum above a thousand powndes old rent escheated unto the saide kinge of famous memory Henry the eight. Nowe for that it is altogeather improbable that the saide Rice Griffith shoulde be guilty of the saide treason, both in respect that there was noe acte accion or attempte by the saide Rice Griffith ageinst the said Kinge Henry the eighte, and for that alsoe the said Rice Griffith did never send speake or writte unto your saide noble grandfather concerninge the said supposed practize neither did the saide Rice Griffith ever goe or sende to Scottlande Ireland or the Yle of Man aboute the same conspiracy, thirdly for that the saide treason was only proved by two meane men of noe reputacion creditt or worth, whereof thone beinge James Griffith not worthe above fower marckes per annum then remained in the towre of London for countergettinge the great seale of Englande beinge detected and apprehended for the same treason by the saide Rice Griffith soe that partely for revenge and partely by the persuasion of the great and heavy adversaries of the saide Rice Griffith (whoe did thirst after his bloodde and Lyvinge) the saide James Griffith was moved falsly to prove the said treason and the other wittnes Edward lloide by persuasion and rewarde of fyve hundred marckes (as it was testified by Katherin countesse of Bridgewater and others) was brought untruely to affirme the saide treason, fowerthly in regarde the saide Rice Griffith lyved in favoure without eny cause of discontentment and was heire unto Sir Rice ap Thomas that brought aide of fower thousande men unto Henry the Seventh att his first landinge and never departed from him untill Richard the third was slaine and the said Sir Rice made by the saide Kinge Henry the seventh knight banneret in the fielde, and then after he and his heires lyved faythfull and true unto Kinge Henry the seventh and Henry the eight untill the attaindor of the saide Rice Griffith. Lastly in regard that the saide Rice Griffith hadde noe coullor of right unto the saide principallity of Wales.

Walter's growing family – he now had eleven offspring whose education was a pressing and expensive concern – led him to beg James I to restore the lands in the Crown's possession, now estimated to be worth £200 per annum.[57] Yet vested interests were still too powerful, even for the combined weight of Walter's historical research and legal suits, and the efforts of his patrons. Although (according to Walter) the king expressed himself in favour of granting the petition, the privy councillors to whom it was submitted seem not to have commended it.

[57] NLW, Dynevor, A 96 (e and f). NLW, Dynevor, A 94 (d) is a copy of a survey of those of Rhys ap Gruffydd's estates in Pembrokeshire and Carmarthenshire, amounting in value to £140. 9s. 9½d., which were still in the Crown's hands; it probably dates from Walter's lifetime.

Walter had modest success more privately when, on 23 October 1607, he was able to arrange the marriage of his younger son, Edward, to Sage, the daughter of John Gwynne William, of Derwydd in Carmarthenshire. John settled on the couple a quarter of the Derwydd estate and other properties in the parish of Llandybïe.[58] It was only towards the end of his life, on 30 May 1623, that Sir Walter Rice at last secured James I's confirmation to himself and his son and heir, Henry, of the reversionary grants of lands in Iscennen and Newton made to Gruffydd Rice decades before.[59] By then, he had taken the decision, seemingly with the reluctant agreement of his son Henry, to dispose of his lands and claims in Pembrokeshire and henceforward concentrate on the Vale of Tywi, where the family's fortune had originally been laid. Seeking influence and pleading the law were expensive for a man like Sir Walter, who also had a taste for 'immoderate living'. His costs, including loans from London merchants, forced him to conclude mortgages on portions of his estate and even to contemplate relinquishing control of large parts of it. On 5 April 1617 Henry Rice, who then lived at Newton, had been granted in his own right the manor of Angle and other Pembrokeshire properties in his family's possession; yet not long afterwards, he found himself under pressure from his father to relinquish these claims. By January 1619 negotiations were well advanced with Sir Thomas Button (died 1634), one of the king's admirals and the explorer of Hudson Bay, who hailed from Glamorgan and was married to Sir Walter Rice's daughter, Mary. Button agreed to pay £2,000 for all the Pembrokeshire properties provided Henry would assign his and his heirs' rights in them to Button in return for an annuity of £120 payable during Mary's lifetime. Three years later, Sir Walter's indebtedness (to the extent of over £3,000) led him to turn again to his relatives for salvation. His son, Henry, his two wealthy kinsmen, Sir Robert Mansel, his brother-in-law, and Sir Thomas Button, his son-in-law, undertook to pay him £3,000 in cash and £200 a year for his life, in return for a mortgage on the estate, which then comprised 700 acres at Newton, 120 acres of 'outlands' nearby, and 150 acres of castle demesne.[60] Sir Walter (died 1636) had shown determination and ingenuity in advancing his cause, and he certainly cut a respectable figure as MP for Carmarthenshire in 1584–5 and for Carmarthen Boroughs in 1601 and again in 1604–11. Yet the progress he made in restoring the family's fortunes was far from spectacular, and his personal circumstances were precarious.

[58] CRO, Cawdor, Box 67/6737; NLW, Dynevor, B 337. Walter's daughter, Barbara, married Walter, son and heir of Morgan Johnes of Llandeilo Fawr, by an agreement made on 29 January 1600: ibid., 328–9.
[59] CRO, Dynevor, Box 338/5; PRO, C66/2320 part 26.
[60] PRO, C66/2149 no.16; CRO, Dynevor, Box 154/1; A 97A; B (i) 212; *DWB*, p.60; Lloyd, *Gentry of South-West Wales*, p.45.

Sir Walter's fascination with his family's history was shared – perhaps even surpassed – by that of his son, Henry Rice, who used his antiquarian knowledge to continue the campaign to rehabilitate the Rices of Newton. A 'paternoll pedigree' was compiled for Henry as early as 1604, well before the Life of Sir Rhys ap Thomas and the Objections to Rhys ap Gruffydd's treason were written.[61] He naturally knew of the brief historical commentary which his grandfather and father had penned, as well as the pedigrees produced by Ralph Brooke and Welsh antiquarians like Thomas Jones of Fountain Gate. Furthermore, Henry and his brother Thomas took BA degrees at Oxford in 1607 and had opportunity to make contact with humanist learning.[62] By October 1620 Henry had secured appointment as a gentleman of the king's Privy Chamber. Henry was living in London at this time, in 'Marquis Howse', Broad Street, and there his uncle, Sir Robert Mansel, the vice-admiral, wrote to him to keep in touch with events at home (especially in the capital and at the royal court) while Mansel was at sea.[63] The Life and the Objections were prepared for publication by Richard Fenton in 1796, and in one of Fenton's surviving notebooks, which contains a copy of the Objections, Henry Rice's petition to Charles I for the return of the Rice estates still in Crown hands (said to be worth about £200 per annum) also appears.[64] This petition is dated 27 May 1625, barely two months after the new king's accession. To begin with, Henry composed a petition to James I; but the king's death on 27 March upset his plans. The revised petition to King Charles was referred for consideration to the Lord High Treasurer (Lord Ley), the Lord Marshal, the Lord Chamberlain (the duke of Buckingham) and Sir Richard Weston, the chancellor of the Exchequer. The Life and the Objections were written about the same time, part of the same propagandist enterprise.

By 13 January 1629, Charles I had signified his assent to yet another petition.[65] On that day, it was confirmed that the Crown had disposed of all the remaining forfeited lands of the Rices in the most recent sales commission and that therefore it was pointless trying to seek their return. Instead, Henry Rice sought an appointment as gentleman in ordinary of the Privy Chamber, and a pension. After almost a century, and with no lands now being requested by the Rice family, the earls of Arundel and Pembroke felt able to report favourably on the quality of Henry's ancestors, his own good service to the Crown, and the lamentable circumstances into which his family had fallen. They

---

[61] CRO, Dynevor, Add. MS 73.
[62] See below p.141. Their sister Jane had married Dr John Williams, principal of Jesus College, Oxford, from 1602 (Dwnn, I, 210). Himself a Carmarthenshire man, he encouraged greater numbers of south Walians to attend Jesus College, among them perhaps the Rices. *DWB, s.n.*
[63] CRO, Dynevor, Add. MS 73; Box 154/1.
[64] CCL MS 4.20; Williams, *Y Cymmrodor*, XVI (1902), 2 n.l; NLW, Dynevor, A 97 (b).
[65] NLW, Dynevor, A 97 (c).

commended Henry Rice, and the king accordingly gave his assent to the petition. It was a triumph of persistence, though we need not assume that Charles I or his advisers read the Life of Sir Rhys ap Thomas or the Objections to Rhys ap Gruffydd's treason. They may have done so. In any case, by then the principal elements of these compositions must have been familiar at court, along with the claim that Henry Rice had himself served James I since about 1617.[66]

Nevertheless, the petitions to Charles I added, for good measure, a novel claim on Stuart gratitude, one which was doubtless current in the Rice household: it was the story that Thomas Rice had been slain (in 1544) in the service of the king's grandmother, Mary, Queen of Scots. It also asserted – building on Sir Walter's claims – that Mary I and Elizabeth I had promised to restore the family's lands that the Crown still held. Henry Rice further maintained that James I had asked for details of the treason of 1531, doubtless implying that 'the wisest fool in Christendom' was prepared to entertain his petition, which was submitted to certain royal councillors 'with a singular commendatyion'. It was only rising costs which, Henry claimed, forced his father temporarily to abandon the cause.[67] If all this were true, then it is possible that Henry Rice's voluminous writings on family history were prompted, at least in part, by the king himself. When Henry Rice was in the course of preparing the petition of *c*.1628 to Charles I, what amounted to his working papers contained some of the same cullings from chronicles and royal records that were utilized in the writing of the Life at about the same time.[68]

The Life of Sir Rhys ap Thomas and the Objections to the charges against Rhys ap Gruffydd blended family tradition and antiquarian researches with the aim of restoring the reputation and material fortunes of the Rices of Newton. Seldom has a family in such dire straits been so well served by the intellectual accomplishments of the English and Welsh Renaissance.

---

[66] CCL MS 4.20; Williams, *Y Cymmrodor*, XVI (1902), 2 n.l; *TCASFC*, X (1914–15), 63.

[67] Williams, *Y Cymmrodor*, XVI (1902), 2 n.l; CCL MS 4.20; NLW, Dynevor, A 97 (c).

[68] BL, Add. MS 23113 f.3–3*d*, seemingly a paper with marginal annotations and source references which was written in support of Henry Rice's petition to Charles I, perhaps by someone whom he employed for purposes of historical research; these references were utilized in the Life itself. It is included, perhaps because of the Scottish episode, in a collection of papers relating to John Maitland, earl of Lauderdale (died 1645), and his family.

PART II

The Life of Sir Rhys ap Thomas

Introduction

(a) The Writing of Family History

'A short view of the long life' of Sir Rhys ap Thomas (c.1449–1525) was first published in its entirety in 1796, in the inaugural volume of *The Cambrian Register*. It has not been republished or edited since. The author of the Life and of the Objections to the alleged treason in 1531 of Sir Rhys's grandson, Rhys ap Gruffydd, was their direct descendant, Henry Rice (c.1590–c.1651).[1] At the time when he composed both works, the writing of substantial, connected, family history was in its infancy. As a *genre*, early family histories had a number of purposes, and the motives of individual authors varied from family to family and according to family circumstances and requirements. The Life of Sir Rhys ap Thomas is an example of this *genre*, the roots of whose component characteristics can be identified in the two centuries before Henry Rice brought his intelligence, education and researches to bear in the 1620s on the writing of his family's history.

Descent was a medieval preoccupation which, in England, was not confined to the aristocracy; in the later Middle Ages, and with growing frequency, it was adapted to meet the aspirations, and to define the status, of a broader group of country landowners and influential subjects.[2] The early recording of descent took two related utilitarian forms: reports of births, marriages and deaths, often in family calendars, and title deeds to property. Taking their cue from the perpetual corporations of monastery, college and cathedral chapter, a number of

---

[1] The identification of the author of the Objections with Henry Rice was first made by Williams, *Y Cymmodor*, XVI (1902), 1–2. At the end of the nineteenth century, J. E. Lloyd (*DNB*, s.n. Sir Rhys ap Thomas) believed that the Life was written about 1635 by a descendant of Sir Rhys; G. Roberts (*DWB*, p.847) accepted that he was Henry Rice.

[2] D. A. L. Morgan, 'The individual style of the gentlemen', in M. Jones (ed.), *Gentry and Lesser Nobility in Later Medieval Europe* (Gloucester, 1986), pp.15–35 (especially pp.16–19); J. Rosenthal, *Patriarchy and Families of Privilege in Fifteenth-Century England* (Philadelphia, 1991), pp.59–60.

families in the later Middle Ages compiled cartularies of deeds, charters and other documents (including relevant pedigrees), some of the cartularies crude and rudimentary, others large and sophisticated.[3] Other considerations gradually gave family history a more compelling interest. Pride of family and ancestry was a growing sentiment that focused especially on patrimonial lineage, whilst the extension of literacy, education and book-collecting among lay people facilitated the transmission of family history. The antiquarian movement from the fifteenth century enabled certain individuals – educated gentlemen as well as clerics – to underpin and extend their interest in ancestry and family by archival investigation.[4] This trend was encouraged by heralds and their official status as arbiters of claims to birth and arms which they came to enjoy in the course of the fifteenth and sixteenth centuries, even if their investigations and verifications of pedigrees sometimes outran the quest for accuracy. Heralds were incorporated as a college by Richard III in 1484. They received a new charter from Philip and Mary in 1555, and the tools of their trade, an archive and a library, were organized and protected from Elizabeth I's reign onwards.[5] Fact and fancy were reflected, too, in the passion for distinctive seals, coats of arms and elaborate representations in church windows and on tombs and monuments. The publication in the sixteenth century of popular humanist histories by such writers as Polydore Vergil, Edward Hall and Raphael Holinshed enabled the activities of an ancestor or a relative to be located to good advantage in the unfolding of England's story.

In Wales, there was a long tradition, dating from at least the ninth century (and scarcely present in medieval English literature), of recording and lauding the sagas of kings and princes. After the death of Prince Llywelyn ap Gruffydd in 1282, it shifted its focus to individuals and families of lesser station who thrived in the changed world of later medieval Wales. Welsh poets became the remembrancers of lore, tradition and history, keepers of family consciences and self-knowledge, and the publicists of the place of their patrons and their families in the wider scheme of things.[6]

[3] G. R. C. Davis, *Medieval Cartularies of Great Britain* (1st edn., London, 1951), Part II. For the sole surviving Welsh lay cartulary, see Griffiths, *BBCS*, XIV (1971), 311–84. For a family pedigree included in a family cartulary, see 'The petygre of the lyfelode' of William Langley (died 1483), in P. R. Coss (ed.), *The Langley Cartulary* (Dugdale Society, 32, 1980), pp.127–8 (*c.*1477–78). The mainly devotional 'Haroldston Calender' of fifteenth-century date contains genealogical notes of the Perrots of Pembrokeshire: BL, Add. MS 22720; E. L. Barnwell, 'Notes on the Perrot family', *Arch. Camb.*, 3rd series, XII (1866), 178–81.

[4] A. Gransden, *Historical Writing in England*, II (London, 1982), ch.11.

[5] A. Wagner, *English Genealogy* (3rd edn., Chichester, 1983), pp.355ff.; R. Marks and A. Payne, *British Heraldry* (London, 1978), pp.43–8. See L. Stone, *The Crisis of the Aristocracy, 1558–1641* (Oxford, 1965), pp.23–7.

[6] Jarman and Hughes, *Welsh Literature*, II, chs. II, IV, XIV.

In the fifteenth and sixteenth centuries, certain particular factors encouraged the recording of family history both for utilitarian purposes and for reasons of sentiment. They promoted self-knowledge among prominent families in England and Wales, and sought to justify the actions of individuals. The establishment of new ruling dynasties, especially the triumphant Tudors, led some families to record (or contrive) relationships with the Lancastrian, Yorkist or Tudor houses, and others to explain why they had not supported a victor. Take, for example, the metrical chronicle of the Stanley earls of Derby, which was written early in Elizabeth's reign and described the rise of the Stanleys in such a selective and inventive fashion as to underscore their crucial role in the establishment and consolidation of the Tudor dynasty.[7] The religious changes of the sixteenth and early seventeenth centuries, and the political struggles with which they were entwined, provided a similar impetus to record. Some families were eager to demonstrate their loyalty and service to the Crown; yet others wished to teach posterity the secret of their own success.[8] Particular families sought to justify or excuse an act of decisive familial importance, selecting, distorting and inventing what they willed from the storehouse of tradition and history. Some individuals were bent on asserting property claims that had slender or unclear foundations; others wished to recover a position lost or usurped by rivals; and all families made prominent by marriage, inheritance or other means strove to demonstrate their credentials of legitimacy and respectability by whatever means they could discover. As Sir John Wynn of Gwydir (1553–1627) wrote in the history designed to establish his family's descent from Gruffydd ap Cynan, king of Gwynedd (died 1137),

> Yet a great temporal blessing it is, and a great heart's ease to a man to find that he is well descended and a greater grief it is for upstarts and gentlemen of the first head to look back unto their descents, being base in such sort, as I have known many such hate gentlemen in their hearts for no other cause but that they were gentlemen.[9]

[7] M. K. Jones, 'Richard III and the Stanleys', in R. Horrox (ed.), *Richard III and the North* (Hull, 1986), pp.32–5. See M. Maclagan, 'Genealogy and heraldry in the sixteenth and seventeenth centuries', in L. Fox (ed.), *English Historical Scholarship in the Sixteenth and Seventeenth Centuries* (Oxford, 1956), pp.43–4; F. S. Fussner, *The Historical Revolution: English Historical Writing and Thought, 1580–1640* (London, 1962), pp.187–8.

[8] For the grafting of noble lineages on royal pedigrees, see R. A. Griffiths, 'The sense of dynasty in the reign of Henry VI', in C. D. Ross (ed.), *Patronage, Pedigree and Power in Later Medieval England* (Gloucester, 1979), pp.24–5, 34–5, reprinted in R. A. Griffiths, *King and Country: England and Wales in the Fifteenth Century* (London, 1991), ch.5; A. Allan, 'Political propaganda employed by the House of York in England in the mid-fifteenth century, 1450–1471' (unpublished University of Wales Ph.D. thesis, 1981), ch.IX.

[9] Jones, *History of the Gwydir Family and Memoirs*, p.35. Sir John is thought to have compiled the History between 1580 and 1616 (ibid., pp.xxiii–xxv).

'The Booke of Sir John Wynn' (Cardiff MS 83), which included his History of the Gwydir Family, contained poetry, tradition and copies of official records, as well as historical writing, and Sir John appears to have been helped in compiling the book (and perhaps his family history) by Huw Machno (died 1637), a popular poet and elegist among leading families of north Wales.[10] In Wales, where a passion for the past was, if anything, more absorbing and pervasive than it was in English society, several notable contributions were made to the development of family history.

The claim of John Smyth (died 1640) in 1618 that he was the first to write 'a genealogike history of any patrimoniall family', without any ulterior or personal motive that might compromise his work, has some justice to it, and modern scholarly opinion, taking its cue from Smyth, asserts that the writing of family history first became popular in the early seventeenth century.[11] But his *Lives of the Berkeleys* has deeper roots, and Smyth a number of contemporaries – even predecessors – as family historians. Moreover, the writing of family history coincides and corresponds with the emergence of 'county histories', which reflect a sense of locality and community in which influential landowners and citizens and their families were an integral part.[12] The family saga which is the Life of Sir Rhys ap Thomas is a remarkable example of the same *genre*.

Henry Rice and his father, Sir Walter, were members of a circle – or rather a group of interlocking circles – of Renaissance men of letters among the Welsh gentry. Sir John Price, Humphrey Lhuyd, Rhys ap Meurig (better known as Rice Merrick), Elis Gruffudd and William Salesbury of an early generation, Maurice Kyffin, Sir Edward and Sir John Stradling, Lewis Dwnn, Sir Edward Mansel and George Owen in the latter part of the sixteenth and seventeenth centuries, were well-to-do gentlemen, esquires or knights who had a role in public affairs and were also men of letters, collectors of manuscripts and printed books, fascinated by history and genealogy, and encouraging of educational and literary endeavours in both Wales and England.[13] Despite the scandal of treason that dogged their family after 1531, the Rices fitted comfortably into this world, socially and intellectually. The sources used in the Life and the Objections were, in general, similar to those on which

[10] Ibid., p.xxii; *DWB*, p.400.

[11] J. Smyth, *The Lives of the Berkeleys*, ed. J. Maclean (3 vols., London, 1893), II, 440. Smyth, from Nibley (Glos.), was the Berkeleys' steward; he based his study on family archives and public records.

[12] G. Williams, 'Local and national history in Wales', *WHR*, V (1970), 45–66, reprinted in D. H. Owen (ed.), *Settlement and Society in Wales* (Cardiff, 1989), pp.7–26; M. McKisack, *Medieval History in the Tudor Age* (Oxford, 1971), chs. V, VI. See, most recently, S. A. E. Mendyk, *'Speculum Britanniae': Regional Study, Antiquarianism and Science in Britain to 1700* (Toronto, 1989).

[13] G. Williams, *Recovery, Reorientation and Reformation: Wales, c.1415–1642* (Oxford and Cardiff, 1987), ch.18.

Rice Merrick, Sir John Wynn and George Owen drew in their historical, topographical and antiquarian writings.

Yet interesting contrasts can also be drawn. Rice Merrick's 'Morganiae Archaiographia', composed between 1578 and 1584, has been known since the seventeenth century as 'A Booke of the Antiquityes of Glamorganshire'. As the first 'county history' to be written in Wales, it is a bold attempt at a topographical history of Glamorgan and its parishes from the Norman Conquest to the Acts of Union; it focuses on genealogy and family history in so far as they served this purpose. George Owen (died 1611) had even wider interests, those of a geologist and cartographer as well as of an antiquarian, genealogist, topographer and historian. They were directed especially towards the study of the topography and history of his native shire of Pembroke and the constitutional development of Wales and its Marcher lordships. Once again, family history was incidental to his main purpose. Wynn's 'History of the Gwydir Family', completed in 1616, is closer in its design, sources and character to Henry Rice's Life of Sir Rhys ap Thomas, and Sir John had the advantage of being able to rummage through his family's chests of deeds and other documents at Gwydir. As a result, and in the course of vindicating his own claims to honourable descent, he revealed much about the society, economy and landownership of north Wales in the fourteenth and fifteenth centuries, and the relatively minor role which his ancestors played in the Glyndŵr rebellion and the Wars of the Roses. Whereas Henry Rice lacked a comparably rich store of family archives, he was able to place his forebears' more publicly significant story in the broader context of English and Welsh social and political history in the fifteenth and early sixteenth centuries. And Henry Rice wrote with a verve, clarity and richness which the disjointed and somewhat stilted prose of Sir John Wynn cannot match.[14]

Maurice Kyffin, Sir John Stradling, Sir John Wynn and George Owen were in touch with William Camden, and Sir John Wynn helped John Speed in his work. The access which such Welshmen had to gentry circles in England, and especially in London, enabled Henry Rice to make the acquaintance of Bishop Andrewes and Sir Thomas Lake. Moreover, from 1597 onwards, Camden was Clarenceux king of arms, working side by side at the College of Arms with the Rices' kinsman and genealogist, Ralph Brooke. Even closer to hand was the genealogical expertise of Thomas Jones of Fountain Gate, who was as valuable to George Owen and others as he evidently was to Sir Walter and Henry Rice.[15] Such scholarly interests among the gentry served a number of

---

[14] Wagner, *English Genealogy*, pp.365–6. Cf. Jones, *History of the Gwydir Family and Memoirs*; Charles, *George Owen of Henllys*; Rice Merrick, *Morganiae Archaiographia*, ed. B. Ll James (South Wales Record Soc., I, 1983).

[15] Thomas Jones also made pedigrees for Sir Edward Lewis of the Van (College of Arms MS, Box

purposes, though in Wales few families, if any, had quite such compelling motives as the Rices for placing historical and genealogical investigation at their service. Moreover, these gentry met one another from time to time, and exchanged ideas and information, Sir Edward Stradling with George Owen, Henry Rice with some of the Herberts and a Parry. In short, the Rices of Dinefwr were part of that intellectual circle that has been identified in south-west Wales, and has hitherto been focused on George Owen and Thomas Jones. The Life and the Objections, for all their practical purposes and preconceived notions, would not be out of place on the shelf with Merrick's 'Morganiae Archaiographia', George Owen's 'Description of Pembrokeshire' or Stradling's 'Winning of the Lordship of Glamorgan'. Such works are an eloquent reflection of how educated Welshmen in the early modern period viewed their family's medieval past and its place in the wider scheme of things, as well as of the frame of mind in which they approached the writing of history.

(b) *The Authorship of the Life*

The Life makes it crystal clear that it was written by a Welshman who lived in Wales at least for part of the time, and was familiar with the topography and patterns of landholding in south and south-west Wales. He wrote English in the classical and humanist vein that flourished in contemporary England and on the Continent, employing a readable and lively Tacitean style replete with classical (especially Latin), biblical and early Christian allusions which vividly illustrated his assessments of character. To this purpose, Henry Rice relied heavily on Plutarch's Lives, either directly or indirectly, and peppered his text with adages, aphorisms and proverbs, many of them culled from the writings of Erasmus.

In Wales and the English borderland, Henry had an entrée to the houses of fellow gentry families – the Perrots in Herefordshire, the Herberts, and an elderly Parry in Breconshire – as well as connections with Welsh antiquaries like Thomas Jones of Fountain Gate in Cardiganshire. Wider associations were formed with Lancelot Andrewes, the scholar-bishop of Winchester, Lewis Bayly, bishop of Bangor, Sir Thomas Lake, who was James I's principal secretary of state, and William Camden, the famous antiquary. These associations

36/X f.66, 75), John Herbert of Morelacke (1591, CRO, Dynevor 109), Edward ap Maredudd (College of Arms MS I.9 f.38b–40b), and James ap Rhydderch of Laugharne, finished in 1583 (NLW MS 22338G). Copies of Jones's pedigrees are in CCL MS 4.114; NLW MS 1602D, a Welsh manuscript possibly in his own hand, contains Carmarthenshire pedigrees including those of Sir Rhys ap Thomas and his ancestors and descendants as far as Walter Rice's children.

were easily cultivated in the intellectual world inhabited by the Oxford-educated sons, Henry and Thomas, of Sir Walter Rice MP. It may be noted, too, that Camden, Laken and Henry Rice's uncle, Sir Robert Mansel (1573–1656), vice-admiral of the navy, were among proposed members of the 'Academ Roial' (1620), a forerunner of the Society of Antiquaries.[16] When the vice-admiral was at sea in the 1620s, Henry Rice corresponded with him and became sufficiently well-informed about current (especially foreign) affairs to draw contrasts and comparisons with an earlier age. The humiliating English expeditions to Cadiz (1625) and La Rochelle (1627) seemed a far cry from Sir Rhys ap Thomas's achievements and helped to stoke Henry's Francophobia; whilst news of the stunning campaigns of the Swedish king, Gustavus Adolphus, was turned into a comparative illustration of Sir Rhys's prowess.[17]

The known written sources of the Life point in similar directions. These sources range from the works of English chroniclers and 'our historiographers' of the sixteenth century (such as Polydore Vergil, Edward Hall, Raphael Holinshed and John Hardyng's continuator), on whom Henry Rice relied for a general structure for the unfolding of events in which Sir Rhys was involved from 1483 until his death in 1525; contemporary scholars like John Speed, William Camden and Francis Bacon, from whose *History of Henry VII* (1622) Henry Rice appropriated several judgements; Welsh poets of the fifteenth and early sixteenth centuries, and later antiquaries like Thomas Jones; to classical humanist collections, particularly of Erasmus, as well as – either directly or indirectly – printed continental histories of inspiring heroes such as Scanderbeg of Albania and Jan Zizka of Bohemia, with whom Sir Rhys ap Thomas could be compared.[18] Moreover, Henry Rice was no mean family historian. He sifted, often with a sceptical mind, the traditions and stories current in his own circle, providing insights into his family's saga prior to Sir Rhys ap Thomas, as well as rehearsing material which figured in the campaign for the recovery of his family's fortunes. He pored over, or commissioned, genealogical writings from such as Thomas Jones and Ralph Brooke that were in his or his father's possession, as well as collections of Welsh poetry written in his ancestors' honour. Yet at home, he found little in the way of a family archive: this had been seized at the time of Rhys ap Gruffydd's attainder in 1531 and

---

[16] J. Foster, *Alumni Oxonienses, 1500–1714* (4 vols., Oxford, 1892), III, 1250–1; J. McConica, *The History of the University of Oxford*, vol. III: *The Collegiate University* (Oxford, 1986), especially chs. 4, 10; W. P. Griffith, 'Welsh students at Oxford and Cambridge and the Inns of Court during the sixteenth and early seventeenth centuries' (unpublished University of Wales Ph.D. thesis, 1981), especially chs. III, VIII; E.M. Portal, 'The Academ Roial of King James I', *PBA*, VII (1915–16), 189–208. See, in general, J. W. Binns, *Intellectual Culture in Elizabethan and Jacobean England: The Latin Writings of the Age* (Leeds, 1991).

[17] See below pp.153, 185, 207.

[18] See below pp.152–3, 227, 237, 263–4.

then probably perished in the Whitehall fire of 1619. On the other hand, during his periods of residence in London, Henry Rice secured access, doubtless through well-placed acquaintances like Sir Thomas Lake, to the royal archives, most notably The Book of the Knights of the Garter in the king's library in St James's Palace, and also the records of the Exchequer and the courts of King's Bench and Common Pleas which proved especially fruitful in revealing the career of Sir Rhys ap Thomas's grandfather, Gruffydd ap Nicholas.[19]

In his use of these materials, Henry Rice's instincts were generally sound and critical, and he carefully noted his sources with sufficient precision for us to relocate them today. Less dependable was his handling of his forebears' attitudes or actions at certain decisive moments during the Wars of the Roses; for all the scholarly scepticism he showed elsewhere, on these occasions he was tempted into distortion. He placed Gruffydd ap Nicholas at Mortimer's Cross in February 1461, fighting on the winning side with Edward, earl of March, when in reality Gruffydd had probably been dead for several months. He sought to explain away the embarrassment of Morgan ap Thomas ap Gruffydd's siege of Henry Tudor and his uncle, Jasper, in Tenby in 1471 by hinting that he secretly shared his brothers' overt support for the retreating Lancastrians; in reality it seems likely that Morgan had embraced the antipathy of his wife's family, the Vaughans of Tretower, towards the Tudors. In 1485, distant chroniclers of Henry Tudor's march through Wales imply that Rhys ap Thomas held aloof almost until the last moment, whereas Henry Rice not only – and, it must be admitted, plausibly – regards this as prearranged by Rhys and Henry to deceive King Richard III, but also places Rhys among those who welcomed Henry ashore in Mill Bay. Finally, when contemporaries are silent or unclear, Henry Rice stepped in to claim a role for the illustrious Sir Rhys ap Thomas: in capturing the rebel leader, Lord Audley, and Perkyn Warbeck in 1497, and even (though with some scepticism on Henry Rice's part) in the killing of Richard III himself on Bosworth Field. But, then, to some degree Henry Rice was a prisoner not only of family tradition but of his father's and grandfather's imaginative campaign to rehabilitate the Rices, the centrepiece of which was the chivalric deeds of Sir Rhys ap Thomas in the service of the Crown.

As for the composition of the Life, internal evidence would suggest that it took place between the publication of Bacon's *History of Henry VII* in 1622 and the months following the humiliating return of the English expeditionary force to La Rochelle in 1627, an episode which was evidently fresh in the author's mind. At that juncture, Henry Rice was assuming more and more of the responsibilities of his somewhat

---

[19] See below pp.159, 162, 167, 212, 245.

profligate father, and shortly afterwards he would submit his own petition to Charles I in the interest of the Rice family.[20]

A surviving statement of the reasons why Henry Rice presented his second petition to Charles I at the beginning of 1629 includes reference to some of the very sources noted in the Life: Holinshed, Hardyng's continuator, Camden, family records (including Sir Rhys ap Thomas's royal patents of appointment), Gruffydd Rice's petitions and, most telling of all, the Garter Book in St James's Palace.[21] Furthermore, notes and transcripts from fifteenth- and sixteenth-century official documents are still to be found among the archives of the Rices of Dinefwr, and there can be no doubt that these were among the sources of the Life. They include copies of a few of Sir Rhys ap Thomas's papers, transcriptions from royal records relating to Sir Rhys's grandfather, Gruffydd ap Nicholas, passages from John Speed's *Historie of Great Britain* and, once again, a note about Sir Rhys taken from the king's Garter Book in the library of St James's.[22] Inspired by his father's and grandfather's petitions to successive monarchs, and supported by his own extensive research and consultations, as well as by family tradition, Henry Rice produced what amounts to a detailed history of his family, concentrating on the distinguished service given by Sir Rhys ap Thomas to Henry VII and Henry VIII. His motive was precisely that of the petitions presented by his father and grandfather, namely, to place in perspective the attainder for treason of Rhys ap Gruffydd in 1531. We have already noted that the document which itemizes 'Objections' to the treason charges survives in a number of copies in the family archives; it was a natural accompaniment of the Life. In composing both, Henry Rice exploited his scholarship and his interest in history and genealogy, which he shared with other English and Welsh gentlemen of the age, to sustain the long campaign for the restoration of the family fortunes.[23]

(c) *The Cambrian Register*

Prior to its publication in *The Cambrian Register*, the Life of Sir Rhys ap Thomas was unknown to the public. It was, however, consulted in manuscript by David Edwardes (*c.*1630–90), an able genealogist who was appointed deputy-herald for Pembrokeshire, Cardiganshire, Breconshire, Glamorgan and Carmarthenshire on 1 August 1684. Edwardes travelled widely in Wales and England, consulting collections

---

[20] Bishop Andrewes (died 1626) appears to have been alive during the writing: see below p.164.
[21] BL, Add. MS 23113 f.3r–v.
[22] CRO, Dynevor, Add. MS 73.
[23] *CR*, II (1797), 270–7, from CCL MS 14416, one of Richard Fenton's notebooks; NLW, Dynevor, A 94 b and c.

of manuscripts as he went. His home was at Rhyd y Gors, near
Carmarthen, and we can easily imagine him exploring the Rice family
archives at nearby Newton. Certainly he is known to have made
excerpts from, and based notes on, the Life a century before it was
published in 1796.[24]

There is also in existence a short extract from the Life, hitherto
unnoticed and amounting to no more than a page in length, which was
penned by an unknown copyist, probably in the seventeenth century. It
is now bound into a seventeenth-century dictionary of navigation,
written in English in a quite different hand by 'H.M.'. This version of a
passage from the latter part of the Life is closely related to the published
version; its small number of textual variants may be explained by two
different copyists of the original manuscript, one in the seventeenth
century and the other, Richard Fenton, who transcribed the entire
manuscript in the latter part of the eighteenth century and submitted it
for publication in *The Cambrian Register*. This short fragment is
reproduced below as Appendix I.[25]

The Cambrian Register, the vehicle of an enthusiastic group of Welsh
literary patriots, was founded 'to investigate this hidden repository [of
unpublished manuscripts and oral traditions of Wales] and to bring to
light whatever may be deemed most rare and valuable'.[26] Although it
ran to only three issues, which appeared in 1796, 1797 and, after a long
gap, in 1818, it fulfilled its aim in substantial measure, if in a
miscellaneous and somewhat disorderly fashion, publishing articles on
medieval Welsh literature and especially on Welsh poetry, biography,
topography and history, interspersed with what may loosely be called
cultural news, contemporary poetry and reviews. Though published in
London, where it had the patronage of a lively and cultured Welsh
community, including the Gwyneddigion Society, *The Cambrian Register*
ultimately failed 'chiefly for want of support', or so its editor, William
Owen Pughe, sadly claimed.[27]

Owen Pughe (1759–1835), a noted lexicographer from Merioneth
who spent most of his active life among Welsh literati, had many friends
and scholarly acquaintances in London-Welsh literary circles. One of
these was Richard Fenton (1747–1821), a topographical and historical
writer and poet who came from St David's. A civil servant-turned-
lawyer, he found himself turned even further by his passion for writing,
and he proved a frequent contributor to the *Register*. It was he who

[24] *DWB*, p.181; F. Jones, *Report on the Welsh Manuscripts contained in the College of Arms* (London,
n.d.), p.10, noting Box 36/V (g); idem, *A Catalogue of Welsh Manuscripts in the College of Arms*
(Harleian Soc., new series, VII, 1988), p.80.
[25] NLW MS 9098D.
[26] *CR*, I (1796), v; the Life occupies pp.49–144.
[27] G. Carr, *William Owen Pughe* (Cardiff, 1983), pp.57–8; P. Morgan, *The Eighteenth Century
Renaissance* (Llandybïe, 1981).

edited and published, in the first two volumes, the 'Description of Pembrokeshire' which George Owen had written two centuries before. This was the fruit of his retirement from London to Pembrokeshire in 1793. He also prepared the Life of Sir Rhys ap Thomas for publication in the journal's first number in 1796, adding editorial comments which were distinguished, usually with care, by Owen Pughe in the printed edition. And it was Fenton who published, in the second number (1797) of the *Register*, without commentary, the 'Objections' which sought to disprove the alleged treason of Sir Rhys's grandson, Rhys ap Gruffydd, in 1531. Fenton had ample opportunity to consult the Rice family archives at Newton in Carmarthenshire, both before and after his retirement to Pembrokeshire. The second of the documents, or one very like it, is still among the family archives in several copies; the original manuscript of the Life of Sir Rhys ap Thomas has regrettably disappeared.[28]

When his *A Historical Tour through Pembrokeshire* was published in 1811, Richard Fenton expressed his admiration for *The Cambrian Register* 'as a most valuable accession to the literature of Wales, with a sincere hope that the Editor's intention of bringing out the third volume, which we have been for some time led to expect, is only suspended and not abandoned'. Moreover, his description of Carew Castle was augmented by the long account, taken from the Life, of the celebrations and tournaments held at Carew in 1506. Making all allowances for publishers' and authors' licence, it seems likely that in 1811 Fenton did not simply reproduce the account published in *The Cambrian Register* fifteen years before, but relied on 'the original MS it was first communicated in', which may have been the original manuscript of the Life and still in Fenton's possession.[29] The variations between the two published versions of 1796 and 1811 are numerous, if minor, and they suggest an editor transcribing and publishing the same account on separate occasions.

Fenton's interest in this Life may have been stirred by an association with the descendants of Sir Rhys ap Thomas, either in London or in south-west Wales, and it may have been given point by certain events in the family's history of which Fenton would certainly have been aware. In the late eighteenth century, the Rice family of Newton and Dinefwr (or Dynevor, as it was then commonly spelt) in Carmarthenshire was prominent and influential and had long lived down the scandal of treason in Henry VIII's reign. George Rice (1724–79) was a prominent Whig and represented Carmarthenshire in Parliament. In 1756 he married Cecil, only daughter and heiress of the first Earl Talbot of Hensol, in Glamorgan. It was by virtue of this aristocratic connection

---

[28] *CR*, II (1797), 270–7; NLW, Dynevor A 94 b–k; *DWB*, s.n.

[29] Fenton, *Historical Tour through Pembrokeshire*, pp.253–67, and note (x) on p.253; see below p.273.

that the Rices entered the peerage, for when George died in 1779, his father-in-law, Earl Talbot, added the barony of Dynevor to his title, with a special remainder to his daughter, the widowed Cecil, and her male heirs. When Talbot himself died in April 1782, Cecil became (somewhat incongruously) the second Baron Dynevor; eventually, when she died in 1793, the barony passed to her son, George Talbot (1765–1852). The 1780s, therefore, were a turning-point in the history of the Rice family, descendants of Sir Rhys ap Thomas.[30] The barony which some felt Sir Rhys had deserved after the battle of Bosworth in 1485 had at last been conferred, some 300 years later, on one of his descendants.

George Talbot, third Baron Dynevor, was MP for Carmarthenshire during 1790–3. Educated at Oxford, later in life he was sufficiently impressed by his Carmarthenshire forebears to petition the king for permission to add his father's family name of Rice to Talbot – which was duly granted in 1817. Shortly afterwards, he was instrumental in reviving the languishing Cymmrodorion Society, whose crucial meeting in June 1819 was held at his London home. This society resolved to co-ordinate the work of the several Cambrian Societies which had emerged in Wales for the encouragement of Welsh literature and writing. The result was the launching of a reinvigorated Cymmrodorion a year later, in June 1820. Lord Dynevor may have been inspired to take a lead by the formation of the Cambrian Society of Dyfed in October 1818, which sponsored 'the first of the great modern Eisteddfodau' at Carmarthen in 1819.[31] Four years later, another eisteddfod at Carmarthen resounded to the verses which the Revd John Jones (1792–1852), chaplain of Christ Church, Oxford (and later editor of the works of the fifteenth-century poet, Lewys Glyn Cothi), had composed in Welsh on the subject of Gruffydd ap Nicholas and his famous descendants, the Rices.[32] The publication of the Life of Sir Rhys ap Thomas in 1796 in the first number of a London-based journal dedicated to the study of Wales's past was an offshoot of the vigorous Welsh literary culture of the period, and also a reminder of the antiquity and fame of the lineage of George Talbot, who had become the third Baron Dynevor three years before.

For almost a century after its publication, the Life of Sir Rhys ap Thomas was generally accepted as an account reliable in all particulars.[33] James Gairdner (1828–1912), the prolific editor of historical materials, enthused about the Life in his *History of the Life and Reign of Richard the Third*, first published in 1878, though he realized that its character and reliability needed detailed investigation.

[30] *DWB*, pp.847–8; *CP*, IV, 364–5.

[31] R. T. Jenkins and H. M. Ramage, *A History of the Honourable Society of Cymmrodorion* (London, 1951), pp.144–9.

[32] NLW, Dynevor B, parcel 25, includes an English translation of these verses.

[33] Cf. J. Williams, *A History of Wales* (London, 1869), p.469.

... the work bears the marks of much conscientious research. Apparently it was based, to a considerable extent, upon authentic materials, which the writer interpreted by the traditions of Welsh bards and antiquaries; and if the facts may be relied on, their importance rises considerably above that of mere private family history.[34]

Gairdner was inclined to attach exaggerated value to tradition in the writing of history. Although H. T. Evans made some pertinent comments on the Life in his *Wales and the Wars of the Roses* (1915), the vehemence of his views deterred practically all historians from using it thereafter. His judgement that it had been 'the favourite resort of generations of less responsible writers' than Gairdner was patently true, but his criticisms were austere and, in a number of respects, quite misleading: 'a vein of unreality runs through the whole biography, and its details cannot stand the limelight of historical criticism.'[35]

(d) *Editorial Note*

The following edition is based on Richard Fenton's transcription of the original early-seventeenth-century manuscript of the Life, as published in *CR*, I (1796 for 1795). The original manuscript seems to have disappeared. An independent seventeenth-century transcription of a fragment of it is printed below as Appendix I. What appears to be a further independent transcription of part of the Life, made by Richard Fenton and published in *A Historical Tour Through Pembrokeshire* (London, 1811), is reproduced below as Appendix II. A comparison of these three versions reveals only minor variations one from another, mostly in the shape of insignificant spelling differences. Accordingly, and in the absence of the original manuscript, no attempt has been made to correct apparent errors which may have been made by Richard Fenton or the *CR* editor or the printer of 1759 – except in a small number of potentially misleading instances.

Brief reference to the source of certain poems and documents was made by Henry Rice (for example, below p.161 n.16). Richard Fenton's footnote editorial notes and comments are reproduced below as footnotes. These have been supplemented by the present editor's notes and comments. Fenton's section headings have also been preserved, but for ease of reference and reading, the text has been arranged in eight chapters, each with a modern title.

---

[34] J. Gairdner, *History of the Life and Reign of Richard the Third* (London, 1878), pp.274–81.
[35] Evans, *Wales and the Wars of the Roses*, pp.6, 12–14, 23, 93, 129, 211, 220 n.1.

1

'A Short View of the Life of Rice ap Thomas'

A short view of the long life of that ever wise, valiaunt, and fortunat commander Rice ap Thomas, Knight, Constable, and Lieutenant of Brecknock; Chamberlaine of Carmarthen and Cardigan, Seneschall and Chauncellor of Haverfordwest, Rowse and Buelth; Justiciar of South Wales, and Governour of all Wales; Knight Bannerett, and Knight of the most Honourable Order of the Garter, a Privie Councellor to Henrie the VII, and a favourite to Henrie the VIII.[1]

The Proeme or Apparatus to the ensuinge Worke.
GENTLEMEN,[2]
You are eyther nobiles nobiles, or nobiles ignobiles, or ignobiles nobiles; the first of you are they, whoe in a continuall succession for manie generations together, have without speck, blemish, or staine, pursude the stepps of your noble founders in the wayes of virtue and goodness, sometimes adding, ever equalling, never impayring their worthie and high deservings. You see then to be good and continue soe, is the true badge and cognisance of gentilitie. Of the second range, or order, are the nobiles ignobiles, men that have bepissed their father's monuments, such, I mean, who have stained the glorious actions of their

---

[1] For Sir Rhys's offices see p.60; all but 'Governour of all Wales' can be substantiated. However, a century earlier, Polydore Vergil noted that Henry Tudor conferred on Sir Rhys 'the perpetuall lyvetenentship of Wales': Vergil, *English History*, p.217. Edward Hall and Raphael Holinshed, to whom Henry Rice confessed himself indebted, claimed that Henry Tudor made Rhys 'chiefe gouernour of Wales': Hall, *Chronicle*, p.410; *Holinshed's Chronicles*, III, 435. Richard Grafton's continuation of John Hardyng's *Chronicle* (1543), p.542, described the grant as that of 'chiefe ruler of all Wales'.

[2] If the Life was addressed to the gentry circle in which the Rices moved, this would not be unusual: Williams, *Wales, 1415–1642*, p.440. The ensuing discourse on types of nobility reflects late-sixteenth-century opinion, especially among heralds (with whom the Rices had contacts) that virtue was superior to lineage as a qualification of nobility. Families which, like the Rices, originated in obscurity and attained nobility by personal achievements deserved special commendation, provided their methods were honourable ones. See M. E. James, *Society, Politics and Culture* (Cambridge, 1986), especially pp.375ff. Lest Rhys ap Gruffydd's treason be thought to besmirch his line, Henry Rice was ready to forgive aspiring men 'without anie respect to vertue' after three or four generations!

noble progenitors with some horrible foule crimes (*criminibus consputatione dignis*), sinnes of a scarlet hue. With anie, on thus degenerous, I must confess I would have noe commerce, *foenum habet in cornu* [he has hay on his horn, i.e. he is a dangerous fellow].[3]

In the third range, or order, are our *ignobiles nobiles* placed, men, though obscure and darke in their beginnings, yet advanced to places of highest dignitie and preferrment, *per legitimos gradus* [by legitimate steps]. Such, in former times, were Themistocles, Marius, Marcus Cato, and Cicero, a man *novitatis nobilissimae qui omnia incrementa sua sibi debuit* [of most noble new rank who merits all his advancement].[4] If anie of this number be among you, they cannot want their due estimation; and for my part, whenever I meete them, my admiration and affection shall both followe, yea and my finger shall point them to passengers, '*Et pulchrum est digito monstrari et dicere, hic est*' ['It is noble to be pointed out with a finger and to say, this is he'].

There are some of late (and truelie it hath binn soe in all ages), *qui ex thymorum captoribus*, as Synesius saith, *imprimis palam rhedam insiliere* [who, from among the hunters of thyme, first jumped on the wagon]. Men, whose beginnings we are as ignorant off as the heades of Nilus or Achelous, crept notwithstanding into greate honours and eminent places *per saltum* [by a leap], by sinister and indirect courses. Who climes by this ladder may truelie be said *ab asinis ad boves ascendere* [to ascend from asses to oxen].[5] Suidas will have him to be a greate disgrace to the order of this forme, whoe, by the ernest sollicitation of his ambition, without anie respect to vertue, will not stick to cutt his owne purse to purchase himselfe by surreptitious meanes an honourable title, I quite debarr him from having eyther *sortem* or *partem in hoc negotio* [a share or a part in this matter], till for three or four descentes he had well ayred and purged himself from the faeces and dreggs of his *layick cimonie*, contenting myselfe for an age or two to afford him a roome among my *expectanto's* [expectations] nott my *sunto's* [reality].[6] And nowe you knowe to whom I make my addresses, will you be pleased to reflect your eyes upon those former times wherein, for magnanimitie and courage, this island was the subject of the world's discourse, striking an aweful regard of our valour in the hartes of all neighbouring nations, and where ever else our

---

[3] Erasmus, *Adagia*, I, i.81, from Horace, *Satires*, I, 4.34.

[4] This may be a play on Seneca, *De Beneficiis*, 2, 27.2, a suggestion I owe to Mr Ceri Davies.

[5] This phrase comes from Erasmus, *Adagia*, I, vii.30, from Plautus, *Aulularia*, 235.

[6] For Bishop Synesius (died *c*.414) and the Suidas Lexicon (*c*.1000), which were popular sources of aphorisms in the sixteenth century, see F. L. Cross and E. A. Livingstone (eds.), *The Oxford Dictionary of the Christian Church* (2nd edn., Oxford, 1974), pp.1321, 1332. Synesius's works were available in Latin editions by the early seventeenth century; and so was the Lexicon, which included quotations from Synesius. It is likely that Henry Rice culled many of his adages second-hand from Erasmus's *Adagia*, which appeared in a number of editions in the sixteenth century. The headwaters of the River Nile (or Nilus) were unknown in western Europe until modern times; so, perhaps, were those of the River Achelous in Greece.

name was heard off. 'Tis evident then, fortitude from all antiquitie was the *palmaria virtus* [palm of virtue] of this land.

There are yett among us the small remainder of the antient Brittaines, certaine old recordes left (all devouring time as yett wanting time to devoure all), wherein, to our greate comfort, we may behold howe this famous isle for manie centuries of yeares past hath binn beutified and adorned with the honourable title *Ynys y Cedeirn* or Insula Fortium; a most true infallible argument of our undaunted prowess and brave atchievementes in those former ages. Oh! there was a time when we had our Mutii, our Fabritii, and our Reguli, as well as Rome, and we had our Socrates' and our Catos too, men little dredding fine, povertie, exile, torment, poyson, or death, when the saveing or upholding of their countrie's honour weare once in question.[7] That we may nott suffer the fame of our noble progenitors utterlie to perish, let us but imagine this speciouse goodlie island to be a fair triangular garden, and out of each corner thereof, among the maine sweetes there growing, let us select some on choice flower of chivalerie to solace and refresh our too much dejected spirits.[8] Fixe we our eyes first upon that noble chieftaine the stoute Earle Percie, and then upon his noe lesse noble antagonist, the renowned Earle Douglas; examine we their brave actions and doughtie performances in that memorable combate, of braverie and of *gayetè de coeur*, as the French terme it; in Chevie Chase there may we behold Hector against Ajax, and Ajax against Hector, both conquerors, both conquered, equall combatants. Had England and Scotland binn wagered for the garland, then, as Rome and Alba was in time past, there had binn champions for them indeede.[9] Nowe to add unto these two worthies (and soe make up my triangle), give me leave to point you out a third in Wales; for Wales, as that famous commander himself said of the

[7] Mutius (or Mucius), Fabricius and Regulus were courageous Roman generals of outstanding personal qualities; Socrates and Cato were philosophers of strong moral sense: Lemprière, s.n. The concept of an Island of Warriors (Ynys y Cedyrn) had a long pedigree by the seventeenth century: *Geiriadur*, s.n. cedyrn.

[8] The most recent expression of a tripartite division – at least of England and Wales – had occurred during Owain Glyndŵr's rebellion when, in 1405, Welsh, Mortimer and Percy rebels against Henry IV planned to dismember his kingdom with Scottish aid: J. E. Lloyd, *Owen Glendower* (Oxford, 1931), pp.93–5. This Percy connection may have dictated the choice of the Percy–Douglas heroics in the example that follows.

[9] This reference to the encounter, later famous in chivalric contexts, between Henry 'Hotspur', son and heir of the earl of Northumberland, and James, earl of Douglas, at the battle of Otterburn (or Chevy Chase) in August 1388, in which Hotspur was captured and the victorious Douglas slain, was doubtless a tactful tribute to the Stuart dynasty. For the battle, see R. Nicholson, *Scotland: The Later Middle Ages* (Edinburgh, 1974), pp.199, 201ff. For the 'Ballad of Chevy Chase', dating from the fifteenth century and popular in the sixteenth, see *DNB*, s.n. Sir Henry Percy; W. C. Dickinson, *Scotland from the Earliest Times to 1603* (3rd edn., Oxford, 1977), p.224. Ajax the Greek and Hector the Trojan are among the bravest of classical soldiers; they had at least one heroic encounter and both figure in Homer's *Iliad*, which was available in the early seventeenth century. The comparison with Rome and Alba (or Scotland) acknowledges the victories of the one and the continuing independence of the other.

Romans, had its Hannibal too, even the greate *Rice*, the subject of this ensuing discourse, nay more then a Hannibal, carrying yet this advantage with him, that he never mett with a Marcellus to teach him in martiall affaires. He was to doe him but right both a *Marcellus* and a *Fabius Maximus*, for as they of Rome, soe he of Wales might trulie be called their sword and buckler.[10] You shall seldome read in martiall storie of anie man adorned with such high attributes and epithets of honour, as this *Rice* was, both by English historiographers, and especiallie among our Welch bardes; who, in their rithmes and carolls, magnifie him above all that ever weare in those partes. Tudur Aled, a famous poete in those dayes, calls him *Tarian a thâlwas i wlâd*, the shield and buckler of his countrie;[11] Rys Nanmor entitles him *Bronddor y Brutanniaid*, the shield of Britaine.[12] Lewis Môn will have him to be *Campiwr y Cymry*, the champion of Wales;[13] Iorwerth Fynglwyd, flying beyond his circle, stiles him (forsooth) *Pen y Byd*, caput mundi [the head of the world], and thus he begins his song:

> Pwy sy benn kwmpas y byd
> Piau pwfer pawb hefyd
>
> [Who is chief of the world's limits,
> And at whose disposal is everyone's strength?]

And in this high phrase he continues to the end, where, it seemes, he will goe noe lesse, for thus he concludes:

> Tapr hyllfawr topia'r hollfyd
> Top ag oll ti piau gyd.[14]
>
> [May you surmount the whole world, most
> generous leader,
> It is yours entirely, top and all.]

[10] Presumably, the comparison here is between Sir Rhys ap Thomas's advance with Henry Tudor against Richard III and Hannibal's invasion of Italy. Like Claudius Marcellus and Fabius Maximus, Rome's defenders against Hannibal, Sir Rhys later helped to secure Henry VII's rule. Plutarch wrote the Life of both Claudius Marcellus and Fabius Maximus; his *Parallel Lives* was popular in Renaissance England, following Sir Thomas North's edition of 1579.

[11] Tudur Aled (*fl.*1480–1525): *DWB*, pp.986–7. This phrase does not appear in any of the poems addressed to Sir Rhys ap Thomas in Jones, *Tudur Aled*, nos. VII, XII, XIII, XIV, CXXXVII. On the other hand, an unpublished poem, addressed to Sir Rhys, is attributed in one manuscript to Tudur Aled, but in others to Iorwerth Fynglwyd: *Mynegai*, pp.4124, 1903 ('Pwy sy ben cwmpas y byd'). It is also possible that Sir Rhys ap Thomas's family kept copies of poems addressed to its prominent members, but that these poems did not have wider currency.

[12] Rhys Nanmor (*fl.*1480–1513): *DWB*, p.843. For his poems to Sir Rhys, see *Mynegai*, pp.3345–50, and E. R. Ll. Davies, thesis cited, pp.115–20. But this particular phrase does not appear in the poems edited by Headley, thesis cited.

[13] Lewys Môn (*fl. c.*1480–1527): *DWB*, p.545. This phrase does not appear in those of his poems which mention Sir Rhys ap Thomas, in Rowlands, *Lewys Môn*.

[14] Iorwerth Fynglwyd (*fl. c.*1500–25): *DWB*, p.417; Pugh, *Glamorgan County History*, III, pp.511–15. For this poem addressed to Sir Rhys and composed after 1513, see Jones and Rowlands, *Iorwerth Fynglwyd*, no.17; for another, no.18.

Another, Gwylim ap Ievan Hên, roughlie termes him *Golchffon y Traws*, the scourge of the obstinate;[15] and David Nanmor calls him, in one place, *Amddiffynnwr y Gwirionedd*, the protector of the innocent, and in another, *Calon y Rhyfelwr*, the hart of the souldier.[16] Christopher Ocland, an Englishman, will have him named *Flos Cambro-Britannûm*;[17] and Mr Camden doth him the honour to call him *Deliciae Henrici Octavi*.[18] Thus may you see, by clapping thes elogiums and favours upon him, of what high estimation that noble gentleman was in those dayes, when his vertues hammered and hewed him out these glorious titles. Nowe should these three brave champions have mett and encountered in a fight, imitating the *matachin daunce*,[19] as that daunce heretofore was invented, in imitation of such a fight, each one having two adversaries; this of necessitie must have followed, England had binn England still; Scotland Scotland, and Wales Wales. But peace, and the God of peace, hath produced those effects by conjoynning these three in one, which (perhaps) otherwise, the doubtfull valour of their invincible swordes, might have perpetuallie severed *trino-uni sit gloria* [in trinity be glory].[20] Nowe to sett an edge upon our appetites, and to give lief and quickening to those good notions which often arise in noble hartes, the shortest and readiest way (noe doubt) is by example, for by precept is a journey some what too far about, besides, our eares are nott of that creditt with us, as our eyes, neyther doe the wordes of menn soe soone take us as their manners. Then lett us call to mind our Bedford, our Salisburie, our Talbot,[21] or this greate Rice, true patternes of wisedome, magnanimitie, and justice, or what else may deserue the name of praise. Oh!

[15] Gwilym ab Ieuan Hen (*fl. c.*1440–80): *DWB*, p.326. This phrase does not appear among Gwilym's *œuvre* in A. E. Davies, 'Gwaith Deio ab Ieuan Du a Gwilym ab Ieuan Hen' (unpublished University of Wales MA thesis, 1979), II.

[16] Dafydd Nanmor (died *c.*1490): *DWB*, p.103. The author may have confused Dafydd Nanmor with Rhys Nanmor (Roberts and Williams, *Dafydd Nanmor*, pp.xxiff.), though these phrases do not appear in the poems addressed to Sir Rhys ap Thomas in Headley, thesis cited.

[17] The *CR* editor adds a note: 'Vide Anglorum Praelia Oclandi'. Christopher Ocland (died *c.*1590) dedicated his *Anglorum Praelia, ab anno . . .1327 . . .usque ad annum . . .1558* (London, 1580), to Elizabeth I: *DNB*, s.n. The reference (p.lii) to *Ricius Thomas flos Cambrobritannum* relates to Henry VIII's invasion of France in 1513.

[18] William Camden (1551–1623): *DNB*, s.n. The phrase is not taken from Camden's *Britannia* (London, 1610 edn.), p.650, noting Newcastle Emlyn castle, 'which Sir Rhise ap Thomas that warlike Knight who assisted Henrie the seventh when he gat the Crowns, and was by him right worthily admitted unto the Societe of the Knights of the Garter, renewed'.

[19] The *CR* editor adds a note: 'Doctor Johnson explains Matachin, by *An Old Dance*, and gives the following quotation from Sir Philip Sidney. "Whoever saw a Matachin Dance to imitate fighting; this was a fight that did imitate the Matachin, for they being but three that fought, everyone had two adversaries striking him who struck the third".' According to *OED* it is of Spanish or Arabic origin; the quotation (1586) is from Sidney's *Arcadia*, I (1590), 74b.

[20] This 'trinity' is a compliment to the accession of James VI and I in 1603.

[21] The reputations of John of Lancaster, duke of Bedford (1389–1435), Thomas Montague, earl of Salisbury (1388–1428), and John Talbot, earl of Shrewsbury (*c.* 1384–1453), England's finest commanders in the latter stages of the Hundred Years' War, were ranked high by sixteenth-century writers. *Holinshed's Chronicles*, III, 137ff.

had we in our late expeditions butt carried the bones of a Bedford about us, as the Turkes did George Castriot's, that invincible Turco-mastix;[22] or cried out, a Talbott! a Talbott! or had we flead this greate Rice, and clapped his skinn upon our drum-head, as Zisca, that greate commaunder, would have had the Bohemians to have don his;[23] we had noe question eyther made absolute conquest of the French, or rattled them away, or (at lest wise) showne ourselves invincible; butt this is a sore too greene, too tender, for the tender touch.[24] What man is he, not alltogether degenerate, who will refuse to clime the craggie and dangerouse passages of honour after his father, were it *per tela vibrantia* [amidst gleaming weapons]? Thos newlie crept into their *magistratus curules* [highest offices], having noe images of their ancestors, may, if please them, take acquaintance, and 'tis worth their labour, with my greate Rice, greate indeede; soe greate, as for ought I read, none greater in all our English storie; standing upon his owne basis and foundation; and soe good likewise as noe force, noe necessitie, could ever drawe him to ill. His mind was ever free and upright, nott unlike the state of the world above the moone, cleare, faire, and peaceable. One man was the parte he plaid, and that parte he plaid exactlie. That this noble gentleman, thus qualified, appeares to the world in thes uglie ragges, lett nott that procure him a slight regard. I doubt not but there are others, when he is knowen to come from his grave, will, eyther for his worth, or for affinitie's sake, affourd him better apparell. He was a man neare mett with ill fortune, till he came under the blotts and dashes of my penn; and yet I may not soe undervalue myself, to thinke that a Hall, a Harding or a Hollinshed, could have donn more for him then I have: or at the worst I may boldly compare with the balett-monger of Chevie-chase, the onlie chronicler I find (worth the while) to register the actes of thos two

[22] George Castriota (1405–68), the Albanian hero, was known as Alexander the Bey ('Scanderbeg') by the Sultan before he converted to Christianity and led resistance against the Turks. He was encouraged by Pope Pius II (1458–64), whose writings doubtless made Castriota's name well known throughout Europe; Pius's *Omnia Opera* was first published in 1551 (Basle), and the *Commentaries* (containing references to Scanderbeg) was first printed in Rome in 1584 (Luigi Tokaro (ed.), *I Commentarii* (2 vols., Milan, 1984)). It may also be noted that M. Barletius's *Historia de vita et gestis Scanderbegi* was published as early as 1520, and a version of it even appeared in English in 1596. 'Our late expeditions' may refer to the disastrous English expeditions to Cadiz (1625) and, more especially, La Rochelle (1627), for which see C. Carlton, *Charles I* (London, 1983), chs. VI–IX. Henry Rice may have been particularly conscious of these ignominious ventures because contingents of men were raised in south-west Wales to serve in them: *Acts PC, March 1625–May 1626*, pp.42–5; *January–August 1627*, pp.455–7.

[23] The story that the dying Jan Zizka (died 1424), the Hussite commander who repelled the Germans from Bohemia, ordered that a drum be made out of his skin in order to frighten his enemies first appeared in print (1503) in the *Historia Bohemica* of Aeneas Sylvius Piccolomini (later Pope Pius II), who visited Bohemia in 1451. In the eighteenth century, a drum with human skin (supposedly Zizka's) was exhibited in the armoury of Glatz fortress. See O. Odlozilik, *The Hussite King* (Rutgers, NJ, 1965), p.57; F. G. Heymann, *John Zizka and the Hussite Revolution* (Princeton, 1969 edn.), p.442.

[24] This is doubtless a reference to the humiliating failure of the attempt to relieve the Huguenots of La Rochelle in 1627: Carlton, *Charles I*, ch.IX.

valorouse peeres, of whom I have heretofore spoken.[25] For my presuming to write his lief, thes are my reasons, first, to revive an auncient custome of writing the lives of worthie men, that soe their fame might not perish; for what greater discouragement cann be to high erected spiritts, covetouse of glorie, and thursting after renowne, then to see us recklesse and carelesse in recording the prowess and magnani-mouse proceedings of our forefathers? Take away praise and praemium and suffer the memorie of our brave performances to dye with us, *et quis virtutem amplectitur ipsam* [and who will cherish virtue itself]?[26] The report and commendation of some remarkable deede of anie of our auncestors (doubtless) hath in it *aliquid vivae voluptatis* [something of the pleasure of life], and doth much delight our cares, and enflame our bloodes with noble desires; soe that, by some such way as this, our dull and drowzie courages must be awakened, otherwise ('tis to be feared) our honour and reputation, with which we are allmost come to an after game, will loose ground, and growe each day more feeble and faint then other.[27] My second reason proceeds from a desire I have to dash in peeces some false forged traditions concerning this *Rice*, which daylie (soe apt, for old affection, we are to beleeve wonders of that man) increaseth among the credulouse multitude, and may hereafter, if not prevented, bring his name, as of others, into suspect: some clapping upon him, as upon divers of our heroes in former times, incredible exploits; others possessed with a delirium will not beleeve (forsooth) he is yett dead (the like conceipt, as I heard from a great person of this land, some of the English heretofore had of Henrie the Seventh), butt translated hence (Romulus like) *per apotheosin* [by transformation], or placed, perhaps, in some repositorie for awhile, whence after some yeares (*anno magno Platonis* [in the great year of Plato],I beleeve), like brave King Arthur, or Sir Guy Heshall, returne againe *tanquam Pater Patriae* [as Father of the Nation].[28]

[25] Edward Hall (died 1547), author of *The Union of the Two Noble and Illustre Families of Lancastre and York* (1542); John Harding (died *c*.1465), author of a *Chronicle* (with a continuation by Richard Grafton, 1548); Raphael Holinshed (died *c*.1580), author of *Chronicles of England, Scotland and Ireland* (1577); see above p.136. See *DNB*, s.n.

[26] Juvenal, 10.141.

[27] For contemporary interest in the inspiring and instructive achievements of heroic and political figures of the past (which was stimulated by the popularity of Tacitus's writings at the end of the sixteenth century), see Guy, *Tudor England*, pp.414–17. Francis Bacon (died 1626), to whom Henry Rice was directly indebted, Sir John Hayward (died 1627), and Bishop Lancelot Andrewes (died 1626), another of Rice's sources, were outstanding exponents of this Tacitean *genre*: P. Burke, 'Tacitism', in T. A. Dorey (ed.), *Tacitus* (London, 1969), pp.149–71.

[28] For the Messianic prophetic tradition relating to Henry VII, see G. Williams, *Harri Tudur a Chymru: Henry Tudor and Wales* (Cardiff, 1985), chs.I and IX; D. Rees, *The Son of Prophecy* (London, 1985), ch.5. The reference to 'Sir Guy Heshall' may refer to the popular romance of Sir Guy of Warwick, mythical ancestor of the earls of Warwick: J. Gupitza (ed.), *The Romance of Guy of Warwick* (EETS, extra series, 25–6, 1875–6). For the concept of the sleeping ruler who would rise again, see R. Folz, *The Concept of Empire in Western Europe from the Fifth to the Fourteenth Century* (London, 1969), pp.162–7.

Sic Britonum ridenda fides et credulus error
Riceaum expectat, expectabitque perenne.

[So the ridiculed faithful and credulous ignorance of the Britons waits for Rhys and will wait forever].

And this follie you must knowe was grounded on this foundation: for, say they (his bodie being removed from the White Friars in Carmarthen, to St Peter's church),[29] his coffin, at the taking up, which was of lead, and stronglie hooped with iron, was found open; wherein there was neyther bones nor ashes, a strange tale to tell! *Sed credat Judaeus apello non ego* [But may the Jew believe, I do not declare].[30] Lastlie, in discharg of the reverence I owe to his memorie (for I may nott denie but that I have an interest in his blood), I could not chuse but lett my penn play the parte of a spade, to digge him (foolishlie, as you see) out of the pitt of oblivion;[31] *et quare ego* (to say as Velleius Paterculus said, speaking in commendation of his greate greate grandfather, Minatius Magius), *verecundia, domestici sanguinis gloriae quidquam, dum verum refero, detraham?* [and how . . . by modesty will I detract anything from the glory of domestic kin so long as I report the truth?] Manie have written the lives of their fathers, their friendes, yea their owne, without anie the lest imputation of arrogancie or vaine glorie. Whie then should I, as upright in my dealing as they, however short in abilitie, expect for a worse fate, soe I keep myself safe from thos accustomed faults of historiographers, love, hate, feare, flattrie, and desire of fame, presuming to thrust noe more upon the world, then what record, historie, or tradition, supported with strong and probable circumstances, shall avowe.

Truth then is the thing I doe ernestlie aime at, which cannott be attayned but by conference with old recordes, of the gentlemen of Wales, especiallie they of the North, who are best preservers of antiquitie, will peruse their moth eaten writings, and communicate their knowledge with mine, they shall doe great honour to Rice ap Thomas, his ashes, and, perhaps, thereby revive the memorie of their owne noble

[29] The *CR* editor adds a note: 'His monument is now to be seen in the chancel of St Peter's Church, Carmarthen, with the effigies of him and his lady recumbent; but the figures, as well as the whole fabric, was composed of such a perishable stone, that no impression remains. And it can hardly be discovered to belong to this great man, but by the garter round the arms, where the family bearings may be faintly made out.' Sir Rhys was in fact buried in the Grey Friars' Church, Carmarthen, where 'a goodly tumbe' stood in the choir at the Dissolution. It had an iron grate round it, together with his banner, coat armour and helmet. The tomb was then moved to St Peter's. The banner and helmet had disappeared by 1803, but in 1865 the tomb (though not the effigies) was restored and renovated by Lord Dynevor, who moved it from the north side of the chancel to its present position on the south side. One of the upper row of figures from the tomb chest is now in Llangynin Church, Carmarthenshire: *RCAHM, Carmarthenshire*, pp.255–6, 259.

[30] Horace, *Satires* I, 5.100–1.

[31] The *CR* editor adds a note: 'Vell. Paterc. Lib. ii.18.' Velleius Paterculus was a soldier-turned-historian of the age of Augustus and Tiberius. Many editions of his *Historiae Romanae* were published before the 1620s; his grandfather, Magius Minatius (rather than his great-great-grandfather) is commended in Book II.16. See also Lemprière, s.n.

auncestors, who ran the fortune of the warres with him, *qui jam illacrimabiles argentur* [recte *urgentur*] *ignotique longa nocte, quia carent vote* [recte *vate*] *sacro* [who now pitiless and unknown are forced through a long night because they lack an inspired poet].[32] In the meane while lett these poor laboures rest upon the file, *quibus ex ingenio quisque suo, demat vel addat fidem* [and let each, according to his disposition, give or withhold faith].[33]

---

[32] Based on Horace, *Odes*, IV, 9.26–8.
[33] Tacitus, *Germania*, 3.4.

2

Gruffydd ap Nicholas

(1) *A summarie Collection of those grievouse Calamities, where with this Land was oppressed during the Division of the Two royall Houses.*
(2) *Of Griffith ap Nicholas, Grandfather to Sir Rice ap Thomas, and what Part he acted in those Times, his Lineage and Death.*

(1) In the russling days of Henrie the Sixt and Edward the Fourth, when we weare at our *Cujus est terre* [whose land is it]? Abner's question: and noe Aedipus then living to resolve the same. When the faire face of this flourishing kingdome was so unnaturallie scratched and disfigured by the uncivill handes of its owne inhabitantes. When our crowne lay betweene the anvill and the hammer, *in extremo discrimine* [in extreme crisis], neyther Yorke's nor Lankester's fortune still like herself, playing at fast and loose with them both, sometimes raysing sometimes depressing the beams of soveraigntie with a false finger. When our king was a true lawefull king to day, and a traitour to-morrowe, and soe adjudged to be by act of parliament; woeful times; when a parliament, the mouth of justice, wrested from its owne true byas, durst speake in noe other language (true or false) but such as the sword did dictate. When our princes of the blood, and our nobles, had noe way of appeasing the furie of Bellona, but with a sacrifice of their owne blood. When our commons, and the whole bodie of this realme, eyther fearing the event, or perplexed with the tedious debatement of the title, or tir'd with the heavie pressures of their lingring calamities, weare even readie to splitt upon a desperate rock, and to conclude (if we guess not amiss) among themselves; *juxta vocem illam meretriciam, nec Eboraco soli, nec Lancastriae soli, sed dividutur* [in accordance with the seductive call, neither York alone, nor Lancaster alone, but divided].[1] Oh! the dayes!

---

[1] This view of the Wars of the Roses could be derived from Tudor historians like Holinshed. The biblical Abner commanded Saul's army in his struggles with King David, but later joined David and was assassinated (*New Catholic Encyclopaedia* [New York, 1967], I, s.n.). The complex story of

(2) In those dayes, I say, tumultuarie, tempestuouse dayes, about the two and thirtieth of Henrie the Sixt. When the flame burst out violentlie between the two royal houses, and that the surges of civill dissention went high within our land; there was of Wales, among the manie that fished in thos troublous seas, one Griffith ap Nicholas, a man for power, riches, and parentage, beyonde all the greate men in thos partes.[2] This Griffith by marriage[3] was linked to three greate houses, having a plentifull issue by all three; valiant and couragiouse sonnes, to second him in all dangers; daughters bestowed upon the men of greatest reckning and account in all South Wales,[4] and his eldest sonne[5] being matched to the chief house in North Wales, drew in likewise to himself a mightie alliance thence, soe that for power and commaund, together with the fastness of his kindred and friendes, in thos countries he had fewe equalls, noe superiours. He was a man alsoe full of welth, and had an estate at lest of seven hundred pownd a year, old rent of assize, seaven strong castles, and seaven houses, for thus said the Bard.

> Saith Gastell, sy ith gostiaw
> A saith lys sy ieth law[6]

> [You have seven castles to provide for you,
> And seven courts under your authority.]

Ther's his riches! For his descent, he was in the fourth degree to Sir Glider, surnamed the *black* knight of the sepulchre,[7] and soe upward in

Oedipus in Greek mythology, popularized by Sophocles's tragedies, included Oedipus killing his father, marrying his mother and blinding himself, with his sons falling to deadly dispute. Not even the Wars of the Roses could rival that!

[2] Griffiths, *NLWJ*, XIII, no.3 (1964), 256–68, and *WHR*, II (1964–5), 213–31; both reprinted in idem, *King and Country*, chs.11, 12.

[3] The *CR* editor adds a note: 'His first wife was Mably, daughter of Meredith ap Henry Donne, of Kidwely, his second was a daughter of Sir John Perrott, of Pembrokeshire, and his third Jane, daughter and co-heiress of Jenkin ap Rees ap David of Gilvach Wen.' His second wife was named Margaret. See Griffiths, *WHR*, II (1964–5), 228–9.

[4] See below pp.164–5. Of his daughters, Joan, daughter of Jane (or Joan), married Philip Mansel of Glamorgan, and her sister Angharad married Jenkin Clement of Carew. Lleucu, daughter of Mabli Dwnn, married Hugh Basset of Gower and, later, Sir John St John, also of Gower; whilst her sister Gwenllian married Gruffydd ap Dafydd ap Thomas. A daughter of Margaret Perrot married John Scudamore of Herefordshire, and another married Maredudd Fychan of Maelienydd. CRO, Dynevor, Add. 73.

[5] The *CR* editor adds a note: 'He married Elizabeth, daughter and heiress of Sir John Griffith of Abermarlais, in Caermarthenshire; which Sir John Griffith was a descendant of Ednyfed Fychan.' Sir John (died 1471) was lord of Llangybi, Betws Bledrws and Llanrhystud in Cardiganshire, as well as of lands in England: Griffiths, *Principality of Wales*, pp.145–6; below p.164.

[6] The *CR* editor adds a note: 'Gwilym ap Ievan hen ai kant', for whom see above p.152 n.15. The quotation from Gwilym's ode is more accurately,

> Saith gastell sy' i'th gostiaw,
> A saith lys y sy' i'th law.

See A. E. Davies, thesis cited, II, 198–9, ll. 27–8. This estimate of Gruffydd's estate, with its repetition of seven, must be regarded as notional.

[7] I.e., Gruffydd ap Nicholas ap Philip ap Syr Elidir Ddu. See Dwnn, I, 210; Griffiths, *NWLJ*,

a direct series and long concatenation of worthie progenitors up to Sir Urian Rheged, king of Gower in Wales, prince of Murriff in Scotland, lord of Kidwelly, and knight of the round table to king Arthur.[8] From this Urian, Griffith ap Nicholas and his successors (nowe the Rices) have the denomination of Fitz Urian, which name hath proved fatall to that house; for in Henrie the Eighth's time, young Rice, grandchild to Sir Rice ap Thomas, within five or six yeares after his grandfather's death (*O quam fragilis favor potentum* [O how fragile is the favour of the powerful]!), among other charges of as small consequence, lost his head, twelve or fourteen hundred pound a yeare, old rent of assize, and thirty thousand pounds in jewells and plate, for assuming to himself this verie name of Fitz Urian.[9] The wordes of the record are these,[10] – '*Quod praefatus Ricaeus ap Griffith novum nomen. Videat Rice ap Griffith Fitz Urian in se praeditorie assumpsit hac intentione videat, quod in se statum et honorem dictae principalitatis Walliae, – dignius et sub pretenso tituli colore praeditorie obtinere proterat et habere.*' – How this name, more then Fitz Herbert, Fitz Hammon, or the like, could give him anie colourable title to the principalitie of Wales, or serve anie way as an enforcement against him for his lief, lett the world judg. But this happened in the time of Henrie the Eight, *truculentissimo illo nobilium procruste, qui fultus suspitionibus ineptis, hominum capitibus insultabat, deque bonorum civium amputatis cervicibus quasi de segetibus hostium lapidatis inter invidiae suae et crudelitatis sequestria laetabatur* [this most cruel torturer of nobles, who fortified with absurd notions reviled men's heads and severed the necks of good citizens, like the stone-covered fields of the enemy, rejoices through envy and cruelty].

But to goe on, there is a remarkable note upon this familie, that from their first founder (to goe no farther than Urian Rheged, which some herauldes, vaunting their skill and knowledge, will scarce allow for the middway) they have ever matched with nobles, noble descendantes, or

XIII, no. 3 (1964), 256. For Elidir Ddu (*fl.*1300–50), a knight of the Holy Sepulchre, see Jones, *JHSCW*, XXXI (1979), 23.

[8] Dwnn, I, 210 (*c.* 1596). Pedigrees compiled for the Rice family by Ralph Brooke in 1600 record the fictitious descent from Urien Rheged, lord of Kidwelly, Carnwyllion and Iscennen, and his wife, Margaret, daughter of the duke of Cornwall. They also claim that Philip ap Syr Elidir Ddu was the first of the family to use the name FitzUrien (CRO, Dynevor, Add. 112). Lewys Dwnn (I, 210) gave this honour to his father, Elidir.

[9] For traditions associating Urien (*fl. c.*570–90) with Gower, Rheged, Moray and elsewhere, see *DNB*, s.n. A recent assessment of Urien's historicity is in A. P. Smyth, *Warlords and Holy Men; Scotland, AD 80–1000* (London, 1984), pp.21–5.

[10] The *CR* editor adds a note: 'Mich. 23. Hen. 8 Rot. 6 inter placita regis', i.e., PRO, KB27/1081, *rex* m.6, published in Williams, *Y Cymmrodor*, XVI (1902), 33–9, with a more accurate version of the passage on p.38: . . . *quod praefatus Ricardus ap Griffith . . . novum nomen videlicet Ryce ap Gruffith ffitzuryen in se proditorie assumpsit hac intentione videlicet quod ipse statum et honorem dictae principalitatis Wallie . . . dignius et sub praetenso tituli colore proditorie optinere poterat et habere* [. . . that the said Richard ap Griffith traitorously adopted a new name, namely, Rhys ap Gruffydd FitzUrien, with the intention, namely, that he could obtain and have, fittingly and by pretence of the title and colour of treason, the state and honour of the principality of Wales]. The original jurors' indictment, made at Westminster on 15 November 1531, is PRO, KB9/517 m.3.

with the children of princes; which gave Mr Camden, by way of discourse, once occasion to say, that they were the best borne gentlemen in Wales, and furthest spread in their branches of anie familie in England; and that he confirmed, allowing them theire alliance with the houses of Northfolk, Worcester, Pembroke, Bullinbrooke, and Barkley, with which five greate houses they have, within this last centurie of yeares, binn mutuallie linked and intermatched.[11] Nowe for Griffith ap Nicholas (to returne againe where I left): I find that in his conception, and before he was borne, he was unwittinglie accessarie both to his father's and his mother's death. His father (Nicholas ap Philipp) being long married, and without issue, to a vertuouse gentlewoman,[12] *fortitudine et sanctimonia insigni* [with extraordinary resolution and piety], it happened he was embroyled in some quarrell, wherin he receaved a dangerous wound, of which despairing (though his surgeons sawe noe such cause), he adventured to lye with his wiefe (soe much did his thoughts worke upon the upholding of his name, that he forgott his owne safetie), and of her then begatt this sonne, which act of his suddenlie hastened him to his end. His noble mother, the lineall descendant of Elystan Glodrydh, earle of Ferlex, and prince of all thos goodlie countries between Wy and Severn, drawing neere her deliverie, dreamt (as if she had a Paris, or a Pericles there) that in her wombe grewe a bay tree, the roote whereof toare up her bowells, and the branches reached from Tawe to Tivy, two rivers, the one on the confines of Glamorgan, the other in Cardiganshire; which gave her occasion propheticallie to say, that sure she was to dye of that birth, yet her hope was, and therein lay her comfort, that out of her loynes one should come, which in those partes should carrie a principall sway; neyther erred she in her divination; for falling into a painfull and desperate labour, and being told that eyther she or her child must perish; well then, said she, with a masculine courage, if it must be soe, lett me perish, but if it be possible, save this poore child of mine for your future comfort, strength, and countenance: where upon her bellie, by the advise of surgeons, was cutt open, and soe the child was preserved; whoe indeede, as she had foretold, grewe in time to be a man of great power and authoritie in his countrie, and soe continued his posteritie for four or five descents after him.[13] This child (nowe Griffith ap Nicholas) growing in yeares, proved

[11] Thomas Jones's pedigree of Walter Rice, 1605 (CRO, Dynevor Add. 111), records the family's descent from these and other English noble houses. Camden, Clarenceux king of arms from 1597 to 1623, knew Ralph Brooke, York herald (died 1625), well: *DNB* s.n.

[12] The *CR* editor adds a note: 'Jenet, daughter of Griffith Llewhelin Voythus'. Its accuracy is confirmed by the 1600 pedigree of the Rices (CRO, Dynevor, Add.112); Lewys Dwnn (I.210) gives her name as Sioned. For Gruffydd ap Llywelyn Foethus, see Griffiths, *Principality of Wales*, p.386; for his legendary ancestor, Elystan Glodrydd, lord of Elfael and Maelienydd, *DNB*, s.n.; and for his daughter's descent, Bartrum, *300–1400*, II, 407.

[13] This story is also told in F. Jones, *TCASFC*, XXIX (1939), 30, from NLW MS 1602 D f.205 (*c.*1609–30), a compilation largely by Thomas Jones of Fountain Gate, Cardiganshire (died 1609),

to be a man of a hott, firie and cholerrick spiritt; one whos counsells weare all *in turbido* [turbulent], and therefore naturallie fitlie composed and framed for the times: verie wise he was, and infinitlie subtile and craftie, ambitiouse beyond measure, of a busie stirring braine, which made manie to conjecture (as Themistocles his schoolmaster did of him) that sure some greate matter hanged over his head; for it could nott be, but one day he should doe some notable good thing, or extreame bad: he was indeede, in his carriage, and the whole course of his lief, nothing butt Themistocles, which drewe upon him mightie adversaries abroad.[14] Three greate Dukes at once attempted to crush and tredd him under foote; Richard, Duke of Yorke, Henrie, Duke of Warwike, or rather Jasper, Earle of Pembrock, to whom he had just cause of quarrell, and Humphry, Duke of Buckingham, with two other greate Judges of the Realme.[15] Will you know howe he valued, and what account he made of the threats and menaces of the's lowde roaring cannons? His Bard will tell you:[16]

> Tri Dûg a geissiodd trwy dwng
> A dau Jystys dy ostwng;
> Nes iddyn noeth i swyddaw
> Dramwy ar draed drimor draw.

> [By means of a fine, three dukes
> And two justices attempted to subdue you;
> And they sooner retreated on foot the length
>   of three oceans
> Rather than depose you.]

By this it appeared there was noe moveing nor stirring of him. The more he was shaken, the more confirm'd, not unlike a tree, subject to wind and weather; *quae ipsa vexatione constringitur, et radices certius figit* [which by its very tossing tightens its grip and fastens its roots more firmly]:[17] The

and possibly once among the Rice archives.

[14] Themistocles (died 459 BC), the Athenian commander and statesman, had the reputation of being bold, ambitious and restless, cunning, resourceful and eloquent (Lemprière, s.n.). Plutarch's Life (ch.II for his teacher's foretelling of future greatness 'for good or evil') was translated into English in 1579.

[15] See Griffiths, *NLWJ*, XIII, no.3 (1964), 256–68, and *WHR*, II (1964–5), 213–31.

[16] The *CR* editor adds a note: 'Gwilym ap Ievan hen ai kant', for whom see above p.152 n.15. For this quotation from Gwilym's ode to Gruffydd, see A. E. Davies, thesis cited, II, 198–9, II.29–32:

> Tri dug a brofes, trwy dwng
> A dau iustus, dy ostwng
> Nes iddynt no'th ddiswyddaw
> Dramwy ar draed dri môr draw.

Both note and quotation are among excerpts from the Life made by David Edwardes (died 1690), which indicates that the note about the source of the poem was already in the copy of the Life used by Edwardes. College of Arms, Box 36 V.

[17] The *CR* editor adds a note: 'Vid: 33. Hen: 6, fol.53. Rot: 673. in communi Banco', i.e. PRO,

Duke of York quarrell'd with Griffith ap Nicholas, for detayning from him one half of two plough lands, and a half of land, with the appurtenances, in Lyesprans and Newhouse,[18] lying and being in the marches of Wales, in the countie of Hereford, for which the said Duke brought a *praecipe quod reddat* [an order that he respond] against him, to which he refus'd to appeare, being often call'd upon and warn'd by the Sheriffes summonitors thereunto. Griffith ap Nicholas was Captaine of the stronge Castle of Kilgarran in Cardiganshire,[19] and held the same by letters patent from the King, which Captaineshipp Jasper, Earle of Pembrock, taking a liking to, wrought soe by his power at court, that the said letters patents were call'd for in, cancell'd and damn'd, and a newe graunt thereof made to the said Earle; and this was the cause of a perpetual hart-burning in them each to the other. The quarrell betweene the Duke of Buckingham and him, was the quarrell of old betweene greate ones neighbourhood, and jelousie of each others power and commaunderie: and that ceased nott betweene their posteritie, till Richard the Thirde's time, when the Duke of Buckingham, and Sir Rice ap Thomas, were wrought to lay aside private spleene for the publique good.[20] As for the two greate Judges, his potent adversaries, I make noe question, butt they stomach'd him, for nott submitting himself to the

CP40/775 m.704*d* (Herefordshire, Michaelmas, 1454–5), for the following suit.

[18] The *CR* editor adds a note: 'Quere – if not Llysyfran and Newhouse in Pembrokeshire'. They may be identified with Llys-y-fran and New Moat in the episcopal lordship of Llawhaden, Pembrokeshire. The two and a half carucates which Roger Mortimer, later earl of March (executed 1330), held there in 1326 were recovered by the Mortimers in 1354 and descended to Richard, duke of York. Bishop John de la Bere of St David's (1447–60) countenanced Gruffydd ap Nicholas's possession of half the property and the duke accordingly instituted proceedings against Gruffydd and the bishop in the court of Common Pleas in the winter of 1454–5. The reference to Hereford arises from the responsibility of the royal officials of Herefordshire for certain matters relating to the south-western Marcher lordships. Willis-Bund, *The Black Book of St David's*, pp.158–9; G. A. Holmes, *The Estates of the Higher Nobility in XIV Century England* (Cambridge, 1957), p.16 n.5. A further cause of tension involved York's nearby lordships of Narberth, St Clears and Traean March. Whether the duke, in financial difficulties, conveyed these lordships to Gruffydd ap Nicholas and the bishop in May 1449 as a mortgage or an enfeoffment, the transaction subsequently soured relations between Gruffydd and Duke Richard: Gruffydd resisted the duke's efforts to assert his authority in west Wales, including an attempt to recover control of these lordships. *CPR, 1446–52*, pp.234–5; *1452–61*, p.71; *LP Henry VIII*, II, part 1, 154; Griffiths, *WHR*, II (1964–5), 217 and n.19; Johnson, *Richard of York*, p.62 and n.73.

[19] The *CR* editor adds a note: 'Kilgarran Castle is in Pembrokeshire overhanging the Tivy.' On 18 April 1451, Gruffydd joined Gruffydd ap Dafydd ap Thomas and William ap John as custodians of the lordships of Cilgerran (including its castle), Emlyn Is Cuch and Dyffryn Breuan; but when Jasper Tudor's creation as earl of Pembroke was confirmed in March 1453, the lordships were surrendered to the new earl (*CFR, 1445–52*, pp.183, 197; *RP*, V, 253). The formal cancellation of the grant that included Gruffydd ap Nicholas was made on 25 February 1454, and duly enrolled 'In memoranda scaccarii inter Recorda de termino Hilarii' of 1454, according to an early-seventeenth-century note (CRO, Dynevor, Add.73). This refers to PRO, E159/230, *adhuc recorda*, Hilary, m.46*d*., which is doubtless the source of the report in the Life. See Griffiths, *NLWJ*, XIII, no.3 (1964), 260; *WHR*, II (1964–5), 215, 218.

[20] Gruffydd may have sought refuge in Buckingham's lordship of Brecon in 1454: ibid., p.219. See Griffiths and Thomas, *Making of the Tudor Dynasty*: Sir Rhys ap Thomas passed through the lordship of Brecon on his way to join Henry Tudor near Welshpool (p.148).

laws which he had soe often infring'd and broken, bobbing them from time to time, with a *non est inventus* [he was not found]; butt what could they otherwise expect in those tymes, when lawes lay asleepe, and all things weare adjudged by the sword, the care of the commonwelth being lay'd aside, and justice and equitie clearlie exiled?[21] This Griffith ap Nicholas knewe right well, being contented to lett both factions shuffle among themselves for a while and to stand himself as neuter, or if at anie time he appear'd, t'was doubtful, and to be taken with eyther hand; sometimes favouring the on partie, sometimes the other, *prout invaluissent* [as they might prevail]. His chiefe spleene was towardes the English, in generall, to whom he ever boare an implacable hate, and they noe lesse to him, which howe lightlie he valued, may appeare by these verses ensuing –

> Ni chryn hwn ni chryna y hâd
> Ni thorir wneythuriad,
> Ni fflyg i'r fais briwdrais bren,
> Ni ddiwraidd mwy na'r dderwen.[22]

> [He will not wither, his stock will not wither,
> His substance will endure,
> He will not bend over to the ground,
> A tree amid shattering violence,
> He will not be uprooted any more than the oak.]

Nowe, this violent bent of Griffith ap Nicholas's inclination being discovered, there wanted not instrumentes among the Welch, to spurr him on in the way of revenge, perswading him the times were nowe fitt and seasonable for such a purpose. Whereupon divers of them building upon his countenance and protection, made somewhat bold with those of the marches (a usuall thing betweene the Scotts and English in the borders upon the like disturbances), robbing and stealing from them their cattle, and what else they could lay handes on, to the greate detriment, losse, and endamagement of those neighbouring counties, which Griffith ap Nicholas, from time to time, passed over and tooke noe notice off.[23] Manie complaintes weare made, butt noe redresse. At

---

[21] Examples abound of his contempt for law, justice and royal commissions: Griffiths, *NLWJ*, XIII, no.3 (1964), 260–4, and *WHR*, II (1964–5), 215, 218–24; see above pp.15ff.

[22] The *CR* editor adds a note: 'Howel David ap Ievan ap Rys ai Kant'. For the poem, addressed by Hywel (*fl. c.*1450–80) to Gruffydd ap Nicholas, see *Mynegai*, p.1600; E. R. Ll. Davies, thesis cited, pp.70–2:

> Ni chrin hwn, ni chrina'i nad,
> Ni thorrir ei wneuthuriad.

This simplistic view of Gruffydd's anti-Englishness derives from prophetic poetry.

[23] This may refer to maintenance by Gruffydd of such as Philip ap Hywel of Knucklas in the Marcher lordship of Maelienydd: see below p.166. For the context of tension between English counties and the March, see Griffiths, 'Wales and the March', especially pp.154–5

length commissioners (the chiefest whereof, as I am told, was the Lord Whittney) were sent into Wales to examine thes abuses.[24] Coming to Lanandiffry,[25] a towne twentie mile distant from Carmarthen, Griffith ap Nicholas, (for soe goes the tale, which I the rather sett downe, because I have heard the same sweetned in the relation by that greate light and ornament of our church, Andrews, Bishop of Winchester, at his owne table; a man much given to the studie of the British tongue in his later dayes, and soe (perchance) by way of discourse with some of that Countrie, might catch up this tradition)[26] Griffith ap Nicholas, I say, having notice thereof, mett them a mile or two beyond, upon the top of a hill, having foure or five in his companie raggedlie attired, and poorelier hors'd, leaving the rest of his trayne at distance to follow him, and to be ever readie at his beck and call upon occasion. In the meane while he salutes the Commissioners, makes himself knowne unto them, and withall desires to attend them for their better guidance and conduction to the end of their journey. The Lord Whittney hearing his name, and glad (as he thought) to have him in his toyle, whom he thought would play lest in sight, yet observing the poorness of his condition, and howe beggarlie he was attended, it would not sinke into the Lord Whittney's head, that this was that greate Nicholas, soe much fam'd at court for the extraordinarie power and authoritie he had in his owne countrie, but rather some excursor or boote hailer, in those unquiett times, flying abroad for pray; or at the best but some scoutes, or espialls, sent out to discover his approach, and soe to give notice to malefactors to stand aloofe. Well, on they goe till they came to Abermarlais Castle,[27] and there all those doubtes and feares were dispelled, and the trewe Griffith ap Nicholas discovered; for Thomas ap Griffith the younger,[28] a stout and hardie gentleman, meeting his Father in that place, with a hundred tall men bravelie mounted, descended there from his horse, and kissed his father's stirrop, and desir'd to receive his commaundes, which the

[24] W. Spurrel, *Carmarthen and its Neighbourhood* (2nd edn., Carmarthen, 1879), p.112, attributes the incident to 1441, when Stephen Gruffydd was mayor of Carmarthen, as he was in 1440–1 (PRO, SC6/1168/1 m.ld); if this is correct, Sir Robert Whitney of Herefordshire (died 1443) was probably the commissioner. On the other hand, H. Melville, *The Ancestry of John Whitney* (New York, 1896), pp.89–96, dates it to *c.*1454, with Sir Robert's son, Eustace, as the commissioner, though he was never knighted (J. S. Roskell, *The Commons in the Parliament of 1422* (Manchester, 1954), pp.236–7). See Griffiths, *NLWJ*, XIII, no.3 (1964), 261–2.

[25] I.e., Llandovery.

[26] Lancelot Andrewes (1555–1626), bishop of Winchester (1618–26) and a noted scholar, had an extraordinary flair for languages – six ancient and fifteen modern, of which Welsh may have been one. He knew William Camden and the Welsh prelates, Gabriel and Gordon Goodman, and was also prominent at James I's court; the connection with the Rices may have been made in this circle. *DNB*, s.n.; P. A. Welsby, *Lancelot Andrewes, 1555–1626* (London, 1958), p.12.

[27] Abermarlais is better described as a fortified manor house, enlarged by Sir Rhys ap Thomas, whose mother Elizabeth was the heiress of Sir John Griffith, its owner. Thomas and Elizabeth may have been married by 1440–1. Jones, *Historic Carms. Homes*, pp.3–4; see above n.5.

[28] This may be an error for Gruffydd's youngest son, John: Griffiths, *Principality of Wales*, p.253; see below p.171 n.1.

Lord Whittney perceaving, newe doubtes and jealousies began to tumble in his braines; for, thought he, if Griffith ap Nicholas appeares thus in a hostile manner unto us, with multitudes of men prepar'd and fitted as for the field, itt is not likelie he will obey our commission, or stand at all to the triall of justice, unlesse he be innocent. They had nott gon above five miles further in their way, to a house of his call'd Newton,[29] but Owen ap Griffith the second sonne saluted them in a farr braver equipage, having two hundred horse attending, well mann'd, well arm'd. This Owen had much of his father's craft and subtiltie in him; he was bold besides, and active; he could, like the Cameleon, or Proteus-like, take all shapes, turne himself into all colours; an excellent artizan in discovering men's secretts, and observing their dispositions; the commissioners had not rested themselves above an hour or two, but he had div'd so farr into their counsells as gave him assurance his father was the cheefe man shott at in that commission, a thing they were ignorant off before.[30] Whereupon consultation was taken for to steale away his commission, which this Owen undertooke, and performed accordinglie. To Carmarthen at last they came, where in their way at Abergwilly,[31] a small village, some mile this side the towne. Thomas ap Griffith the elder,[32] a man of a sweete, mild and gentle disposition, presentes his services first to his father, and then to the commissioners: he had five hundred tall men following him, and they well disciplin'd, whom before in good order on foote he leades, even till they came to the commissioner's lodging, and there Griffith ap Nicholas left them for that night, commaunding his three sonnes to attend them at supper, and to see them fairlie entreated. And nowe the Lord Whittney, and the rest, could have wished themselves safe at home, and their commission at an end, which they had little hope to execute among soe manie violentlie bent (as they thought) for his defence and safeguard; yet fearing lest he should give them the slipp, they send for the maior and Sheriffes, to whom they shewe their commission, requiring them, by vertue thereof, to be their assistant in the attaching of Griffith ap Nicholas, which they promised to obey, appointing the next morning for the fittest season. Nowe you must knowe after the Lord Whittney had read his commission

[29] It is not known when Gruffydd moved from Crug, his father's home near Dinefwr Castle and the borough of Newton, to the fortified manor house of Newton on the site of the present mansion. It may have been soon after he became approver of the royal demesnes at Dinefwr in 1425: Griffiths, *NLWJ*, XIII, no.3 (1964), 257.
[30] For Owen, the younger son of Mabli, Gruffydd's first wife, see ibid., and Griffiths, *WHR*, II (1964–5), 213–31 *passim*.
[31] The *CR* editor adds a note: 'Abergwilly is about the distance of a mile from Carmarthen, where the Bishop of St Davids has his palace, the only habitable episcopal residence now belonging to that See, which once could boast of seven, some of which were truly magnificent, such as that at St Davids, Llawhaden Castle, and Lamphey, all three in Pembrokeshire.' If Henry Rice were composing the Life at Newton, Abergwili would indeed be 'this side of the towne' of Carmarthen.
[32] For Thomas, Gruffydd's eldest son by his first wife Mabli, see Griffiths, *NLWJ*, XIII, no. 3 (1964), 256–68; *WHR*, II (1964–5), 213–31; and *Principality of Wales*, pp.154–5.

to the maior, he clap'd the same up in the sleeve of his cloake, which one of the sheriffes discover'd to Owen ap Griffith; Owen by this time had his desires, to be brief, to supper they goe, where the commissioners were soe well liquor'd, that for that night they forgott quite the errand they came for, by which meanes Owen ap Griffith had a fitt opportunitie cleanlie to ridd them of their commission, of which he gave his father present notice. The next morning the commissioners, the maior and sheriffes goe to the Shire Hall, wheather they sent for Griffith ap Nicholas, whom at his coming they arrested in the king's name, framing certain accusations against him, to which hee was presentlie to answeare. Griffith ap Nicholas, after he had made his obeysance, humbly desir'd his lordship to procede against him in a faire and a legall way, and that his commission mought be publicklie read, otherwise he held himself nott bound to stand to the arrest, or to make anie answere to the charge. Reason good, said the Lord Whitttney, and you shall both see it and heare it read, and soe putting his hand in the sleeve of his cloak for the commission, he found that there t'was nott to be found, neyther did anie of his fellowes or followers knowe what was become of it, or whom they might charge. At length they had noe excuse to make but to cap the miscarriage upon the neglect of servantes. Whereat Griffith ap Nicholas startes up in a furie, clapping his hatt upon his head, and looking about upon his sonnes and friendes: what says he, have we cozeners and cheaters come hither to abuse the kinge's majesty's power, and to disquiet his true harted subjects? then turning about to the commissioners, he rappes out a greate oath, and sayes, ere the next day were at an end, he would hang them up all for traytours and impostors, and soe commaundes handes to be layd on them and to carrie them to prison. The commissioners fearing he would be as good as his word, fell to entreate for pardon, and to desire they might eyther returne or send to court for a true certificate of this their employment: but nothing would serve the turne, unless the Lord Whittney would be bound by oath, to putt on Griffith ap Nicholas's blew coate, and weare his cognizance, and soe goe up to the king, to acknowledge his owne offences, and to justifie the sayd Griffith's proceedings; which (to preserve himself from danger) he willinglie undertooke, and accordingly performed. What was the issue of this greate affront, or howe digested by the state, I could never learne, onlie 'tis to be imagined that it was hush'd up and smothered, as fearing, in thos wavering and tottring times, to procede in a rough and harsh way with on soe potent among the Welch, as this man was. As the quarrell increased dailie betweene the two royall houses, soe did we in each parte of this kingdome increase in disorders, and in Wales they were busie still with their neighbours in the marches. On a time Roger Corbet, Walter Honton, Ralph Lee, and others of prime marke and note in the countie of Salop, made greate complaint against one Philipp ap

Howell, of Knokelas, within the lordship of Molenith, in the marches of Wales, for divers damages and losses that countrie sustayned by the sayd Philipp, and noe justice could be had against him, for that Griffith ap Nicholas did receave, maintaine and comfort, and cherish him from time to time, to the greate derogation and losse of the king's liege people dwelling within the sayd countie, whereupon they were both found guiltie of felonie, as appears by an indictment[33] taken at Salop before William Borley, Thomas Corbet, and others, justices assigned by the king for the keeping of the peace in the said countie.[34] Griffith ap Nicholas, like another Sertorius, *inopinatis casibus semper audax et intrepidus*[in unexpected circumstances always courageous and intrepid],[35] was nothing at all *amated* with the report of these rigorouse proceedings, butt, standing upon his guard, falls to newe counsells, and resolves to stand noe longer neuter, but directlie and resolutelie to thrust himself into the Yorkish cause, and therefore the better liked of his friendes and followers, making his fortune common with their's, both in the danger and honour of the attempt. And nowe thrusting himself into dangers, he, in the first place, makes meanes to be reconciled to Richard, Duke of York, betweene whom and himselfe (as you have heard before) there had passed manie passages of unkindnesse; offering him his service and assistance in the regaining of his right, which was willinglie embraced, and thankfullie accepted by the said duke, in whose good graces from that time forward Griffith ap Nicholas held a principle regard.[36] That being donn, he foorthwith acquaintes his friendes with his determinations, putts himself into armes, furnishing with men,

---

[33] The *CR* editor adds a note: 'See the Crown Office, anno 32. Hen.VI.' Even though the indictment before the Shropshire JPs has not been located (PRO, KB9/271 is fragmentary), for verification of this reported incident (1454), see Griffiths, *WHR*, II (1964–5), 219–20. Philip ap Hywel ap Rhys, of Knucklas in the lordship of Maelienydd, having failed to obey the sheriff of Shropshire's order, was instructed to appear before the court of King's Bench early in 1454 for stealing six cows at Ledbury and driving them across the border to Knucklas on 25 June 1453; Gruffydd ap Nicholas was accused of harbouring him after 1 August 1453 at both Ledbury and Carmarthen. An early-seventeenth-century transcript of the indictment, and its endorsement to the effect that Thomas Horde, one of the JPs, presented the indictment at Westminster on 28 January 1454, is in CRO, Dynevor, Add.73 (surely the source of the report in the Life); and another transcript is NLW, Dynevor, A 99(a). The record of the ensuing trial in King's Bench is PRO, KB27/771 *rex* m.23d. The alleged complainants may be identified with Roger Corbet (died 1467) of Moreton-Corbet and Culseys (Salop), a former MP for Salop; his wife's brother, Walter Hopton of Brome (Salop), one of the duke of York's officers in his nearby Marcher lordships of Montgomery, Chirbury, Ceri and Cydewain; and Ralph Lee of Cheshire, escheator of Merioneth from 1437 to 1469. Wedgwood, *HP*, pp.22–3; Johnson, *Richard of York*, pp.84 n.35, 233; *CPR, 1435–41*, p.34; *1441–6*, pp.22–3. Corbets and Hoptons had their own reasons for wishing to embarrass Gruffydd ap Nicholas: see above pp.18, 24, 112.

[34] William Burley and Thomas Corbet were among JPs appointed for Shropshire on 17 December 1453 and 1 March 1454. *CPR, 1452–61*, pp.675–6.

[35] Sertorius was a heroic rebel general in Spain in the first century BC. Plutarch's Life has many allusions to his bravery.

[36] This is an oversimplification of Gruffydd's attitudes to the king and York from 1454: Griffiths, *WHR*, II (1964–5), 222ff.

monie, and ammunition, and soe ever after (as it was observed) the Lancastrian partie declined, and fell off in thos partes. Going on a time to Hereford to buy necessaries for the warres, he was there, by some accident or other, taken and apprehended, having (as the record saith[37]) about him *quingentas marcas in pecunia numerata in quadam boga contenta* [500 marks in cash contained in a certain bag], which the eschetor, by virtue of his office, seazed upon as forfeited to the king, *quia positus fuit in exigens pro quibusdam feloniis unde in comitatu Salop indictatus fuit coram dicto domino rege, etc.* [because he was placed in custody for certain felonies of which he was indicted in Shropshire *coram rege*, etc.]. Notwithstanding, all this while the officers were busie about his purse, his person was shifted away eyther by the helpe (as some doe report) of Sir John Scudamore[38] his sonn in lawe, a powerfull man in those partes, whoe there gave him the meeting, or else by some prompt and readie wile of his owne, being a man ever *qui in periculis imminentibus praesentis consilii imaginem prae se ferebat* [who in threatening dangers offered the appearance of instant counsel]; and soe somewhat like Mr Flea, the Frenchman,[39] quickly skipping into dangers, and as soone skipping oute againe, being full of quiddities and subtile knackes, not usuallie knowne; which often kept and saved him from destruction. When he was free of troubles, and among his companions, he was verie pleasaunt and merie, and full of wittie conceiptes, an excellent poete, there being manie fine peeces of his yet extant.[40] In the times of his privacie and retiredness he was full of devotion, and a sincere follower of religious preceptes, which his poete intimates in the ensuing verses; saying,

[37] The *CR* editor adds a note: 'Vid. Inq. capt. coram Edmundo Delamare escaetore dni. regis. Anno. 33 Hen. Sexti in Scacc. remanent ac in custodia rememb. regis exist.' Although the record of this inquisition has not been located, Edmund de la Mare's enrolled financial account as escheator for 1453–4 notes the 500 marks seized from Gruffydd at Hereford on 16 August 1454 because of certain felonies of which he had been indicted in Shropshire (PRO, E357/44 m.69*d*, from which the Latin quotations are taken). Griffiths, *WHR*, II (1964–5), 220 n.28; see above p.167 and n.33.

[38] The *CR* editor adds a note: 'Mawd, daughter of Griffith ap Nicholas, by his second wife (who was a daughter of Sir John Perrot, of Pembrokeshire), was married to Scudamore, of Kentchurch in Herefordshire.' The marriage is substantiated by CRO, Dynevor, Add.73. His daughter's name was Maud: *DWB*, p.907.

[39] This is an elusive allusion, but it may be based in part on Peter Woodhouse, *Democritus his Dreame, or The Contention between the Elephant and the Flea* (1605), ed. A. B. Grosart (Manchester, 1877), which stresses the superiority of activity over size and bulk, and the nimbleness of the flea. Although Frenchmen were frequently the subject of contemporary satire, 'Mr Flea the Frenchman' does not figure in T. L. Berger and W. C. Bradford jnr., *An Index of Characters in English Printed Drama to the Restoration* (Englewood, Colorado, 1975).

[40] For Gruffydd's doubtful reputation as a poet himself, see *DWB*, pp.313–14, s.n. Gruffydd Benrhaw. On the other hand, Gruffydd's patronage of the Carmarthen (or Newton) eisteddfod is well attested (G. J. Williams, 'Eisteddfod Caerfyrddin', *Y Llenor*, V (1926), 94–102, based on NLW, Peniarth MS 158 (1587, placing the festival at Newton) and 267 (1636, placing it at Carmarthen)). D. J. Bowen, 'Dafydd ab Edmwnt ac Eisteddfod Caerfyrddin', *Barn*, rh.142 (Awst 1974), 441–8, dates it *c*.1450, quoting contemporary references in Lewys Môn's and Gutun Owain's poetry to an eisteddfod at Carmarthen.

Dy Wên yw pump Llawenydd
Dy galon yw ffynon ffydd.[41]

[Your smile is the five joys (of Mary),
Your heart is the fountain of faith.]

Soe as we may trewlie say of him, as was said of Licinius Mucianus, that he was *bonis malisque artibus mixtus* [a mixture of good and evil skills].[42] When Richard, the valiant Duke of Yorke, receaved that fatall overthrowe at the battle of Wakefield, his eldest sonne, the Earle of March, lay at Gloucester, who, presentlie upon notice of his father's death, invites his friendes in the Marches, and divers others further in Wales, to come in his ayde to revenge his father's murder. He was not long a raysing an armie of three or four and twentie thousand, soe much in those partes did they favour the lineage of the Lord Mortimer.[43] Among the manie that resorted unto him Griffith ap Nicholas was of most eminent note, having seaven or eight hundred men following of him, well armed, well ordered, goodlie of stature, and hartes answerable thereunto. The Earle of March his designe was to have mett and encountered with the Queene, and his father's murderers in the field, butt Jasper, Earle of Pembrocke, stood as a block in his way, who for his honour's sake at that time had binn better emploied elsewhere, although this proved somewhat crosse to the Earle of March his purposes, yett Griffith ap Nicholas was much joyed thereat, hoping nowe to be fullie revenged of the Earle of Pembrocke for old displeasure. To be briefe, both armies meete on a plain neere Mortimer's Crosse, after large demonstrations of prowesse, and magnanimitie of eyther side, Griffith ap Nicholas receaves a mortall wound. Owen ap Griffith, his second sonne (the eldest being left at home to secure his owne fortunes), standes in the head of his father's troopes, maintaines the fight, and pursues the Earle of Pembrocke even to flight; soe the day fell to the Yorkish side. Then Owen ap Griffith making search for his father, found him lying on the ground panting and breathing for life, to whome he made a short relation of the Earle of March his good fortunes, and his enemies

---

[41] The *CR* editor adds a note: 'Gwillim ap Ievan hen ai kant.' But the same couplet, with a very trifling variation, occurs in a *cywydd* of Dafydd ap Gwilym:

Dy Wen yw'r pum llawenydd
Dy gorph hardd amdwg o'r ffydd

For the quotation from Gwilym's ode to Gruffydd, see A. E. Davies, thesis cited, II, 198–9, ll.45–6. As to the alleged Dafydd ap Gwilym poem, Thomas Parry (ed.), *Gwaith Dafydd ap Gwilym* (Cardiff, 1952), p.clxxxv, was inclined to attribute it to Robin Ddu, though Ifor Williams had earlier published it in *Cywyddau Dafydd ap Gwilym a'i Gyfoeswyr* (2nd edn., Cardiff, 1935), pp.32–3.

[42] Licinius Mucianus, governor of Syria in the first century AD, was a nobleman who combined nobility and generalship with lack of ambition and self-effacement. Lemprière, p.331; M. Cary (and A. H. Scullard), *A History of Rome* (3rd edn., London, 1975), p.407.

[43] G. Hodges, *Ludford Bridge and Mortimer's Cross* (Logaston, Herefs., 1989), puts Edward's army more credibly at about 2,000 (p.45).

overthrowe. 'Well then', said he, 'wellcome death, since honour and victorie makes for us'; and soe shaking off his clogge of earth, he soared up in a divine contemplation to Heaven, the place of his rest. And this is more than ever came to the knowledge of Hollingshed, Hall, Grafton, and others, *ejusdem furfures* [of the same ilk].[44]

---

[44] Gruffydd ap Nicholas's presence at Mortimer's Cross seems unlikely (Griffiths, *WHR*, II (1964–5), 227–8). However, two of his sons (including probably Owen) are thought to have fought on Jasper Tudor's side (Evans, *Wales and the Wars of the Roses*, pp.124–30). It is not surprising that Henry Rice should admit that he could find nothing in Tudor chronicles about Gruffydd's death at the battle, implying a certain scepticism on his part.

3

Thomas ap Gruffydd ap Nicholas

(1) *Thomas ap Griffith, eldest Sonne to Griffith ap Nicholas, and Father to Sir Rice ap Thomas, leaves his country and goes to Burgundie, being noe way naturallie enclin'd to civill dissentions. His adventures there, his excellent skill in Monomachie, or single fight. His Death.* (2) *How Morgan Thomas, his eldest Sonne, siding with the house of York, layd siege to the Castle of Pembrocke, and howe David Thomas, his second Sonne, taking part with the House of Lankester, relieved the same; rescuing the Earle of Pembrocke, and the young Earle of Richmond out of his brother's handes, and safelie enshipping them for Britainy. Their Death.*

(1). After the death of Griffith ap Nicholas succeeded Thomas ap Griffith his sonne,[1] heire of his father's fortunes, though somewhat differenced in their qualities and conditions. Both of them were endued with virtues, as well begetting admiration as affection; yet in a severall way of proceeding, the one being sharpe, sterne, and severe, the other milde, sweete, and gracious, the father climing into the hartes and affections of the people, with a majestique authoritie, the sonne endeering and ingraciating himself by that ever humble, yet safe way, of affability and curtesie. This gentleman had the generall applause of all for horseman-shipp, and for true skill at his weapon, he was inferior to none: being commonlie call'd the *Faire Man at Armes*. In his owne inclination he was verie much retir'd, full of thoughts, and ever meditating alone, or conversing with those might best informe his conscience. For matter of lerning he was nott altogether unfurnished; soe that considering those ruder times, he may well passe for a scholler. In the composure of his

---

[1] The *CR* editor adds a note; 'Thomas ap Griffith (*Hynaf*, as he was called), for he had another son of the same name, by his second wife, was the eldest son of Griffith ap Nicholas, by Mably, daughter of Meredith ap Henry Donne of Kidwely, in Caermarthenshire.' Thomas's parentage is well attested, but the existence of a younger Thomas (rather than John), born of Margaret Perrot, is mentioned in some pedigrees but not in others. Bartrum, *300–1400*, II, 330; *1400–1500*, IV, 642; CRO, Dynevor, Add. 112 and 73; see above p.164.

limmes verie strong and active; and a soldier he was indeede, having binn train'd up for manie yeares, wherein, at that time, both for commaunderie, and civill education, he had some advantage of the rest of his family, under two of the most flourishing princes of Christendome in thos days; Philipp the Good and Charles the Worlick, father and sonne, both Dukes of Burgundie,[2] performing there such deedes of chivalrie, as purchas'd him the fame of a Captaine that knew how to doe his worke, and did itt.[3] This Thomas ap Griffith could at noe hand away with the fractures and hurlements then in the state, calling it an unnaturall sway, where the father fought against the sonne, the brother against the brother, the servant against his master, and the subject against his sovereigne, he being otherwise composed by nature and education, and ever wishing peace. Nowe to stand as neuter, and in times of civill uprores be only a looker on, that he dislik'd as much on the other side, holding it noe way suitable with his reputation; ne yet with his safetie soe to do. These considerations drewe him into transmarine partes, there to seeke adventures, serving (as I said before) for manie yeares in the Burgundian Warres,[4] having left be hind him, to manage his affaires in his absence, two of his sonnes, Morgan and David, two men the fittest in all the world, to fish in troubled waters, of whom I may well say, as Tacitus said of Agrippa Posthumus, that they were trulie *bonarum artium rudes et robore corporum stolide feroces, nullius tamen flagitii comperti* [guiltless of virtue and confident brute-like in their physical strength, yet had been convicted of no open scandal].[5] Nowe during the time of his being abroad, there befell him a sudden accident, which forc'd him to looke homewards, otherwise, noe doubt, he would have followed the fortunes of those three memorable Battayles of Grauson, Morat and Nancie, and there have concluded his days, rather then

[2] R. Vaughan, *Philip the Good* (London, 1970), and *Charles the Bold* (London, 1973). Philip died in 1467, Charles in 1477.

[3] There is apparently no trace of him among the surviving Burgundian archives. The 'Thomas, maistre bombardier anglois', who was paid 72 livres on 31 January 1477 for services to the duke of Burgundy at the siege of Nancy and elsewhere is unlikely to be Thomas ap Gruffydd ap Nicholas, Archives Départementales du Nord, Lille, recette générale, B2106 no. 67754. On the other hand, Gwilym ab Ieuan Hen's contemporary ode to Thomas associates him with Burgundy: 'Heb satyn Burgwyn ynghylch pargod – f'ais' [Without Burgundy satin around the eaves of my heart]: A. E. Davies, thesis cited, II, 209–10, 1.3.

[4] He and his brother Owain garrisoned Carreg Cennen Castle for Henry VI in 1461–2, but after it was captured by Sir Richard Herbert, his only official position was as farmer of the castles and towns of Dinefwr (1462–5) and Dryslwyn (1464–5). He may have gone abroad *c.*1465. Griffiths, *WHR*, II (1964–5), 229; idem, *Principality of Wales*, pp. 206, 253. There seems to have been Burgundian support for Lancastrian landings in Wales in the early 1460s, and one of these unsuccessful raids may have been the occasion when Thomas fled: Evans, *Wales and the Wars of the Roses*, p.145.

[5] According to CRO, Dynevor, Add.75, Thomas had five sons, Morgan, Jenkin (or John), Henry, David and Rhys, and a daughter Margaret. John may have been illegitimate: ibid., 112. But Bartrum, *1400–1500*, IV, 643, credits him with twelve sons (six of them illegitimate) and eight daughters (three illegitimate). For the quotation, see Tacitus, *Annals*, I, 3: *rudem sane bonarum artium et robore corporis stolide ferocem, nullius tamen flagitii conpertum.*

return'd into England;[6] when all thinges weare in the hight of disorder, and in a way soe averse, soe diametrically repugnant to his nature. It happen'd while he resided in the duke's court, there fell a liking betweene him and a neare kingswoman of the Duke's (Cupid, it seemes clayming an interest in him as well as Mars), from liking it grewe to a familiaritie, and what followed, that we may easilie guesse. He being a personable gentlemen, well spoken, and on who was his crafts-master in winning of women's favour: in somme among others, he wonn this Ladies good graces, which, in the end, she was pleased, *quinta parte suae suavitatis sui nectaris imbuere* [to imbue with the quintessence of her own sweetness], and than 'twas high time to be gonn.[7] This gentlewoman (as I find in the collection of one Perrot, of Herefordshire),[8] was daughter to Francis, second sonn to Philip, Duke of Burgundie; but (for ought I can read) that duke had butt one legitimate sonn, which was the Earle of Charolois, and therefore this must needes be a *Latene*,[9] if at all. Perrott likewise says, she was one of the Maides of Honour to Queene Katherin, in her later time, who was Dowager to Henrie the Fifth.[10] Others (and among them one Thomas Johns, of Fountaine Gate, a knowne herauld), will have her to be one of the duke's owne daughters.[11] To satisfie my

---

[6] I.e., the battles of Grandson (2 March 1476) and Nancy (5 January 1477). 'Morat' probably refers to the battle of Murten (22 June 1476) rather than that of Moret (August 1465). This suggests a return to Wales before 1476.

[7] The *CR* editor adds a note: 'In most of the pedigrees I have seen of this family, Thomas ap Griffith's second wife is call'd Elizabeth, daughter of James De Burgoigne, second son of Philip, Duke of Burgundy, whom he married by a dispensation from the Pope, his first wife living, by whom he had one son John, and from whom Thomas Johnes, Esq. of Hafod in Cardiganshire is descended.

Thomas ap Griffith's first wife was a daughter of Sir John Griffith, of Abermarlais in Carmarthenshire.'

Duke Philip had one surviving legitimate son, his heir Charles. For his ample (if often exaggerated) supply of bastards, see Vaughan, *Philip the Good*, pp. 132–5; J.-J. de Smet (ed.), *Recueil des Antiquités de Flandre par le Président Ph. Wielant* (Recueil des Chroniques de Flandre, vol.IV, Brussels, 1865), pp.78–81. Although S. R. Meyrick, *The History and Antiquities of the County of Cardigan* (Brecon, 1907), pp. 290–3, offers a pedigree in which Thomas Johnes descends from Thomas ap Gruffydd ap Nicholas and his alleged second wife, Elizabeth, daughter of Francis, the duke of Burgundy's brother, this connection cannot be unequivocally established. Henry Rice's scepticism is commendable. For the Latin quotation, see Horace, *Odes*, I, 13.16: *quinta parte sui nectaris imbuit*.

[8] 'Perrot of Herefordshire' may be Robert Perrot esquire, of Morton-on-Lugg, near Hereford, and his 'collection' may refer to Lewys Dwnn's handiwork. Bartrum, *1400–1500*, IV, 643, records the suggestions (mainly from Lewys Dwnn) of a Burgundian match, producing a son John. Such a romantic story may have a germ of truth in it, to judge by the number of Thomas's bastards, but it was also doubtless congenial to Walter Rice in Dwnn's day to popularize the story.

[9] I.e., concealed or hidden; see above nn.7, 8.

[10] The *CR* editor adds a note: 'It was her sister Margaret, who came into England in that capacity, and was married to Sir Hugh Lutterel of Dunster Castle, in Devonshire' (*recte* Somerset). The connection with Catherine of Valois (died 1437) seems unlikely, and no Luttrell married a Burgundian; Sir Hugh (died 1428) married Catherine, daughter of Sir John Beaumont of Devon. Maxwell-Lyte, *History of Dunster*, I, 104–5 (and pp.114, 120–2, for later Luttrells).

[11] See above p.139. A pedigree made by Thomas Jones which notes the Burgundian marriage is not known, but CRO, Dynevor, Add.73, notes that Thomas ap Gruffydd married a daughter of Francis, second son of the duke of Burgundy, and that she was maid of honour to Catherine of

owne curiositie in this point, I have looked over divers of the Burgundian writers, and cann receave noe light; onlie Pontus Heuterus Delphicus, who writt the lives of those later dukes, and Reusnerius,[12] out of him produce a catalogue of the duke's illegitimate children, and there they say, *quod Philippus bonus Burgundiae Dux quatuor habuit filias illegitimas anonymas quarum una nupsit apud Britones* [that Philip the Good, duke of Burgundy, had four illegitimate daughters, names unknown, one of whom married a Briton], where I beleeve they harpe and guess somewhat at this businesse. Nowe upon this occasion Thomas ap Griffith returning home both from his martiall and venereall affaires, he did nott long enjoy anie true peace or contentment there, being presentlie engaged in feudes, and divers single combates, which he ever perform'd on horsebacke, an exercise in those days, wherein he was singular, and ever victorious. The first that provoked him in duell, was Henrie ap Gwilim of Court-Henrie,[13] a gentleman of an ancient linage, welthie and full of magnanimitie and courage, one who, in the height of stature and proceritie of his bodie, had as much advantage of him as the proud Pautaucus had of the valiant Pyrrhus.[14] Thomas ap Griffith was a man of a well regulated valour, better skill'd at his weapon, and ever warie in his proceedings, the other had an invincible spiritt, but withall temerarious, rash, and headie. I cannott think of Thomas ap Griffith, but suddenlie Fabius Maximus comes into my mind, and soe doth L. Minutius, when I thinke of Henrie ap Gwilim.[15] Eight or ten times did they drawe their swordes each against the other in single fight, wherein Thomas ap Griffith was ever conqueror; but the other would

Valois; a more modern pedigree refers to her as Elizabeth, daughter of James, second son of the duke. This Dynevor Pedigree Book may be based on the researches of Thomas Jones in the early seventeenth century.

[12] Pontus Heuterus Delfius, *Rerum Burgundicarum Libri Sex* (Antwerp, 1584), p.153 (and *Libri sexti*, [Antwerp, 1583] p.67), notes that one of Duke Philip's illegitimate daughters married an English lord (with the quotation ibid., p.67), but of course another among his at least five illegitimate daughters could have had a liaison with Thomas ap Gruffydd. This seems to be the source for Elias Reusnerus, *Genealogia Imperatorum, Regum, Principum, Comitum, Baronum et Dynasticarum Germanorum* . . . (Frankfurt, 1612), pp.332–3 (with the same quotation on p. 333). Elias Reusnerus was a German historian whose works were published in Germany from the 1570s onwards.

[13] The *CR* editor adds a note: 'Henry ap Gwilim built Court Henry in Carmarthenshire, which was call'd after his name, his family having lived before at a place in that neighbourhood, called Lanlash, he left two daughters, one of whom married Sir Rice ap Thomas, and the other Sir William Mathews, Knt.' For Llanlais (Llangathen) and Court Henry, see Jones, *Historic Carms. Homes*, pp. 42–3, 96. Henry's pedigree and the association with Llangathen are in Bartrum, *300–1400*, II, 405.

[14] Henry ap Gwilym had been associated with Thomas ap Gruffydd ap Nicholas as farmers of Dryslwyn Castle and town in 1464–5; he evidently accommodated himself to Yorkist rule (hence perhaps the subsequent hostility between the two men) but the two families grew closer later when Henry's daughter Efa married Thomas's son Rhys: Griffiths, *Principality of Wales*, pp. 265–6; see below p.187. The battle of equals between Pyrrhus and Pautauchus is related in Plutarch's Life of Pyrrhus, ch. VII.

[15] Fabius Maximus was Roman general and dictator during the second Punic War. See Plutarch's Life, chs.Vff., for examples of tension with L. Minucius.

never be conquered. Henrie ap Gwilim, presuming, fall after fall, of a reparation, would still be a challenging, therein shewing a rise of courage in the declination of fortune. Thomas ap Griffith trusting to his skill and cunning, and soe forgetting the true rules of wisedome, would still be as nimble in his answeare, as the other in his objection; whereby he transgress'd that discrete lawe, made to the purpose by Lycurgus, wherein he adviseth, *ut non saepius cum eodem Hoste congrederemur, ne bellicosior fieret* [that we should not often confront the same enemy, lest he become more warlike], which in the end he found true by the experience of manie a broken pate.[16] Once coming home grievouslie hurt, his brother Owen mett him, and desirous to know the cause of his woundes; in good faith, saith he, I have binn at cuffes with my old adversarie, who hath given me a bloodie nose; well, are you appas'd, and I would twear worse with you, said his brother, for teaching him to outskill you at your owne weapon, an answeare not unlike to that of Antaludas to Agesilaus returning home well beaten by the Boeotians, with whom he had often bicker'd, *digna* (said he) *institutionis praemia capis, qui Boeotios ex ignavis pugnaces reddidisti*[17] [you reap the reward worthy of the manner, you who have turned the Boeotians from cowards into brave men]. At another time there fell out some difference, betweene Thomas ap Griffith, and William the First, Earl of Pembrock, of the noble Family of the Herberts; but for what cause I cannot learne; and it seemes they were flowne to such high termes, that one Turberville would needes combate Thomas ap Griffith, on the Earle's behalf.[18] This Turberville was an arrogant cracker, and a notable Swash-buckler, one that would fight on anie slight occasion, nott much heeding the cause. He, on a time, sends his cartel, or letter of defiance to the said Thomas, with the rodo-mantade, that if he did nott suddenlie doe him reason, he would ferret him out of his cunnie berrie, the castle of Abermarlais.[19] Thomas ap Griffith smiled at the message, and shaping him an answeare, suitable to his humour, that for his parte, he knew him nott, neyther had he ever cause for quarrelling him; and therefore pray'd him that, if he had a desire to be kill'd, he would make choice of some other, rather than

---

[16] Lycurgus, the legendary legislator of Sparta, was noted for the wisdom of his precepts. Little is really known about him; but see Plutarch's Life, ch.XIII, for this, the third of his laws, illustrated with reference to King Agesilaus's repeated attacks on the Boeotians (n.17 below).

[17] This presumably refers to the withdrawal of the Spartan ruler Agesilaus (died 361 BC) from Boeotia after one of his expeditions, during which he was wounded. For his chiding by Antalcidas, a Spartan politician, see Plutarch's Life of Agesilaus, ch.XXVI.

[18] For William Herbert, earl of Pembroke (died 1469), see *DWB*, s.n. Turberville may be identified with Richard ap Jankyn Turberville of Pen-llin, Glamorgan. He was still living in 1479 and married, as his third wife, Margaret, daughter of Pembroke's son, Sir Richard Herbert of Ewias: Bartrum, *1400–1500*, X, 1733; V, 780. Turberville's association with Glamorgan a few lines later supports this identification.

[19] 'Rodomantade' (or 'rodo montade'), an exaggerated boast: probably popularized in English by Sir John Harrington's translation (1591) of Ariosto's *Orlando Furioso* (first published 1532), in which Rodomont is the boastful Saracen.

himself; for at that time he had neyther will nor leasure to undertake so butcherlie an office: this scornfull returne soe much incens'd and provok'd the insufferable pride and haughtie stomack of Turberville, that foorth with, in a headlong furie, he hyes him to Abermarlais, and comming in at the gate, the first man he sawe was Thomas ap Griffith himself, sitting by the gate in a gray frocke gowne, whom he tooke for the porter, demanding of him weather Thomas ap Griffith weare within or noe? Sir, said Thomas ap Griffith, he is not far off, and if you would ought with him, lett me receave your commands. Then prethee, fellowe, sayd he (twirling his mustachoes, and sparkling out furie and fier from his eyes), tell him here is one Turberville would speake with him. Thomas ap Griffith, hearing his name, and observing his deportment, had much adoe to hold from laughing outright, yet containing himself, he said he would acquaint his master, and soe going into his parlour, presentlie sendes two or three of his servants to call him in. Turberville noe sooner sawe Thomas ap Griffith, but without anie apologie made for his mistaking, he tells him of his unmannerlinesse, and that he was come thither to correct him for his sawsinesse towardes soe great a person as the Earle of Pembrocke. In good time, Sir, said Thomas ap Griffith; but I pray, said he, is nott my Lord of courage sufficient to undergoe that office of correction without the help of others? Yes, certainlie; but you too meane a copesmate[20] for one of his place and dignitie, he hath left to my chastisement, said Turberville. Well, then, said Thomas ap Griffith (though I might justlie except against my Tutor), where is't your pleasure to have me to Schoole? Nay, where thou wilt or dars't, said Turberville; a harsh compliment, said Thomas ap Griffith; I am not ignorant, said he, as I am defendant, that both time, place, and weapons are in my choice; but speaking in the person of a school boy, (for noe higher account you seeme to make of me) I weene 'tis nott the fashion for schollers to appoint, where their masters shall correct them, yett seeing you leave it to me, lett it be at Arthurstone in Herefordshire, a place indifferent for both (for in Glamorganshire, perhaps, you may think, it is nott safe for me, and heare in Carmarthenshire I am sure 'tis nott for you), there I will attend with my sword at my side, and my launce in my rest on such a day.[21] A match, cried Turberville, and soe abruptlie for the present they parted. To be short, both these combatants mett according to appointment, where at the verie first encounter 'twas Thomas ap Griffith's fortune to breake the other's back, and there leave him. This overthrowe caus'd a nottable hartburning for a while betweene their houses; wittness that memorable battle at Trampton-

---

[20] 'Copesmate', or one with whom one copes, i.e., an adversary.
[21] For the remains of the prehistoric barrow known as Arthur's Stone, near Moccas, see *RCAHM An Inventory of the Historic Monuments in Herefordshire*, vol.I. *South-West* (London, 1931), pp.55–6 and plate 89.

Plate 1 Dinefwr Castle from the south, before 1660. This painting by an unknown artist shows, on the right, the Tywi bridge at Llandeilo Fawr and, in the distance, perhaps the buildings which predated the present mansion and occupied the site of medieval Newton. (*National Museum of Wales: Welsh Folk Museum*)

Plate 2   Carreg Cennen Castle, Carmarthenshire. This fortress was built in the late thirteenth century and remained impregnable until its demolition in 1462. (*Cadw: Welsh Historic Monuments. Crown copyright*)

Plate 3   a) Dinefwr Mansion from the north, *c*.1660. The earlier buildings stood to the south and west (right), and the remains of a few of Newton's burgage plots may be seen. The medieval castle looms in the distance. (*National Museum of Wales: Welsh Folk Museum*)

b) The inner court of Weobley Castle, Gower. Sir Rhys ap Thomas or his son added the hall porch (right) and other buildings to improve this residence. The castle dates from the late thirteenth century. (*Cadw: Welsh Historic Monuments. Crown copyright*)

Plate 4 a) Carew Castle, Pembrokeshire, from the south-west. Built in the late thirteenth century, it became Sir Rhys ap Thomas's grandest residence. Its enclosures and parks were the scene of the Garter celebrations in 1506. (*Ralph A. Griffiths*)

b) One of two surviving chairs decorated with Sir Rhys ap Thomas's arms and the Garter. There are minor differences in the carving of the arms and legs of the two chairs, but they are companion pieces. (*National Museum of Wales: Welsh Folk Museum*)

Plate 5 Sir Rhys ap Thomas's Garter plate in the twelfth stall on the Sovereign's side of the choir of St George's Chapel, Windsor. Sir Rhys was elevated to the Order in 1505. His motto, *Secret et Hardy*, the coat of arms and raven badge, and the inscription, *Msr. Ris ap Thomas*, are contemporary. (*Dean and Chapter of St George's Chapel*)

Plate 6   Carved oak tester valances of the bed said to have belonged to Sir Rhys ap Thomas, now at Derwydd House, Carmarthenshire. They appear to portray Sir Rhys's part in Henry VIII's campaign against the French in 1513. The Garter and the raven (for Sir Rhys) and the fleur-de-lys (for the French) are displayed. (*National Museum of Wales: Welsh Folk Museum*)

Plate 7 The carved oak-panelled cupboard at Cotehele House, Cornwall, where it was probably taken by Catherine St John, Sir Gruffydd ap Rhys's widow, in 1524–5 when she married Sir Richard Edgecombe. It was carved by Harri ap Gruffydd and depicts, *inter alia*, two harpists strumming their harps (top right). (*National Museum of Wales: Welsh Folk Museum, by courtesy of the National Trust*)

Plate 8 a) Portrait of Henry Rice (1586–*c*.1656), author of the Life of Sir Rhys ap Thomas and other writings designed to rehabilitate his family's reputation. The painter is unknown. (*The Lord Dynevor, by courtesy of A.C. Cooper Ltd.*)

b) Portrait of Richard Fenton (1747–1821), the antiquary, by the fashionable court painter, Sir William Beachey (1753–1839), painted *c*.1775–6. Fenton published the Life of Sir Rhys ap Thomas and the Objections to Rhys ap Gruffydd's attainder in 1796–7. (*National Museum of Wales*)

field in Glamorganshire, fought betweene the Mathews and the Turbervilles in the quarrell of Sir Rice ap Thomas, wherein the Mathewes got the better of the day, as appeares by their pardon yett extant, for that dayes bloodie service.[22] The last combate he perform'd was with one David Gough,[23] a man in disposition nott unlike the former. The two mett at a place called Pennal, in the Countie of Merioneth, where, after a long and bloodie fight, this David Gough fell by the sword of Thomas ap Griffith, and the place to this day is call'd Pennal Field.[24] Thomas ap Griffith, not able to goe farr in respect of his woundes, shakes off his armes, and layes him downe flatt on his face to breath himself, after a tediouse and wearisome encounter; in the meane time (woe worth the while), there comes behind him some base fellow (a servant noe doubt, or friend of the others), and runns him through: where at turning him about, and looking upon his murderer (with such a looke, I imagine, as Marius cast upon that base Minturnian, or the noble Pyrrhus, on the servant of Antigonus, comming for the like wile and inglorious office),[25] he used these wordes. Ah! my Friend, had I remember'd to have layn upon my back, thou durst not thus cowardlie have kill'd Thomas ap Griffith, intimating thereby, that with the verie sight of his countenance, he would have terrified him from soe foule a fact, and so he died. In honour of his memorie, there was in the place a Cenotaph of stones and turfes erected,[26] wheather the gentlemen of the

[22] Sir Rhys ap Thomas married Jenet, daughter of Thomas Mathew of Radyr and widow of Thomas Stradling of St Donat's (died 1480). But a skirmish at Trampton-field, Glamorgan, is not otherwise known. Frampton, about a mile north of Llantwit Major in Turberville country, may be intended, and David Edwardes (died 1690) identified it as such when he made excerpts from the Life (College of Arms, Box 36 V). On the other hand, Clark, *Limbus*, p.8, claims that Sir David Mathew was 'slain by the Turbervilles in a riot at Neath'; if Sir David died *c*.1484 (*DWB*, p.618), this would fit generally the time-scale suggested by the Life – after Thomas ap Gruffydd's skirmish and during Rhys ap Thomas's time.

[23] The *CR* editor adds a note: 'This David Gough is supposed to be a near kinsman of that Mathew Gough, a famous warrior in the times of Henry Fifth and Sixth, slain in the civil tumult, raised by Jack Cade.' A David Gough, of Maelienydd in the March, served the Yorkist kings: he was one of Edward IV's serjeants at arms, and Richard III confirmed him in office as constable of Radnor Castle. Evans, *Wales and the Wars of the Roses*, p.148; *Harleian 433*, I, 155, 257; II, 209–10; III, 198. The events at Pennal may have had political undertones; otherwise, it is worth noting that a Dafydd Goch ap Maredudd ap Gruffydd ab Adda of Llanbadarn, Cardiganshire, was addressed by Lewys Glyn Cothi in a poem (Griffiths, *Principality of Wales*, p.500). A later note among the Dynevor muniments identifies Thomas's adversary as Dafydd Goch ab Ieuan ab Owain, who is otherwise unknown: NLW, Dynevor, A 103 (m).

[24] The site of this skirmish is not known; see n.26.

[25] While under arrest at Minturnae, in Italy, the Roman general Marius (died 86 BC), who was noted for his cruelty, unnerved his executioner with a penetrating look (Plutarch's Life of Caius Marius, ch.XXXIX). Antigonus Pyrrhus, wounded, did likewise to a servant of his enemy, Antigonus, king of Macedonia, as recorded in Plutarch's Life of Pyrrhus, ch.XXXIV; see above n.14.

[26] The *CR* editor adds a note: 'In a meadow below the village of Pennal, in the County of Merioneth, there is, at this day, to be seen a Tumulus, which in all probability is the very spot here referr'd to; but no tradition now remains amongst the inhabitants of that neighbourhood, to countenance this piece of history.' No such cairn or mound is now known in Pennal parish:

countie, upon a certaine day, for manie yeares after resorted, where they spent the time in jumping, wrestling, running at the quinteine, and other manlie exercises. And thus have you the storie of Thomas ap Griffith, commonlie call'd the curteouse ennemie, his bodie being bravelie accompanied, was conveyd to the abbey of Bardsey, in the county of Carnarvon, and there solemnlie interr'd, the beholders all, with a universall conclamation, giving an assured testimonie of their hartes overflowing sorrowe.[27]

(2). Nowe to continue my discourse, Thomas ap Griffith, by foule play, finishing his daies somewhat untimelie, left a plentifull issue after him. Morgan Thomas, and David were home-bredd men, far diffring from their father in the true temperature of their mindes. Morgan was the better man; David the better souldier, Morgan I had rather have for my friend, David I would more feare as an enemy, Morgan had more vertue in him, the other more strength and force: right Brutus and Cassius.[28] These two, guided by severall starres, rann contrarie courses, the one siding with the house of Yorke, the other with that of Lankester. During their being abroad in those embroilments, they were much improv'd in their knowledge and civill deportment, experience having taught their valour good manners, soe that in a short time they purchas'd to themselves the fame of good Captaines, and for proof it was nott long ere a fitt occasion was offer'd to manifest what stuff they were made of. When that irreparable overthrowe was given to Queene Margaret and Prince Edward her sonne, at Tewkesburie, of which when Jasper, Earle of Pembrocke, on his waye with new succours had notice, he was forced to retire himself to his castle of Chepstowe, and from thence to his castle of Pembrocke, having his nephew Henrie, the young Earl of Richmond,

RCAHM, vol. VI, *The County of Merioneth* (London, 1921), pp.157–60; E. G. Bowen and C. A. Gresham, *History of Merioneth*, vol. I (Dolgellau, 1967), *passim*.

[27] Bardsey, with its Augustinian abbey, is famous as the burial-place of 20,000 legendary saints, confessors and martyrs. *RCAHM, An Inventory of the Ancient Monuments in Caernarvonshire*, vol. III (London, 1964), 17–20. Thomas ap Gruffydd ap Nicholas is known to have died by 1474, when the escheator of Carmarthenshire disposed of some of his property: PRO, SC6/1169/6 m.9; /8 m.10*d*; Griffiths, *Principality of Wales*, p.155. Sir John Wynn also knew of the Pennal encounter, at which his forebear, John ap Maredudd, was thought by some to have been present on Thomas ap Gruffydd's side, 'which field was fought betweene Thomas Gruffith ap Nicolas and Henry ap gwilim; and the earle of Penbrookes captaynes where Thomas ap gruffith gott the field, but received there his deathes wounde'. Jones, *History of the Gwydir Family and Memoirs*, p.27. Sir John seems to have produced one incident from the three which Henry Rice recorded. There are other conflations in the early-seventeenth-century account in NLW MS 1602 D f.205 (Jones, *TCASFC*, XXIX [1939], 30), which ostensibly associates Thomas's death with the siege of Harlech Castle by William Herbert, earl of Pembroke, in 1468: 'Whereupon the Erle sware he wold see Thomas ap Gr hanged, and therefore when he came to Harlech and laide seige to the Castle; and heeringe that Thomas ap Gr was dead, he made inquisition where his bodie was buried, meaninge to hange his bodie to save his oath . . . his ffriendes having intelligence of the Erles meaning, stole a waite his bodie out of the grave, and Conveyed thirtie myles of to the Ilande of Bardesey and theire buried him secretlye.' See above pp.32–3, with slight differences of detail.

[28] See Plutarch's Life of Brutus, chs.VII and XXXIV (for example).

in his companie, which made him the more unsafe, being a pray greedilie look'd after.[29] They rested nott long at Pembrocke castle, for Morgan Thomas, by speciall command from the King, had raised great forces, and soe stronglie beseeg'd the said castle, as there was no possible meanes of escape;[30] soe that they were driven to this hard choice, eyther to perish through famine, or else to putt themselves into such handes from whom they could expect for little mercie or favour. Amid these extreames, David Thomas, the second brother, a faithfull friend to the Earle of Pembrocke, and in hart a sworne servant to the familie of Lankaster, had his wittes whollie emploid, howe he might safelie fetch off these distress'd Princes, and to that purpose he presentlie flies over the countrie, sometimes to the Earle's wellwishers and servants, who instantlie follow'd him, sometimes to his brother's owne friendes and followers, whom he possessed, that though his brother made shewe of besieging the castle, yett he would be willing thos noble lordes might be rescued, soe he did not appeare to have a hand in the businesse, by which meanes he had suddenlie gathered together a rude rabble, to the number of two thousand within the compass of eight dayes, and soe attended by his ragged regiment, with hookes, prongs and glaives, and other rustick weapons, *ad subitum usum properatis* [with haste to set to], he setts upon the besiegers, and forceth his brother from the siege, rescueth the two Earles, and soe convaies them to Tenbie,[31] a maritime towne, and ther safelie enshipped them for Britany. Thus have we our soveraigne or pomeroyall tree miserablie rent and torne with storme and tempest, supported by a poore willowe stake, or a crab tree forke. Whence, O! you great ones, yea the greatest among you, kinges learne this lesson, nott to slight or under value, at anie hand, your inferiours, there being such a mutuall relation betweene us, while we walk on the stage of this earth, that the greatest may have use of the meanest, and those (as here for instance) ordeyned for emperie, may, at one time or other, fall in debt to a subject for the preservation of their lives.[32]

[29] Griffiths and Thomas, *Making of the Tudor Dynasty*, pp. 71–7. Chepstow was not one of Earl Jasper's lordships; it belonged to the Mowbray duke of Norfolk in 1471.

[30] Ibid., pp.75–6. The essentials of this story, perhaps learned from Henry Tudor himself or one of his entourage, first appeared in Polydore Vergil's *English History* and was repeated by Hall and, with less detail, by Holinshed. The author of the Life copes with the embarrassment to the family by suggesting that Morgan secretly sympathized with the besieged; it is more likely that he was swayed by his wife, a daughter of Sir Roger Vaughan, whom Jasper Tudor had executed at Chepstow a short time before. Vergil, *English History*, p.155; Hall's *Chronicle*, pp.302–3; Holinshed, *Chronicles*, III, 328. Henry Rice elaborates on the dire straits in which Jasper and Henry were placed, and the size and source of Dafydd ap Thomas's relieving force; but he omits the digging of ditches and trenches before Pembroke Castle by the besiegers.

[31] The *CR* editor adds a note: 'Tenby, a corporate town and contributory borough to Pembroke, is situated at the southern extremity of Pembrokeshire, about ten miles distance from the county town.'

[32] This was a pertinent reminder in the England of the mid-1620s; it also echoes Henry Rice's account of services which his family had done to monarchs (the royal apple tree of 'pomeroy') in the

Nowe Jasper, Earle of Pembrock, and his nephew Henrie, Earle of Richmond, being fledd the kingdome, who weare the onlie remainder left, of feare king Edward, using alltogether loose the raynes, yielded himself whollie to the pleasures and contentments of his mind. In the meane while those turbulent, factiouse, and high-working spiritts of the time, unused, unaccustomed to peace and idlenesse, began in all corners of the kingdome to fall to jars among themselves, in which (amongst the rest), those two noble brothers were unfortunately embroyled, which brought them both, not long after, to an untimely end; *Utinam! potius pro republica, quam in republica periissent* [O! better they had perished for the commonwealth than in the commonwealth].[33] And here, I pray, give me leave to tell you a tale of this David Thomas, which, howe ridiculous and trifling soever it may appear, will serve much for the setting foorth of the bold and all-daring spiritt of that heroicall gentleman. It hath binn a common thing in all ages (none, from the highest to the lowest, being able to escape the lash of a maliciouse tongue) to frame agnominations and impropriums, and to give nick-names to men though never so well deserving; soe Thomas, Earle of Lancaster, by Peers Gaveston, was called *The Stage Player*; Aymer de Valence, Earle of Pembroke, *Joseph, the Jew*; Guy, Earle of Warwick, *the Black Dog of Arden*;[34] and, soe David Thomas heare was called, *David Keffil Cwtta*, or *David with the Curtail Horse*. The occasion of this mis-naming him thus first began: There was a neighbour of this David's had a brave young horse, of whose goodness he was a better judge than the owner, and therefore taking a fancie to the beast he gave for the same foure and twentie kine, with pasturage for them a whole yeare, which was held a prodigall act, and gave his enemies cause of sport. Having gotten this horse he croppes his eares, slits his nose, and cutts his tayle, and withall, as our Picts heretofore were wont to paint their bodies, soe he with marking irons imprinted diverse uglie and monstrouse shapes upon this horse, to make him seeme more fearfull and terrible to his enemies. Being on a time told howe in a deriding manner his adversaries had nick-named him for curtailing his horse, 'Well, then,' said he, 'I hope, nowe they will leave off talking of me, seeing I have bought me a horse, whose taile they may plaie withall.' At another time his enemies having notice of a jorney he intended, they broke downe parte of a bridge he was to pass over, thereby to interrupt his passage and way lay him; but he comming to the place of danger, and close pursude, there being no other remedie, he putts spurres to his horse, and over he goes cleere (the report of which lepp is somewhat

past: BL, Add. MS 23113 f.3–3*d*; see above pp.130–1.

[33] When the brothers died is not known, though it may have been before, or at the same time as, their father *c*.1474; after all, the youngest son, Rhys, became Thomas ap Gruffydd's heir.

[34] William Caxton, *The Chronicles of England*, published in 1480 and based on the earlier Brut Chronicle, made Gaveston's use of nicknames well known. David is known as 'Ceffyl Cwta' in some pedigrees: Bartrum, *1400–1500*, IV, 643.

incredible; but, to use no other wordes then those of a poete of those times, 'twas, *Naid ar March na neidir mwy* [A leap with a steed that will never be repeated],[35] and which certainlie none there durst second), then wheeling about, and calling to his enemies on the other side, after exchanging divers scornfull speeches with them, at length, dared them to follow him on with the cowes they ridd on, or that they would meete him midd way in the river and he would stand them all, and that they mought see that he spoke noe more than he intended, into the river he swims a great way, but seeing none make towards him, back he comes bidding them adue for cowardlie dastards and cravens, and soe leaves them, as I heare leave my tale, for recommending of which to the world (it having somewhat of honour and braverie in it), I hope, I have a better plea than Plutarch for telling us the tale of Alcibiades and his dogg, or at lest wise then that foolish chronicler of our's, who, among the gloriouse actions of our kings, will needes present us with a superfluous relation of the Lord Maior's shewe, or the lamentable downfall (on some speciall daye) of his Lordshippe's custard, by the negligence of one of his tadpoles, who had forgotten (as it seemes) the chiefest point of his office, *To hold fast.*[36] And nowe of course, and in orderlie proceeding; we are come to yong Rice ap Thomas, the true heire (nowe his two elder brothers weare gone) both of his father's fortunes and vertues, who in processe of time grewe to be a man of a wider note, and more eminent mark abroad, then anie of the rest of his familie; their vertues being for the most parte restrained and narrowed within the bounds of Wales onlie. But his growing of a greater latitude, and longer expansion, made him beloved among the English, and admired and feared among the French. And whereas I have hitherto tired you, perhaps, with an expectation of my promise, touching this noble gentleman, I must begg your pardon, my desire being first to bring you in acquaintance with some of his ancestors, that soe you might see he was noe hawke flowne from a kestrell's nest, nor yet a pearle raked off the dunghill.

---

[35] The source of this quotation has not been located.

[36] Plutarch, in his Life of Alcibiades, ch.IX, records how the Athenian general cut off the beautiful tail of his dog; when chided for doing so, he replied that at least it diverted criticism from his other deeds. For the scorn with which the pageants in the Lord Mayor's show (including the 'tappoles') were regarded in the early seventeenth century, see S. Williams, 'The Lord Mayor's Show in Tudor and Stuart Times', *Guildhall Miscellany*, X (1959), 6–18.

4

The Young Rhys ap Thomas

(1) *The Birth and Breeding of yong Rice ap Thomas. (2) His wise, discreete, and judiciouse Carriage, when first he was possest of his Fortunes.*

(1). Having offered to your view a summarie relation of the genealogie and parentage of yong Rice ap Thomas, together with certaine noble deedes and famouse exploites of some of his worthie ancestors, that you mought not be ignorant of what concerned him, even before he *was*, the next thing falling under our consideration, is *himself*, whom I represent unto you, as I find him at this day recorded in men's memories, and among the best writers and hypemnematographists[1] of the times, those cabanetts and safe conservors of actes formerlie donne.

You must then first knowe that this Rice was begotten and borne in a tumultuouse season, among the clashing of armes, and the dispositions of men's mindes and constitutions of their bodies naturallie fierie and furiouse, when *meum* and *tuum* were fluctuate and wavering, neyther *mine* nor *thine*, and the whole frame of this kingdome loose and disjointed: at whose birth[2] his father (stirred thereunto, as it seems, by some illumination) proceeded to that height of curiositie, as to consult with mathematicians and prognosticks, touching the nativitie of this child, whose horoscope, as they concluded, promised greate matters: that in time he should growe to be a man of a high active and martiall spiritt: that he was designed for high atchievementes and doughtie performances in the warres; that he should attain to greate honours at courte, and for popular affection in his countrie out goe all his forefathers, which in the end, proved accordinglie true.[3]

---

[1] 'Hypemnematographists' presumably meant writers who assist remembrance by artificial aids.

[2] The date of Sir Rhys ap Thomas's birth is thought to have been *c.*1449 (*DWB*, p.840). The Life suggests that as a boy he accompanied his father to Burgundy *c.*1465.

[3] Such consultation is quite plausible, and if (see n.4) Lewis Caerleon indeed served the family, he, as a noted astrologer, could well have cast Rhys's horoscope. On the other hand, Henry Rice

His father, ravished with a kind of delight in these happie presages, and finding as the child grewe of yeares, by a watchful observance, that what of one so yong could be promised, was like enough by him to be performed. The first thing he took care of, was to give him a breeding semblable to those vertues beginning to peepe out and appeare in the verie gemm and budd of his infancie, sparing noe cost to procure him the best instructors. Manie were recommended, and fewe chose, among whom, one Edward Lewis, a gentleman of North Wales, was in greatest esteeme, and gave him his first entrance into letters. This Lewis was a man of a readie witt, cleere judgment, and well redd in the liberall sciences, as having had most of his breeding in Italie, in the universitie of Padua, the verie same (as is supposed) who was afterwardes servant and physitian to the Lady Elizabeth, queene dowager to Edward the Fourth; and used as a speciall instrument, or one of those links in that chaine which drewe on this yong pupil of his, to side with Henrie, Earle of Richmond, against Richard, the Usurper.[4] Nowe while Rice ap Thomas's tutors were marking him (as it is in the French proverb)[5] with the letter A, to distinguish him from inferiour metalls, his father in the meane while falls into an humour of travelling; not but that he was stayed enough and well attempered, but because he could nott away with our civill jarres (nowe at the hotest), therefore to Burgundie he goes (as you heard allreadie), taking this sonn of his along with him, to acquaint him with the fashions of that court, at that time, one of the best schooles in Christendome, both for civill deportment and warlick direction;[6] to initiate him betimes in the principles of warr (a profession his starres pointed him unto), to prepare and arme him with resolution against those difficulties and rubbs, he was to shoulder withall, in the craggie wayes to honour, noe charges being spared, noe care neglected, nothing omitted that might make him everie way trulie accomplished. Rice had nott long continued in this schoole, but, like yong Scipio, bredd under a sedulouse father,[7] he profited soe much, and ripened soe

may have been displaying wisdom after the event. See the copies of horoscopes in Cambridge University Library MS Ee. III. 61 f.159ff., 108*v*ff.; this manuscript belonged to Lewis Caerleon later in the fifteenth century.

[4] This identification with Dr Lewis Caerleon may or may not be well founded; Henry Rice sounds a note of uncertainty, partly perhaps because he believed him to be a north Walian (though this may be an error of the *CR* editor). No record has been found that he was educated in Padua: R. J. Mitchell, 'English students at Padua, 1460–75', *TRHS*, 4th series, XIX (1936), 101–18. For his service to Elizabeth Wydeville in 1483 and his relations with Henry Tudor, see P. Kibre, 'Lewis of Caerleon, Doctor of Medicine, Astronomer and Mathematician (d.1494)', *Isis*, XLIII, part 1 (1952), 100–8; A. B. Emden, *A Biographical Register of the University of Cambridge to 1500* (Cambridge, 1963), pp.116–17; Griffiths and Thomas, *Making of the Tudor Dynasty*, pp.91–6.

[5] For the French proverb, 'Il est des bons, il est marqué à l'"A"', first recorded in 1579, see *Dictionnaire de la Langue Française du seizième siècle*, I (Paris, 1925), *s.* 'A'; *Französisches Etymologisches Wörterbuch*, XXIV (Basle, 1969–83), 1.

[6] See Vaughan, *Philip the Good*, ch.5.

[7] This may be a reference to Scipio Africanus (died 183 BC), who saved his father's life in battle

fast, that through the whole armie he grewe to be of speciall regard; the gentlemen and the gallanter sort still courting him, and the wiser and graver men delighting in his conversation.

One time Duke Philip taking a view of his armie, he fortuned to find yong Rice at the manage, and observing the gracefulness of his riding, the comeliness of his person, and the settled soberness of his behaviour, he sendes for Thomas ap Griffith, the father, whom he had long knowne, and ever highlie favoured, both for his curtesie and courageous carriage, on all occasions; making it an earnest suite unto him to have this young gentleman, his sonn, for his servant, which the father yeelded to, though with much unwillingness, fearing, lest his intimacie with one of the Duke's blood,[8] being once discovered, might turne to the ruine and destruction of his sonne, whom he so deerely loved. This the Duke observing, and nott knowing Thomas ap Griffith's secrett reason, but imputing it to his indulgencie; 'Well', says he, 'courteous Thomas (for soe the Duke ever called him, and soe did we in Wales, ever after, as long as he lived, which faire addition is, at this day, not quite forgotten), I see you are loath to part with this your jewell, and you have good cause, for never, in all my lief, have I seen a more hopefull gentleman; but nowe, seeing I may call him mine, by your free donation, assure yourself he shall doe noe worse than my onlie sonne.' And soe the Duke placeth him with the Earle of Charoloys, where he was with all grace and favour verie nobly entreated.[9] Within a while after the Earle finding him capable of emploiments above his yeares, would needes, for his more encouragement, bestowe on him a troope of horse, which he modestlie refused, professing his ignorance and want of experience to undergoe soe greate a charge; that, his care should be, his meritts might ever have the upper hand of his emploimentes, that he would never doe any thing, eyther privately or publicklie, that exceeded his forces, that for the present he would think himself highlie advanced, if his Lordship would vouchsafe him the place of a gentleman in his companie, which, according to the trust reposed in him, he did nott doubt but he should be able to discharge.

The Earle, commending the moderation of his answere and the humbleness of his request, presentes him forthwith with a publique horse and admittes him unto pay, following him in his owne wayes, from which his lordshipp sawe noe reason to disagree. And nowe young Rice b[e]ginns to shewe what mettall he was made of, and that to be in continuall action was his cheefe delight; for he was ever eyther practising of armes, or playing att his weapons, running, wrestling, riding,

by an act of great bravery.

[8] See above p.173.

[9] Charles, count of Charolais succeeded his father as duke of Burgundy in 1467. There is no known record placing Rhys in Charles's personal service.

swimming, walcking, and undergoing all those militarie duties imposed upon him, with cheerfullness and alacritie.

Thus continued this yong sparke running in a faire even course, till, passing through all inferior offices, he was nowe climed up that step as gave him the title of a captaine, and I would the earlie upstart captaines[10] of our times had taken a lesson out of this man's courses for their imitation, and suffered their over-greedie ambition to receave some sweete allay from that wise moderation he used in all his proceedings; soe had our late expeditions binn better ordered, and more bravelie performed, and nott protested against upon our exchanges for their insufficiencie, to the dishonour of our nation; but this nose must nott be wrung and wiped too hard, *ne sanguis eliciatur* [lest blood be drawn]. As Rice ap Thomas was hitherunto bred up in courte and campe, under the best tutors in the schoole of obedience and vertue; all began heedfullie to eye him, and expecting what fruit this towardlinesse of his would bring forth, and anxious to see what he would write on the other side of the leafe; neyther were they soe eager, as he forward to give the lowdest testimonie to the world of his proficience in the profession of armes, seeking out all occasions that might advance him to the highest pitch of glorie. Butt while menn were in the heate of expectancie, fortune, fearing least the wheele of Rice his fame should make away too fast, comes nowe with her trigger, to stopp the swiftness of the motion, soe that for the present all those brave actions he was like to have undertaken receav'd a checke, for his father having trodd awry (as I have hinted before), and the businesse nott able anie longer to be concealed, both father and sonne were forc'd to fly, and to make a faire retreate to their own home, leaving Burgundie, as a ground where on their valour was nott ordain'd to take roote.

(2). Nott long after their returne Thomas ap Griffith the father, and Morgan and David his two eldest sonnes, being unfortunatelie cutt off by untimelie death,[11] yong Rice ap Thomas, as heire of right, possess'd himself of all their fortunes, for the right management whereof as likewise for his farther guidance in the affaires of the world, eyther in peace or warr, at home or abroad; he at his verie first entrance gave a most assur'd testimonie both of his wisdome and discreate moderation in the choice of his companions, to whose grave counsells he had recourse, which ever made him walk secure and free from the stroak of thunder.

[10] The *CR* editor adds a note: 'The writer here levells a very just satyr at the many ill-concerted, and as badly prosecuted expeditions, which marked the reign of James the First, and the administration of his favourite Buckingham.' The 'late expeditions' referred to may be the ill-fated English adventure to La Rochelle in 1627, and the recriminations that accompanied its failure: see above p.153 n.24.

[11] Their return to Wales seems to have taken place shortly before 1474: see above p.32. According to Bartrum, *1400–1500*, IV, 643, Morgan had no children and David only one daughter.

The chiefest of them I find to bee John Bishopp of St Davids,[12] a learned, grave, and reverend prelate; Robert, Abbott of Talley,[13] and John, Prior of Carmarthen,[14] two sound politicians, and both well seene in state affaires; Morgan of Kidwelly,[15] a man deeplie read in the common lawes of the Realme; Richard Griffith,[16] and Arnold Butler,[17] two ancient captaines, verie famous in those partes for their skill in souldierie; and Robin of the Dale, a profound astrologer, and a notable

[12] The *CR* editor adds a note: 'I apprehend the writer must be mistaken here, respecting the name of the Bishop of St Davids; there was a bishop of that see in the time of Henry the 6th, named John Delabere, but who was, I presume, dead before the period here referr'd to, one Robert Tully filling the see in the latter years of Edward, and John Morgan bishop of that see (whom he, farther on, refers to by his surname) not having acceded to it till the year 1503.' John de la Bere ceased to be bishop in 1460. Bishop Tully (1460–81) was Lancastrian in sympathy; Edward IV did not allow him to occupy the see but he lived at Tre-fin and Tenby in Pembrokeshire and could have counselled the young Rhys ap Thomas. John Morgan was archdeacon of Carmarthen from 1488 to 1494 and bishop from 1496 to 1504; he seems to have become close to Sir Rhys, though he had no Welsh benefice before 1488. See A. B. Emden, *A Biographical Register of the University of Oxford to 1500* (3 vols., Oxford, 1957–9), II, s.n.; *Le Neve*, XI, 55, 65. This may be a retrospective use of Morgan's episcopal title (see below p.212.). It may be noted that two poets patronized by Rhys ap Thomas also addressed poems to one of the bishops: Lewys Glyn Cothi to Robert Tully, and Ieuan Deulwyn to John Morgan. E. R. Ll. Davies, thesis cited, pp.393–4, 489.

[13] The *CR* editor adds a note: 'Robert ap Gwillim, Harry ap Jevan Gwyn of Mydhifinych, by whose sister Gwellian, Sir Rice ap Thomas had illegitimate issue five daughters, and as many sons.' Of fifteenth-century abbots of Talley, only Lewis (1435) and David (1488, 1493, 1504) are known: W. Dugdale, *Monasticon Anglicanum* (6 vols. in 8, London, 1846), IV, 161; Isaacson, *Episcopal Registers*, II, 514, 538, 658. But for the liaison with Gwenllian, sister of the abbot of Talley, see Bartrum, *1400–1500*, IV, 645. Myddynfych, near Llandybïe, was occupied by a family descended from Syr Elidir Ddu and, therefore, related to that of Rhys ap Thomas: Jones, *Historic Carms. Homes*, pp.135–6. Ieuan Deulwyn, whom Rhys patronized, addressed a poem to one of Talley's abbots: E. R. Ll. Davies, thesis cited, pp.443–6, 491.

[14] Thomas Wynter was prior of St John's Augustinian Priory at Carmarthen from about 1472 and for several years after 1476 (Williams, *Welsh Church*, p.401). He must have been reinstated after resigning in 1471 for uncanonical behaviour (*Cal. Papal Reg.*, XIII, part 2 [1471–84], p.508); his successor is not known.

[15] Trahaearn ap Morgan, whom Lewys Dwnn described as 'skilled and qualified in the laws of England', was one of the Morgans of Tredegar and married to a co-heiress of Henry Dwnn of Kidwelly; he was favoured by Henry VII and Henry VIII. He is to be distinguished from Morgan Kidwelly, a lawyer in Richard III's service both before and after 1483. Evans, *Wales and the Wars of the Roses*, pp.216–18; Horrox, *Richard III*, pp.86–7, 210–11, 250, 286–7; Jones, *Historic Carms. Homes*, pp.134–5; Bartrum, *1400–1500*, III, 394–6; see above p.38.

[16] The identification of Richard Griffith is uncertain, but he may have been the younger brother of Sir Walter Griffith (*c.*1431–81), lord of Llangybi, Betws Bledrws and Llanrhystud (Cards.), as well as of more extensive estates in Yorkshire and Staffordshire (*Testamenta Eboracensia*, ed. J. Raine *et al.* (6 vols., Surtees Soc., 1836–1902), III (1865), 269–70). This would make him the brother of Elizabeth, Rhys ap Thomas's mother. Griffiths, *Principality of Wales*, I, 145–6, 274–5; see above p.16.

[17] The *CR* editor adds a note: 'A descendant of Sir Arnold Butler of Dunraven Castle in Glamorganshire (by the gift of Wm. de Londres, one of the twelve Norman knights, who possess'd themselves of that country), whose immediate ancestor, John Butler, came into Pembrokeshire, and married Elizabeth, daughter and sole-heiress of Philip Percival, of Coedcantlais, where his posterity remained for many years.' John Butler of Dunraven was living in Henry VII's reign and his son and heir, Arnold, died *c.*1540–1; the latter may have been Rhys's companion in arms. Rice Merrick, *Morganiae Archaiographia*, pp.52, 157, 160, 186. A John Butler was bailiff of Carmarthen in 1499–1500: Griffiths, *Principality of Wales*, I, 344. To describe Griffith and Arnold as 'ancient captaines' may have been a retrospective judgement, at least in the latter's case.

prophett,[18] one on whose sayings young Rice repos'd much confidence, as being with the rest of those blinder times, somewhat too farr transported that way. Having nowe made choice of such friendes, and they, on the other side, thinking themselves bound, by the confidence he had reposed in them, to returne him semblable faith and assurance of their love, buckled themselves stronglie to him, and furnish'd him with the wisest counsels, to make him trulie capable of those ornamentes due to his highe deservinges. Upon the first consultation had betweene these grave and wise gentlemen touching the advancing this brave yong spiritt in the way of honour, they mett with on manie rubbs, which stood in opposition to their designes, chieflie occasioned by reason of that long and deadlie feud betweene his father and Henrie ap Gwillim, the chief of court Henrie, a man of ancient nobilitie, and greate in power:[19] to remove which obstacle, and quite to putt out the fine [*recte* fire] that for many yeares had raged and almost devoured both their houses, a motion is made for the conclusion of a marriage betweene the said Rice and Eva, one of the co-heiresses of the aforesaid Henrie, a thing willinglie condescended unto by both parties;[20] a happie match, by which there came to Rice a strong and mightie alliance, and a fortune, if nott equall, yet nott much inferiour to his owne, which gave him a more wide support, and enabled him nowe with both winges, (whereas before, we may say, he had but one) to go on in his night to the hill of honour. And nowe having gotten him to wief a woman of honorable birth and virtues answerable, it concern'd him in the next place to take care of his familie, and to settle his house in order, a thing which in short time by the labouriouse endeavours of his friendes, and the well made choice of his officers, he soe trulie accomplish'd, that the gentrie did continuallie flock thither as to some academie, for their civill nurture and education, by which meanes his house was soe much frequented, and he soe well attended, that wherever he came in respect of the greatnesse of his traine, he bare shewe rather of a prince than a private subject; and though this drewe him to an extraordinarie expence, yet hee ever held the reynes in his owne handes, moderatelie and wiselie restrayning himself within the limitts of his yearlie revenues, his disposition ever inclining to frugall courses, and to the looking narrowlie into his œconomical affaires, and the contracting his domestic charge, wherein he used so warie a proceeding, that, as his judgment and moderation were everie day more and more applauded, soe his hospitalitie noe way abated or diminished, shewing us the middle way, betweene base avarice and vitiouse prodigalitie.[21] For his apparell servantes and diett

---

[18] For astrologers, see above p.182.

[19] See above pp.174–5.

[20] Efa was Rhys's first wife: see above pp.62–3.

[21] Practically none of his administrative archive survives; for his household, estates and income,

(the three most considerable thinges in houehold [*recte* household]
government) he wiselie proportion'd himself after this manner: he never
wore garment at home (for abroad and in the warres, you must know he
was ever *ex capsulâ totus* [exceedingly neat], verie rich and sumptuouse)
but was cheape and homelie; proper for the time, nott greatlie
distinguishing him from his other followers; in the keeping and wearing
of which there needed noe great care to be had or taken, eyther by
servant or master. As touching his servantes, they were nott soe manie in
number, as they were serviceable in their condition. And as for his diett,
it was neyther costlie nor sparing, nor fetched from farr. And thus
having settled and order'd his affaires at home, and taking care for able
ministers, wheather he were absent or present to manage his fortunes,
soe that for his owne little private commonweale he neede take no
further thought. He betooke himself thenceforth whollie to the
government of the publique, refusing noe paine or labour for the
reducing of his countriemen to civilitie and good order, whom he
perceaved (like others in all partes of this kingdome) to be growne rough
and unrulie, by reason of the long continued intestine garboiles within
this land, which are wont, whereever they lay their rude handes, to
counfound and perverte both lawe, learning and all good manners. To
reforme therefore all abuses, and to bring things againe to a settled
government, two wayes weare thought of as most convenient, the one by
religion, the other by conversation. As for religion, which during those
civill warrs was forc'd to flie to some desarte place, leaving neyther
sanctitie nor innocence, nor faith nor justice behind her, he made it his
masterpiece, calling to his assistance the good and wise bishop of St
Davids[22] to recall both her and her vertuouse companions againe, and
soe to restore them to their pristinate state and glorie; and to winn them
more willinglie to returne, a strict survey is taken of all the churches in
the diocese, for the furnishing of which with sufficient and able ministers,
they omitted noe circumspection, and when there wanted meanes for
anie one of them to discharge his function, there was provision made by
the willing contribution of their friendes, to enable him to wade through
his charge, soe that in their time, religion may be said to be of a more
flourishing grouth then had binn knowne for manie ages before:[23] And
because by conversation familiaritie is encreas'd, and curtesie

and the poets he patronized, see above pp.59ff.
[22] See above n.12.
[23] Of the surviving registers of Bishops Hugh Pavy (1484–96) and John Morgan (1496–1504),
Pavy's reveals an especially vigorous traffic in clerical appointments; moreover, his policy statement
of 30 July 1493 on the appropriation and union of benefices and churches accords with comments in
the Life. What is not clear is Sir Rhys ap Thomas's role in all but a minority of benefices where he
was the patron. Isaacson, *Episcopal Registers*, II, especially pp.660–3. Williams, *Welsh Church*, p.269,
suggests that Pavy enforced discipline, and R. W. Dunning, 'Patronage and promotion in the later
medieval Church', in R. A. Griffiths (ed.), *Patronage, the Crown and the Provinces in Later Medieval
England* (Gloucester, 1981), pp.174–6, has an assessment of Pavy.

engender'd, and amitie continued, they, in imitation of the antient law-makers, instituted certaine festivall dayes, to the end that men should assemble together to entertaine publike sportes, and places of meetings weare appointed, and summer-houses erected, where the women with dancing, and other allowable recreations, passed the time, and the men exercised all manlie actions, as running, quoiting, lepping, wrestling, and the like; among whom this youg [*recte* yong] Rice ever made one, nott refusing sometimes to decline his gravitie and to dance among his neighbours, but that was seldome, and then too with a decent and comlie behaviour. And this manner of proceeding to civilize the people was not his owne invention, but grounded (as it seemes) on that old institution of Numa Pompilius, who finding the Romans at his coming to the kingdome to be both proud, fierce, and cruell, could thinke of noe better way to lenify and allay their stomackes *quam ludis ac choreis plurima graviate etc. urbanitate conditis* [than with many games and dances, in a serious and elegant fashion].[24] Semblable to these as I take it, were our paganalls or country feasts first instituted, and nowe againe revived by the appointmente and instructions of our graciouse sovereigne,[25] and our summer-houses, and may-poles erected, and church-ales frequented, which certainlie may serve to good use if executed according to his majestie's true intention.

Now you must understand, though Edward the 4th. in his later dayes gave himself up wholie to his pleasure and repose, yong Rice wiselie foresàw (as upon everie shift of princes most commonlie it falls out) there might happen an alteration in the state, and therefore made his preparations, as if an enemie had binn at his door. Richard Griffith and Arnold Butler,[26] men of approv'd knowledge and skill in souldierie, were the cheefest he made use of to traine up the yong gentlemen, and all others of the better sorte, according to the true militarie discipline of those times, in which they emploid much labour, accustoming them daylie (as if they had been in field) to the hardest duties of a soldier, which at the first seem'd harsh and unpleasant to them, being in former times bredd but to a tumultuarie kind of fighting with hookes, pronges and glaives, without anie order or method, but when once they had

[24] Numa Pompilius, the legendary successor of Romulus as king of Rome, introduced festivals and other arts of peace during his tranquil reign. See (e.g.) Plutarch's Life, ch. VIII.

[25] The *CR* editor adds a note: 'James the 1st whose declaration, as printed in the year 1618, this paragraph occurs –"And as for our good peoples lawful recreation, our pleasure likewise is, that after the ende of divine service our good people be not disturbed, letted or discouraged, from any lawful recreation, such as dancing, either men or women, archery, for men leaping, vaulting, or any such harmless recreations, nor from having of May games, Whitsun-ales, and Morris dancers, and the setting up of May-poles, etc.". 'James's Declaration of Sports, issued on 24 May 1618, arose from his rebuke of 'some Puritans and precise people' when he passed through Lancashire in 1617. The Declaration was later reissued by Charles I in 1633. J. R. Tanner (ed.), *Constitutional Documents of the Reign of James I* (Cambridge, 1952 repr.), pp.54–6.

[26] See above nn.16, 17.

attayned to some insight in that noble science, it is said they tooke soe
much pleasure therein, that scarse they afforded their leaders anie time
of rest, and gentlemen often had their sett meetinges where they
discoursed most commonlie of nothing else butt fortifications,
entrenchments, and the ordering of battles, as if by way of divination
they foresaw there would, ere long, be some use of the art, of which they
held it a dishonour to be anie way ignorant, neyther indeed were they, as
the meanest in the company for a shift, could have dischar'd the office of
a captaine, which gave occasion (as I take it) of that old said saw, that
when Rice ap Thomas went to Bosworth field, there followed him as
manie captaines as soldiers,[27] that is, men as able to direct as to execute:
and alluding to this, I heard a greate privie counsellor of this kingdome
once say, that he thought in Rice ap Thomas his time more able and
expert commanders might have been chosen out of Wales alone than
nowe (woe worth the while) through this whole land – butt to procedde:
the care which yong Rice daylie shew'd of the publique good and benefit
redownding to all by this care, wonn him more and more ground in the
hartes of the people, soe that he began to carrie all cleere before him,
everie man striving with a friendlie emulation to make a neerer
approach to his favour, and to ingratiate themselves the more they were
desirous to hold something or other under him, tying themselves thereby
with lief and fortune ever to be at his command, which, when he once
assuredlie found, he fell upon a fine devise and politicke way to endeere
and fasten his countriemen unto him, which was to turne all such landes
as he had in demesnes, into horse races, as that of Carewe, Narberth,
Emlyn, Abermarlais, Wibley or of other his greate houses,[28] and as they
increas'd he would bestowe on this and that man a horse, by which
meanes drawing inn those of the best abilities in all the adjacent
counties, he tyed them stronglie to their former proffers, soe that nowe,
with the help of his tenants (which I find upon record[29] to be betweene

[27] The source of this story is unknown.
[28] The *CR* editor adds a note: 'Carew Castle is situated on a branch of the harbour of Milford, in a
rich beautiful country, the ruins of which at this day exhibit a magnificent appearance; Sir Rice ap
Thomas, was at the time referr'd to above, mortgagee in possession of it, and made it his favourite
residence for many years, as is evident from the sumptuous additions he made to that noble fabrick,
particularly the bow-window front: this castle is memorable for the celebration of a tilt and
tournement solemnly held there, by Sir Rice, being the only regular exhibition of this kind on
record in the principality; an account of which, will be given at large in this history.' See below
pp.247ff; Walker, *Arch. Camb.*, CV (1956), 81–95; King and Perks, *Archaeological Journal*, CXIX
(1962), 270–307.
[29] The *CR* editor adds a note: 'Vid. Record: Dom: Regis, in Thesauro Receptoris, Scaccarii sui,
sub Custodia Dom: Thesauror: et Camerar: remanent.' This may refer to records forfeited at the
time of Rhys ap Gruffydd's treason in 1531 (see below n.31). PRO, DL43/12/14, is a detailed survey
of the lordship of Kidwelly dating from Sir Rhys's lifetime and revealing his numerous plots of land,
most of which seem not to have been held by his forebears but had been acquired from many
individuals. It is partly edited by Morris, *Carms. Antiquary*, XI (1975), 55–87. Echoes of such
methods used by Sir Rhys to establish his lordship by manipulating land tenure are sounded in Elis
Gruffudd's Chronicle (*c.*1552) and in NLW MS 1602 D f.153 (*c.*1609–30): Jones, *TCASFC*, XXIX

eighteen or nineteen hundred, and all of them bound by their leases to be readie with a horse when he call'd upon them), he was by report able to bring into the field foure or five thousand horse, upon a verie shorte summons, which popularitie of his, had it happen'd in the time of a jealouse and unbragiouse prince, might easilie have wrought his confusion; but Edward the 4th. being well assur'd of the loiall intentions of his hart, thought himself happie in the strength of soe powerfull a subject, neyther did the people suffer their desires here to rest; (as if nott to goe forward in love were to goe backward) for as he gave them horses, soe they gave him certain patches of land within their estates,[30] and that at their verie doores (as if in some doting or roving humour they intended to erect some newe tenure to envassell themselves unto him) and this they did nott onlie for his countenance and protection, butt to express likewise the interest he had in their hartes to love him, handes to fight for him, and in their fortunes to supplie all his occasions, for confirmation of which traditional report, we find by an inquisition of this estate, taken in the 23d of Henry 8th.,[31] it did appeare that this Rice left to his heire, twelve hundred pound land a yeare old rent of assize, and upward, all which, save onlie his castles and mannors, and the demesnes belonging unto them, was dispersed here and there over all South Wales, in quilletts and small tenements, and at this day the modicum left of that greate estate, is thus scatterr'd up and downe in several places, fewe or none of those tenements being conterminant each with the other.

Nowe in this soe prosperous a condition, and in this height of felicitie, it had binn no newe thing, if this yong Rice, together with his fortunes, had rays'd his cogitations above the lowlie orbe of a subject, and soe to have forgotten the dutie and allegiance due to his sovereigne, but soe well did he compose his spiritt, and soe trulie fitt his saile to his boate, that noe puffe of greatnesse, or vaine flash of popular applause, could at any hand oerturne him, being built up, even from his verie cradle, with the pure materialls of honour and honestie, his thoughts ever ayming at greatness for good endes, to serve his king and countrie, and to preserve the reputation of his house and familie. Yett notwithstanding we may

---

(1939), 31–2; see above, pp.72–3.

[30] The *CR* editor adds a note: 'And this perhaps may account for the otherwise very unaccountable mixture of property, particularly in the counties of Carmarthen, Pembroke and Cardigan at this day, where it is common to find half an acre, or an acre of land, in the midst of a large tract of contiguous property, belonging to a person having no other land but that, within several miles of it.' The general circumstances in which landowners in Pembrokeshire (including Rhys ap Thomas) bought large numbers of small customary tenements are outlined in Howells, thesis cited, I, 120–2, 140. As a result, Rhys ap Gruffydd could rally a large force of tenantry against Walter Devereux, Lord Ferrers, in 1531 (see above p.97).

[31] This is very likely a reference to PRO, Exchequer, Treasury of Receipt (E36), 151, 'The booke of viewes of the castells and manors places late apperteynyng to Res ap Griffith atteynted'. The properties were situated in the lordship of Builth as well as in the counties of Carmarthen, Cardigan and Pembroke. See also the valor of Rhys ap Gruffydd's lands (SC12/23/43), and the accounts of royal keepers of the estate from 1531 (e.g., SC6/Henry VIII/4882ff.)

nott imagine him soe stupid and senselesse as not to feel the favourable gale of his happie fortune, or refuse sometimes to be tickled with the musicall acclamations of the manie, only thus much we may gather by the whole course of his lief, that he never did put anie confidence in those fickle and slipperie commodities, for proofe whereof I heard Doctor Baylie, Bishop of Bangor, my verie noble friend,[32] once in a sermon speaking of privadoes and minions to princes, and then of your demagoge popular men, such as are darlings of the multitude, give instance of young Rice, for one of the most generall belov'd men, and of greatest authoritie that ever was in Wales, and yett never anie man (in shewe) more neglected and lesse studied to winn in the people a love and observance of him then he did; for he, by a rigid and severe way of proceeding, enforc'd them to resigne unto him the full interest of their hartes; nay, some will not sticke to say, that when he came to hold place of authoritie under Henrie the 7th, and Henrie the 8th, he grewe cruell in his charge. Severe he might well be, for severite we know, is *proximum justitiae bonum* [next to justice]. And as he was severe, soe, when he had donn his dutie, and laid aside his authoritie, he was affable and courteous withall, carrying himself so equall betweene, that neyther his courteous behaviour weaken'd the reverence due to his person, nor his severitie the love, a thing rarely to be seene. I doe not doubt butt he was well read in the disposition of his countriemen, as being by nature a people rather enclin'd to libertie then servitude, and therefore forc'd to hold a hard hand over them. By this newefound way of popularitie he was now growne to such a height, as higher he could not goe in the esteeme of the people, soe that hereupon presentlie they gave him the surname of Greate, calling him ever after the Greate Rice of Wales.[33] 'Twas a bold hyperbole of that proud Bard,[34] when thus he sung of him,

> Y Brenin biau'r ynys
> Ond fy o ran i Syr Rys.

Which thus may be Englished:

> All the Kingdome is the Kings,
> Save where Rice doth spredd his wings.

The poett tells us a lye, that thereby we may attayne unto the truth. He affirmes yong Rice to be greater than he was, to the end we should beleeve how greate he was. Poetts and historiographers take to themselves sometimes superlative prerogatives; and in that age, among

[32] Lewis Bayly, the reformist bishop of Bangor (1616–31), may have been a native of Carmarthen. He encouraged the use of Welsh in his diocese. *DWB*, pp.28–9; J. G. Jones, 'Bishop Lewis Bayly and the Wynns of Gwydir, 1616–27', *WHR*, VI (1973), 404–23.

[33] This phrase has not been located. But cf. BL, Add.MS 23113 f.3, the contemporaneous explanation of Henry Rice's motives in petitioning Charles I: 'Sir Rice ap Thomas, commonly called the Great Rice of Wales' (see above p.131).

[34] The *CR* editor adds a note: 'Rhys Nanmor ai Kant'. But the following lines do not appear in the poems edited by Headley, thesis cited.

us, our Bardes especiallie, were too excessive, as if they had libertie to think what they would, and to say what they thought. Yett I find that this Greate Rice (see still the faithfulness and loyalty of his hart) did question the lief of his poete for the pride and arrogancie of his perfidiouse rithmes; who, coming to his triall stood upon his justification, and said they were all mistaken for my wordes, said he were these.

> Y Brenin biau'r ynys,
> A chyriau Fraink, a chors Rhys.

Which may be thus translated:

> The Kingdom is, the King's (I wis)
> The skirts of France and Rice is his.[35]

Which sudden and quick invention sav'd his lief, and soe he was dismissed; young Rice being glad of anie occasion to save his beloved Bard. And thus you have a true relation of Greate Rice, his deportment, both in his owne private, as well as in the publique, during the last tenn yeares of King Edwardes reigne;[36] we shall next proceed to the time of that bloodie usurper Richard, against whom he seemes to be the man ordained by divine providence to throwe the first stone, and to open the gate to that monster's destruction.

---

[35] Nor do these lines appear in Headley, thesis cited.
[36] For Rhys Nanmor (*c.*1480–1513), see *Companion to Welsh Lit.*, s.n.; E. R. Ll. Davies, thesis cited.

5

The Reign of Richard III

(1) *The Duke of Buckingham and the Bishop of Ely, consult att Brecknock, and there lay the Plot for Richard the Usurper's destruction. (2). An old Quarrel reconciled betweene the Duke of Buckingham and Sir Rice ap Thomas. (3) Morgan of Kidwelly undertakes to use his utmost endeavour to drawe Rice ap Thomas into the confederacie.*

(1) Maorke the ill success of a stolne crowne, poore Prince Edward was robb'd of his; and heere the thieves begin to wrangle. When theeves fall out, true men, wee say, have hope to recover their goodes.[1] The Duke of Buckingham, of late the usurpers coadjutor in all ungodlie practizes, is now become his mortall ennimie, whoe could expect lesse? Actors in Villainie never love themselves; such they ware: fellowes they might well be called, friendes they could be at noe hand. This Duke, another Caius Julius Vindex, first stirred the stone, which rowling along tumbled the traytour out of his seate.[2] Hee, together with the wise advise of the Bishop of Ely, hammered out and layed the groundwork of a most gloriouse edifice.[3] For the corner stone, when the Duke's owne title failed him, (for you must know he looked asquint sometimes that way himself)[4] Henrie, Earle of Richmond, as most worthie, was held the fittest man, being next of blood on the Lancastrian side, for strengthening of which might, and taking away all of all scruple, they held it most

[1] The first notice of the proverb, 'When theeves fall out, trewe men come to their good', is dated 1546, and it was popular in the second half of the sixteenth century. M. P. Tilley, *A Dictionary of the Proverbs in England in the Sixteenth and Seventeenth Centuries* (Ann Arbor, 1950), p.656.

[2] This refers to the precipitate rising against Nero by the governor of Gallia, C. Julius Vindex, which, though it failed, set in train more serious opposition: Plutarch, Life of Galba, chs.IV–VI, XXII, with comment in Cary (and Scullard), *History of Rome*, pp.403–4.

[3] For John Morton, bishop of Ely (1478–86), and his part in the downfall of Richard III, see C. Ross, *Richard III* (London, 1981), ch.4; C. S. L. Davies, 'Bishop John Morton, the Holy See, and the accession of Henry VII', *EHR*, CII (1987), 2–30.

[4] For the possibility that Buckingham had designs on Richard III's throne in the autumn of 1483, see Griffiths and Thomas, *Making of the Tudor Dynasty*, ch.8.

safe, to make overture of a match betwixt the sayd Earl and the Ladie Elizabeth, eldest daughter to Edward the Fourth, nowe next heire of the house of York.[5] The first admitted to this consultation, was, Reginald Brag, to whom this secrett was no sooner disclosed, than he undertook, with all faith, to recommend the same to his mistresse the Countesse of Richmond.[6] Long it remayned not with her before she made Doctor Lewis partaker of the counsell. This Lewis was an active stirring man, of strong abilities, by profession a Physician, and therefore under colour of his art often used in secrett conferences. Him of all others the Countesse made choice, both for his fidelitie and soundnesse of judgment, as likewise (in respect of his profession) the fittest minister to passe up and downe with private passages from partie to partie, without suspition, as a mediatour betwixt herself and the Queen Dowager, touching the accoupling her sonne in marriage with the Ladie Elizabeth; which employment the Doctor faithfullie discharged, to the full contentation of both parties.[7] After this manie were drawne in and interested in the cause, till they had finished a chaine, soe strong, that neyther the subtle prankes of the usurper, ne yett his bitter threatts and loud fulminations weare ever able to dissolve or breake asunder. The maine doubt nowe remayning which puzled their counsells, was to designe a place for the Earle Henrie his landing. In England it was not safe, in Wales it was impossible; unlesse greate Rice and Herbert, men mightie for power and commaunderie in those partes, could be wrought upon to espouse the cause.[8] Milford Haven was held most commodiouse for the Earl's first footing, a place where, in a manner, Rice ap Thomas was growne absolute, encircling all with the wideness of his power; it was then resolved, that if the said Rice could be tampered withall, the day were half wonn.

(2) At this time you must knowe, there was a deadlie quarrell betweene the Duke of Buckingham and Rice ap Thomas, and both flowne to soe high a pitch of defiance, as that the Duke some fewe dayes before, had sent him a cartell, threatning him withall, in a loftie and arrogant

[5] For Henry Tudor's claim, see S. B. Chrimes, *Henry VII* (London, 1972), ch.2.
[6] Griffiths and Thomas, *Making of the Tudor Dynasty*, pp.91ff.
[7] Ibid., pp.91ff., and see above p.183.
[8] The Herbert mentioned is Sir Walter Herbert, the younger (and abler) brother of William, second Herbert earl of Pembroke, for whom see Griffiths and Thomas, *Making of the Tudor Dynasty*, pp.128–9; Evans, *Wales and the Wars of the Roses*, pp.215–16. This paragraph owes much to Polydore Vergil's *English History*, pp.194–8. The Life's additional suggestion that Milford Haven was designated as Henry Tudor's prospective landing point in the secret discussions beforehand is interesting; rumours to that effect seem to have reached Richard's ears, though it was felt that they might refer to Milford-on-Sea in Hampshire: Evans, *Wales and the Wars of the Roses*, pp.213–14; Horrox, *Richard III*, pp.208–11.

language, to come and cudgell him out of his castle of Carmarthen;[9] if soe be, that some speedy satisfaction weare not given his Lordshipp for injuries received, to whom Rice ap Thomas in a manner stoute enough, tho' somewhat better season'd with curtesie (a virtue inherited by him from his father, who never was rough and boysterous, save when his sword was out), made answeare; that the wayes being mountaynous and craggie, his Grace might spare the labour; for that hee intended in person shortlie to attend his Lordship at Brecknock; there to receave his commandes, intimating thereby, that he doubted nott with the assistance of the Vaughans[10] and the Games[11] (two noble families then swaying those countries) together with his other fast friends, to be able to mate the Duke at his owne doores, and soe he was indeede: the Duke onlie having a bare authoritie of commaunding their persons and nott their affections, the other with their unanime consent having the disposall of their persons, fortunes, lives, and all.

Thes two roaring lions (fitt pillars to support the greate worke nowe in hand) thus in heate of blood, and spurn'd on in the way of revenge, did unjustlie dishearten the confederates insoemuch, as in all likelihood this hitherunto well erected building was neere to fall asunder, if soe, a firme reconciliation weare not made presentlie betweene them. Whereupon newe counsells were taken, and Doctor Lewis, a Welchman borne, and once a Tutor to Rice ap Thomas in his younger dayes, thought the ablest and most convenient messenger to be employed on such a piece of service.[12] The Doctor glad of anie occasion to effurther the enterprize afoote, undertoke to use his best endevours in that behalf, and for that purpose made a journey into Wales, to the said Rice, lying then at his Castle of Abermarlais;[13] where he found him readie to shape his course

[9] At the heart of this dispute may have been Buckingham's enormous accession of authority in Wales in May 1483, including the constableship of Carmarthen Castle for life: Griffiths, *Principality of Wales*, I, 203.

[10] The *CR* editor adds a note: 'These Vaughans were of Tretwr Castle in Brecknockshire: Sir Thomas Vaughan beheaded at Pomfret by order of Richard the Third. was of this family.' The Vaughans of the lordship of Brecon were a prolific brood: a daughter of Sir Roger Vaughan of Tretower (executed in 1471 at Chepstow by Jasper Tudor) married Rhys ap Thomas's brother Morgan. Sir Roger's mother was Gwladus, daughter of Dafydd Gam (died 1415), from whom the Games family of Brecon descended (see n.11). The connection with Sir Thomas Vaughan whom Richard III executed at Pontefract in 1483 is less certain. See *DWB*, pp.101, 992, 997, 1000–1, 1008.

[11] The *CR* editor adds a note: 'Descendants of Sir David Gam, knighted for his services at the battle of Agincourt.' Dafydd Gam was in fact slain at Agincourt, the record of his death poignantly immortalized by Shakespeare, *Henry V*, Act IV, Scene 8. The claim that he was knighted while lying mortally wounded on the battlefield has some imprecise support: N. H. Nicolas, *History of the Battle of Agincourt* (2nd edn., London, 1832), pp.135–6, 168, 174, 279–80, 290, 369, 379, and appendix p.60.

[12] See above p.195 for intrigues by this ubiquitous scholar. The possibility that such a mission took place need not be dismissed out of hand; it is hardly surprising that it left no corroborative record in view of the secrecy involved.

[13] Rhys seems to have occupied Abermarlais during the minority of Walter, son and heir of Sir Walter Griffith (died 1481), at least until 1489: Griffiths, *Principality of Wales*, I, 162, 274–5.

for Brecknock, there to putt that old inventerate difference betwixt him and the Duke to the decision of their swordes. And here this good Doctor was putt to the height of his skill; who being an expert philosopher and a physician both, well read in the causes and remedies of disordered affections and unrulie passions, began to applie his best receipts for the cooling and allaying of these overhott and fierie spiritts; leaving noe arguments unus'd to pursuade, to concord, and unitie, and further giving his (nowe patient) Rice ap Thomas to understand, that greate preparations were afoote for the good of the weall publique, which, ere long, should be imparted to him, and therefore besought him to reserve his well knowne valour to better purpose; or at lest wise for the present to beare himself a man of peace; such and soe forcible were the Doctor's reasons, that in the end, as some great benefitt weare like to accrue to the common wealth by their accord, Rice ap Thomas did willinglie assent to a peaceable conclusion. This parte being well plaid, and the Doctor seeing his physicke to work so powerfullie with Rice ap Thomas, to the Duke then he goes, with whom his medicinal applications produced the same effects, and so beating the Yron when it was hott[14], he brought them in the end to be so flexible, that they condescended to give each other the meeting at a place called Trecastle, middway betwixt Brecknock and Abermarlais, where with mutual embraceings they gave assured testimonie to all the beholders of a hartie reconcilement.[15]

(3) The Doctor having successfullie hitherunto performed the errand for which he came into those partes, namely, the reconciliation of the Duke and Rice ap Thomas, yet thought his message lame of a legg, for that the latter was not interested in their counsels, or anieway laboured to favour the cause, wherefore he closeth with his old acquaintance, Morgan of Kidwelly, a discreete man, and a cabanett close friend to the said Rice,[16] to whom, after long communication (first taking of him an oath *sub sigillo* [under his seal] for his fidelities), he delivered the true state of the businesse, and howe farr all things were advanced in England for the common good, imploring him for God's cause, whose honour was highlie abused by Richard's unjust usurpation, for his countries sake, for his owne safety, and the preservation of all good men who were joynt sufferers in these grievous calamities, to employ all his witt and industrie

---

[14] Cf. Chaucer's 'The Tale of Melibeus', §70 (*c*.1386): 'Right so as whil that Iren is hoot men sholden smyte'; Tilley, *Dictionary of Proverbs in England*, p.342 (for its common use in the sixteenth century).

[15] Trecastell was situated close to the border between the lordship of Brecon and Cantref Bychan in Carmarthenshire. Meetings on such common borders to solve disputes between neighbouring lords were a well-established practice. Griffiths, 'Wales and the March', pp.156–7, 169.

[16] For Trahaearn ap Morgan of Kidwelly and his relationship with Rhys, see above p.38.

to imprint in Rice ap Thomas a true feeling of this soe pious, just, and honourable undertaking, so that he might deliver up the keyes of that parte of the kingdom (nowe in his custodie)[17] to the assured pledg' of our weall, the renowned Earl of Richmond, the retayning whereof, being the price of blood, might, in the end, worke him more mischief then ever the wrongfull gould, sacrilegiously stolne from the temples of Toloux, did to thos wicked miscreants the souldiers of Cepio the Roman Consull,[18] likewise enforcing the fitt opportunitie nowe offer'd for the uniting the two royall houses, that had caused the shedding of soe much innocent blood; and last of all, tho' not lest of all, to a spiritt affecting glorie, to lett him knowe what fame and reputation 'twould add to himself and his whole posteritie, to be anie way assistant in this case, which noe doubt in time should be amplie rewarded by Earle Henrie, when he weare fullie invested in the Diademe. Morgan of Kidwellie hearing this relation of Doctor Lewis, howe his partizans were resolved to goe through, stitch with what they had soe carefully begun, and prosperously labour'd, and considering with himself howe much it would make for Rice ap Thomas his advancement (a thing he speciallie eyed) to have a hand in soe gloriouse a work; he could not chuse but take it to hart, giving a willing avouch unto the Doctor's reasonable desires, soe to rayse himself a ladder to clime by, in discharging such offices, as should be acceptable to both parties, provided likewise, that the Bishop of St David, and the Abbot of Tallye, might share in the counsells, two men, who for wisdome and greate experience in affaires of state, might justlie claime a larger interest in the said Rice, to direct his actions then himself, to which the Doctor agreed. And soe, for the present they parted, the one to his mistresse, the Countesse of Richmond, the other to the Bishop of St David's and the Abbot of Talye.[19]

(1) *King Richard requires from Rice ap Thomas on Oath of Allegiance, and his Sonn, Griffith Rice, for a Pledge of his Fidelitie. (2) Rice ap Thomas his answeare*

[17] Lewis's apparent stress on piety, justice and honour in the conspiracy against Richard III echoes the terms of Henry Tudor's manifesto after his landing in August 1485; cf. Jones, *History of the Gwydir Family and Memoirs*, pp.27–8.

[18] In 106 BC, the consul, Q. Servilius Caepio, looted the chief sanctuary of the Gaulish tribe of the Tectosages at Tolosa (Toulouse); but the treasure disappeared mysteriously on its way to Rome and Caepio was believed to have embezzled it. Cary (and Scullard), *History of Rome*, pp.217–18.

[19] See above p.186. If these intrigues took place in 1483, the bishop would have been Thomas Langton (1483–5), one of Richard III's appointees who, at least in the summer of 1483, thought well of the king: A. R. Myers (ed.), *English Historical Documents*, III (1327–1485) (London, 1969), pp.336–7, from J. B. Sheppard (ed.), *Christ Church Letters* (Camden Society, 1877), p.45. In any case, Langton seems to have accompanied Richard on his tour of midland England from 20 July and to have been with him still in Yorkshire in September when he sent this letter to William Sellyng, prior of Christ Church, Canterbury. See R. Edwards, *The Itinerary of King Richard III, 1483– 1485* (London, 1983), pp.4–8. The reference is more likely to be a retrospective one to either Bishop Pavy or Bishop Morgan (1496–1504).

to the King. (3) The Bishop of St David's, the Abbott of Talye, and Morgan of Kidwely, seeke to drawe Rice ap Thomas to side with the Earl of Richmond. (4) The effectes of their persuasions.

(1) While businesses weare thus on motion for Henrie, we must knowe, Richard had nott his handes in his bosome, as one that were idle, having, by his emissaries, continuall advertizement from time to time of his enemies walkes.

In the first place he labours ernestlie by large promises to regaine the ringleaders of the confederacie, the Duke of Buckingham, or if that failed, by threates and menacing wordes to teare him from the adverse partie, butt all would not doe, for the Duke being well acquainted with the slye cast of Richard's bowe, was growne too old a bird to be caught with chaffe, and therefore little caring for his glozing speeches, under which he knewe there lay nothing but poyson and fraud, ne yett regarding his taunting termes, which he was well assured, paid home where they laid hold, he held it his safest course nott onlie to stand on his owne guard, butt declare himself an enimie. Richard frustrated of the lest hope of catching the Duke in his toyle was surrounded on each side with apprehensions of danger, and had no other way of fortifying himself, but by ministring of others and taking of hostages from those who were of greatest power to displesure him. The Lord Stanly was the man he most feared, as being married to Earle Henrie's mother, whom at noe hand he would licence to depart the court, until he had enpledged the Lord Strange his eldest sonne for his indemnitie.[20] These strict courses being taken with the English, he falls upon the like with us in Wales; directing his commissioners for Carmarthen to Rice ap Thomas, there to take of him an oth of fidelitie, and further requiring his onlie sonne Griffith Rice as a gage for the true performance of his future loyaltie. The oth Rice ap Thomas stood not upon: as for his sonne, he humbly besought the commissioners not to bereave him of that comfort, having noe more but that one, and he nott above four or five yeares of age, not doubting butt by letter to give his Majestie such satisfaction as should well suite with the kinge's desires, and his dutie to all, which the commissioners freely gave way, and accepting his letter to this effect, departed.[21]

---

[20] This story, whose essentials are corroborated by the Croyland Chronicle (N. Pronay and J. Cox (eds.), *The Crowland Chronicle Continuations, 1459–1486* (London, 1986), p.179), is derived from Polydore Vergil's *English History*, p.212, but attributed to 1483 rather than to 1485. Jones, 'Richard III and the Stanleys', in Horrox, *Richard III and the North*, p.34.

[21] There is no available corroboration of this story, but it is significant that William Griffith of Penrhyn was a hostage for the loyalty of his father to Richard at the same time as Lord Strange was in Richard's custody at Nottingham. *DWB*, p.1125. The date of Gruffydd ap Rhys's birth is unknown; according to this account, it took place *c*.1478–9, which is plausible.

(2) *Rice ap Thomas his letter to Richard the Third, penned by the Abbot of Talye.*[22]

Sir,

I have received letters mandatorie from your Majestie, wherein I am enjoyned to use my best endeavours for the conservation of your royall authoritie in these partes, and to applie likewise my soundest forces for the safe guarding of Milford Haven from all forraigne invasion; especially to impeach and stopp the passage of the Earle of Richmond, if soe by anie treacherouse meanes he should attempt our coustes: and withall, Sir, an othe of allegiance hath binn tendered me in your Majesties name by certain commissioners, deputed (as it seemes) for that purpose, requiring alsoe my onlie sonne as an hostage and pledge of my fidelitie. Touching the first, Sir, nowe an enemie is declared, I hold myself obliged, without further looking into the cause, faithfullie to observe the same, by a necessarie relation my obedience hath to your Majestie's commandes, to which I deeme it nott unseasonable to annexe this voluntarie protestation; that whoever, ill affected to the state, shall dare to land in those partes of Wales, where I have anie emploiments under your Majestie, must resolve with himself to make his entrance and irruption over my bellie. As for my othe, Sir, in observance to your Majestie's will, which shall ever regulate mine, I have (though with some hartes griefe I confesse, and reluctancie of spiritt), as was required, taken the same before your Majestie's commissioners, and if stronger trialls, than eyther faith or othe might be layd upon me to confirme my most loyall affection, I should make noe delay to enmannacle and fetter myself in the strictest obligations for your Majestie's bettter assurance. And heare I beseech your Majestie give me leave without offence to disburden myself of certaine cogitations, whereby I am persuaded, that these pressings of vowes and othes upon subjects, noe way held in suspect, hath often times wrought even in thos of soundest affections, a sensibilitie of some injurie don to their faith: a thing which hearetofore hath binn prejudiciall to manie great princes, whoe, while they shewed themselves distrustful, and feared subtile dealing, have redd to some of fickle minds and unstable thoughts evil lessons against themselves. I speake nott this, Sir, as repining at what I have donn; butt to give your Majestie, to witt, that I feare some ill offices have bin done me, which might you thinke yourself unsure of my service without this manner of

[22] There is no other known version of this letter, but its general orthography would not be out of place in the late fifteenth century. On another occasion when a letter is included in the Life (see below p.212), Henry Rice is scrupulous in noting that he had not seen it himself: no such caveat is entered here. The opening lines may rehearse a proclamation and set of instructions sent to Rhys in respect of the south-west Wales coast comparable with those sent to sheriffs and commissioners in English shires on 7–8 December 1484, with the aim of resisting an invasion by Henry Tudor and his allies: *Harleian 433*, III, 124–8. Cf. similar proclamations and instructions on 22 June 1485, on the eve of Henry's invasion: ibid., II, 228–30.

proceeding. Whatever, Sir, other men reckon of me, this is my religion, that noe vowe can lay a stronger obligation upon me in anie matter of performance, then my conscience. My conscience bindes me to love and serve my King and country, my vowe can doe noe more. He that makes shipwrack of the one, will (I believe) make little account of the other. For my owne part, Sir, I am resolutelie bent, while I am to spinn out my dayes in well doing; and soe, God willing to conclude the last actions of my lief. And sure, Sir, could I find myself culpable of one single cogitation, repugnant to the allegiance I owe to your Majestie, I should think the lief alreadie I have lived overlong.[23] Nowe, Sir, for the delivering of my sonne to your Majestie's commissioners as a gage of my fealty, I have as yett, presumed on this shorte pause, nott in way of opposition to your commandes, but to fit myself with such reasons, as shall, I hope, in noe sorte seeme discordant with your will. The yeares, Sir, my poore child beares on his backe are butt fewe, scarce exceeding the number of foure, which I conceaved, mought well privilege him, being more fitt for the present to be enbosomed in a mother's care, then exposed to the world; nature as yet, not having the leasure to initiate him in that first lecture of feeding himself. Againe, Sir, be pleased to consider, he is the onlie prop and support of my house nowe in being; and therefore may justlie challenge at my handes a more tender regarde, then I can anie way expect he shall find among strangers, and in a place so farr remote from his natural parents.[24] And lastly, Sir, I may well call him the one half of myself, nay to speake more trulie the better parte of me, so that if your Majeste should deprive me of this comforte, I were then divided in my strength, which united, might perhaps serve as most useful weare I called to some waightie employments for the good of your service. I humblie beseech your Majestie to reflect upon these necessities with an impartial eye, and in the meane while to be fullie assured, that without these hard injunctions, I reallie am, and will, how badlie soever I be entreated, still continue,

        Sir, your most humble,
          Most obedient,
            And most faithfull
              Subject and servant
              RICE AP THOMAS   From Carmarthen Castle, 1484.[25]

[23] Rhys may have had in mind the special oaths of loyalty demanded of 'alle the knightes squiers gentilmen and othere oure subgiettes' in north Wales on 8 February 1484, to be received by William Griffith, chamberlain there (*Harleian 433*, II, 90). It is likely that a similar instruction was sent to Richard Mynors, chamberlain of south Wales. Drafts of special oaths of loyalty to Richard, especially directed against his 'ennemyes Rebelles and traytors', are in *Harleian 433*, I, 2–3.

[24] This may suggest that Rhys's first wife, Efa, daughter of Henry ap Gwilym, was alive in 1484, and that consequently his marriage to Jenet Mathew, widow of Thomas Stradling (died 1480), took place rather later.

[25] It is not known who was appointed to succeed Henry, duke of Buckingham, as constable of Carmarthen Castle after the duke's execution on 2 November 1483; that Rhys should be in effective

To this letter I could never learne of anie returne made, onlie I heard of divers commaundes that followed, to confirme the said Rice in his allegiance; exhorting him to vigilance in his charge. The reasons, if we conjecture aright, whie King Richard prest him noe further for his hostage, weare, because of the dangers now beginning to discover themselves in everie corner of the kingdome, or that he thought Rice his bare protestations and letter of force sufficient for confirmation of his securities in those partes, or else was desirous to make his distrust under a simulated guise of being well satisfied, lest, by discovering his doubts, he should teach Rice a way warrantably to be false.

(3) Whatever then became of his letter, or howe accepted, it is acknowledged by most, that hereupon Rice ap Thomas grewe verie discontented, still fearing what sinister interpretation might be made of the wordes he had written, and well knowing, that anie slight occasion would serve the turne where the tyrant was bent to ruine: whereupon the Bishop of St David's and the Abbot of Talye, noting his perturbed thoughts and discomposed gestures, concluded this a fitt season to performe what Morgan of Kidwellie, with their assistance, had undertaken to Doctor Lewis, in behalf of the Earle of Richmond, and soe gentlie laying their handes on his pulse, as he was in the fitt or intermission, soe they applied their counsels, till at length by little and little, ere he was aware, they had fullie acquainted him, a thing hitherunto he was utterly ignorant of, with the whole proceedinges, pressing him further, the cause being so good, and the meanes so easie, to have an eye to his owne honour, and that he would consider the greate riches and power he had, was butt lent him, to be emploid for God's glorie and his countries safetie; the former whereof was nowe highlie abused through usurped authoritie; the other grievously bleeding under the heavy hand of tyrannie and oppression, requiring the help of all good men for its deliverance. Rice ap Thomas having somewhat recollected himself, though he hartilie wished the tyrants destruction, whom he had just cause to feare; yet being taken unprovided, gave the Bishop and the rest noe other answeare at that time, but that King Richard, however an ill man, and possessed of the crowne by oblique courses, was notwithstanding, his King *in esse* [at present], and therefore he held himself bound, rather with submission, to endure the worst of tyrannies, then in a rebellious way to resist the Lord's annointed.[26] The Lord's annointed? the Devill's rather, said the Bishop. And I pray, Sir, said hee, for instance in myself: weare I your Bishop nowe *in esse*, or in fact onlie, without anie lawfull calling, would you hold my absolutions or excommunications, or anie other ministeriall injunctions of mine of

charge of the fortress need cause no surprise. Griffiths, *Principality of Wales*, I, 203.

[26] This is the classic dilemma of a subject.

anie validitie? or that my diocesans weare at all obliged to yield me canonical obedience? why, this is your case, you have a King who is a cruell tyrant, a bloodie butcher, a most unjust usurper, another Nero, under whom to doe ill was nott alwayes safe, alwayes unsafe to doe well; O monstrous! and can you be soe voyd of understanding, as to imagine, that by anie lawe of God or man we owe him anie faith or allegiance, more than an hereticke or infidel? It seemes Rice ap Thomas was nott at all displeased with this discourse of the Bishop's; whereupon, said he, my Lord, I pray what thinke you of the othe I have taken? for my conscience tells me I should not falsifie it besides, my letters sent of late to his Majestie, replenished with most loyal protestation, to affurther his service, will stand up as witnesses against me before men. The good Bishop knowing that he undertooke nothing, which first receaved nott an inward approbation from that counsellour which in all extremities he had recourse to his conscience, prepared nowe to discharge his dutie as a divine, and soe to enlarge himself somewhat upon the nature of a vowe, which he gave him to understand, was legitimate or illegitimate, to be broken or kept as it is good or bad in its foundation. To breake an inconsiderate vowe, is a far lesse sinne then to perform it. Holie David vowed rashlie to Abigail, he would not leave Nabal by morning, a man to pisse against the wall, and yett David broke that vowe, and God and all good men allowed thereof for well donn.[27] Sir, you have taken an oath faithfully to serve King Richard, a most bloodie assassinate, O! execrable oath! and can you be soe deprived of all reason, as to think yourself obliged in conscience to make good the same? noe, noe, Sir, recant rather what you have unadvisedlie, nay, coactitiouslie donn, and further, as your spirituall and gostlie father, I heare disenchaine you of these bondes, and give you free absolution, and as touching your letter to that faithless miscreant, I knowe nothing contained therein (and I appeal to my Lord Abbott who drewe the same) but you may well dispense withall, without anie the least impeachment to your honour. And for that particular branch of your letter, where you undertake by oath, that none (ill affected) shall enter at Milford, without he make his passage over your bellie, my answeare is, that the Earle of Richmond can be no ill affected man to the state, comming in pursuite of his owne right, and withall to release us of our heavie bondage; or if you bee further scrupulous herein, I shall never hold it for anie disparagement to your humilitie, to lay yourself prostrate on the ground for the true and indubitate Lord of us all to make an easie entrance over you. Although Rice ap Thomas was nowe growne somewhat more flexible, being by these forcible reasons of the Bishop's, satisfied of all doubts that mought assault the peace of his conscience, yet nothing could be wrought out of him for the present, more then that

[27] 1 Samuel ch.25.

wordes fell from him sometimes, which gave them half an assurance, he loved nott the tyrant; whereby they be gathered, he was nott soe much troubled in mind, for the nullifying of his vowe, as that he expected in a matter of soe greate importance to be solicited from better handes, therefore they left him for a while to frame out his owne resolves, from such private debatementes, as best suited with the true rules of that perfitt wisedome he was naturally endude withall.

(4) About this time the Countess of Richmond was dispatching away for Brittany, great sommes of monie to her sonne, with packetts of intelligence concerning the good inclinations of the nobilitie, gentrie, and communaltie of this realme, for the promoting of his cause.[28] The person emploid for this service, was one Hugh Conway, who began nowe to pine, that, though he had particular instructions for the Earle Henrie his landing at Milford Haven, yett he mought well reckon without his host, if Rice ap Thomas (the very hinge about which this greate worke was to turne, and without whose ayde and assistance there was noe looking upon those coastes) was not made a partizan in the businesse, and therefore thinking his message lame of the better legg, he delayed his journey for a while of going to Plimouth, where he was to take shipping, in expectation of further advertizement, howe Morgan of Kidwellyes labours succeeded in that behalf, and as good lucke was, it turned all to the best: for to remove the doubtes and feares with which Hugh Conwey was soare troubled, Doctor Lewis came in seasonably to the farewell, with a relation of the said Morgan's endeavours, as alsoe the Bishope of St David's and the Abbott's judiciouse carriage in working and moulding of Rice ap Thomas to their desires, with whom, as they had nott absolutelie prevailed, soe they sawe no cause to despaire, were the businesse fairlie urged, eyther by letters from the Earle himselfe, or by some person of authoritie entrusted for that purpose. The Countesse of Richmond hearing this, thought now the forte half won, and therefore nott to lett things coole, she gave Hugh Conwey second instructions for advising her son, speedilie to write unto the sayd Rice, wishing him withall to season his complimentes with large promises of honour, and to sett downe the true state of the cause, being by Doctor Lewis his reporte a likelier way to endeere him then anie other. Hugh Conwey, nowe a glad man, and furnished with such dispatches, goes for Plimmouth, and soone arrived in Brittany.[29]

---

[28] Vergil, *English History*, p.197; Griffiths and Thomas, *Making of the Tudor Dynasty*, pp.96, 103.

[29] See above p.202. See Vergil, *English History*, p.197, and Griffiths and Thomas, *Making of the Tudor Dynasty*, pp.93–6, for Hugh Conway's mission to Brittany; for Conway, a former servant of Edward IV, and one of the Stanley circle by 1483, see N. Tucker, 'Bodrhyddan and the families of Conwy, Shipley-Conwy and Rowley-Conwy', *Flintshire Historical Society Publ.*, XIX (1961), 61–85.

(1) *The Duke of Buckingham takes armes, and declares himself an enemie to Richard, which rash attempt cost him his life. (2) An answeare to a most false and maliciouse slander layd by Raphael Holinshed upon the Welchmen.*

(1) It was a saying of Augustus, that, they who take upon them the conduction of greate and weightie affaires must be warie, want of consideration and foresight being unpardonable errors in a perfitt and well accomplish'd commander.[30] Well had it fared with the Duke of Buckingham, if he had follow'd this wise direction: first, in examining his owne forces, then the businesse he had in hand, and lastlie, for whom he was to undertake this action, and with whom he had to deale. His forces, God wott, weare but weake, his whole armie being compos'd but of the riff-raffe of the Welch, and those too enforc'd and compell'd rather by imperious menaces then courteous behaviour or liberal entertainment;[31] againe the businesse he was to pursue, was of noe lesse consequence then a crowne, a thing not likelie to be procured with weake handes and cold affections. Thirdlie, the person for whom he was to runn the present danger, was beyond the seas, and far from giving him eyther succour or countenance. Last of all he had to doe at this time with a man of noe meaner condition then a King, who was nowe in the fielde, with a mightie hoste readie to bid him to battaile. Yett notwithstanding the duke, out of a temerariouse ardor of spiritt, would needes goe on till he came to Severne, where he mett with a fierce inundation (a far more powerfull adversarie then Richard), and there the poore Welchmen, I meane the refuse and drosse of the Welch, (for to say truth, of the better sorte he had none to attend him, their hartes as then being wholie bent to followe the fortunes of Rice ap Thomas, the Mars of Wales, as they call'd him, and the onlie planett then ruling them) worne out with cruell usage, having neyther monie, victualls, nor wages, were of meere necessitie forc'd to departe and leave this their unbeloved generall, at which time, had he likewise retir'd himself to his castle of Brecknock, he mought perhaps have promis'd himself a more safe protection among the Welch then he found in the handes of his servant Humphrey Bannastar, a man whom he had tenderlie brought up, and whom of all men he had most deerlie lov'd, favour'd and trusted; yett, notwithstanding all which, this falseharted Bannaster, the scorne of men, eyther for hope of reward, or feare of losse, most villanouslie and trecherouslie betraid him, which brought him to his inglorious end, a fact soe foule, that Richard (as verie a devill as he was), seem'd to blush thereat, saying, that hee which would be untrue to so

---

[30] Cf. Suetonius, *Augustus*, c.25.

[31] For Duke Henry's unpopularity among his own tenantry of Brecon, especially gentry families such as the Vaughans, see Pugh, *Marcher Lordships*, pp.340–1. The Life (see above p.196) noted that the Vaughans and the Gameses were inclined to attach themselves to Rhys ap Thomas rather than to the duke.

good a master, would be false to all others; so odiouse are traytors even to those whose instruments they are.[32] And this was the wofull conclusion of this great Duke of Buckingham, another Sempronius Gracchus, of princlie blood, quick witted, *sed prave facundus* [but perversely eloquent], who, noe question, mought have outlived all his staines, and seene the scale of honour rise againe with him, had he learned this one rule, *omissis praecipitibus, tuta ac salubria compescere* [in avoiding pitfalls, hold back safe and sound], or have had such a companion with him as Rice ap Thomas.[33]

(2) And heare I must be bold to borrowe a word with Raphael Holinshed, whoe in this place (I know not howe) by head and shoulders brings in both *Cowardlynesse* and *Falsehartednesse*, and would faine (unseasonablie) clapp them both upon the Welchmen, a hard censure![34] Though I account it an undervaluing of myself to undertake the protection of the scumme of anie nation (for these were noe better); yett in this, soe innocent, I find my countriemen to be, that I cannot chuse, but advocate for them. An *officious* lye may well be dispens'd withall in anie man; a *malicious*, that at noe hand, especiallie in an historiographer. Wheather Holinshed were malicious or sencelesse, or both in these two contumeliouse and reproachfull wordes, let the world judge. 'Tis the quarrel of the vulgar I undertake, nay (to go yett lower) the shavings, filings and offall of the vulgar, for of the better sorte (as I told you before), such who had given as large demonstrations of their braverie to the world, as ever anie Roman did, none appeared at all in this action. Hollinshed, you will say, is dead, and cannott answeare for himself; I will therefore spare him. Yet give me leave to examine his writings, and then make an equall judgment of both. The Duke of Buckingham, as is confessed, enforced and compell'd the Welchmen, in spite of their hartes, to attend him in this expedition, and they being ignobly used, forsooke him. Doe you call this falsehartedness? Why, they had noe hartes at all; and this Duke, therefore, may well be said to be a Lord of phantasticall bodies without soules, hartless, but not falseharted as Hollinshed would inferr. And as for the Welchmen's cowardly forsaking (as he sayes) of the Duke, speake you, O! the weakest of Welch spiritts, for I want line to fathome your prowesse! Cowardlinesse, as I conceave it, implies a flight from some enemie; and here werre noe

[32] Griffiths and Thomas, *Making of the Tudor Dynasty*, ch.8; Horrox, *Richard III*, ch.3. The Life repeats the common error that it was Humphrey (rather then Ralph) Banaster who betrayed the duke.

[33] Tiberius Sempronius Gracchus was rumoured to be seeking a crown and was accordingly murdered. His brother, Caius Sempronius Gracchus, became very powerful, but when he lost his power he was killed while seeking refuge with a servant. Plutarch's Life of Tiberius and Caius Gracchus.

[34] Holinshed, *Chronicles*, III, 417, for the untrustworthiness of the Welsh.

enemies but such as Gustavus Adolphus himself would have fledd from, famine and furiouse waters.[35] As for master Hollinshed, or anie other favouring his opinion in matter of cowardize or trecherie (of which there is not much to chuse), my answeare is, if I weare putt to that base choice (as I hope I shall never) I had rather yett bee a Welch coward, and forsake my generall, then an English Bannaster, and betray my master: I say, I had rather be a coward, then a traytour: and yett, I had rather bee noe man, then eyther of them.

[35] Here Henry Rice perhaps mingles his historian's instincts and his patriotism as a Welshman. This may refer to the campaign of Gustavus Adolphus, king of Sweden, in Livonia in the late summer of 1625. In a race against time, an impending shortage of supplies, and the autumn rains, he successfully completed the campaign before autumn (M. Roberts, *Gustavus Adolphus* (2 vols., London, 1953–8), I, 247–8). For the availability in England and Wales of news of the Thirty Years War, via newsbooks, see J. Frank, *The Beginning of the English Newspaper, 1620–1660* (Cambridge, Mass., 1961), pp.11, 13.

6

Henry Tudor's Enterprise

(1) *Rice ap Thomas declares himself for the Earle of Richmond to his private friends.* (2) *The Commons, though nott knowing his designs, were yet willing to second him with their lives and fortunes.*

(1) But now to return to the order of my storie, while the Duke of Buckingham was in the full heate of his overash undertakings spinning out (with more hast then good speede) the fatall webb of his own woe; we must understand Rice ap Thomas was busilie gnawing upon that hard and dangerous bone, which the bishop of St Davids and the rest had cast in his way. First he sawe all in destruction, the whole kingdom wearie of the insupportable burthen it sustayned; a notable alteration intended, noe lesse than the pulling downe of one king and putting up of another, parties at worke on all handes; high time to looke about him! Wherefore he fell to weigh the true condition of the present affaires, wheather, if undertaken, they tended to God's glorie, or weare any way profitable to the commonwelth, honorable for himself, and easie to be effected, in all which debatements, each thing answeared soe well to his desires, as he sawe noe reason whie the embarking in soe good a business, should anie way prejudice his reputation, or give the lest checke to his conscience; and therefore resolved forthwith to declare himself for the Earle Henrie, carying with him this assurance, that, if things succeeded well, as he was of speciall use in the service, soe a proportionable reward would nott be denied him; if otherwise, the worst that could befall him was death, and that therefore if he must, his opinion was *acrioris viri esse, merito perire* [the violent man perishes accordingly]. Standing thus in the highest elevation of his braverie of spiritt, newes was brought him of the Duke of Buckingham's downfall,[1] which startled him somewhat on the

---

[1] Buckingham was executed at Salisbury on 2 November 1483 (Griffiths and Thomas, *Making of the Tudor Dynasty*, pp.96–101; Horrox, *Richard III*, p.155). The source of the Latin proverb has not been traced. For an English version, see Shakespeare's *Romeo and Juliet*, Act II, scene vi, 9 (mid-1590s):

suddaine, not soe much for the Duke's death, as that he fear'd the partie might be discourag'd therewith, and so the cause weaken'd: wherefore beholding his neighbour's house on fire, he held it nowe high time to looke to his owne.[2] Hereupon convoking his forenamed friends togither, the bishop of St Davids, the abbott of Talley, and Morgan of Kidwelly, with whom he desired to joyne in counsell; Arnold Butler, Richard Griffith, and John Morgan, old and experienced souldiers,[3] he acquainted them with the duke's fall, and though he could nott readilie weene what alteration would follow of that, yett this he was sure of, that as the duke's attendants in his unfortunate jorney to Severne side, were for the most parte all Welchmen, king Richard might well be jelouse of the whole countrie, and soe noe man sure in what state and condition he stoode; and further, if anie were shott at, he himself was likeliest to be the first man: therefore he besought them to assist him with their best advise, howe in this case he should carrie himself; for by the violent manner of proceeding against the duke, he well sawe *Sic volo* [So I will] bore the sway, and every man held his life by curtesie, a thing he liked nott, nor would anie way trust to. The bishop and the rest observing his speeches carefullie, and not knowing what second counsells the Earle Henrie the *primum mobile* [the prime mover] in this action would nowe fall upon, weather he meant, as was first concluded to fixe upon Milford Haven for the certaine place of his landing, or wheather changing his resolution, he intended to give over the enterprize, and sitt downe in the cause, began to flitt and waver in their opinions, some advising him to save his owne stake, and nott to hazard fortune, lief and all at a cast; but stay and attend, to what head the humours in England now stirred, would gather; others urging him to take armes, some againe giving him counsell to stand for the king, some for the Earle; and some there wanted nott who would have him play a double part, as Valerius Festus did betweene Vitellius and Vespasian, soe holding both in hand, agreeable to our old proverbe:

> Good riding at two anchors, men have told;
> For if the one faile, the other may hold.[4]

These violent delights have violent ends,
        And in their triumph die.

[2] Horace, *Epistles*, I, 18.84 (*Tunc tua res agitur paries dum proximus ardet*). For an earlier use of this metaphor in relation to Brecon and the revolt of Llywelyn Bren (1316), see N. Denholm-Young (ed.), *Vita Edwardi Secundi* (London, 1957), pp. 66–7.

[3] For Trahaearn ap Morgan of Kidwelly, see above p.186. John Morgan, to be distinguished from the later bishop, may be identified with Trahaearn's younger brother: Bartrum, *1400–1500*, III, 394–6. It is even more likely that John (died *c*.1492), the son of Evan (or Ieuan) Morgan, is intended; his journey to the Holy Land and his knighthood of the Holy Sepulchre qualify him as one of the 'experienced souldiers'. *DWB*, pp.635–6; see above p.41.

[4] Erasmus, *Adagia*, 1139D. For the proverb's popularity in English in the late sixteenth and seventeenth centuries, see Tilley, *Dictionary of Proverbs*, p.571.

Each of these consults stood with some reason, all of them tending to safetie, though nott soe honourable as safe. 'Tis true safetie and honour were ever both of them the objects of Rice ap Thomas his care, and as he ever heeded the one, soe he never neglected the other; yett seeing he was nowe to make triall of himself, he determined rather to jeopardize his safetie then shipwreck his honour: and therefore told them plainlie, he liked nott this ambiguous manner of expressing themselves, with intention to interprete things afterward, as they sawe best for their purpose; that it was noe time nowe to halt betwixt two opinions: that they had nott long since, with all earnestness, advised him on the Earle of Richmond's behalf, and he sawe noe reason whie the fall of one man should thus on a suddaine enfeeble their courage, or stagger their constancie: 'twas nott to an arme of flesh they weare to trust, but to an Allmightie Arme. The cause, noe doubt, is good, and dishonour and shame to him that declines it. I am confident, said he, God is with us, and we shall prevaile; not we, but *El* with us. *Immanu-el*, and Immanu-all, God with us and all with us. In which galiard resolution he told them, that he ment directlie and resolutelie to espouse the cause, and if they would followe him therein, they should see he would make his lief and fortune common with theirs, both in the danger and honor of the attempt. Glad they weare all of this his free declaration, as jumping aright with their wishes; for however severall opinions were deliver'd by them, thereby to worke out of Rice ap Thomas a discoverie of his owne, yett weare they, as at first, ever of one mind, still for the advancing of the Earle Henrie's service, soe the said Rice could noe way better have fitted their humours then by thus ingenuouslie manifesting of his pleasure, which they nowe express'd both in their lookes and language, assuring him of their faith and furtherance in all his purposes. Here upon Rice ap Thomas (to take them at their wordes) would faine have presentlie putt himself into the field, and soe have proclaimed the Earle of Richmond King, by the name of Henrie the Seventh, which they instantlie persuaded him to forbeare, untill Hugh Conway were return'd out of Brittanie, for with out the Earle's presence or approbation at lest, 'tweare meere fool hardinesse to appeare for him at all; neyther could the taking of armes beare anie other shewe, butt of plaine rebellion, the readie way to their destruction. Yett because they understood by secrett intelligence from their friendes above, that the tyrant began to have an ill conceipt of Rice ap Thomas, and of all other his subjects, to hold him in greatest jelousie, they advised him to stand upon his guard, and to have his friendes continuallie about him, soe to prevent any suddaine surprize which mought be made upon his person, and this counsell was followed; for under colour of guarding the coastes, the said Rice had often meetings with those of best abilitie for service in the countrie, who, togither with the help of Arnold Butler, Richard Griffith, and John

Morgan, did soe well discipline and traine up in feates of armes, as in shorte time for their experience, they seem'd so manie captaines as soldiers.[5] Neyther wanted he at those times his secrett instruments to sound the affections of the people, using every way that could be devised, to stirr up and alter the vulgar: yea, Rice himself did not sticke sometimes, to lett fall certaine doubtfull speeches whereby they might easilie perceave which way he looked. Besides sundrie libells and defamatorie rhithmes were framed against king Richard, and suffered to be divulged, and by and by the same were forbidden and called in againe, which increased them the more.[6] With these manner of proceedings the generalitie began to be disquieted in mind, not knowing what to trust to, sometimes (as the nature of feare is) flocking togither, and then againe severing themselves and appointing private meetings, wherein their secrett conventicles they were readie to affirme and to expresse their cogitations with more audacitie, ever discoursing of those immenent dangers then hanging over them. The welthiest were for safe-seeming wayes and stood for Richard, a middle sorte were for Richmond, and those of desprate fortunes, as loveing to fish in troubled waters, cared nott which way the world went, soe all were in combustion; yet all concluded to fixe on Rice ap Thomas for their anchor hold, directing their course by his compasse, and without further dispute to insist in his steppes and followe his directions.

Rice ap Thomas, all this while, having given them line enough, yet still he kept the raines in his owne handes; and nowe obtayning what he aymed at, he made his perambulation into all partes where he had anie authoritie, rewarding some with his purse, feeding others with hopes, and all with assurance that their perill and wellfare should be to him in equall regard with his owne; then telling them of their duties, he persuaded them each to depart to his owne home, wishing them, upon the lest notice given eyther by firing of beacons or otherwise to be in a readiness,[7] and bring along with them good armes, and courageouse hartes, and as for the directing of their valour, that they might leave to himself, whoe would be ever studiouse of their good, and never suffer them to runn into the lest danger, save when their owne honour, and their countrie's safetie should urge them on.

About this time Hugh Conway returned out of Britanny, with letters from Earle Henrie to the Countesse of Richmond, and divers others, who were principall actors for him both in England and Wales; among

---

[5] See above p.200 for Rhys's probable involvement in coastal defence, at King Richard's behest.

[6] For seditious rumours concerning Richard, see Ross, *Richard III*, pp. xxxiii, xlvii, 145–6, 202; idem, 'Rumour, propaganda and public opinion during the Wars of the Roses', in Griffiths, *Patronage, the Crown and the Provinces in Later Medieval England*, pp.20–2.

[7] Polydore Vergil's *English History*, pp.213–14, notes the placing of beacons along the Pembrokeshire coast.

whom[8] one was to Rice ap Thomas, which he receaved by the handes of Morgan of Kidwelly, whoe likewise at that verie time, and to the verie same effect, receaved letters himself from one Evan Morgan, his neere cosen and intimate friend.[9] This Evan was a man of an antient and noble house, as anie gentleman in Monmouthshire, the chiefe of Tredegar and Machan, and the lineall descendant of Bledri, the Greate, Lord of Kilsant and Gwinvay. He fledd with the Earle Jasper from Chepstowe to Pembrock, and thence attended the Earle of Richmond, whom he served, into Brittany, where he continued in high favour with his master, for his true love and faithfull service, untill they returned for Milford Haven, and soe followed him on to the battle of Bosworth. There were foure of this worthie familie (the Bishop of St Davids,[10] Morgan, of Kidwellye, John Morgan, and this Evan, the topp of them all), who were speciall actors, and contrivers of this business, for as much as concerned us in Wales, and the onlie men that wrought Rice ap Thomas to the partie, which must needes clapp a wide marke of honour upon the name, and nott, without injurie, to be passed over in silence.

[8] The *CR* editor adds a note: 'Which letter the editor has not inserted, as the compiler of these memoirs confesses (to use his own words), "That he never had the honour to see the originall, but, that he had been informed by Sir Thomas Lakes, a principall secretarie of state, that, amongst young Rice's evidences (who was grandchild to Rice ap Thomas) in the signett office, when he was cleark there, he had seen such an one, written with the Earle of Richmond's own hand, and which, with other papers, were all unfortunately lost, at what time the banquetting house of Whitehall, under which that office then stood, was consumed with fire." Presuming therefore on such evidence and traditions in the country, to corroborate it, he had, in imitation of Thucydides, Dionysius Halicarnassus, and other historiographers, introduced a letter of his own composition to suit the circumstances.' Sir Thomas Lake (died 1630), principal secretary of state in 1616–19, was an Oxford MA, clerk of the signet *c.*1600, and keeper of the records at Whitehall from 1603. He would have had direct access to the forfeited archives of Rhys ap Gruffydd, and there is no reason to doubt that he saw a letter from Henry Tudor to Rhys ap Thomas among them (*DNB*, s.n.). The banqueting hall at Whitehall was destroyed by fire in 1619, which explains why few of Rhys ap Gruffydd's records survive in the Public Record Office. The writings of Thucydides and Dionysius of Halicarnassus were known in England by the sixteenth century: Binns, *Intellectual Culture*, pp.180, 217; M.C. Howatson, *The Oxford Companion to Classical Literature* (2nd edn., Oxford, 1989), s.n.
[9] For Evan (or Ieuan) Morgan of Tredegar, whose son, John, was knighted by Henry VII, see Evans, *Wales and the Wars of the Roses*, p.216; *DWB*, pp.635–6; see above p.209 n.3.
[10] Henry Rice is referring to John Morgan (or Young), who became bishop in 1496; earlier references to a bishop of St David's (see above p.198) may intend him retrospectively. He is thought to have been the son of Morgan ap Jenkin of Langstone and Pencoed (Gwent): Bartrum, *1400–1500*, III, 394–6; Emden, *Oxford*, II, 1311; *DWB*, p.646; see above p.186. The rapid advancement of several of the Morgans, including the later bishop, after Bosworth strongly suggests that they played a significant role in or before 1485. John the cleric was chaplain and councillor to Henry VII by October 1485, clerk of Parliament from 9 October 1485, and ecclesiastical preferment quickly followed (Emden, *Oxford*, II, s.n.; *DWB*, s.n.). John Morgan (died *c.*1492), Evan's son, was made steward of the lordship of Ebbw for life on 7 November 1485 and was knighted by Henry VII; he was occasionally called a knight before 1485 because he was a knight of the Holy Sepulchre (Pugh, *Marcher Lordships*, pp.99–100, 295; *DWB*, pp.635–6; Evans, *Wales and the Wars of the Roses*, pp.216–17). See G. B. Morgan, *Historical and Genealogical Memoirs of the Morgan Family . . .* (2 vols. in 1, London, 1891–5), II, 7–15, 119–25, for Morgans in early Tudor service.

Rice ap Thomas sendes Letters in answeare to the Earle of Richmond, to be forwarded by Morgan of Kidwellye, wherein he declares that he would with all his power partake of his quarrell. Rice conferrs with Robert of the Dale his Prophet. The Earle of Richmond landes at Milford.

Noe sooner was Rice ap Thomas's answeare written, but Morgan of Kidwellye posts the same away for France to the Earle of Richmond, signifying alsoe unto him with what alacritie and cheerfulness Rice ap Thomas had embraced his quarrell; howe readie he was, and howe able for service; what a choice selected band of soldiers he had in readinesse, the goodness of his armes, and the bravenesse of his cavallerie; there being nothing wanting in the sight of man, save onlie his presence to make them invincible; and therefore humblie besought his Lordshipp to foresloe no time, but that he would take opportunitie by the forelocke,[11] and nott suffer these enflamed spiritts in their first heate through further delayes to be evaporated. The Earle having receaved Rice ap Thomas's answeare, with other joyfull and comfortable advertizements from Morgan of Kidwellie, he was soe greatlie encoraged herewith, that noe hopes of auxiliarie forces from the French King,[12] or anie other necessarie provisions whatsoever, could make him anie longer to disappoint his friendes and confederatts with an expectation of his coming, and therefore with all convenient speed furnishing himself with such men, monie, and munition, as he could readilie procure, he enshipp'd himself and wayed anchor from Harfleet, having butt two thousand men in all, and they (God wott) poorlie provided:[13] and soe in seven dayes, with a prosperous gale, he landed at Milford. In the interim Rice ap Thomas stood all upon thornes, as conceaving there might be some private compacte and underhand working betweene the usurper and the French King, whereby the just pretences of Richmond should be for ever confounded, and that which increas'd his jealousies the more, was, that his master should be forc'd to trifle out the time in a suite of small moment for that king to graunt, and which being obtayned could add little strength to his cause.[14] Hereupon he often complain'd to his secrett friendes, of the French King's ignoble dealings, and discover'd the implacable hate he conceaved against him and his, wishing (and

[11] The earliest recorded usage in English of this proverb is in Robert Green's *Menaphon* of 1589 (p.65): *OED*, s.v.

[12] A. V. Antonovics, 'Henry VII, King of England, "By the Grace of Charles VIII of France" ', in R. A. Griffiths and J. W. Sherborne (eds.), *Kings and Nobles in the Later Middle Ages* (Gloucester, 1986), pp.169–84; Griffiths and Thomas, *Making of the Tudor Dynasty*, pp.127–31.

[13] There are grounds for thinking that Henry sailed from Honfleur with about 4,000 men. It is likely that the force supplied by Charles VIII was indeed about 2,000 strong, partly recruited in a hurry among discharged and possibly unruly soldiers from the military base at Pont de l'Arche. The remainder included English exiles, some of the French king's Scots guard, and assorted Bretons. Ibid., pp.129–30; Antonovics, 'Henry VII, King of England', pp.175–7.

[14] Henry's alleged distrust of the French and apprehension at Richard's diplomacy reflect Vergil, *English History*, pp.215–16; Antonovics, 'Henry VII, King of England', p.174.

indeede he had his wishes, for he grewe a terror to them in future times, as you shall hear) that it might one day be his good fortune to revenge these injuries, and soundlie to cudgell those French dogges, as he call'd them.[15] While he was in this heate of passion (an enemie of which he ever heald the upper hand) and being somewhat entangled in a laberinth of doubtfull cogitations, he sendes for Robert of the Dale, his prophett, to come unto him.[16] This Robert, in those blinder times, was taken for a verie understanding man, as having wonne some fame in foretelling divers things, which accordinglie came to passe; by which meanes he had insinuated himself soe farr into Rice ap Thomas his good opinion, that oftentimes he was made partaker even of his neerest touching secretts. Being nowe togither, Rice ap Thomas desir'd him to deliver his opinion frealy of Richmond, and what he thought would be the issue of those greate designs he had in hand, to which the prophet would make no answeare, excusing himself, that though he could speak something in that kind of inferior persons, yett he was carefull nott to look too narrowlie into princes matters, as being dangerous to deale withall, Rice ap Thomas taking his silence as a presage of ill lucke, still importuned him by prayers and promises of greate rewardes, that he would not conceale his knowledge of this businesse. The prophett seeing Rice soe vehement, and thinking it best nott to provoke his anger, which by his countenance he found him apt to fall into, and therefore deliver'd his mind unto him in this manner,

> Full well I wend,
> That in the end,
> Richmond sprung from Brittish race
> From out this land the Boare shall chace;[17]

all which might verie well be, and yett Rice ap Thomas nothing the wiser, unless the Earle continued in a resolution to land at Milford. For if he made his entrie some other way, noe parte of the glorie (which he soe greedilie thirsted after) was like to fall to his share, soe that all his endevours and the infinite charges he had been at, vanished away *in fumo*; wherefore he falls upon his prophet againe, urging him to deliver his opinion touching the Earle's landing, and wheather he would come for Milford or noe. To give him satisfaction herein the prophett required a day to deliberate, which being graunted, and the next day come, the

---

[15] A certain element of hindsight springs from this reference to Henry VII's rupture with France in 1489 and his invasion three years later. Chrimes, *Henry VII*, pp.279–82; Antonovics, 'Henry VII, King of England', pp.169–70. Nevertheless, despite Henry's Francophile instincts, by 1489 Frenchmen were already accusing him of ingratitude.

[16] For Rhys's earlier connection with Robin (or Robert) of the Dale, see above p.186.

[17] The source of this and the following prophecy is not known. For a strikingly similar dilemma in which the poet Dafydd Llwyd was allegedly placed by Henry Tudor himself during his march through Wales in August 1485, see Griffiths and Thomas, *Making of the Tudor Dynasty*, pp.142–3. Dafydd also thought discretion the better part of honesty in telling Henry what he wanted to hear.

prophett saluted Rice ap Thomas betimes, but without declaring himself would faine have taken his leave, whereat the said Rice grewe into a rage, threatning to hang him if he perform'd nott his promise first; well then, replied the prophett, to save thee that labour,

> Hie thee to the dale,
> I'le to the vale,
> To drink gude ale
> And soe I pre, han a care of us all,

everie man concluding by his speech, that the Earle would come for Milford and land at the dale, and that the lives and fortunes of them all were in Rice ap Thomas his hands, of which the prophett desir'd him to have a speciall care. Hereupon Rice ap Thomas musters up all his forces, calls all his friends about him, and where he found anie want among them, eyther of armes or other necessaries for the wars, he supplied with his owne store, whereof he had sufficient, as well for ornament as use; soe that in fewe dayes he had gathered togither, to the number of two thousand horse and upward, of his owne followers and retayners, bearing his name and liverie. His kinsmen and friendes, who came besides with brave companies to doe him honour, were Sir Thomas Perrott,[18] Sir John Wogan[19] and John Savage, a man of noe lesse valiantness than activitie, and much emploid by the earle after he came to be king, in the wars of France and else where;[20] Arnold Butler, Richard Griffith, John Morgan and two of his owne brothers, David the younger, and John, all of them worthie soldiers and verie expert commaunders,[21] with divers others, *Qui omnes urgentur longa nocte, quia carent vate sacro* [who are all forced through a long night because they

[18] The *CR* editor adds a note: 'Sir Thomas Perrott was of Haroldston, near Haverfordwest, Pembrokeshire, father to Sir John Perrott, Lord Deputy of Ireland in the reign of Queen Elizabeth.' Bindoff, *HC*, III, 86–8. It was a tradition in Rhys's family during the following century that he had led 1,800 mounted men (of 4,000, many of them presumably on foot) to join Henry Tudor: NLW, Dynevor, A 14; BL, Add. MS 23113 f.3; NLW, Dynevor, A 96e, A 97b.
[19] The *CR* editor adds a note: 'Sir John Wogan, of Wiston Castle, Pembrokeshire, a man of immense possessions and command in that country in those days.' See Griffiths, *Principality of Wales*, p.542, which notes his later service in Sir Rhys ap Thomas's retinue in 1513.
[20] The connection with France indicates that this refers to Sir John Savage, nephew of Thomas, Lord Stanley, who was killed at the siege of Boulogne in 1492. There may have been a link with Rhys ap Thomas, for both he and Savage were in secret contact with Henry Tudor before Bosworth, and afterwards Savage was well rewarded by the new king. Knighted by Edward IV and patronized by Richard III, it is possible (despite Horrox, *Richard III*, p.323 n.219) that he was the John Savage captured by Richard's servant, Richard Williams, steward of the lordship of Pembroke, and on whom Richard was eager to lay hands in May 1485. *DNB*, s.n.; *Harleian 433*, III, 172–3; Griffiths and Thomas, *Making of the Tudor Dynasty*, p.131.
[21] See above p.209. Rhys's brothers, Dafydd the younger (to be distinguished from Dafydd 'Ceffyl Cwta', above p.180) and one of two Johns, born illegitimately to Thomas ap Gruffydd, are noted in the pedigrees: Bartrum, *1400–1500*, IV, 643. One of these Johns cemented the link with Breconshire by marrying Elizabeth, daughter of Sir Thomas ap Watkin Vaughan of Bredwardine (ibid., p.647). For the Latin quotation, also quoted above p.156, see Horace, *Odes*, IV, 9.26–8: *sed omnes illacrimabiles urgentur ignotique longa nocte, carent quia vate sacro*.

lack an inspired poet]. There came likewise out of North Wales to this service, manie worthie gentlemen both of name and note, especially of the Salisburies, under the conduct of Robert Salisburie, a fast friend to Rice ap Thomas in the French warrs, and whoe for his well deservings there, was knighted in the field by Charles Brandon, Duke of Suffolk.[22] These Salisburies were ever firmlie united to Rice and his familie, whereby they purchased to themselves the name of *Salsbriod y Brain*, friendes to the raven,[23] which name was given them first at the battle of Pennal, where Thomas ap Griffith, father to Rice ap Thomas, lost his lief, and manie of this noble familie in the said quarrell, to the eternall praise of their true affection.[24] Rice ap Thomas, being in this brave equipage, encompass'd with most able commaunders, and furnish'd with all things necessarie, as well for armour as horse (whereof a hundred and upward were out of his owne stables), word was brought him by his conspicillos or spies,[25] whoe kept continuall watch on the coast for that purpose, that they had descried a small fleete of shippes making towards the haven's mouth; whereupon incontinently he bate up his drum, putt his men in order, and mounted on a goodlie courser, call'd *Lwyd Baxe*,[26] or *Grey Fetter Locks*, he set forth in most martial manner towards the Dale, as his prophett whilome had advised him, a place nott farr from his castle of Carew,[27] from whence, at that time, he led his armie, and there meeting with the Earle of Richmond readie to take land, he receav'd him ashore, to whom he made humble tender of his service, both in his owne, and in all their names who were there present, and laying him downe on the ground, suffer'd the Earle to pass over him;[28] soe to make good his promise to King Richard, that none

---

[22] Robert Salusbury was probably of Plas Isa, Llanrwst, and the younger son of Thomas Salusbury (died 1471). He had four brothers; the eldest, Thomas, though patronized by Richard III, fought at Blackheath (1497) with Sir Rhys ap Thomas and was knighted by Henry VII for his services. Evans, *Wales and the Wars of the Roses*, p.210; *DWB*, p.899. The occasion for the knighting of Robert Salusbury for service in France presumably arose during the 1513 campaign, during which both Robert and Sir Rhys ap Thomas were present and as a result of which Brandon was created duke of Suffolk. Gunn, *Charles Brandon, Duke of Suffolk*, pp.16ff.

[23] The *CR* editor adds a note: 'Alluding to the armorial bearing of Rice ap Thomas's house.' Both families were particular patrons of the poet Tudur Aled, among whose poems addressed to the Salusburies this phrase may appear. Jarman and Hughes, *Welsh Literature*, II, 325–6, 328, 330, 332, 335; *Tudur Aled, passim*.

[24] See above p.177. Thomas Salusbury was apparently killed at the battle of Barnet in 1471, not in Merioneth a little later: *DWB*, p.899.

[25] From Latin *conspicillum*, a watching. For the large number of horses which Rhys kept, and his fame as a commander of light cavalry, see above p.73.

[26] The *CR* editor adds a note: 'The Word should be written *Bacseu*, but the orthography of the original has been observed throughout.' For this horse in 1497, see below p.244.

[27] S. B. Chrimes, 'The landing place of Henry of Richmond, 1485', *WHR*, II (1964–5), 173–80, establishes the likelihood that the landing was at Mill Bay, little more than a mile south of Dale. Regardless of whether Rhys ap Thomas welcomed Henry soon after his landing, or was still struggling with his conscience, or was calculating his best interest, Rhys could well have been at Carew Castle, one of his favourite residences and could have taken his men to meet Henry.

[28] The *CR* editor adds a note: 'There is a tradition in that country, which seems to contradict the

should enter in at Milford, onlesse he came first over his bellie. The Earle forthwith lifting him up by the arme, and most affectionately embracing him, told him, that he well hoped it would never be his ill hap, to see him brought soe lowe as the earth again for his cause; if I bee, Sir, (said Rice ap Thomas, with a cheerfull countenance) I trust you will rayse me a second time, with as much ease as you doe nowe: if I did nott my best endevours, replied the earle, for soe noble a friend, I were much to blame, and should wish myself rather nott to be, then want meanes to gratifie such high deservings: I well perceave, answered Rice, you are borne to be victorious, and therefore I pray, said he, reserve your strength, and employ your forces to conquer your enemies, for amongst us you have none; whereupon the earle walked forward with a silent and majestike pace through the midst of them, noting and observing of each side the demeanour of his countrymen, and the manner of Rice ap Thomas his discipline, with which he was soe much taken, that he thought he had wonn the field, before he had scarce entered the land: for never did he meete with a more goodlie personage, (as he did often say) fuller of alacritie or a stouter commaunder in all his lief, then Rice ap Thomas was, he yett with souldiers better schooled in the principles of war, with couragious hartes and able bodies. Being overjoyed with soe glorious a sight, and transported with such an auspicious beginning. The Earle of Richmond after some pause, delivered himself thus, 'My deere cozen, and you my beloved countriemen, and fellowe souldiers, it is nowe upward of fourteene yeares, since my uncle Jasper and myself escaped out of these partes, and hither at length we are returned againe.[29] I fledd *then* for my lief, I returne *nowe* for a crowne – a crowne my undoubted right. My lief and my crowne are inseparable, I must eyther enjoy both or neyther. David Thomas, your noble brother, Sir, as all men heere present, and I shall ever acknowledge above – beyond all hope, most miraculously preserved my lief:[30] and you, my deere cosen, with the assistance of these valerouse gentlemen, under your discreete

fact as here stated, namely, that Rice ap Thomas did not literally suffer the Earle to pass over his belly, but that in consequence of the declaration he had made in his letter to Richard, as a salvo to his conscience, he went under the arch of a small bridge, called Mullock Bridge, near Dale, over which their passage lay, and there remained till Richmond had crossed it.' The stream near Mullock which the insurgents needed to cross was about a mile north of Dale. This is a nice tradition, though it corresponds closely with alleged events when Henry Tudor reached Shrewsbury on 17 August and demanded entry. One of the bailiffs, Thomas Mitton, refused, saying (according to the town's chronicle) that 'before he should enter there he should go over his belly, meaning thereby that he would be slain to the ground and so to run over him before he entered, and that he protested vehemently upon the oath he had taken [to Richard III]'. Next day, Shrewsbury relented, and Mitton 'lay along the ground and his belly upward and so the said Earl stepped over him and saved his oath' (H. Owen and J. B. Blakeway, *A History of Shrewsbuury* (2 vols., London, 1825), I, 246–7). It may be that this was a well-known method of avoiding the implications of an inconvenient oath!

[29] It was indeed fourteen years since the escape from Tenby in May 1471: see above p.31.

[30] This is a reference to the elder Dafydd ('Ceffyl Cwta') among Rhys's brothers, and his role in Henry Tudor's escape in 1471: see above pp.179–80.

conduct, may serve as speciall instrumentes to help me to my crowne, injuriouslie witheld from me by a most tyrannical and bloodie usurpation. Performe you the latter, Sir, which I am confident of, as he hath trulie accomplished the former, and you leave nott the world curtesie equivalent to these to bestowe upon me. Oh! the miserable afflictions, and heavie calamities we have sustayned, since last I trod upon this earth! it strikes me with horrour to thinke of them, and all neighbouring nations tremble at the reporte. What hath that cruell butcher, Richard,[31] Duke of Glocester left unattempted, that might make way for his outragious ambition? Howe manie of our nobles and others, have perished by his bloodie commaundes without anie legal triall? Five kinges and princes of the blood miserablie murdered, two vertuous Queens, baselie traduced, a third, even his owne wife, empoysened; incest likewise purposed; myself forced to live in the state of a pilgrim or banished man, to leave my fortune and my countrie, and live upon the almes of strangers; a prise sett upon my head, and wicked ministers suborned to worke my confusion, and all to raise a stair to his ungracious promotion.[32] My deere countriemen, you are all assembled heere, at this time, for the same purpose. I reade it in your lookes; 'tis your valour and vertue which I principallie heede, you are the men who add strength to good causes. Heere I am come, fellow souldiers, more in your right than my owne; what shall I say? Heere I stand before you, but what name to give myself, I am altogether to seeke. A private man I will not be termed, seeing I am by the best of the nobilitie and gentrie of this kingdom, yea by all the world besides, that have heard of my just title and pretence, allowed for a prince,[33] and yett a prince you cannott well call me, whilst another possesseth my right; besides, a question may be raysed, wheather you yourselves be traytours or true subjects, till it be decided, what manner of man you have amongst you, a true lawful

---

[31] The *CR* editor adds a note: 'In a letter of Henry the Seventh, when Earle of Richmond, to John ap Meredith, ap Jevan, ap Meredith, of the house of Gwidir, Carnarvonshire, in the editor's possession, the usurper is styled, *"that odious tyrant, Richard, late Earl* of Gloucester;" on what ground I know not, that being the only instance I recollect of such a title being applied to him.' This letter was inserted in Sir John Wynn's *History of the Gwydir Family*, p.28 (though in this copy Richard is correctly styled 'late duke of Gloucester'); it is possible that Henry Rice used it as the basis for the speech which he put into Henry Tudor's mouth on landing, for a number of the letter's sentiments echo the pretender's reported words. In earlier letters, sent from France, Henry described Richard as 'that homicide and unnatural tyrant': Griffiths and Thomas, *Making of the Tudor Dynasty*, p.120.

[32] The reference is presumably to the deaths of Henry VI and his son Edward (1471), Edward V and his brother Richard (*c.*1483), and Henry Stafford, duke of Buckingham (1483); to the treatment of Henry VI's queen, Margaret of Anjou, and Edward IV's queen, Elizabeth Wydeville; and to the death (1485) of Richard's own consort, Anne Neville, and the rumour that he planned to marry his niece Elizabeth of York or her sister. Such accusations were common currency throughout the sixteenth century. For Richard's efforts to winkle Henry Tudor out of Brittany, see Griffiths and Thomas, *Making of the Tudor Dynasty*, pp.86–8, 110–12, 118–21.

[33] For Henry's adoption of the style of king from about November 1484, see Griffiths and Thomas, *Making of the Tudor Dynasty*, pp.124–6.

prince, or an enemie.[34] What remayneth then, butt that we joyntlie use our best endeavours for the cleering of this point, and shewe to all partes, wherever we come by an invincible demonstration of our prowess, that the Lord of Hostes is patrone of our cause. To second us doubt ye nott. Continue therefore in that height of courage and resolution you nowe are, and lett us either in liveing together, procure the peace and welfare of this commonwelth, or by our death conclude our miseries; in both lett us have a care of the honour of our ancestrie and posteritie.

(1) *The Welshmen, with all joy, receave the Earle at Milford Haven. (2) Rice ap Thomas his speech at the Dale.*

(1) The Earle had no sooner finished his oration, but all flocked unto him in a confused manner, mingle mangle, without all order, as being transported with his eloquence, and ravished with his presence, some kissing his handes, some his feete; and some adoring the ground he trod upon, as if hee were some angelical creature, and noe terrestriall personage: then beating up their drumms, sounding their trumpetts, winding their cornetts, and to expresse their inward joy and content-ment, they fell to shoutes and acclamations, clapping their handes, and crying up to heaven, King Henrie, King Henrie, downe with the bragging white boare. After this they betake them to their orisons, praising God, and saying, nowe is the accepted time, nowe are those happie dayes come, will recover againe that deluge of blood spilt within our land; here is the pledge of our peace and welfare; 'tis butt an adventure we are to make, to make all this good; let us goe on in God's name, and St David, and we shall prevail.[35] When they had for a while, in these lowde plauses, and sweetest jubilyes, penetrated the aire, and echoed forth their loving affections in the most pleasing manner of expressions; Rice ap Thomas, when he sawe his time, drewe them backe, commanding every man to his colours; whereby the Earle might see, in what order and obedience he held them, to their places of service; then, he made up presentlie to the Earle, in a grave march, and in an humble straine thus spoke to him.

[34] This echoes Henry's sensitivity to the dilemma facing his followers in challenging Richard, the acknowledged king. He consequently declared himself king beforehand and denounced Richard as a tyrant and usurper. After Bosworth, he regarded his reign as beginning on the day before the battle. Wynn, *History of the Gwydir Family*, p.28; Chrimes, *Henry VII*, p.50. Henry's reliance on God's help is also reflected in his appeal to Welsh landowners (Wynn, *History of the Gwydir Family*, p.28; Griffiths and Thomas, *Making of the Tudor Dynasty*, pp.139–41).

[35] Sources from the early sixteenth century report that he invoked the name of St George rather than that of St David: A. H. Thomas and I. D. Thornley (eds.), *The Great Chronicle of London* (London, 1935), p.237; R. Fabyan, *The New Chronicles of England and France*, ed. Henry Ellis (London, 1811), p.672.

(2) My Lord and Master; you are heere (you see) with the generall applause of these my fellow souldiers in a kind of militarie election, or recognition, saluted King; and our suite, nowe is, you will take us to your protection; we are, as yet, but in a storme, and it much concernes both you and us, speedilie to provide for each other's safetie. While we have you at the helme, we are confident, Sir, by God's helpe, and your wise discretion, to arrive, ere long, at our wished porte. Let us, therefore, if we meane to doe well and goe through, stick with our business, strike while the yron is hot.[36] We have furniture of arms sufficient, and to spare, and I assure you, our hartes are as well furnished within, as our bodies without. God hath given you the absolute commaunderie of both; with us, remaines onlie the glorie of obedience. Weare we nowe, Sir, upon some private attempt of our owne, we could proceede, and stop, goe on, and come off, at pleasure, with you my Lord, who are designed for Emperie, it is otherwise; there being noe middle course to runn, a King or a beggar. You are, God be thanked, in a good way to putt things out of doubt; goe on, then, Sir, and lose noe time, it's ill dallying with edge tooles. As for our well wishes towards the advancement of your service, I hope wee have satisfied you in wordes; action (the onlie thing we would be at) must nowe be the true touchstone, to try us thoughout; that will shewe us whole unto you, whoe, for the present, you see but in parte. Let us, then, Sir, pray be a doing, and let us, noe further boast ourselves at the buckling on our armour, but reserve ourselves, until we put it off. Call, then, my Lord, for your French forces ashore, and let them take some ease and refreachment, examine what defects they may have in their armes, or otherwise, and according to our meanes, we shall not be wanting to minister a supplie, then may you dispose of both them and us, as shall best suite with your affaires, soe God prosper our proceedings.[37]

(1) *The French Armie is landed and supplied with necessaries. (2) The Earle of Richmond, and Rice ap Thomas, consult together, for the right ordering of their business. (3) The Bishop of St David's preacheth to the whole Armie. (4) They march several wayes, and meete againe about Shrewsburie.*

(1) RICE AP THOMAS having made an end of what he would say, the Frenchmen lying abord all this while, were sent for to land; whoe, upon

[36] For this metaphor, see above p.197.

[37] For the French contingent in the army, under the command of Philibert de Chandée, see Griffiths and Thomas, *Making of the Tudor Dynasty*, pp.129–30; Antonovics, 'Henry VII, King of England', pp.175–8. Behind the invitation to the French to land and be refreshed may lie the reluctance of some soldiers to disembark, as reported by a Scottish chronicler: Griffiths and Thomas, *Making of the Tudor Dynasty*, p.135.

their coming, were marvelouslie well and kindlie receaved by Welchmen, and entreated with all curtesie, each man striving (and indeede, to do them but right, for that sole virtue of curtesie towards strangers, I thinke the Welch goe beyond all the nations of the world); everie man, I say, striving to give them all contentment, and cheering them up with fresh victuals, or what other way they could devise, to encrease and continue this new begun acquaintance. The Earle of Richmond, then entreated the Earles of Oxford and Pembrock, to muster the French, and take a view of their defects, whoe, upon enquirie, found they wanted both necessarie furniture of armes, and other munition, besides that, they were verie rawe and ignorant in shooting, handling of their weapons, and discharging the ordinarie dutie of souldiers; men, as it seemed, raysed out of the refuse of the people, and clap'd upon the Earle, to avoyd his further importunities;[38] which coming to Rice ap Thomas his eares, he was not soe wroth with the French King's former delayes, as nowe, with the poornesse of his supplies; yet containing himself, he, for the present, furnished them with all such things, as he could spare, without the damage of his own particular, though in hart, he wished them backe againe in France, there being nott one man of qualitie among them, to endeere future ages to make mention, eyther of his name or service.

(2) This being done, after the Earle of Richmond had embraced, and thanked Rice ap Thomas, for his forwardnesse in affurthering his service, they, both together, with the Earles of Oxford and Pembrock, drewe aside, to consider of their present state and condition, and what course was best to be taken, for their putting forward. In fine, they concluded, the Earle should shape his course by Cardigan,[39] and Rice ap Thomas by Carmarthen, that soe going several wayes, the Welch and the French mought be kept asunder, to prevent such jarres and quarrels,

---

[38] For the French forces, see above p.213. John de Vere, earl of Oxford (died 1513) and Henry's uncle, Jasper Tudor, earl of Pembroke (died 1495), were the principal commanders.

[39] The *CR* editor adds a note: 'There have been frequent enquiries instituted, with regard to the different routes which Charles the First took, whilst he traversed the kingdom in various directions during the civil war, many of which have been settled with accuracy. The certainty would be no less curious and interesting, to ascertain the different stages of Richmond's march through Wales, in his way to Bosworth. Two of his resting places are well authenticated; which I shall here mention, as an inducement to such as may be possessed of ampler means of information, to add to the catalogue. David ap Evan, of Llwyn Dafydd, in the parish of Landissilio Gogo, Cardiganshire, entertained Richmond and his followers, one night, which the Earl acknowledged by several presents, particularly a drinking horn, richly mounted on a silver stand which was afterwards presented to Richard Earl of Carbery, and is now in the possession of John Vaughan, Esq. of Golden Grove, Carmarthenshire. The following night, Inon ap David Llwyd, Esq. of Wernnewyd, in the parish of Llannarth, Cardiganshire, received the Earl in a style of hospitality, suited to the high rank of his guest.' See Griffiths and Thomas, *Making of the Tudor Dynasty*, pp.143–8 (and map pp.140–1). Richard Vaughan, second earl of Carbery, died in 1686 (*CP*, III, 7–8); John Vaughan, esquire, lord lieutenant of Carmarthenshire, was descended from a related line and died in 1804. Jones, *Historic Carms. Homes*, p.84.

as commonlie arise betweene strangers; appointing Shrewsburie for
their rendezvous, and place of meeting againe. In the meane while,
Arnold Butler, Richard Griffith, and John Morgan, men forward in their
charge, weare appointed to meete the Earle in severall places; soe to
strengthen his partie, if occasion were offered;[40] to direct and convoy
him over those uncouth wayes and fastnesses; to call in for such
provisions, as the countrie could afford, for the reliefe of their armie; and
lastlie, to inform the people as they went along, what side Rice ap
Thomas ment to stick to; by which meanes, a world of companie flocked
unto him, not caring wheather they went, soe they went along with him.

(3) When all things weare thus in a readinesse, the Bishop of St David's
stepps up, and makes a learned sermon to the whole armie, taking for his
text, that of the Psalmist.[41] '*The Earth is weak and all the Inhabitants thereof;*
I bear up the pillars of it.' Pointing out to them, in the fore part of the verse,
the wicked raigne of King Saul, to whom he likened King Richard; and
in the latter part of the verse, the happie succession of King David,
whom he wished the Earle of Richmond to imitate, in re-establishing the
pillars, which Richard, by his bloodie tyrannie, had put out of frame,
that is, that he would have a care, when he were in perfect authoritie, for
the true worshipping of God, and the administration of justice; the two
maine pillars, wherewith all good commonwelths are supported;[42] that
nowe having taken armes, however, for the regaining of his owne right,
he should not putt his trust in charotts or horses, or in the strength of
man, butt in the name of the Lord; for by that way onlie, David proved
victorious, whose example he advised the Earle to followe; and then, the
next newes, said the Bishop, wee shall hear, will be,[43] '*Our Enemies are*
brought downe and fallen; but we are risen, and stand upright.' Going on in this
kind, with manie other profitable admonitions, both divine and morall;
the Bishop concluded, praying, and wishing the Earle in all his wayes,
the strength of Jacob, and the strength of Israel; of Jacob to prevaile over
men, and of Israel to prevaile with God; that the Lord of Hostes would
shewe himself *El nekamoth*, a God of vengeance against his enemies, and
but a letter changed, *El nechamoth*, a God of comfort unto this whole
nation.[44] When the sermon was ended, everie man buckled on his

---

[40] Arnold Butler joined Henry at Haverfordwest *c.*8 August, Richard Griffith and John Savage at
Cardigan two days later: Griffiths and Thomas, *Making of the Tudor Dynasty*, pp.143, 145; see above
p.215. This could have been a means whereby Henry Tudor was enabled to keep in touch with
Rhys ap Thomas during these first days of the march through Wales.

[41] The *CR* editor adds a note: 'Psalm lxxv.ver.4'. In the authorized King James version, Psalm 75,
verse 3, reads: 'The earth and all the inhabitants thereof are dissolved: I bear up the pillars of it.'
John Morgan, the later bishop, is likely to be the preacher intended.

[42] Both obligations were contained in the English coronation oath: S. B. Chrimes and A. L. Brown
(eds.), *Select Documents of English Constitutional History, 1307–1485* (London, 1961), pp.4–5.

[43] The *CR* editor adds a note: 'Psalm xx.ver.8'. The authorized King James version, Psalm 20,
verse 8, reads: 'They are brought down and fallen: but we are risen, and stand upright.'

[44] Jacob, the Hebrew patriarch, received from an angel the divinely given name of Israel after

armes, and betook him to his weapons, clapping their hands, and crying out a fresh, King Henrie, King Henrie, none but Henrie should be their King, soe they fell upon their march, the Earle, as was resolved before, towards Cardigan, and Rice ap Thomas to Carmarthen.

(4) The Earle having taken Liverie and Seisin of parte of his kingdom, and nowe in the way of possessing himself with the whole, Rice ap Thomas forthwith commanded the beakons to be sett on fire, thereby to give notice to all the countries adjacent, of his landing, and withall to summon his friendes and kinsmen from all partes, where his power was extended, to come in with their forces, and meete him, some in one place, some in another, in his way to Shrewsburie. By that time he came to Carmarthen, his number was much increased; from thence to a place called Lanimdiffry he goes, his snoweball gathering more and more in the rowling, and soe to Brecknocke, where divers of the Vaughans and Gamess gave him the meeting, men of noble families, and verie powerful in those countries, with manie tall and able followers: some of them as being his neare kinsmen and fast friends, doing him the honour to goe along with him in those his brave adventures.[45] During the short time of his being at Brecknock, there happened a passage both wittie and stoute, betwixt one Richard Games,[46] of the house of Aberbrane, and himself, which I may nott omit. This Richard was a very valiant Gentleman, and soe pleasant a companion withall, that (as the report goes) he could doe nothing butt in jest, save onlie fight; *that* he ever did in earnest: which earnestnesse of his cost him one of his leggs in the end. Notwithstanding, there was noe man more forward to goe on the present service, then himselfe; a thing Rice ap Thomas would noe way heare of, allthough the said Games was his neere kinsman, and intimate friend, and one in whose merrie and facete conversation (as alwayes free from offence) he tooke much delight. This Richard Games began to take in ill part, as thinking himselfe slighted therein, and therefore desired to know a reason of his repulse, to which Rice ap Thomas made answeare, that it was not for anie doubt he had of his valour and courage (of which he had alreadie given to the world sufficient testimonie) that he desired to leave him behind, butt because he would spare him, in respect he was growne lame and defective in one of his leggs. I am, therefore, replied Games, the fitter for your companie, for if I be not deceived, said he, the service

confronting a mysterious divine stranger. The name came to be equated with the Hebrew nation in its special relationship with God (El). See Cross, *Oxford Dictionary of the Christian Church*, pp.718, 720.

[45] The road from Carmarthen to Llanymddyfri (Llandovery) and then to Brecon was a well travelled one. For the Vaughans and Gameses and their relationship with Rhys, see above p.196.

[46] The *CR* editor adds a note: 'A lineal descendant of Sir David Gam, who was knighted, and slain at the battle of Agincourt.' One branch of the Gameses was settled at Aberbrân (Bartrum, *1400–1500*, II, 215). For Dafydd Gam (died 1415), see above p.196 n.11. Theophilus Jones, *The History of the County of Brecknock* (4 vols., in 2, Brecknock, 1909–11), IV, 154 n.l, was unable to identify Richard, but suggested that he was an illegitimate brother of John Games of Aberbrân.

you are upon, requires, as well men that will abide by it, as such who can runn away. Say you soe, cozen, said Rice ap Thomas, why then I see, you and I must never parte, for such as you are who will abide by it, are the men to whom we must trust: whereupon, Richard Games incontinently made himselfe readie to goe along, being well provided aforehand, both of horse and armes, to encounter with all dangers. By that time, Rice ap Thomas was come to Brecknocke, his traine was grown soe long, that it was high time to cut it shorter, the companie that followed him growing cumbersome; for 'tis almost incredible, with howe much ernest affection from all quarters they came to him, even women and children, to their power expressing as much courage and resolution, as the tallest souldier there, to undergoe the service. Notwithstanding which, Rice ap Thomas was nothing inflated, with these palpations and applauses of the giddie multitude, but heeding the worke he had in hand, fell presentlie to examine his forces, that, as ther were assembled, calling out of the best of them, soe manie, as made up his number full 2000 horse well manned, and well armed at all pointes, such and soe excellent, as, which way soever they went, drewe with a kind of ravishing delight, the eyes of all beholders; and indeede, all English writers, whenever they make mention of Rice ap Thomas, doe still annexe some epithet of honour to his brave troupes of horse.[47] Having thus made his provision for the war, he began to thinke of his owne fortunes at home; and howe to secure that, and make a safe retreate in case of extremitie. Therefore to make good his stake, he made choice of 500 more, out of the remainder and overplus of his armie, whom he recommended to the charge of his two brothers,[48] David the younger, and John, togither with the tuition of his onlie son, young Griffith Rice, commaunding them to keepe togither, and nott lay by their armes until his pleasure were further signified; and withall, that they would take care in his absence, to protect those from injurie, who come in soe loving a manner to expresse their affections towards him. With the assurance heereof, the residue of his followers went away to their homes well satisfied, yet shedding abundance of teares, and filling the ayre with doleful lamentations at his departure. Being in this glorious equipage, and soe stronglie provided on all handes, Rice ap Thomas made with all speed for Shrewsburie, and as he went, mett with the Earle of Richmond in his way, to whom he made humble obeysance, vowing to followe him

---

[47] For the 1,800 horse in Rhys's retinue mentioned in the sixteenth century by Rhys's descendants, see above p.123; and for his reputation as a commander of light cavalry, see above p.53.

[48] The *CR* editor adds a note: 'This constantly occurs in our Welsh pedigrees, where two children bear the same Christian name, with the distinction only of elder and younger; the elder David, has been already mentioned, with the addition of *Ceffyl Cwtta*': see above p.180. Rhys's son, Gruffydd, would have been seven or eight in 1485.

through all dangers, to the utter subversion both of the tyrant and his wicked complices.[49]

(1) *The Author in the continuation of his, of this storie hitherunto hath, for the most Part told you, what the Welch alone say of Rice ap Thomas: hereafter he meanes the English and the Welch togither shall speake for him; his reasons for both.*

(1) As yet, I am but in the confines of Wales, and therefore bound to sett downe the passages of their affaires there, according to those relations I have receaved thence, holding them (as good reason, in what may concerne themselves) as more authenticke and certaine guides than anie other. For noe doubt, the proofes of busnesses which are derived from the source and well-head, where they were primarily acted, doe much more worke upon our beleefe, and carrieth a greater share of truth, than what we find in bookes, obtruded to the world by common writers; whoe have bought their ware upon trust, relying upon fame, augmenting ever to the worse, the farther it goeth. I must confesse, I have taken some paines in the disquisition of the truth; I have conferred with divers antiquaries of good repute, and of ablest judgments that way, I meane our Welch Bardes; to whom I must subscribe the rather, because for the most parte, I find them all in a tale.[50] The same libertie we take we give. And nowe I am entring the borders of England, I shall as gladlie followe the course of English historie, as heretofore I have don of the Welch; that soe from the testimonie of both, Rice ap Thomas may receave a double confirmation of his heroicke proceedinges; wherein, laying aside all partialitie, you will find hee came not short of anie, that lived in those times.

(1) *The Earle of Richmond and Rice ap Thomas, meete at the place appointed. They march togither to Shrewsburie, and thence by degrees to Adderstone. A briefe touch of the passages in their jorney.*

(1) When the Earle of Richmond was, as I said, in his way to Shrewsburie, mett and saluted by Rice ap Thomas, with soe goodlie a band of Welchmen, it was noe small joy unto him, to receave a full assurance of the aide and succour of soe powerfull a commaunder; for you must knowe, the Earle all this while (notwithstanding all those reall

---

[49] The junction of the two forces is traditionally said to have taken place on Long Mountain, east of Welshpool, probably on 16 August: Griffiths and Thomas, *Making of the Tudor Dynasty*, p.148.

[50] If this allusion to Welsh poets implies consultation with poets living in Henry Rice's time, as opposed to his reading of their poetry, it is worth noting that Edward Dafydd, the most prominent of the Glamorgan poets of his day, addressed works to both Henry Rice and his father Walter (died 1636): E. R. Ll. Davies, thesis cited, pp.154–9; *DWB*, pp.104–5.

promises made unto him at Milford) was much appaled and troubled in
mind; not knowing well what to thinke of Rice ap Thomas, there being
divers rumours dispersed, up and downe, through his armie, that the
said Rice ment to side with Richard; and for that purpose was readie to
give him battaile, and to interrupt his passage, which rumour indeede,
Rice himselfe, out of policie, had caused to be blowne abroad, to
hoodwinke the tyrant, untill he were in his full strength.[51] And this his
devise, he acquainted the Earle withall, at their first meeting, which
presentlie removed all jealousie, and cause of distrust; and soe togither
they marched on to Shrewsburie, where the Earle was receaved with an
ave chaire,[52] and God speede the well, the streetes being strewed with
herbes and flowers, and their doores adorned with greene boughes, in
testimonie of a true hartie reception. And here I pray, observe the
manner of Rice ap Thomas, his ordering and arraying his men, which
for the rareness thereof, is worthie of a note. The first thing he would ever
doe, when he were to rayse anie forces, was to search into the nature and
disposition of his souldiers, and as he found them enclined in their
affections, soe to place and arrange them, each by the other; brothers he
would joyne, and associate to brothers, cozens to cozens, and friendes to
friendes, soe to stir an emulation in them, to excell the one the other,
when they were to fall upon anie notable piece of service: as for
strangers, whose spiritts he knewe to be less eager and hott (as nott
having the like motives) in so friendlie a contention, those he ever placed
last, leaving allways to them the precedencie, whoe were likeliest to be
most active in the pursuite of glorie, and this course he continuallie
practised in all his future employments, which made him soe strong, that
like *Silurus* his sheafe of arrowes, he could never be broken, being still
victoriouse in whatever he undertooke;[53] for soe fortunate he was in the
atchieving of greate and weightie matters, wheather civill or militarie,
that noe action of his, butt was held worthie of some newe honour or
office, especiallie his warlike actions. And certainlie, this singularitie of
ordering his armie must needes be a great cause of making him soe
invincible, a lesson it seemes, he had learned from Pammenes, in
Plutarch, whose counsell was ever '*Ut in bello amatores amatos juxta
locarentur, quo firmius esset vinculum*' [So that in war lovers might be placed

---

[51] Rhys's apparent equivocation before joining Henry Tudor near Welshpool is amply conveyed
by the chronicles of Polydore Vergil, Edward Hall and Raphael Holinshed, on which Henry Rice
relied: see above p.40. To regard such rumours as deliberately publicized by Rhys ap Thomas may
(or may not) be a device to reconcile the narratives at this point with the earlier account of Rhys's
reception of Henry Tudor near Dale.
[52] The *CR* editor adds a note in Greek, 'χαῖρε' meaning Latin *ave*. The reception at Shrewsbury
was far less warm, and only with difficulty were the bailiffs of the town persuaded to allow Henry
and his army to march through; they were discouraged from staying. Griffiths and Thomas, *Making
of the Tudor Dynasty*, p.150; Owen and Blakeway, *A History of Shrewsbury*, I, 246–7.
[53] This allusion has not been traced.

next to those loved, wherefore the bond might be the firmer].[54] But, to goe on. From Shrewsburie they went to a small village, called Newport, and there Sir George Talbot came unto the Earle, with 2000 tall men, which still gave him more encouragement, insoemuch that he hoped his game hitherunto being soe fairlie plaied, he could not chuse but rise a winner in the end.[55] After this for Stafford they goe; thence to Lichfield and soe to Adderstone, where he and his father-in-lawe, the Lord Stanley, met and consulted touching the ordering of their affaires, and howe to give battaile to king Richard, which donn, they departed each to his charge.[56]

(1) *King Richard is advertized of the Earle of Richmond his landing at Milford. – He raiseth a greate armie, and soe marcheth on to the Towne of Leycester.*

(1) RICHARD, all this while, relying on the fastnesse of his friendes in Wales, lay carelesse at Nottingham, where, it seemes, his intelligence was but poore, or his espialls verie false and trecherouse: for the Earle was come beyond Shrewsburie before he hard anie word of his landing;[57] soe as we may easilie perceave all things did conspire the confusion of this monster. It was not long ere he was advertized of the Earle's arrivall at Milford, and that all things necessarie for his enterprize were unprovided and verie weake, which made him rechlesse of what soe neerlie concerned him, as being confident that Sir Walter Herbert and Rice ap Thomas would soone defeate soe poor a company. I take it there is an error committed here by all our historiographers in joyning Sir Walter Herbert[58] and Rice ap Thomas togither in this place;

[54] Cf. Plutarch, Life of Pelopidas, 18.2.

[55] Polydore Vergil notes that, after landing, Henry Tudor wrote to Sir Gilbert Talbot, uncle of the young earl of Shrewsbury, presumably to inform him of his route and to request aid. Talbot's arrival at Newport (Salop) on 19 August is well attested, though his force is said to be in excess of 500 armed men, rather than as large as 2,000. Vergil, *English History*, p.218; Griffiths and Thomas, *Making of the Tudor Dynasty*, pp.146, 150. 'The Song of Lady Bessy' notes that Talbot had been in touch with Henry Tudor as early as May 1485: M. Bennett, *The Battle of Bosworth* (Gloucester, 1985), p.83.

[56] Griffiths and Thomas, *Making of the Tudor Dynasty*, pp.151–5; Bennett, *Bosworth*, pp. 90–7.

[57] This is a very doubtful assertion. At Nottingham, Richard received news on 11 August of Henry Tudor's landing, as his summons to the Vernons of Derbyshire makes clear; Henry probably did not reach Shrewsbury until 17 August. Griffiths and Thomas, *Making of the Tudor Dynasty*, p.155; see above p.42.

[58] The *CR* editor adds a note: 'I take this Sir Walter Herbert to be the son of William Herbert, first Earl of Pembroke, of that name. – Sir Walter married a daughter of the Duke of Buckingham, and died, without issue, in his father's life-time.' Henry Rice was unduly sceptical of Sir Walter Herbert's importance in south Wales to both Richard III and Henry Tudor; he was the most energetic representative of the Herbert clan at this juncture, his wife was Anne, daughter of Henry Stafford, duke of Buckingham, and he had known Henry Tudor when both were youngsters (Griffiths and Thomas, *Making of the Tudor Dynasty*, pp.128–9). Like Rhys ap Thomas, he seems to have given a public impression of equivocation early in August 1485, as Polydore Vergil's *English*

for although Sir Walter was a man of great commaund in Glamorgan and Monmouthshires, yet in those partes where Rice ap Thomas bare sway he had nothing to doe. The report goes, that these two noble gentlemen, being neere kinsmen and faithful friendes, took severall sides, the one with Richard, the other with Richmond, and that they both (careful of their owne safeties, however the world went) did mutuallie compact to procure each other's pardon, what side so-ever prevailed; and this tradition I have bin the more bold to sett down here, having heard the same allowed, and confirmed, by divers of that honourable familie.[59] Nowe, to proceed, by and by, a second message was brought to the king, that the Earle was on his way beiond Shrewsburie, and, that Rice ap Thomas attended him with all his power, at which name the tyrant startled, crying out for vengeance on him who, contrarie to his oath, had thus deceaved him. Being thus affrighted, he began to think it high time to looke about him; therefore, in all haste, he sendes for his most trustie friends, Norfolk, Northumberland, and others. And soe raising a puisant armie, like an experte commaunder (as indeede in feates of armes, and matters of chivalrie, to give the devill his dewe, he was nothing inferiour to the best), falls, forthwith, to dispose them with a great deale of judgment.[60] Then calling for his horse, a goodlie white courser,[61] with as much speede as the downe pressing plummets of his villainies would give leave, attended by his footmen, and guarded with wings of horse, with a meagre and dreadful countenance, he comes to the towne of Leycester.

(1) *Richard and Richmond prepare for Battaile. – They fight. – Richard is slain*

(1) By this time both armies were come within view, the one of the other, neere the village of Bosworth. Richard committed the vauntguard of his armie to that approved cheeftaine, Northfolke, after him the king followed himself with the bodie of the armie, consisting of veteran souldiers, and approved men of war, such as were like enough to have carried the day, had their hartes and bodies walked in the same course. Hereupon Richmond leades forth his men; his vauntguard was fronted with archers, over which the Earle of Oxford was in cheefe, the right

---

History reports, on whose account Henry Rice heavily depended. Rhys's sister was married to Sir Richard Herbert: Bartrum, *1400–1500*, IV, 643.

[59] This tradition of a compact between Rhys ap Thomas and Sir Walter Herbert is reminiscent of the brothers-in-arms agreements made for mutual protection in wartime and noted by K. B. McFarlane, 'A business-partnership in war and administration, 1421–1445', *EHR*, LXXVIII (1963), 290–308, reprinted in his *England in the Fifteenth Century* (London, 1981), ch.VIII.

[60] Summonses to such as Norfolk and Northumberland had already been issued: Griffiths and Thomas, *Making of the Tudor Dynasty*, pp.155–6; Bennett, *Bosworth*, p.89.

[61] The *CR* editor adds a note: 'Saddle white Surrey for the field to-morrow. Shakespeare's Richard III.' Cf. *Richard III*, Act V, scene iii, 1.65.

wing Sir Gilbert Talbot had designed unto him, and Sir John Savage had the left, the Earle himself governed the battalion, having with him his uncle Jasper, Earle of Pembrocke, and Rice ap Thomas, in whose brave cavallerie the Earle reposed much confidence, for as yet the Stanleys stood aloofe.[62] And nowe the time was come, appointed by God, in his secret judgment, to determine for the garland, soe that without anie further delay, these two royall combatants, by their prayers, recommended themselves to the protection of the Highest, whetting the valerouse spiritts of their followers, with cheerfull orations, large promises, and their owne personal braverie. And soe, upon summons from the death-menacing trumpett, they encounter and fall to blowes.

> – Pede pes et cuspide cuspis
> Arma sonant armis, vir petiturque viro.[63]
>
> [Foot by foot and point by point
> Arms sound on arms, and man assails man.]

While the avantguardes were in this hott chase, the one of the other, King Richard held not his hands in his pocket;[64] but grinding and gnashing his teeth, up and downe he goes in quest of Richmond, whom noe sooner espying than he makes at him, and, by the way, in his furie manfullie overthrewe Sir William Brandon, the Earle's standard-bearer, as also Sir John Cheney, both men of mightie force, and knowne valiancie.[65] In Wales we say, that Rice ap Thomas, whoe from the beginning closelie followed the Earle, and ever had an eye to his person, seeing his partie begin to quaile, and the King's gaine ground, took this occasion to send unto Sir William Stanley, giving him to understand the danger they were in, and entreating him to joyne his forces for the disengaging the Earle, who was not only in despaire of victorie, but allmost of his liefe. Whereupon (for it seemes he understood not the danger before) Sir William Stanley made up to Rice ap Thomas, and joyning both togither rushed in upon their adversaries and routed them, by which meanes the glorie of the day fell on the Earle's side, King Richard, as a just guerdon for all his facinorouse actions and horrible murders, being slaine in the field. Our Welch tradition sayes, that Rice

---

[62] This account is based on Vergil's *English History*, p.223. Bennett, *Bosworth*, p.104, suggests that Rhys ap Thomas was in the vanguard under Oxford's command, but there is no evidence for this. There is no reason to reject the Life's statement that Rhys was with the king and Jasper Tudor towards the rear at this early juncture. Although there is no earlier reference to Jasper's presence at the battle than that in J. Speed, *The History of Great Britain . . .* (1st edn., London, 1611), p.724, on which Henry Rice seems to have relied, there is none at all for the suggestion that he remained in Wales 'to safeguard his nephew's line of retreat': T. B. Pugh, 'Henry VII and the English nobility', in G. W. Bernard (ed.), *The Tudor Nobility* (Manchester, 1992), p.50

[63] The source of this quotation has not been located.

[64] Cf. above p.199.

[65] Vergil, *English History*, p.224.

ap Thomas slue Richard, manfullie fighting with him hand to hand; and we have one strong argument in defence of our tradition, to prove that he was the man who, in all likelihood, had don the deede, for, from that time forward, the Earle of Richmond as long as he lived did ever honour him with the title of Father Rice. And seldome, or never, shall we read that our kings have given these *honorifica gratulationis cognomina* [honourable names of congratulation] to their subjects, but for some singular and transcendent meritt; and therefore we may, probably, conjecture, that eyther Rice ap Thomas (as the speech goes) slue Richard, or else, without doubt, he performed some meritoriouse peece of service in that place, which made the Earle give soe honourable an addition to his name.[66] I will not heere minister occasion of discourse, though it hath binn a question often argued, and the case putt home on both sides by some of the wisest statists of our times, wheather Stanley or Rice, in this service, merited most from Richmond? 'Tis true, Sir William Stanley set the crowne upon the Earle his head; but the keyes hung at Rice ap Thomas his girdle, which lett him in, and could have shut him out.[67] Stanley, I say, putt the crown upon his head; yet, in the Earle's owne conceipt, though he came in time innough soe to doe, he stayed soe long as to endanger it; but Rice ap Thomas followed him *per saxa per ignes* [through rock and fire], through thick and thin, from first to last, to his infinite charge. The truth is, they were both men of high deserving, therefore let them devide the honour betweene them, as they did the spoiles of King Richard's tent. Of which though Stanley had the greatest share (a thing Richmond rather winked at, than liked) yet the portion which Rice ap Thomas had, was delivered him by the Earle's owne appointment.[68]

Well, nowe the tragedie being ended, and the tyrant slaine, I shall fitt him with an epitaph out of Doctor Case, in his Prolegomenon on Aristotle's politicks, whoe notes him for one, '*Qui vulpis caput, et caudam Leonis habuit; sanguine suorum petiit sceptrum, sanguine suo amisit regnum*' [who had the head of a wolf and the tail of a lion; he grasped the sceptre with his relatives' blood and lost the kingdom with his own blood]; – and there I leave him.[69] Being thus ridd of Richard, the most pestilent

---

[66] The Life is cautious about accepting Welsh tradition that it was Rhys who summoned Sir William Stanley to save the day – and indeed dispatched Richard III. But the fact remains that we do not know the precise reason why Sir William intervened when he did to save the day for Henry Tudor, or who struck Richard dead: Bennett, *Bosworth*, p.116; see above p.43.

[67] For the story that Sir William Stanley (and his brother, Lord Stanley) placed the crown on Henry's head, see Bennett, *Bosworth*, pp.121, 187 n.26, relying on Vergil, *English History*, p.226, and *Great Chronicle of London*, p.238.

[68] For the spoil acquired by Sir William Stanley after the battle, and transported to his castle at Holt, see Bennett, *Bosworth*, p.121. The suggestion that Rhys received some too, and with the specific approval of Henry Tudor, is intriguing.

[69] A quotation from John Case, *Sphera Civitatis* (Oxford, 1588), p.4. Dr Case (*c*.1546–1600) taught at Oxford from 1567 and was a friend of William Camden. Henry Rice evidently knew his *Sphera*

disease this land was ever infested withall, we are nowe fallen into the hands of a more careful shepherd, Henrie, Earle of Richmond, henceforth stiled Henrie the Seventh, who hath, by the helpe of God, laid a firm foundation both of our present and future peace in this our kingdom, to all posteritie; though, afterwards, nowe and then certain flushings and whelkes appeared in the face of our state, which argued an ill affected liver as yet not thoroughlie sound. – After *Te Deum* sung, the Earle being saluted king, he resolved to lay some speciall markes of his favour upon certaine gentlemen, who that day had well deserved, for their fidelitie and courage, wherefore he began with Rice ap Thomas, and there knighted him in the place. The like honour he did to some fewe others, whoe weare of prime note and noble blood.[70] After which he setts forward for London.

Civitatis, a popular student textbook based loosely on Aristotle's *Politics*; its *Prolegomena* contained a condemnation of Machiavelli and tyranny. C. B. Schmitt, *John Case and Aristotelianism in Renaissance England* (Kingston, Ont., and Montreal, 1983), especially pp.87, 135–6, 178–86.

[70] Bennett, *Bosworth*, pp.123–32. Sir Rhys was knighted on 25 August, three days after the battle: see above p.45; Shaw, *Knights*, II, 22–3.

7

The Reign of Henry VII

(1) *A brief Touch of Henrie the Seventh. – His wise and orderlie Proceeding on first attayning the Crowne. (2) Of the Honours and Offices conferred upon Sir Rice ap Thomas then, with his other Employments.*

(1) NOVUM *imperium inchoantibus utilis clementiae fama* [At the beginning of a new regime the value of clemency is well known], said Tacitus,[1] there is nothing more expedient to a king, recente and fresh in government, than to use his best endeavours for the gaining, from all sortes of people, an opinion of his clemencie. King Henrie, well read in this maxime, made good use thereof, for at his first entrance, to make sure of the affections of his subjects, he shewed a disposition worthie of a graciouse prince by publishing his royal proclamation with a generall pardon to all such as had taken armes against him, soe as they submitted to his mercie by a day, and tooke the oath of allegiance, by which meanes he ridd the offenders of their fears, and gained much love.[2] His next care was to chose such counsellors as might shewe to the world his wisdome, judgment, and capabilitie of rule. The chiefest he made choice of to receave the complaintes of the aggrieved, and to reforme the abuses of the commonwelth, weare Jasper, Duke of Bedford, the Earles of Oxford, Shrewsburie, and Darbie,[3] Richard, Bishop of London,[4] and

---

[1] Tacitus, *Histories*, IV, 63.

[2] For the only known general pardon issued at the outset of the reign, on 24 September 1485, see W. Busch, *England under the Tudors*, vol.I , *King Henry VII* (London, 1895), p.23. Clemency or mercy was regarded as an essential quality of the 'gracious prince' in fifteenth-century England.

[3] This is a somewhat unusual list. Granted that Henry's uncle, Jasper Tudor, created duke of Bedford on 27 October 1485; his step-father, Thomas Stanley, created earl of Derby on the same day; and John de Vere, earl of Oxford, are commonly regarded as the king's close advisers from the outset, George Talbot, earl of Shrewsbury (born 1468), on the other hand, did not enter the king's inner circle until appointed steward of the royal household in 1506 (*CP*, XI, 706–9). M. M. Condon, 'Ruling élites in the reign of Henry VII', in C. Ross (ed.), *Patronage, Pedigree and Power in Later Medieval England* (Gloucester, 1979), pp.121, 139 n.61. These four nobles may appear here in the *Life* because of their military role in Henry's reign, suppressing rebellion and leading expeditions abroad, in which Rhys ap Thomas also took part.

[4] The *CR* editor adds a note: 'Richard Hill, Bishop of London'. Richard Hill (died 1496) received

Richard, Bishop of Norwich[5], Sir Rice, his trustie Welchman (as Speede calls him)[6], and Morgan of Kidwellie, a fast friend of the kinge's, when first he had the crowne in designment. Things being thus well regulated in England, the next thing which fell under the kinge's consideration, was the rectifying abuses in the principalitie of Wales. Nowe there was none seemed soe fit unto him to undergoe that charge, as Sir Rice ap Thomas, and he, therefore, resolved to make choice of him for the administration of justice in those partes. Whereupon Sir Rice was presentlie sent for, to whom the king, in performance of his former promise, forthwith gave him the praefecture and cheefe government of all Wales.[7] And there the king rested not, for within a fewe dayes after he graunted Sir Rice three patentes besides. In the first, he made him constable and lieutenant of Brecknock: in the second, he did constitute him Chamberlaine of South Wales, *in comitatu* Carmarthen, and Cardigan, and by the same graunt appointed him Seneschal of his Lordship of Buelth: in the third, he gave him *Allocationem Feodi*, and all within the compasse of one month; whereby we may gather the meritts were very extraordinarie, the favours being soe overpressing, especiallie from a king who was close-fisted, and ever cautiouse in the disposing of his rewardes.[8] With these honours and offices thus heaped upon him, Sir Rice was commaunded to goe for Wales, to rectifie such disorders as had crept in there during his absence, which were verie manie, for the people wanting their head, were nowe growne unrulie and falne to deadlie feudes among themselves, which was chieflie occasioned through the turbulencie of those souldiers, whom Sir Rice upon his going for Bosworth, had left under the charge of his two brothers, David the younger, and John, for the safe garding his onlie son, Griffith Rice. To compose these differences, Sir Rice spent some time, and that to good purpose, for by pardoning some, and punishing others, and doing justice

no preferment between 1477 and 1486, when he became dean of the chapel royal; in 1489 he was appointed bishop of London: Emden, *Oxford*, II, 934.

[5] The *CR* editor adds a note: 'Richard Nix, Bishop of Norwich'. Richard Nykke (died 1536) received no preferment between 1473 and 1488. He was appointed registrar of the Order of the Garter (1496) and, like Richard Hill, became dean of the chapel royal (1497); in 1501 he was appointed bishop of Norwich. Emden, *Oxford*, II, 1381–2.

[6] John Speed, *The History of Great Britain* . . . (?2nd edn., London, 1625), pp.947–8, describes Rhys rather as a man 'of great command in Wales . . . in whom he conceyved no little trust'. For Trahaearn ap Morgan of Kidwelly's earlier contacts with Henry Tudor, who made him chancellor of Glamorgan soon after Bosworth, see Evans, *Wales and the Wars of the Roses*, p.217; see above p.186.

[7] In terms of formal office-holding, this is an exaggeration; but it is likely that informally the king regarded Rhys – and told him so – as his principal lieutenant in Wales. Hence the high-sounding phrases which sixteenth-century writers used of Rhys's position after 1485.

[8] On 3 November 1485, Rhys was appointed constable, lieutenant and steward of the lordship of Brecon for life, with the profits attached thereto. Three days later, he was appointed chamberlain of south Wales, and the steward of the lordship of Builth for life, with the usual fees; and on 17 November the auditors of south Wales were instructed to allow him his fees, wages and allowances as chamberlain. Griffiths, *Principality of Wales*, p.189; NLW, Dynevor, A 93 (a copy, perhaps made in the early seventeenth century, of all the royal grants to Sir Rhys ap Thomas).

to all, those fierie spiritts weare presentlie allayed.[9] Nowe for the manner of Sir Rice, his proceeding in the time of his civill government, thus, in briefe, he bore himself. Whenever delinquents were brought before him, his fashion was to begin with gentle wordes and persuasions seasoning them ever and anon with comfortable admonitions out of the scriptures, soe to imprint in the hartes of the offenders the love of justice and honestie, when this was don, the partie was dismissed. Againe, if that wrought nott, he would growe more rough, betaking him to menaces; lastlie, if all fail'd, and that they persevered in ill-doing, remaining stiff and incorrigible, he eyther cutt them off with the sword of justice, or carried them to the warrs, theare to end them, or amend them.[10] Yet for all this, he seldome proceeded thus farr: but against his will, and ever he would putt them off as long as he could. When he ascended the tribunal or judgment seate, he ever came thither free from passion *Vultu Legis* [in the likeness of the law]: and he allwayes pronounced the sentence of death, *voce magis leniter severâ, quam rabida* [in a voice gently stern rather than fierce]. Such was his deportment, when he sate *in magisterio*, and there are manie particular instances to confirme the same; but, for the present, I onlie tye myself to speake of his militarie actions.[11]

(1) The Lord Lovell and the two Staffords rebell against the King, and are suddenlie put to flight. Lambert Simnell, the counterfeit Plantagenat overthrowne in Battaile. Sir Rice ap Thomas his manlie resolution and courage in the said Battaile.

(1) The king being firmlie established on the throne, begins nowe to be confident and full of assurance, the rest of his reigne would passe away in pleasure and contentment, wherein he outreached his owne judgment through over much credulitie. For however he made accompt of peace and calmes, yet his fortunes for manie yeares after proved verie tempestuouse and full of broken seas. To checke the rashnesse of his beleafe, and point him to his aberration, a present occasion happened that disturbed his securitie, which was a revolt made by the Lord Lovell

[9] This interesting passage may in part refer to the suppression of risings in the March in 1486: see above p.47.

[10] This is an interesting passage, with its gloss on the common practice in the later Middle Ages of recruiting trouble-makers for the king's wars.

[11] The *CR* editor adds a note: 'My Author, from several hints thrown out in the margin, had evidently an intention of reserving the history of Sir Rice's civil government for a second volume, which must have proved a source of very interesting information respecting the state of the principality, and the manners of its inhabitants in those days. It is therefore much to be regretted, that it was either never executed, or lost; yet, it is probable, that the work referred to may still be extant amongst musty family papers, in the possession of such as are too indolent to examine them, or when examined, illiberally tenacious of any thing curious that might turn up.' And if such a work were ever written it still has not come to light.

and the two Staffordes, who, like small pustles, began nowe to appeare in the ensmothed countenance of this region. The reporte of their rebellion made manie of the king's faithfull and well-affected subjects take armes and prepare for his defence, among whom Sir Rice ap Thomas was one of the foremost, having raised to the number of 500 horse, and well onward on his way; but before he or anie of the rest could come with their forces to the field, newes was brought them that the fire was extinguished, and all turned to smoke; for the Duke of Bedford proclaiming the king's graciouse pardon to all that would come in and sue for mercie, divers submitted, others fledd, and all disbanded, soe that the king was master of the field, before he scarce knewe that he had an enemie.[12]

In the necke of this there followed a more boistrouse raging surge raysed and provoked by the malevolouse aspect of a base counterfeit, one Lambert Simnell, whoe took upon him the person of Richard, Duke of Yorke, second son to Edward the Fourth, or Edward Plantagenett, son to the Duke of Clarence, nott caring wheather this Simnell, (a fitt name for a baker's son) though somewhat with the finest for soe grosse an imposter, Simnell, being a kind of bread *ex flore seu polline purissimae farinae conflato* [made from flower or flour of the purest quality]: *Cheate* made of a more furfuraceouse stuffe, noe question had binn more proper for him; for I am sure he laid hard to have cheated us of our king, and our king of his crowne. This Simnell, I say, or *Ignis fatuus* [will-o'-the-wisp] blowne up and downe with everie blast from countrie to countrie, presumed at length to come to England, and soe gathering somewhat to his partie by rouling, encamped at Stoke, with full desire to make purchase of noe lesse than a crowne. How forward soever this jugler and his adherents were, the true king (as reason good) took the field first, attended by his two approved generalls, the Duke of Bedford, and the Earle of Oxford, as likewise the Earle of Shrewsburie, and the Lord Strange, with divers Knights and Gentlemen, namelie, Sir Rice ap Thomas, upon whom, that day, the king had bestowed a troop of English horse, the business requiring such hast, soe that he could nott suddenlie be provided out of Wales. This favour, among the manie, receaved from his gracious master, Sir Rice held for the greatest, as being the meanes whereby the English and the Welch were for ever after tyed in an indissoluble knott of true affection: for till this king's raigne wee allwayes looked awry each on the other, rather inclined to enmitie

[12] C. H. Williams, 'The rebellion of Humphrey Stafford in 1486', *EHR*, XLIII (1928), 181–9; Bennett, *Lambert Simnel and the Battle of Stoke*. The implication of the Life is that as a result of the premature rising of 1486 and its sudden collapse, Rhys raised 500 mounted men. On 3 May, whilst he was at Nottingham, Henry VII included the duke of Bedford among commissioners to enquire into treasons, felonies and conspiracies in Warwickshire and Worcestershire; if Bedford were indeed in the king's entourage, then his proclamation of the king's pardon at this time might well have been instrumental in dispersing the Staffords and their men: ibid., p.38.

than amitie.[13] And hence, upon this verie occasion (as the report goes) grewe the first concord betweene us; Sir Rice giving such invincible demonstrations of prowesse in his owne person, and complying soe wiselie with the disposition of the English, that from that time forward divers of prime marke among them, vouchsafed to honour him with their companie, who followe him in all their expeditions: an act alone worthie to eternize his memorie. Well, to be short, both armies meete and joyne battaile, where all went to wracke on the impostor's side: 4000 and upward of his men being slaine, all his commanders cut off, and himself taken prisoner.[14] On the king's parte, half the vauntgard miscarried, divers were hurt; butt none of note, save the valiant Sir Rice ap Thomas, who that day onlie fought for his liefe, elsewhere for his honour, for eyther to give testimonie of his braverie to his newe companions, or upon a hurt receaved by an Irish dart of skeine[15] from the hand of a common souldier, while he was in the heate of a single encounter with the Earle of Kildare; being somewhat transported with furie, and further carried than wisedome gave him commission, he fell from fighting with one, to fight with manie, among whom, noe question, oppressed with numbers, he had lost his liefe, had not the Earle of Shrewsburie rescued him out of the handes of the merciless rabble, at the sight of whose presence, inspired with fresh courage, he flies at his enemies, doing such slaughter among them, and performing such deeds of armes, as contributed much to that daye's victorie. This tragedie ended; the king was told of the bitter banquet Sir Rice had binn at, to whom in merriment he said, howe nowe father Rice? Howe likest thou of the entertainment here? Wheather ther is better eating leeks in Wales, or shamrocke among the Irish? Both, certainlie butt coarse fare, said Rice; yett eyther would seeme a feast with such a companion, pointing at the Earle of Shrewsburie.[16] Of this memorable peece of service, our

---

[13] See Bennett, *Lambert Simnel*; see above p.47. The Life is dependent on Polydore Vergil's account of the rebellion, with the identification of the impostor as a baker's son (hence perhaps his name) derived from Francis Bacon, one of Henry Rice's acknowledged sources, who in turn was following a suggestion by Bernard André, Henry VII's historiographer. See Bennett, *Lambert Simnel*, p.47. The implication of the Life is that Rhys was with the king before the royal army was raised and therefore could not go to Wales to recruit. The author nicely uses Rhys's command of an English contingent of soldiers as a metaphor for the hopes that some Welshmen placed in Henry Tudor after 1485. 'Cheat' was wheaten bread of the second quality.

[14] For the 4,000 rebels killed, see Molinet, *Chroniques*, I, 564. Henry Rice highlights the role of the earl of Shrewsbury and Lord Strange among the nobles present in the king's army because Bacon does so: *The History of the Reign of King Henry the Seventh*, ed. R. Lockyer (London, 1971), p.66.

[15] Ibid., pp.66–7, for the Irish 'only armed with darts *and* skeins' [knives]', which may have suggested a personal encounter with Kildare.

[16] The *CR* editor adds a note: 'My Author (in a marginal note, by way of confirmation of what he here has advanced), says that he chanc'd to fall in company with a grave Welch Gentleman, well versed in antiquities, when, among other discourses, stumbling (to use his own words) on the subject in hand, he gathered that Sir Rice was once in danger of his life upon some service against the Irish, and that must needs be at this time, for he was never elsewhere embarked against them: and likewise, that the Irish were then under the command of a great man of England, one John

common history makes noe mention at all, neyther doe I much wonder thereat: for the English themselves doe acknowledge their relations touching this battaile to be both lame, naked and imperfect, rather declaring the success of the day, than the manner of the fight: soe that I, therefore, have herein laboured to follow my Lord Verulam, his steppes in making search for that parte which concernes Sir Rice ap Thomas in this particular, digging truth as he did (soe neere as I can) out of the mine.[17]

(1) Henrie the Seventh bickers with the French King, laieth siege to Bulloigne, and for a summ of money rayseth it againe with some blemish to his honour.

(1) Henrie the VII. standes upon record for a covetous prince, and we cannott alltogether excuse him, for in the carriage and conduction of affaires betwixt himself and the French king, he somewhat plaied the parte of a merchant, both with his subjects and enimies, gaining from the one, by an inchoation and shewe of warr, from the other, by an acceptation of peace: a foule staine to his honour, and which lost him much in the estimation of the world abroad, and in the hartes and affections of his subjects at home.[18] The first discoverie of Henrie's tenaciousnesse and love of lucre was on this occasion. Charles the Eight, of France, a prince altogether as covetouse to enlarge his dominions, as ever Henrie was to fill his coffers, finding a sweetnesse in the expansion of his empire began to look with a wishfull eye upon the Dutchy of Brittanie, which aspiring thoughts the king of England would faine have

Powel, in a battle against the King, which name of John Powel, no doubt, he corruptly used for John De La Pole, Earl of Lincoln. Further, he says, this old Gentleman told him of that very question after the battle, merrily proposed by the King to Sir Rice, and for the author of this tradition, cited by one Parry, a Brecknockshire man, very studious, of antient things, who was a hundred years old and upward.'

If Rhys personally engaged a FitzGerald, it would have been Thomas, the brother of the earl of Kildare and one of the rebel captains at Stoke rather than the earl himself who remained in Ireland (Bennett, *Lambert Simnel*, pp.91, 101). Bacon (*Reign of Henry VII*, p.57) mistakenly calls the earl of Kildare Thomas, having the earl himself take part in the invasion (ibid., pp.64, 67). FitzGerald was slain in the battle. George Talbot, the young earl of Shrewsbury (1468–1538), was certainly present in the king's army and was among the commanders who bore the brunt of the fighting (*CP*, XI, 706–9; Bennett, *Lambert Simnel*, p.95).

As to Henry Rice's informant, Parry the centenarian may have been one of the three brothers of Queen Elizabeth's lady-in-waiting, Blanche Parry, whose family came from Llandyfaelog Tre'r-Graig in Breconshire and Poston in Herefordshire. Longevity may have run in the family for Blanche herself died well over eighty years of age. *DWB*, pp.730–1; E. Jones, *History of Brecknock*, IV, 2–3.

[17] Bacon, *History of Henry VII*, ch.2. Francis Bacon was created Lord Verulam on 12 July 1618 and Viscount St Albans on 27 January 1621: *CP*, XI, 282–5.

[18] Bacon (*History of Henry VII*, pp.207, 229) expressed a common contemporary view of Henry VII as rapacious for treasure. Henry Rice seems to have had specifically in mind the preparations for the king's expedition to France in October 1492, the grants by Parliament and the financial provisions of the peace concluded with Charles VIII. Cf. Bacon, *History of Henry VII*, pp.120–9.

suppressed, had he not been soe close fisted, that he could not away with
the least noise of expence; and therefore not intending reallie to warr
with France to save charge, much time was trifled in negociations, till
the Bretons received a great overthrowe, and the tardie expedition
under Lord Brooke proved of noe effect.[19] However, Henrie now his
sword (which indeede was not drawne in good ernest) failing him,
thought to master his enemies by pollicie, encouraging Maximilian the
Emperor, to goe on with his suite to the Ladie Ann, Heire of Brittanie,
who soe far follows Henrie's advise, that they were married by solemn
proxie, which the French king laboured to render invalid, by the
sentence of divines and civilians, that in the end, he obtained her for
himself.[20] Affrontes thus multiplying, and Henrie seeing the Emperor
soe shamefully baffled, he puts his own title afoote to Normandie, Guien,
and Anjou, yea to the whole kingdom of France.[21] Wherefore refusing
all further conference with the French ambassadors, he summons
parliament, and rayseth a puisant armie of 25,000 foote, and 1,500
horse, under the commaund of Jasper, Duke of Bedford, John, Earle of
Oxford, Thomas, Marquiss of Dorsett, Thomas, Earle of Derbie,
George, Earle of Shewsburie, Edmond, Earle of Suffolke, Edward,
Earle of Devonshire, George, Earle of Kent, the Earle of Essex, and Sir
Rice ap Thomas, much noted for the *brave* troupes that he brought out of
Wales.[22] *Ah! pulcrum est digito monstrari et dicier hic est* [Ah! it is noble to be
pointed out with a finger and have it said, this is he]. Heere Sir Rice, by
way of excellencie, hath an apospragisme, a seale of honour claped upon
his faire and glorious companions, and by whom? By an *Os Angliae vere
aureum* [spokesman of England, true gold], the Viscount St Albans.
Verbum regium [regal words] delivered in his language, makes a man
more than a peere; and Sir Rice is the onlie gentleman named among
the nobilitie here, and that emphaticallie, with a magnification of the

---

[19] This interpretation of Henry's reluctance to aid Brittany to resist Charles VIII of France is
hardly fair. The Bretons were defeated at St Aubin du Cormier on 28 July 1488, and the belated
expedition to France under Lord Daubeney in June 1489 was of little avail. The expedition in
which John Brooke, Lord Cobham (died 1512), served seems to have been that led by the king
himself to Boulogne in October 1492: *CP*, III, 346; Chrimes, *Henry VII*, pp.280–2.

[20] Early in 1491, the Emperor Maximilian renewed his suit to marry Anne, duchess of Brittany
since the death of her father, Francis II, in September 1488, but on 6 December 1491 she married
Charles VIII of France: Bacon, *History of Henry VII*, pp.103, 115; Chrimes, *Henry VII*, pp.280–1.
Bacon (*History of Henry VII*, p.106) notes Charles VIII's consultations 'with his divines' in view of
the proxy marriage with Maximilian.

[21] In 1492 he declared it his intention to resurrect the claims of English kings to the crown of
France: Chrimes, *Henry VII*, pp.281–2; Bacon, *History of Henry VII*, p.116.

[22] The *CR* editor adds a note: 'See the Life of Henry the Seventh, written by the Lord Verulam,
Viscount St Albans, page 108.' See Bacon, *History of Henry VII*, p.126, where all these nobles are
mentioned, along with Sir Rhys ap Thomas, though the army is said by Bacon to have included
1,600 horse. The earl of Arundel and Thomas, earl of Ormond, are the only omissions from Henry
Rice's list. Sir Rhys ap Thomas is said by Bacon (*History of Henry VII*, p.126) to be 'much noted for
the brave troops he brought out of Wales'. For the Latin which follows, see its earlier use above
p.149.

braverie of his troupes. Yet my Lord of St Albans, for all this, amidst his favours, mistakes Sir Rice, his name calling him Richard Thomas, a slight mistake, and *easie* to be amended, though *Hard*: blott out these foure letters, and we are all right. I dare swere, if Sir Rice weare alive, hearing his souldiers praised by soe excellent a penn, he would easilie remitt the indignitie don to his name.[23] The continuer of Harding, indeede, doth not onelie misname him, but superadds withall, calling him Richard Thomas Ddy, or Black Richard Thomas; the first place that ever I read of his complexion. The king nowe having in readinesse his armie, sails for Calais, with desire rather to shewe war, than to make itt. From there he makes for Bulloigne, to which he laid siege allmost for a yeare together, during which there passed noe memorable action of warr at all, neyther was it likelie there should, Henrie being otherwise disposed, and ayming at peace.[24] And as he wished the calme windes of peace begann to blowe; bad windes for those, who upon this occasion had much empayr'd their estates, and putt their fortunes upon the venture, good onlie for both kings; the one satisfying his desires in the increase of his treasure; the other his ambition in the quiet possession of Brittany. And thus Henrie growne fullhanded as having receaved in present 745,000 ducketts for his charges in that jorney, and 25,000 crownes more, promised to be paid him yeerelie for his charges sustayned in aide of the Bretons, away he departes for England, full well contented in himself; however, generallie through the whole armie they began to speake somewhat broadlie of his rapaciouse disposition, not sticking further to say: He cared not whom he polled and pilled to fill his owne coffers, with manie other reproaches, which the king little heeded, comforting himself, I believe, with those wordes of that melancholicke and morose Athenian:

> Populus me sibilat, at mihi plaudo,
> Ipse domi, simul ac nummos contemplor in arcâ.[25]
> [The people hiss at me, but I applaud myself at home
> when I contemplate the amount in the cash box.]

There were manie of his principall counsellors at the same time, had greate presentes given them, amongst whom Sir Rice ap Thomas was offered a pension of 200 markes by the yeare, which he with some indignation refused, telling the messenger, that if his master intended to releave his wantes, he had sent him too little, and if to corrupt his mind,

---

[23] The *CR* editor adds a note: 'See the Continuation of John Harding's Chronicle, page 122.' Cf. John Hardyng, *The Chronicle from the firste begynnying of Englande. 2 parts* (London, 1543), with A Continuation, f.122.

[24] The siege in fact lasted less than a month: M. V. C. Alexander, *The First of the Tudors* (London, 1981), pp.102–3. Henry Rice has taken his figures for the payments to Henry VII from Bacon, *History of Henry VII*, p.128.

[25] Ibid., pp.128–9. The quotation has not been identified.

or stagger his fidelitie, his kingdom would not be enough.[26] Withall, 'tis said of this great man, Sir Rice, that when his souldiers began to mutter, and mutinie with the rest, he did noe more; but hold his finger, saying, *St.* or *silete* unto them, and all was hushed; soe much was the love and reverence they boare him, as I may safelie say, that neyther Julius Caesar himself with his bare word, *Quirites*, nor Augustus with his *frowne*; nor Pompey the Greate with his *Ore venerando*, could commaund more among their mightie legions, than Sir Rice with his *silete* over the small number he had in charge.[27] And thus you have an end of this cold peece of service, which in effect was as fruitlesse to the common souldier, as that idle expedition of Caligula's, whoe imbattailing upon the sea-shore (and noe man wist what he went about) ordered his armie on a suddaine to gather cockle skells.[28]

(1) *The historie of Perkin Warbeck epitomized. The Cornish men rebell, and side with Warbeck, and are overthrowne. The parte Sir Rice ap Thomas acted in that businesse.*

(1) The storme which the king foresaw, and feard when he was abroad, came nowe violentlie showring downe upon him; for no sooner did he returne out of France, but he was presentlie haunted with the ghost of another, Richard, Duke of Yorke, raysed by the magick spells and subtile machinations of the Ladie Margaret, Dutchess of Burgundie, the old inveterate enemie of the house of Lancaster.[29] This Ladie far stricken in yeares, when other women of her age had given over child-bearing, brought forth two monsters Lambert Simnell and Perkin Warbeck;[30] striplings of strength, as soon as they came into the world, to

---

[26] This is a nice gloss, in Sir Rhys's favour, on Bacon's statement (ibid., p.128) to the effect that 'great pensions were offered to Henry's counsellors'.

[27] It was a reproach for soldiers to be addressed in a civil capacity as Quirites. Caesar is said to have quelled a rebellion by doing so: Howatson, *Companion to Classical Lit.*, p.479. For Augustus's famous piercing eyes and fierce gaze, see Lemprière, s.n.; for Pompey's qualities of leadership, see Plutarch's Life.

[28] This is presumably a reference to Caligula's abrupt abandonment of his planned invasion of Britain in AD 40: Cary (and Scullard), *History of Rome*, p.371.

[29] Chrimes, *Henry VII*, pp.81–92; and for the duchess of Burgundy's role, C. Weightman, *Margaret of York, Duchess of Burgundy, 1446–1503* (Gloucester, 1989), ch.6. Her bitter denunciation by Tudor historians is demonstrated, ibid., pp.153–5

[30] The *CR* editor adds a note: 'As it may be a matter of some curiosity, to know the origin of a man of such singular fortunes, and to trace his posterity, I shall subjoin a short pedigree of his family. As it occurs amongst the genealogies of Glamorganshire, where it settled, on the marriage of Perkin's widow with a gentleman of that country.

Dirick Osbeck; of the town of Tournay, in Flanders; John Osbeck comptroller of the town of Tournay, married Catherine, daughter of Peter de Faro, keeper of the keys of the gates of St John, in Tournay.

Peter Osbeck, commonly call'd Perkin Warbeck, son to John aforesaid married Catherine, daughter of Alexander Gordon, Earl of Huntley. She secondly married Sir Matthew Cradock.

bidd battaile to the mightiest monarkes. Having had ill successe with the former, and making a right use to herself of the errors committed then, in the conduction of those affaires, she became now more cautiouse and after long search, fitted herself with a subject everie way answearable to her owne desires, which she carved and cutt out to the life, setting forth her counterfeite and false ware, with soe artificiall a foile, that both France, Germanie, Scotland, Ireland, yea and a greate parte of England too, were taken with her curiouse and sly conveighances. Nowe, (that I may take noe more of this storie, than leades me to such exploites and services, as were perform'd by Sir Rice ap Thomas during the said disturbance, it being a peece allreadie excellentlie woven, by the most skilful artizan of our times) we must knowe after the dutchesse had for a while kept this Pseudo-Richard in private, and furnished him with some cabinett-instructions, and observing over and besides, that he was a handsome youth and of a winning behaviour, dexterouslie and featlie witted, and withall well seene for his yeares in making apposite answears, and fencing himself from the tempting objections, so as he was likelie to play his owne parte well innough, if at anie time he were putt unto it, she became much transported with the conceite of her owne handie worke; her next care was howe to conveigh him handsomelie into some other region, whence he mought first arise and shewe himself to the world. As lucke serv'd, the Ladie Brampton, an English Ladie was about this time embarquing for Portugall, by which meanes the dutchess had a fitt opportunitie to shift him thither, there to stay, and abide her further directions.[31] In the interim she wrought meanes to disperse abroad, both in England and in other kingdoms adjoining, that Richard, the true duke of Yorke, was nott murther'd with his brother, as was imagined, butt was yett alive, to which rumour manie farr and neere were willing to lend their eares for old affection to that familie. The dutchess finding this good effect of her labours, sends forthwith unto

Richard Perkin married . . .
John Perkin, married Isabel, daughter and heiress of Richard Rogers.
Robert Perkin of Rhos y gelly, son of the said John, married Alson, daughter of Griffith Thomas, of Landemore.
Margaret, daughter and coheiress married Richard Bydder. Anne, daughter and coheiress married Henry Bydder, of Pennard.'
Taken into Queen Elizabeth's household after Warbeck's execution on 23 November 1499, Warbeck's widow, Catherine Gordon (died 1537), a kinswoman of James IV of Scotland, later married, as his second wife, Sir Matthew Cradock (died 1531), one of the most influential men in Swansea and Gower. The details which the *CR* editor gives seem to be taken from Warbeck's confession made when he was captured in September 1497; the subsequent line of Perkins of Gower may or may not be well founded, though in Stuart times it might have suited a Welsh family to claim descent from Catherine Gordon. *DWB*, pp.85–6; Chrimes, *Henry VII*, pp.91–2; for the confessor, C. L. Kingsford (ed.), *Chronicles of London* (Oxford, 1905), pp.219–21; and *Limbus*, p.500, reproducing this pedigree probably from *CR*.
[31] This paragraph owes much to Bacon, *History of Henry VII*, pp.132–4. For Sir Edward Brampton, a converted Jew from Portugal, and his part in Warbeck's early training for imposture, see Weightman, *Margaret, Duchess of Burgundy*, pp.158, 169, 180, 234 n.32; Chrimes, *Henry VII*, p.81 n.2.

Perkin, that he should hasten to Ireland, which commaundes he obey'd, arriving not long after at Corke. The first who apprised the king of his landing, were his faithfull subjects, the maior and Brethren of the cittie of Waterford, as appeares by the king's letter of thankes to them for that particular intelligence; which I here sett downe as well suiting with the businesse in hand, faithfullie transcribed out of the originall.

BY THE KING

Tour trustie and well beloved the Maior and Brethren of the citie of Waterford.[32]

Trustie and well beloved, we greete you well, and have receiv'd your writing bearing date, the first day of this instant month; whereby we conceave that Perkin Warbecke came into the haven of Corke, the 26th day of Julie last past. And that he intendeth to make saile from thence, towardes our countie of Cornwall, for the which your certificate in this partie, and for the true mind that you have allwayes borne towards us, and nowe especially for the speedie sending of your said writing, which we receaved the fifth day of this said month, in this wee give unto you our right heartie thankes, as we have singular cause soe to doe, praying you of your good perseverance in the same: and also to send to us by your writing, such newes, from time to time, as shall be occurrent in those partes; whereby ye shall minister unto us full good pleasure, and cause us nott to forget your said good mindes unto us, in anie your reasonable desires for time to come. Given under our signett, our mannour of Woodstocke, the 6th day of August.

P.S.[33] Over this, we pray you putt you in effectuall diligence for the taking of the said Perkin, and him soe taken, to send unto us, wherein you shall not onelie singularlie please us, butt shall have alsoe for the same in monie content the somm of 1000 markes sterling, for your rewarde, whereunto you may verilie trust; for soe we assure you, by these our present letters; and therefore wee thinke it behooful, that ye sett forth shipps to the sea for the taking of Perkin aforesaid; for they that take him, and bring or send him surely unto us, shall have undoubtedlie the said reward.

While Perkin remayned in Ireland, he took upon him the person of the Duke of Yorke, which the Irish, fooles, as they were, verilie beleev'd

---

[32] The *CR* editor adds a note: 'The original of this letter is to be seen amongst the records of the city of Waterford.' A copy of the king's letter in Waterford's archives is among the papers of Sir George Carew (1558–1629), who spent much of his career in Ireland, partly in association with Sir John Perrot; after returning to England in 1603, he seems to have spent his last years arranging his extensive Irish materials, to which Henry Rice may have had access. J. S. Brewer and W. Bullen (eds.), *Calendar of Carew Manuscripts* (London, 1871), p.468. For Carew, see ibid. (1515–74) (London, 1867), introduction; and *DNB*, s.n; cf. *HMC*, X (1885), appendix V, pp.265ff.
[33] The *CR* editor adds a note: 'This postscript was written with the king's own hand.'

to be true. The King of France, loveing the sporte of blind-man buffe, as well as the Irish, must needes be hoodwinked with the rest, and makes hast by solemn ambassie, to invite this *quidam videtur* [certain impostor] to come for France, where he was entertain'd with all the compliments due to a greate prince, but there on some discoverie made of his Legerdemain, he staid not long, soe that this airie bodie was blowne into Flanders, and thence into Scotland, where he cast such a mist before that kinge's eyes (for he was one could handsomelie tell a lie, and winn it credit) that he obtayned the Lady Katherine Gordon, a kinswoman of the kinges in marriage, and withall persuaded him with a great armie to make an invasion upon England.[34] King Henrie impatient of these indignities, summons a parliament, whence he was supplied with one subsidie and two fifteenes, in the levying whereof the Cornish men fell to open rebellion, who, with the Lord Audley[35] at their head, came even as far as Blackheath, where they encamped, thinking the time long till they had given a full manifestation of their disloyaltie.

The king, as God would have it, was at this time well provided for them, (however the noise of a Pretender, the discontents of subjects, and the armes of a foreigner (a dangerous triplicitie to a monarchie) weare of force to confound the stoutest resolution) for having an armie in redinesse to warr with the Scotts, he made stay of those forces for his owne defence, which he presentlie divided into three partes.[36] The first was leadde by the Earle of Oxford in chiefe, assisted by the Earles of Essex and Suffolk, Sir Rice ap Thomas and Sir Humphrey Stanley; these environed the hill on the right side, and on the left, to intercept the enemie's passage, and take away from them all hope of flight. The second, was under the command of the Lord Daubinie, who had the charge to sett upon them in front. The third remained with the king, to minister fresh supplies as there were cause: to be shorte, both armies meete, and fall to hott fight, shewing such equall courage, that awhile it grewe doubtfull on which side the victorie would rest; for the Cornish-men never gave over to the last, and certainlie had they binn well

---

[34] See above n.30. For Catherine's father, George, earl of Huntly (died 1501), see *CP*, VI, 676–7. Huntly married, as his second wife, a daughter of King James I.

[35] The *CR* editor adds a note: 'My author, in a marginal reference, represents Lord Audley, as *one troubled in his mind, and soe the fitter to be the ringleader of the faction*, but on what authority I know not; as our historians in general, say no more than that he was popular, vain, ambitious, and restless in his temper.' The information about the parliamentary grants was available in Bacon, *History of Henry VII*, p.168, who also noted that Lord Audley was 'unquiet and popular [seeking popularity], and aspiring to ruin' (ibid., p.170). See Arthurson, 'The rising of 1497: a revolt of the peasantry?', in Rosenthal and Richmond, *People, Politics and Community in the Later Middle Ages*, pp.1–18; see above p.48.

[36] For this paragraph's debt to Bacon, cf. *History of Henry VII*, pp.171–5. The Life adds Sir Rhys ap Thomas and Sir Humphrey Stanley to the nobles commanding the first part of the king's army. It also follows Bacon (ibid., p.175) in putting the rebel dead at about 2,000 and the king's losses at about 300, whereas the consensus among modern historians has figures of 1,000 and 300 respectively (Chrimes, *Henry VII*, p.90).

armed, and their cause answearable to their stomackes, they had gon neere to have endanger'd the day, butt in the end were overcome and putt to flight, leaving 2000 and upward of their companions dead in the field. At this battaile, Sir Rice ap Thomas had the commaund of 1500 horse,[37] where he performed the dutie of a right noble valerouse and redoubted chieftaine; for having his horse twise slaine under him, and mounted on the third, called *Llwyd y Bacseu*, in English *Grey Fetter Lockes* (a horse he ever reserved for a sure piece of service) he made through the thickest of the enemie to the Lord Audley, whom, after a fierce encounter, 'twas his good happ to take, and present to the King as his prisoner, for which brave exploite, the King gave him, by way of reward, the goodes of the said Lord, and withall, for his more honour, created him Bannerett in the field, having then manie woundes about him, scarce bound up *adhuc rubens ab hoste* [bloody from the enemy].[38]

The victorie thus obtained, a peace soon after was concluded betwixt England and Scotland, the Scotch king being persuaded to discard Perkin Warbeck out of his dominions. Perkin embarkes againe for Ireland, whither he was no sooner come, then letters were brought him from the discontented partie in Cornwall, who with their lives and fortunes, were readie to undergoe his quarrell. Glad of these joyful advertizements, hastend with onlie sixe or seven score of his wicked adherents, to England, landed at Whitsand Bay, and from hence to Bodmin, the blacksmiths towne, where 3000 of the rabble gave him the meeting, which soe puffed him up, that he begins to slight the title of duke of Yorke, and putts forth his proclamations in the name and stile of king Richard the Fourth, and thus marching forward in a regall manner with his rascall regiments, laid siege to the strong citie of Exeter.[39]

The king understanding of his proceedings, though he made but sporte thereat, yett he neglected not the sending of speedie supplies to relieve the towne, under the commaund of Robert, Lord Brooke, Lord Steward of his House, Giles, Lord Daubinie, his Chiefe Chamberlain, and Sir Rice ap Thomas, the noyse of whose coming made Perkin King of Rakehells, steale away from Taunton in the dead of night, to Bewley in the Newe Forest, where he registered himself a sanctuarie man. The King hearing of his flight, commaunded Sir Rice ap Thomas, with 500

---

[37] The *CR* editor adds a note: 'Griffith Rice, the lineal descendant of Sir Rhys ap Thomas and son of Rice Griffith, beheaded in the reign of Henry the Eighth, in his petition to Queen Mary, and Queen Elizabeth, for the restoration of his father's possessions, forfeited by his attainder, in enumerating the services of his ancestors, mentions this in particular, which exactly corresponds with the account given of it here.' For Gruffydd Rice's petition to Queen Elizabeth, noting Sir Rhys ap Thomas's 'XV^en' hundred horsemenne at Blakhethe feeld where he tocke the Lord Awdley prisoner', NLW, Dynevor, A 14, 95a (copy); see above p.123.

[38] See Shaw, *Knights*, II, 29, for confirmation (17 June) of the honour conferred after the battle of Blackheath.

[39] This paragraph is based on Bacon, *History of Henry VII*, pp.182–3. The blacksmith of Bodmin was Michael Joseph, one of the Cornish rebels' leaders: Alexander, *First of the Tudors*, pp.116–18.

horse, to pursue and apprehend him; butt coming too late, he could not at that time doe noe further service, than onlie besett the sanctuary, till the King's pleasure were farther knowne. I know some of our writers clapt this employment upon the Lord Daubeney; but we may not suffer them to robb Sir Rice of that honour, who in the verie Eulogie and testimonie of his praise,[40] is stiled by the name of the pursuer of Perkin Warbeck, which is sufficient to convince this error, and make good my assertion.

(1) *The peaceable conclusion of the later Parte of Henrie the Seventh his Raigne. The Order of the Garter was conferred upon Sir Rice ap Thomas, Anno Vicesimo Primo, Henrici septimi. The next year following, Sir Rice feasted divers of his Friends and Kinsmen, at his Castle of Carew, in Pembrokeshire, where was helde solemn Justs and Tournaments, with other warlike pastimes, to the honour of St George, chiefe Patron of Men of Warre.*

After the King had, for the space well nigh of fifteene yeares, binn haunted with these fanatical spirits, he at length arrived to safe harbour: for with that final overthrow of Perkin Warbecke, all false-fained practices, and mischievous attempts against his sacred person, were come to their period, soe that time forward, to his last, he ever lived free from those feares and fevers which commonly attend on Princes, whose crowns and titles are continually liable to question.

By this meanes, souldierie, and the exercise of warr, grewe out of request, and was little sett by; everie man nowe being necessitated, that had not otherwise wherewith to subsist of himselfe, to betake to some newe course of liefe for his better supporte. The King thus ridd of all dangers, and eased of the burdens of his cares, he spends the rest of his dayes, which, within a while after expired, in the well ordering the commonwelth, and filling of his coffers. Howe carefull he was of the later may easilie appeare, by the greate masse of treasures he left behind him, and as for the former, he shewed himselfe a most wise Prince, in the choice of able and sufficient ministers, for the administration of justice.[41] Sir Rice ap Thomas, ever well approved of by the King, for his manie

---

[40] The *CR* editor adds a note: 'See the book of the Knights of the Garter, created in the time of Henry the Seventh, where Sir Rice, in the preamble to his patent is stiled thus.' A loose paper of the early sevententh century in CRO, Dynevor, Add. 73, purports to be copied from one of the 'kinges bookes of the knights of the Garter in his Majesty's Cabinet at St James'. This is presumably the source of the report in the Life. The Garter Book is likely to have been the first known register of the Order of the Garter which recorded ceremonies and installations from Henry V's reign to that of Henry VIII; it has been lost, but its successor is still at Windsor: Marks and Payne, *British Heraldry*, p.125. For Robert, Lord Willoughby de Broke (died 1502), steward of the household from 1488, see *CP*, XII, part 2, 683–6; Lord Daubeney (died 1508), chamberlain of the household from 1495, ibid., IV, 102–5. Rhys's role in the extraction of Warbeck from sanctuary at Beaulieu is not otherwise attested, though Warbeck's captor is not known either. Bacon, *History of Henry VII*, p.186, notes the sending of 500 horse to apprehend the rebel leader.

[41] Cf. Bacon, *History of Henry VII*, pp.227–36.

faithful services, was still continued in his government, and during the rest of the King's raigne was whollie occupied about the affaires of Wales, using soe much vigilance and circumspection in those his employments, that noe just grievance, or complaint, all that while, was presented, eyther to the King or the counsell board, touching the lest disorder in those partes.[42] Suffice it for the present, businesses there by him were soe judiciously handled, to the King's good liking, that some time after he was sent for to court, where for his more grace and in acknowledgement of his high deservings, he, together with the Earle of Kent, and the Lord Stafford, was admitted a companion of the noble order of the garter, and the better to enable him with meanes for the support of that dignitie, he had at the same time the Lordshipp of Narberth[43] bestowed upon him. Nowe the report goes, that when he accepted of that honour, the Earldome of Pembroke or of Essex was offered him. Notwithstanding he made rather choice to be confrere of the order; and being asked whether he preferred a temporarie title before what by continuance would enoble his posteritie; he made answeare, that his profession was armes, and the greatest honour could be conferred upon a souldier, was knighthood. As for his sonne, and his sonne's sonne, and for the rest of his posteritie, if they were ambitiouse of further advancement, his desire was for their more glorie, they should sweate for the same as he had donn.[44]

[42] The deaths of Jasper Tudor (1495) and Prince Arthur (1502) left Sir Rhys with unchallenged practical authority, especially in south Wales. See above pp.48–9.

[43] The *CR* editor adds a note: 'Narberth is a market town in Pembrokeshire situated within 4 or 5 miles of a navigable branch of Milford Haven, through which the great road leads from London to Haverfordwest, and Milford; on the South side of the town, appear the ruins of a castle, built by Sir Andrew Perrott, son of Stephen Le Perrott, who first came into this country, with Arnulph de Montgomery, who was son of Adam Le Perrott, who came over with William the Conqueror.

By several antient writings I have seen, it appears, that the Lordship of Narberth, had been in the possession of Griffith Nicholas, the grandfather of Sir Rice ap Thomas. An inquisition taken in the 8th of Henry the Sixth, ascertains it to be the possession of Richard, Duke of York, as cozen, and heir at law, to Roger Mortimer, who died, seized of the same without issue; then follows a licence of alienation to the Duke of York, to sell the said Lordship, to John, Bishop of St David's and Griffith ap Nicholas, which Griffith conveyed it to Owen ap Griffith, his youngest son, the founder of the families of Upton, in Pembrockshire, and of Llechdonny in Carmarthenshire, and uncle to Sir Rice ap Thomas. How, in so short a time it got back to the crown, so as to admit of the grant, to Sir Rice I know not, but with the posterity it rested not long, for it was forfeited on the attainder of his grandson, Rice Griffith, and soon after granted to the Barlows of Slebech, in Pembrokeshire, in which family it continued, till within these few years it became, by purchase, the property of William Knox Esq.'

Sir Rhys was created a knight of the Garter on 22 April 1505: see above p.50. For the chequered history of Narberth in the fifteenth century, and especially of Gruffydd ap Nicholas's interest in it after 1449, see above p.17. The inquisition *c.*1431 presumably refers to one taken before Richard, duke of York, was granted livery of his estates the following year: Johnson, *Duke Richard of York*, p.10. Owen ap Gruffydd's descendants in Llechdwni (Carmarthenshire) are shown in Bartrum, *1400–1500*, IV, 649.

[44] The earldom of Pembroke had been in abeyance since the death, without heirs, of Jasper Tudor in 1495, but Henry Bourgchier, earl of Essex (died 1540), was very much alive in 1505 and not out of favour with Henry VII. Henry Rice may have intended the earldom of Exeter, for the last duke of

The next year following, being returned again to his charge, Sir Rice held solemne justs and tournaments at his castle of Carewe, in commemoration of that anniversarie greate feast of St George's, at court, where at that time he could not give his attendance, by reason of other more weightie employments. The preparations he made were both sumptuouse and magnificent well fitted to the occasion. Plentie, I meane, he had of all sortes of provision, but noe superfluitie, neyther scantie nor deare, such was his fare that mought be found in all places; a souldier's diett well ordered, and therein he shewed as much skill, as in arraying his armie. Neyther, indeede (if we believe Paulus Emilius, whom in that, Sir Rice did trulie imitate), is there less *arte convivium exhibendo quam aciem bene instruendo* [skill in showing entertainment than in successfully drawing up a battle line]:[45] so farr as in the one we would become formidable to our enemies, so in the other, we should strive to please and hold a complaceancie with our friendes. Nowe for the manner and setting forth of his shewes, with other civil respects of entertainment, it is thus traditionallie given out, which, I pray, be pleased to accept by peece meales, as I have gathered the same from several discourses, and thereupon make your judgment, both of worth and greatness of this man. Sir Rice, as I told you, being at his castle of Carewe, in Pembrockshire, made publication of a solemn just and turnament, with other marshall exercises, he went to hold for the honour of St George, Patrone of that noble Order of the Garter. The fame hereof, being blowne abroad, manie worthie and valerouse gentlemen of his blood, some to doe him honour, others to make triall of their abilities in feates of armes, came unto him from all partes of Wales. The first that presented his service, was his owne sonn, Sir Griffith Rice, one of the Knights of the Bath to Prince Arthur;[46] then came Sir Thomes Parrott, and Sir William Wogan, men of eminent note, and his neere neighbours; likewise Arnold Butler, Richard Griffith, and John Morgan, old beaten souldiers, and verie expert commaunders;[47] after them followed Griffith

Exeter, Henry Holand, died in 1475. The suggestion that either could have been offered to Sir Rhys is most intriguing. See *CP*, V, 138–9, 212–15.

[45] This may be a reference to Lucius Aemilius Paullus (*c*. 230–160 BC), the Roman general who, after the sack of Epirus, scrupulously paid the enormous booty into the Roman treasury, keeping for himself only the captured books of the Macedonian king: Howatson, *Companion to Classical Lit.*, p.413. There is no independent evidence for these celebrations at Carew Castle round about 23 April 1506, commemorating not only St George's day but also Sir Rhys's elevation to the Order of the Garter the previous year, but see above p.50.

[46] For Gruffydd ap Rhys's knighthood and his service with Prince Arthur, see above p.51.

[47] The Life appears to have misnamed Sir Owen Perrot (died 1521) of Haroldston and Sir John Wogan (died 1557) of Wiston: Bartrum, *1400–1500*, IX, 1435–6; R. K. Turvey, 'The Perrot family and their circle in south-west Wales during the later Middle Ages' (unpublished University of Wales Ph.D. thesis, 1988), p.259; Lewis, *WWHR*, II (1911–12), 94; F. Green, 'The Wogans of Pembrokeshire', ibid., VI (1916), 195–8. For Butler, Griffith and Morgan, long-standing associates of Sir Rhys, see above p.209.

Dunn,[48] a brave man at armes, and one of Diana's champions against the schollers of Pallas, at the coronation of Henrie the Eighth; he was afterwards by Sir Edward Howard, High Admiral, knighted in Brittany, for his good service against the French. From Brecknockshire there came Vaughan of Tre-towre, granchild to Roger Vaughan the Marshall, beheaded by Jasper, Earle of Pembroke, at his castle of Chepstowe.[49] From Glamorgan and Monmouthshires, Jenkin Mansell,[50] surnamed the valiant, the same who procured the repeale of his father Philipp's attaindour, slaine in the quarrel between the houses of Yorke and Lancaster; and Sir William Herbert of Colebrooke,[51] sonn to that thrice noble warrior, Sir Richard Herbert, beheaded at Banburie: all these weare of South Wales. Out of North Wales their repaired thither, Young ____ Griffith, sonn to Sir John Griffith,[52] Lord of

---

[48] The *CR* editor adds a note: 'Sir Griffith Dunn, son of Sir John Donne, who lies buried at Windsor, ap Griffith, ap Meredid, ap Henry Dun, ap Griffith Gethin, ap Kadwgan Llwyd, ap Griffith, ap Cadwgan of Kidwelly, ap Llewhelin, ap Gwrgant'. K. B. McFarlane, *Hans Memling*, (Oxford, 1971), pp.54–5, places the birth of Gruffydd Dwnn (or Donne) (died 1543) in about 1487; he was a skilled horseman and one of Henry VIII's jousting friends. For his distinguished father, Sir John Donne (died 1503), who made his peace with Henry VII and was buried in St George's Chapel, Windsor, see Griffiths, *Principality of Wales*, pp.187–8; McFarlane, *Hans Memling*, pp.1–10. The above pedigree is sound, at least in its later generations: ibid., pp.56–7. For the jousts following Henry VIII's coronation, see Scarisbrick, *Henry VIII*, p.18; *Hall's Chronicle*, pp.510–12. At this tournament, a group of knights posing as champions of Diana, the virgin goddess of the hunt, challenged the followers (or scholars) of the goddess Pallas Athene, patron of arts and learning. A. Young, *Tudor and Jacobean Tournaments* (London, 1987), pp.146–7, 197.
  Sir Edward Howard, the English admiral, commanded a fleet that made for Brittany in March 1513 (Scarisbrick, *Henry VIII*, p.34); Gruffydd Dwnn may have accompanied it and been knighted by Sir Edward before the latter's untimely drowning. Alternatively, he may have accompanied the second fleet to Brittany under Sir Edward's brother, Thomas, shortly afterwards.
[49] Vaughan of Tretower would have been one of the three sons of Sir Thomas Vaughan – Roger, Watkyn or his eventual heir, Henry: *DWB*, pp.1000–1. Their sister married Sir Rhys's brother Morgan: see above p.179 n.30.
[50] The *CR* editor adds a note: 'This Jenkin Mansell, mentioned in some genealogical charts, to have been beheaded at Chepstow, was son to Philip Mansell, by Mably, daughter of Griffith ap Nicholas, therefore Welch uncle to Sir Rice ap Thomas.' For Jenkin, 'the valiant', son of Philip Mansel of Oxwich in Gower, see *DWB*, p.611. Philip was erroneously said to have been executed after the battle of Mortimer's Cross (1461), though he may have perished later during the Wars of the Roses. His attainder (1464) was reversed by Henry VII, at which point Jenkin recovered his father's estates: Evans, *Wales and the Wars of the Roses*, pp.128, 152. A Welsh uncle was the first cousin of a parent.
[51] The *CR* editor adds a note: 'Sir William Herbert, was nephew to Sir Rice ap Thomas, the son of his sister Margaret, who married Sir Richard Herbert of Colebrook; Sir William Herbert married Jane, Daughter of Sir William Griffith, Knt. chamberlain of North Wales.' William Herbert was the son of Sir Richard Herbert of Coldbrook (died 1469), younger brother of William Herbert, earl of Pembroke (died 1469), and his wife, Margaret, daughter of Thomas ap Gruffydd ap Nicholas. Bartrum, *1400–1500*, IV, 643. He seems to have been under age when his father was killed at Edgecote in 1469; his support for Henry Tudor in 1485 was rewarded with appointment as receiver, chancellor and approver of the lordships of Monmouth and the Three Castles on 27 November 1485: Somerville, *Duchy of Lancaster*, I, 651. He married Jane, daughter of Sir William Griffith of Penrhyn (Caernarfonshire) (died 1506), who was chamberlain of north Wales from 1483 to 1490 and was knighted in 1489. *DWB*, p.1125.
[52] The *CR* editor adds a note: 'It must be a mistake, I apprehend, to call Sir John Griffith Lord of Llansadwrn as Sir John Griffith of Abermarlais, who was Lord of Llansadwrn, left only a daughter,

Lansdown, and yong Wynn,. of Gwidir, his kinsman, two hopefull gentlemen, of good towardlinesse, and with them the lusty Robert Salisburie, a man much noted for his greate strength of bodie, a fast friend and companion to Sir Rice, in manie of his warlike adventures.[53] He was afterwards knighted by Charles Brandon, Duke of Suffolke, in the chiefe church of Roy, for his prowesse and loftie courage, shewne in that expedition. These men of prime marke weare all lodged within the castle. Besides these, manie more, to the number of five or six hundred weare assembled and drawne together, at that meeting, men, most of them of good ranke and qualitie (for those of the meaner sorte, who were the greater number, were passed over as not regarded) to be spectators of those rare solemnities, never before knowne in those partes, nor, for ought I remember, practised by anie of the order, in their private hereto fore.[54] For them, tentes and pavillions were pitched in the parke, neere to the castle, wheare they quartered all the time, everie man according to his qualities, the place being furnished aforehand, with all sortes of provisions for that purpose. This festival and time of jollitie continued the space of five dayes. On St George's eve's eve [21 April], which was the first day of their meeting, Sir Rice tooke a view of all the companie, chusing out five hundred of the tallest and ablest among them; those he divided into five troopes a hundred to each troope, over whom he appointed captaines, David the younger, and John, two of his brothers, Arnold Butler, Richard Griffith, and John Morgan, all tried men and readie in their profession.[55] The next day being the eve, these five captaines drewe forth their forces into the field, exercising them in all pointes, as if they had bid suddenlie to goe upon some notable piece of service, in which delightfull shewe, that whole dayes allowance was spent, with the full contentation of all those noble gentlemen there

who was Sir Rice ap Thomas's mother, he must therefore have been one of the family of Penrhyn in Carnarvonshire, now the seat of Lord Penrhyn.' The editor could be right in doubting that a relative of Sir John Gruffydd (died 1471) was invited to Carew, though he did have a son, Sir Walter (died 1481), whose own son and heir, Walter, was born *c.*1473: Griffiths, *Principality of Wales*, pp.145–6, 274–5. On the other hand, William Griffith of Penrhyn (died 1531) had a close relationship with Sir Rhys ap Thomas, and G. Roberts was inclined to accept that this William, son of William Griffith (died 1506), took part in the Carew festivities – after all, he is described as 'out of North Wales' (*DWB*, pp.1125–6, which assigns his birth to *c.*1480, though see below p.252). Like Sir Rhys, he served in the king's expedition to France in 1513.

John [Wyn] ap Maredudd ab Ieuan (died 1559) could be described as 'of Gwydir', which his father purchased *c.*1500; later in the Life he is said to have been no more than sixteen years of age in 1506: *DWB*, p.1097; see below p.256.

[53] For Robert Salusbury, and his knighting in France, see above p.238 n.22. By 'Roy' the Life probably intends Thérouanne, which was besieged during this campaign in 1513; its 'chiefe church' may have been the church in which a *Te Deum* was sung on 24 August as Henry VIII and the Emperor Maximilian made their triumphant entry into the town. Scarisbrick, *Henry VIII*, p.36.

[54] Not without justice are these festivities described not only as 'rare' but unprecedented in southwest Wales among the gentle classes. Indeed, it is difficult to think of any earlier private festivals organized in Henry VII's reign other than in association with the king's court. Young, *Tudor and Jacobean Tournaments*, p.70, with a useful list on pp.196–7.

[55] See above pp.209, 215.

present. The third day, St George his day, earlie in the morning, the
drummes beat up, and trumpets sounded, everie man with the
summons, betaking him to his charge; first the captaines ledd forth their
companies, in a militarie array, well armed at all pointes: then followed
Sir Rice himself, upon a goodlie courser, having two pages and a herald
on horseback, before him richly cladd, after whom the rest of the
gentlemen followed, being all bravelie mounted in a most decent and
seemlie manner, and soe in a silent and grave march, they passed on to
the Bishop's palace, at Lamphey[56] a mile or thereabouts distant from
Carewe castle. At their comming thither, they bidd good morrowe to the
Bishopp in the language of souldiers, with Arquebusses, Musketts, and
Calivers, and then dividing themselves, they made a lane for Sir Rice to
passe onward to the gates, which (as yett) weare nott suffered to be
opened.[57] Upon his approach, the Bishop's subsidiarie (the businesse
being soe ordered among them, before hand) came out at the wickett,
demanding what he was, why in armes, and the cause of his coming
thither? to which Sir Rice made answeere, that he was one of St George
his knights, who ever shew'd himself a trustie patron and protector of
marchialists: and therefore he held it most suitable to his profession
especiallie on the verie day (as that was) dedicated to the honour of that
renowned Saint, to appeare in harness and militarie equipage. Notwithstanding, he willed the messenger to assure the Bishop that (as then)
he was a man of peace, for he came thither to pray for the peace and rest
of St George's soul, and for the wellfare and prosperitie of his graciouse
master, sole sovereign of that honourable order, whereof himselfe was an
unworthie companion: in which hartie and devoted excercise, he
earnestlie desired the Bishop would be pleased to come with him. Noe
doubt, replied the messenger, but my Lord, besides the dutie of his
calling, will easilie assent to such pious and religious motions: yet ere I
give you admittance, said he, it is necessarie you change your habit, it
being a thing ill beseeming our scholeastical militarie course of lief, and
the sanctimonie of this place, to consorte and joyne in devotion, with the
rough and all disturbing disciples of Mars: in the meane while I shall

[56] The *CR* editor adds a note: 'Lamphey Palace, in the parish of that name, near Pembroke, was
once the magnificent residence of the Bishops of St Davids, three of which they had in the county of
Pembroke; viz. St Davids, Llewhaden castle, and Lamphey, not long after the time referred to here,
it was alienated from the see, but how, I know not; in Queen Elizabeth's time, we find it in the
possession of the Earl of Essex, who occasionally resided there. It afterwards became the property of
the Owens of Orielton, in which family it now continues.' Bishop Barlow alienated the manor of
Lamphey to the Devereux family, later earls of Essex, in 1546 (Williams, *Wales, 1415–1642*, p.299);
and for the Owens of Orielton, see Owen, *Old Pembroke Families*, pp.104–16. Like many of the
nobility, Sir Rhys evidently had his own herald to organize not only the events at Carew but also
the visit to Lamphey; he may have penned at least part of the account of these festivities. Siddons,
Welsh Heraldry, pp.306–7; *CP*, XI, appendix C.
[57] The bishop would have been Robert Sherborn (1505–8), later bishop of Chichester (1508–36),
who was a king's clerk, secretary and councillor to Henry VII by 1496: Emden, *Oxford*, III, s.n. See
C. A. Ralegh Radford, *The Bishop's Palace, Lamphey, Pembrokeshire* (London, 1948).

imparte unto my Lord, the summe of your desires.[58] Sir Rice hereupon passed by, with all his companie, and rid up unto the Bishop's parke, where he had a faire tent of purpose provided for him, over which was written *cedant arma toga* [let arms give way to the toga].[59] There he alighted, and forthwith enrobed himself, in St George his livery; after some small repose, he walked on foote downe to the palace, having a trumpeter before him, and a herald of armes; two pages carrying his traine. And the choicest of gentlemen, to be his associates, the rest during the time of the ceremonie, he left behind him, to cheere up and make merrie; for their was foisons and plentie, both of wine and all other necessarie provision, laid out in a readinesse for their solace and refreshment, at the Bishop's charge. Sir Rice drawing neere to the palace, he caused his trumpet to sound, thereby to give notice of his approach, and then the gates were opened; the Bishopp, having with him the Abbott of Talley, and the Prior of Carmarthen, all with rich copes, stood there to give him entrance.[60] And soe some fewe compliments first passing betweene them, they walked forward in a solemn procession, *canentes et supplicantes* [singing and praying], twice or thrice round the court, and then to the chapel. There Sir Rice was desired to stay for a while, at the door, till first the quire were placed, and the Bishop had taken his seate. Within a while the herauld comes unto him, and ushers him in. When they weare allmost in the middle of the chapel, they turned about, and made, each of them, two humble *congés* to the king's seate, and soe in like manner againe when Sir Rice went into his stall. Presentlie upon, the Bishopp ascends to the high altar, and reades divine service: after which much good musick followed: manie new hymnes and anthemes they had made of purpose for that solemnittie, and there sung; some for the long life, peace, and prosperitie of the king; others for the rest of St George his soule, and his safe deliverance out of purgatorie. Divers and sundrie superstitious ceremonies they had besides, which are now growne obsolete and out of use.[61] To be shorte, Sir Rice, having donn his offering, and all religious formes observed and ended, he tooke the Bishop, Abbott, and Prior along with him to dinner, and soe backe againe he goes to Carewe, in the

---

[58] Mars, the god of war. Fenton's 1811 version of the account of the Carew celebrations has more appropriately 'our scholasticall *unmilitarie* course of life' (below p.275).

[59] A Ciceronian tag (cf. Cicero, *De Officiis*, I.22.82).

[60] See above p.209. For the inner and outer courts and the chapel at Lamphey, see Ralegh Radford, *Lamphey, passim*.

[61] Here speaks the post-Reformation author of the Life. For popular church music and pre-Reformation hymns in Latin and Welsh, see Williams, *Welsh Church*, pp.94–5, 450–2. Two notable Welsh composers, John Lloyd (*c*.1475–1523) and Robert Jones, were members of Henry VII's chapel and may have been known to Sir Rhys: S. Sadie (ed.), *New Grove Dictionary of Music and Musicians* (London, 1980), IX, 703; XI, 99; *DWB*, s.n. Henry VIII's formal arrangement (1522) for Garter celebrations by knights absent from Windsor included a religious service at which a herald should be present and a seat reserved for the sovereign: Ashmole, *Order of the Garter*, pp. 614–17.

same decent and comelie march that he sett forth. Drawing neere, the captaines saluted the castle with a brave volley of shott, and the like was returned them againe from the walles. That donn, they, and their troopes, passed into the parke, where each had his particular tent to entertaine his souldiers and friendes: a thing Sir Rice had a principall care of from the beginning. When these were gone and provided for, Sir Rice having reserved a great companie of the better sort for his guests, he leads them to the castle, with drummes, trumpetts, and other warlike musicke. Over the gate, at the entrance, was hung up a goodlie faire table, wherein was represented the species and pourtraiture of St George and St David embracing one another with this mottoe, *Nodo plus quam Gordiano* [Knot stronger than the Gordian].[62] In the first court, which was the *Platea* or common place wherein people did use to walke; two hundred talemen were arranged all in blewe coates, who made them a lane into another lesse court, called the *pinacotheca*, in which the images, scutcheons, and coat armours, of certaine of Sir Rice's auncestors stood, and soe they passed into the greate hall, which hall was a goodlie, spaciouse, roome, richlie hanged with cloath of Arras and tapistry.[63] At the upper end under a plain cloath of state, of crimson velvet, was provided a cross-table for the king: on each side, downe the length of the hall, two other tables, the one for Sir Rice alone, the other for the rest of the gentlemen. Here everie man stood bare, as in the king's presence. Within a while after the trumpetts sounded, and the herald called for the king's service; whereupon all the gentlemen went presentlie downe to waite upon the Sewer. The Sewer for the time, Sir Rice appointed his sonn, Sir Griffith Rice, who had binn bred up at court, and therefore had some advantage of the rest in point of curialitie and courtlinesse:[64] Sir William Herbert, of Colebrooke, the carver, and young Griffith, of Penrhyn,[65] the pocillator or cupbearer. When the king's meate was brought to the table, the bishop stood on the right side of the chaire, and Sir Rice on the left, and all the while the meate was a laying downe, the cornetts, hautbois, and other wind instruments were not silent. After the table was served and all sett, the bishop made his humble obeysance to the king's chaire, and then descended to say grace, which donn, he returned againe to his former station. Much pleasant discourse passed

[62] This motto expressed the strength of the bond – greater than that of the Gordian knot – between St George and St David, England and Wales.

[63] For Carew Castle, see above p.74. In general, see M. Howard, *The Early Tudor Country House: Architecture and Politics, 1490–1550* (London, 1987), esp. ch.4 ('The Courtyard and the Household').

[64] Sir Rhys's son, Gruffydd, was in Prince Arthur's service: see above p.51.

[65] The *CR* editor adds a note: 'There seems to be some mistake about this gentleman, which it is not easy to rectify, a little before he is called son of Sir John Griffith, Lord of Lansadwrn, which could not be, as Sir John Griffith left only a daughter, who was Sir Rice ap Thomas's mother, and here he is stiled young Griffith of Penrhyn; yet another difficulty arises, for in the pedigrees of that family, no Sir John Griffith occurs; but perhaps it may be safe to correct the pedigrees by this account, as better evidence.' See above p.248.

betweene them for a time, which ever and anon was seasoned with diversitie of musick. When they sawe their time, the table was voyded, and the meate removed to the sideboard for the wayters. Then the king's chaire was turned, and so everie man at libertie to putt on his hatt. The king's service being finished, Sir Rice went to his owne table, taking onelie the bishop along with him, whom he placed at the upper end, at a messe all alone, and himself at some distance sate him downe at another. All the gentlemen there present were pleased; for Sir Rice's more honour, to stand by and give him the looking on, untill his first course was served: then Sir Griffith Rice the king's Sewer, his two fellow Officers, and the rest by the name of wayters, went to the king's reversion. The fare they had, you will easilie believe was good, being provided as for the king. Such cheere as they had, was attended with much pleasant discourse: divers passages of mirth, free of all offence, passed from one to the other. The King, Queene, and Prince's healths were often drunk among them; and the bardes and *prydydd's* accompanied by the harp, sung manie a song in commemoration of the vertues and famous atchievements of those gentlemen's ancestors there present, a custome used long before, even by Achilles himself, *qui in conviviis ingentium virorum facta canebat ad citharam* [who at feasts sang to the lyre of the deeds of great men].[66] By that time these conviviall merriments were ended, the day was well nigh spent, soe that they could fall to noe disports for the rest of the afternoone; but onlie walke abroad, and take the fresh aire of the parke; Sir Rice in the meane while betakes him to his privacie; but soon after comes into the field, where he entertained the gentlemen with some polemicall discourse, which was his proper element, a thing most delectable to the hearers, whoe were all of them professors of armes. Here upon having a fit opportunitie, Sir William Herbert steps forth and makes challenge to all comers, foure to foure, at justs and turnaments, the next morning, for the honour of ladies. This challenge was presentlie accepted by Sir Griffith Rice. The appellant names for his assistants, Robert Salisburie, Jenkin Mansell, and Vaughan of Tretower, the defendant, Sir Thomas Perrott, Sir William Wogan, and Griffith Dwnn.[67] The ordering of the whole business was referred to Sir Rice himself, whom they all jointlie desired to sit as judge: Sir Rice gave way to the motion, and provided for them accordinglie. All parties agreed, and growing late besides, Sir Rice sawe it high time to goe home; soe in they went; first to the chapel, where they heard solemn service, then to supper, observing the same decorum and order at night, that they had done at dinner; for the king's table in all points, as likewise for the observation of those his civill lawes and complementall shewes of hospitalitie. Thus this daye's pleasing labour, or laboursome pleasure

[66] This quotation has not been identified. '*Prydydd*' = 'poet'.
[67] See above pp.247–9.

was ended; the first day of this pompe and ceremonie, the third of their meeting. The next morning, by sound of trumpet, Sir Rice was summoned to play the judges parte, which accordinglie he did. He had on that day a faire gilt armour; two pages well provided on horseback before him, with a herauld and two trumpeters; himself mounted on a goodlie steed, richlie barbed and trapped, with foure footmen, two on each side attending him. Two hundred tall men in blewe coates, some before and some behind him. In this manner he went into the parke, where a tilt was made readie for the purpose, riding about the same twice or thrice, for the well accommodating the enterprize then in hand. At one end of the tilt there was a tent for the appellants to rest them, at the other for the defendants. Sir Rice perceaving all things well ordered, he presentlie took him to the judgment seate, about the middle of the tilt, over against the breaking place; his servants standing round about him, everie one having a halbert in his hand, and a good baskett-hilt sword at his side. When time served, the trumpetts sounded, and then the appellants came in sight. The first that appeared was Sir William Herbert, the challenger having a trumpeter before him, and a page carrying his shield without anie devise, the motto – '*Et quae non fecimus ipsi*' [And those things we have not done]. The next was Robert Salisburie, who had for an impresse on his shield, a Gyant running at a Pigmie, with this motto, '*Pudet congredi cum homine vinci parato*' [Shameful to meet a man ready to be subdued]. Then came Jenkin Mansell the valiant, whose sentence was – '*Perit sine adversario virtus*' [Courage perishes without an enemy]. After followed Vaughan of Tretower, who tooke this for his dicton – '*Ingens gloria calcar habet*' [Glory is a great spur].[68] After these the inceptors, or enterprisers followed the noe lesse brave defendants or propugnators. Their manner was the same, Sir Griffith Rice had written on his scutcheon, '*Et vinci et vincere pulchrum*' [It is noble to conquer and be conquered]. Sir Thomas Perrott, in a more loftie language, made choice of this for his motto: '*Si non invenio singulos pares, pluribus simul objicior*' [If I do not find an equal, then I offer myself to many]. Sir William Wogan, meaning to do honour to his noble adversarie, tooke yet a more humble motto, which was this: '*Profuit hoc vincente capi*' [Noble to be taken by this victor]. And Sir Griffith Dwnn, a man of an active spiritt, used these wordes to express his inclination: '*Industrioso otium paena*' [To the industrious, leisure is a punishment].[69]

---

[68] For the use of mottoes in Wales before 1700, see Siddons, *Welsh Heraldry*, I, 237, 245, 247, though none of the examples cited accords with those noted in the Life; it seems possible that they were devised for the occasion. The motto on Sir Gruffydd ap Rhys's banner, *c.*1510–25, was taken from Psalm 147, verse 9, *Et pullis corvorum invocantibus eum*: Lord Howard de Walden (ed.), *Banners, Standards and Badges from a Tudor Manuscript in the College of Arms* (De Walden Library, 1904), p.90 (College of Arms MS, I.2).

[69] The lack of a device on Herbert's shield, Salusbury's taking of an allegorical *imprese* for his, and the personal choice of mottoes in other cases suggest ephemeral insignia for a colourful and grand

These gallant gentlemen, in good order, ridd twice or thrice about the tilt, and as they passed along, they by their pages presented their shields to the judge, which done, both parties severed and took their stand, the one at one end, the other at the other end of the tilt. Then the trumpetts sounded; whereupon the two first combatants putt their launces into their restes, and soe rann each their six courses. In like sorte followed the rest, who charged the one, the other with equall ardour, ever and anon devidinge manie a shrewd counterbuffe among them, and performing their devoirs with much judgment and agilitie. Noe sooner had they made an end with their speares, but they fall to Turney with their swordes all at once, which was a most delightful spectacle to the standers by. This exercise was performed by them in the plaine field, and sound knockes, you may be sure, were receaved and returned on both sides, butt noe harme at all done; for Sir Rice had taken order with the stickes to parte them, and prevent all cause of jarr, if anie the least occasion in that kind were offered. All which needed nott more than to shew Sir Rice's care for the preservation of love and amitie betweene those, soe neere him in blood, and who were mett at that time, for noe other end but to doe him honour, that care being taken afore hand among themselves, not to esteeme of knockes valerouslie receaved and manfullie bestowed in the number of injuries, *sed quicquid accideret boni consulere* [but whatever happened was well regarded]. Having performed their devoirs, both with sword and speare, they mutuallie embraced each other, and soe hand in hand they went to the judge to receave a definitive sentence of their activities. Sir Rice, whose office was to arbitrate the cause, after long deliberation with himself, grewe doubtfull in opinion; for some of them were excellent at the speare, and some at the sword: some who were well with the sword failed with the speare, and they that surmounted with the speard [*sic*], fell shorte with the sword. This bredd much difficultie in the judgment, soe that Sir Rice to draw the thread even, when first he had commended them for their heroicall deedes, and given a large testimonie of their skill and valour in the performance of them, concluded in the language of Virgil's Shepherd:

> Non nostrum inter vos tantas componere lites,
> Et vitulâ tu dignus, et hic, et quisquis amores
> Aut metuet dulces, aut experietur amaros.[70]
> [It is not for me to settle so high a contest between you.
> You deserve the heifer, and he also, and whoever shall
> Feel the sweetness or taste the bitterness of love.]

occasion. R. Barber and J. Barker, *Tournaments* (Woodbridge, 1989), p.136; A. R. Young, *English Tournament Imprese* (New York, 1988), *passim*.
[70] See Virgil, *Eclogues*, III, 108–10. The *CR* editor adds a note: 'Vergil, Eclogue, 3d.'

Willing them merrilie, as you see by way of caution warilie to take heede of those said Dames, whose honours that day they had soe faithfullie maintayned.

Thus the emploiments and excercises of the morning ended; and soe in they went first to hear divine service, as they were wont to doe, and then to dinner, where they wanted for nothing that mought give them all assurance of hartie wellcome. Robert Salisburie, Jenkin Mansell, and Vaughan of Tretower, were appointed for this day the honorarie officers of cupbearer, carver, and sewer, Sir Rice having a cane [*recte* care] in the matter of forme to grace them all equallie; and soe to stave off all cause of envie, and other sinister interpretation. When they had dined, they went visitt each captain in his quarter, where they found everie man in action, some wrestling, some hurling of the barr, some tossing of the pike, some running at the quinteine,[71] everie man striving in a friendly emulation, to performe some act or other worthie the name of souldiour. With these and the like delights, the afternoon vanished.

At Supper, Sir Griffith Rice, in the presence of his father, made challenge to Sir William Herbert, foure to foure, at the ring next morning, for a supper, which the losers should pay at Carmarthen for theyre farewell at parting. Sir William forthwith undertooke him, onlie wishing the yong heirs of Penrhyn and Guidir[72] mought be added to their number, whom he sawe to be gentlemen of a faire expectation and clearlie spirited, and who had bore noe parte in all those activities, which, indeede, was not their fault; for willinglie they would have both given some demonstration of their youthful courage, at the justs and turnaments, had nott Sir Rice, in respect of their greenesse (the eldest being not above sixteene yeares of age), perswaded the contrarie.[73] The motion nowe being reasonable, and those two galliard yong spiritts besides forward of themselves, Sir Rice easilie gave his assent; the rather, because in that exercise they were not soe much to employ their strength, as to shewe they were gentlemen at armes, gracefull in behaviour, dexterouse and skillfull, both in running and taking of the ring. The next morning, Sir Rice having taken his seate, the trumpetts were commanded to sound, to which these rivall knights obeyed,

[71] Quintain, a tilting post for practice.

[72] The *CR* editor adds a note: 'This young Heir of Gwidir, here mentioned, was afterwards the famous Sir John Wynn, a man of the greatest fortune and command in all North Wales, a very full account of whom, together with a fine print of him, is given in Mr Pennant's Tour. There is another curious and scarce print of this Gentleman by his countryman, Vaughan, the celebrated Engraver, in the early part of the last century.' The editor mistakes John Wyn ap Maredudd (died 1559), the young heir of Gwydir here mentioned, for his grandson, Sir John Wynn (1553–1627), the author of *History of the Gwydir Family*: *DWB*, pp.1097–8. See T. Pennant, *The Journey to Snowdon* (London, 1781), opposite p.140 (the portrait at Wynnstay of Sir John Wynn, by William Sharp). The engraving of Sir John by Robert Vaughan (died 1667), is in Jones, *History of the Gwydir Family and Memoirs*, p.43.

[73] For the implication of this estimate of the birth of John Wyn ap Maredudd and William Griffith, see above pp.248 n.52.

running each of them theire six courses, with such indifference, soe as to perplex the nicest judgment; butt in the end, Sir Rice gave sentence against his sonn, a thing agreed upon beforehand betweene him and his father; however, the cause went, that soe he mought shewe his friendes the towne of Carmarthen before they went away, and what entertainment that place was able to afford, which, at that time, was thought to be verie good;[74] Sir Griffith said noe more, but tould his father, the decree should be obeyed: and soe to dinner they goe, observing the same order they had donne before, save onlie the changing of sewer, cupbearer, and carver, which offices that day, Sir Thomas Perrott, Sir William Wogan, and Sir Griffith Dwnn did execute. After dinner, Sir Rice leads his noble guests into the parke a hunting, where they killed divers bucks, all which he bestowed among them towards the furnishing out of their festivall metting at Carmarthen. To supper then they come, after which they had a comedie acted by some of Sir Rice his owne servants, with which these majesticall sights and triumphs were concluded.[75] This meeting was, for some years after, called by the name of St George, his pilgrimage to St Davids, where one thing is noteworthie, that for the space of five days among a thousand people,[76] (for soe manie at the least were thought to be assembled togither at that time) there was not one quarrell, crosse word, or unkind looke that happened betweene them, such care Sir Rice had taken for the well-ordering of what he intended, merely in commemoration of the famous Patron and gloriouse sovereigne of the Garter, whereof himself was an unworthie companion. Early in the morning, before they parted, the bishop bestowed a sermon upon them, tending all to loyall admonitions, obedience to superiours, love and charity one towards another. His text was out of Eclesiastes, cap.x.ver.20.[77] 'Curse not the king! no, not in thy thought, and curse not the rich in thy bed-chamber: for a bird of the air shall carry the voice, and that which hath wings shall tell the matter.' After the sermon was ended, when the gentlemen came to take leave, Sir

[74] R. A. Griffiths, 'Carmarthen', in idem (ed.), *Boroughs of Medieval Wales* (Cardiff, 1978), pp.152–63; T. James, *Carmarthen* (Carmarthen, 1980), chs.4, 5.

[75] What could such a 'comedie' have been? For hints – but no more – see Williams, *Wales, 1415–1642*, pp.114–16, 163.

[76] The *CR* editor adds a note: 'It were well for England, if, at this time, we have a few, Sir Rice's men of fortune, birth, and power, who, with a popularity well directed, and a loyalty more than skin deep, would employ those distinctions to make their fellow creatures, and particularly their inferiors, happy, by encouraging them to be peaceable subjects, and setting them the example of duty and subordination, and not by Utopian doctrines and wild theories, incapable of being reduced to practice, prostitute their time and talents to purchase the applause of the multitude, at the expence of insulted Majesty, the disarranging that nicely balanced system of Government, the envy of the world, and the subversion of those happy laws which hold the life and property of the Peer and Peasant in equal estimation.' This is a rare outburst from the editor *c*.1795!

For the use of St George and St David to symbolize the honour done to Sir Rhys – and Wales – by his election to the Order of the Garter, see above p.252.

[77] This is a precise quotation from the King James authorized version: a sobering exhortation to respect the king and the nobility.

Rice bestowed upon divers of the choicest of them, a ribband of true blewe colour, which he desired them to weare for their more honour. At each ribband there was a medaile, the impresse of which was that true symbol of Faith, '*Dextrae Manus mutuo implicatae*' [Right hands mutually entwined], with this motto: '*Nec poterat ferrum*' [Nor could the sword], which they kindlie accepted, and for manie years wore for his sake; and soe giving them his thankes, he recommended them to his sonn, Sir Griffith Rice, who was engaged to be their Symposiastes the night following.[78] Thus in Wales did we honour St George, which made the English ever after earnestly to affect and higly [*sic*] to regard, the societies, love and friendship of the Welch, and their Patron St David, a thing well pleasing to the king, and for which he gave Sir Rice manie thankes the yeare following, when he came to give his attendance at courte.[79] Within a few months after the king died, leaving an earthly crowne to enjoy an heavenly: in whose place as his lawfull successor Henrie the Eight followed, by whom Sir Rice was yett more and more graced, than ever he had bin by his father for nowe we find him enstiled *Deliciae Henrici Octavi* [Beloved of Henry VIII].[80] He was growne on a suddaine, so great a privadoe, that 'twas thought Themistocles himself could not doe more with Xerxes, than he with king Henrie; for soone after his entrance to the crowne, he appointed him *Justiciarium suum Southwalliae*,[81] which office was, as I take it, much of the same nature with the justiciars of Ireland, onelie *ad pacem servandam et justitiam singulis universis exhibendam* [to serve peace and show justice to all], much like that of Propraetors, or Proconsuls of the Romans.

---

[78] Symposiastes, a drinking companion.

[79] For the gifts sent by Sir Rhys and his son to the king at court in 1506–7, see above p.49 and n.27.

[80] The *CR* editor adds a note: 'Camden's Britannia, Latin, 4to. p.586.' But this precise reference has not been located. For Sir Rhys's patents from Henry VIII, see above p.52.

[81] The *CR* editor adds a note: 'Vide Rot. Anno primo. Hen. 8.' The grant of 11 May 1509 was confirmation of his tenure of the office, which he had originally been granted on 4 January 1496 during the prince's pleasure: Griffiths, *Principality of Wales*, p.162; see above p.49.

The classical allusion seems to be to Themistocles the Athenian (died *c*. 459 BC) who, towards the end of his life, entered the service of Artaxerxes, king of Persia, from whom he received many honours and responsibilities. Howatson, *Companion to Classical Lit.*, p.563. Thucydides wrote a famous assessment of Themistocles's character (1.138); for lectures on Thucydides in sixteenth-century Oxford, see Binns, *Intellectual Culture*, p.217.

Henry VIII and Sir Rhys ap Thomas

The death of King Henrie the Seventh. Henrie the Eighth is advanced to the crowne. He quarrells the French King, passeth over into France, and taketh the two strong Townes of Terwin and Tourney, and the exploits of Sir Rice ap Thomas in that expedition.

King Henrie the Eight, after the death of his renowned father, coming at once to a flourishing kingdome and a plentifull fortune, spent most part of the two first yeares of his reigne in masques and revells, and those other oblectations which usually attend youthfull and galliard spiritts.[1] In his third yeare there fell out some difference between Pope Julius the Second, and Lewis the Twelfth of France, and that difference in the end turned to a most furiouse and bloodie war, which King Henrie, by all meanes possible tried to compose: but nott finding himself able to performe what he intended there, he fell into choler, and stood upon rough termes with the French king, demanding restitution of the Dutchie of Normandie, Guienne, and the countrie of Angouleme, yea of the crowne of France, as his lawfull inheritance.[2] Hereupon great preparations were made, both by sea and land. By sea, that puissant Captain, Sir Edward Howard, was Admiral, having manie brave gentlemen in his companie. By land the Lord Marquesse Dorsett was in Chiefe, and to goe along with him, there were appointed the Lord Howard, sonne and heire to the Earl of Surrey, the Lord Brooke, the Lord Willoughby, and yong Sir Griffith Rice, the onelie sonne of Sir Rice ap Thomas, who was one of the Knights of the Bath to Prince Arthur, a gentleman upon whom no unfaithfulness could ever take hold, though bredd of a child at courte, a rare felicitie![3] Of these preparations

[1] This exaggerated comment is placed in context in S. Anglo, *Spectacle, Pageantry, and Early Tudor Policy* (Oxford, 1969), pp.108ff.; Henry VIII's personal role in court festivals, including masques and revels, in the early years of his reign is well described.

[2] For the drift (1510–13) towards war with France, see Scarisbrick, *Henry VIII*, pp.24ff.

[3] This ironic comment on court life was commonplace. For the 1512 expedition to Fuenterrabia,

made by the King of England, Ferdinand, King of Arragon, made good use, being alsoe himself in termes of hostilitie with the French King, and having likewise other private designes upon the kingdom of Navarre. Wherefore he persuades his son-in-lawe, under promise of great assistance, to land his army at Guipiscou, as a place convenient to open the way into Guienne, which done, Ferdinand makes no more ado forsooth, but under pretence of coming himself in person to joine with Dorsett, chopps into Navarre, taking possession of the strong citie of Panpelona, and that without anie stroake strucke, and soe that mock expedition cost the King of England the expence of more treasure than the King of Arragon had given him in marriage with his daughter.[4] Howe Harrie, digested this affront cleaves nott by the storie; but it did not abate his resolution of falling upon France, for which purpose he rayseth a puissant armie. Over the advantgarde the Earle of Shrewsburie, high steward of the king's house, had commaund, having with him the Earle of Darbie, Decowrcé, Prior of St Johns, the Lord Fitz-Walter, the Lord Hastings, the Lord Cobham, and Sir Rice ap Thomas, amounting to 8,000 men, which sailed for Callice, a towne, which while we held it, the French themselves acknowledged the keyes of France hung at our girdles. Within a while after followed the retaguardia or rereward of the king's armie, under conduct of the Lord Chamberlain Herbert, the Earles of Northumberland, Kent, and Stafford, with manie more of prime marke.[5] There were foure men (above the rest) distinguished on this expedition.

> . . . 'Talbotus belliger [the warlike], audax [bold]
> Poiningus, Ricaeus Thomas flos Cambro Britannum [flower of the Britons],
> Et Somersetus.'[6]

These corageouse warriors having rested a fewe dayes at Callice, and consulted for the well-ordering of their affaires, presentlie drewe their forces into the field, commaunding everie souldiour by sound of trumpett to depart the towne, and speedilie to repaire to his charge. The first, according to his place, went the Earle of Shrewsburie, Captain General, then followed the Lord Herbert; next after the valiant Sir Rice ap Thomas, *Campiur y Brutanniaid*[7] [Champion of the Britons] tooke the field with his light horse men and archers, and soe they marched forward till they came before the stronge towne of Terwin, to the north west side of which the Earle of Shrewsburie layed present siege, as likewise the

---

see above p.53.

  [4] *Hall's Chronicle*, p.528, carries a vivid account of this disastrous expedition.

  [5] Scarisbrick, *Henry VIII*, pp.34–9; see above pp.53ff.

  [6] The *CR* editor adds a note: 'Christopher Ocland in his Praelia'. Cf. Ocland, *Anglorum Praelia*, p. lii: 'Ricius Thomas flos Cambrobitannum' in relation to the invasion of France.

  [7] See above p.151.

Lord Herbert to the east side; whilst Sir Rice scoured the coast with his horse, holding the French in such awe, as none of them durst approach the towne to releave it. It fortuned at this time, as the Callicians were comming with necessaries for the armie, their companies fell to drinking and disorder, of which the Duke of Vandosme, governor of Picardie, having notice, with 800 light horsemen came upon them, and cutt manie of them off. Yet the French had little cause to brag of their winnings; for Sir Rice having heard the newes, all enraged thereat, caused his trumpett to blowe to the stirropp, pursuing the Duke of Vandome from place to place, who, not disposed to stay to heare his Welch compliments, which he well knewe would prove both harsh and unpleasant, takes him to his heeles, and hyes him backe to Bangey Abbey, where the French armie lay to shelter the storme.[8] By this time the king himself was landed, and on his march towards Terwin. The French king, startled to hear it, makes sudden preparations to give him the encounter. Both were come within a small distance each of the other, and manie hott skirmishes passed betweene them. As they were thus exchanging these harsh salutes, there appeared in sight on a suddaine a companie of horse men, which somewhat appalled the English, as imagining the whole power of France had followed, neyther did the king himself well knowe what to make of it: butt within a while, by his colours, they perceaved it was Sir Rice ap Thomas, who in a most glittering and brilliant manner, came (the first man) from the siege with his cavelleria to attend the king's commaundes. The king, glad of the accesse of soe experte a commaunder, especiallie at such a time, himself being in action, receaves him gentlie, and soe forthwith sends him to the Earle of Essex, Captaine of the speares, wishing them both to join and sett upon the Frenchmen. Sir Rice, having receaved his instructions, presentlie departed and went to the Earle, both returning incontinentlie to do what they had in charge. The French perceaving their design, and nott caring greatly for such unpleasant acquaince, retire them with speede and avoide battaile. The Earle and Sir Rice having notice hereof, they drewe neere to the enemie and there *staled*, but hearing for certaine that both foot and horse recoyled, they brake up their ground, and returned to the king to give accounte of their proceedinges.[9] It happened, as the king proceeded in his march, that one of his greate bombardes called the Redd Gunn,[10] was overthrowne, and left by the

---

[8] See above p.54.

[9] For descriptions of this incident in *Hall's Chronicle* and other contemporary sources, see above p.55.

[10] See above p.55. The *CR* editor adds a note: 'It is curious to trace the improvement in the structure and management of artillery since that time, when the replacing a dismounted gun, was a service so arduous, as to require the most experienced generals with a large body of the bravest troops to cover it, and entitle those who were employed on that occasion to the thanks of their sovereign.'

way. The French having taken the John Evangelist, another greate piece of ordnance some fewe dayes before, thought to doe the like by this; but the lord Barnes, Capt. of the Pioneers, lying in wait for them, prevented their designs, to whose aide came presentlie the Earle of Essex with his speares, Sir Rice with his horse, and Sir John Nevill with the Northumberland men. They had not gone farr, butt they ascribe the whole armie of France, where upon the Earle sendes to Sir John Peachie, Lieutenant of the speares who was in place, where the said Gunn was to be mindfull of his charge. Meane while, Sir Rice politickly takes the advantage of the ground where he sawe most likelihood of gauling the enemie. This example of his the earle alsoe followed, knowing him to be a man of a most excellent judgment, and for matter of discretion with the best, and therefore worthie of imitation. By this time the Lord Barnes had got up and carted the gunn. And nowe the whole French armie appeared, comming on in a most glorious array with standardes, penens, and banners, displaid to give them chase: which noe sooner perceav'd by Sir Rice, but forthwith he calls to my Lord of Essex, giving him to understand, that to quarrell and attack the whole power of France with soe small a parte of their forces would savour rather of temeritie, and meere foolhardiness, than of anie true judgment or well-grounded valour; besides, they were nott authorised by anie warrant to runn such a course, their commission onlie being to fetch off the gunn and noe further. The earle being happie to be directed by a man of soe greate experience, presentlie gave way to his admonitions, and soe with a soft and warie retreate they followed the gunn, which the French mistaking for feare, thought the day was theirs. Here upon they sett upon the English with a large body of their best horse, which the Earle and Sir Rice whealing about upon the suddaine, encountered with such unfriendlie demeanure, as to make the enemie take to their heeles. The sight whereof, together with the dreadfulnesse of the chase, startled the whole host of France, and made them turne taile. When this was ended, the Earle and Sir Rice returned to the king, with the said gunn, making report unto him of their dangerouse adventures, for which the king gave them hartie thankes, with manie promises of other condigne rewards, suitable to their high deservings.[11] The king then layes his siege to the towne of Terwin, battering the same on everie side with his greate ordnance. In the meane while, newes was brought him that the French king had an intention of relieving the citie, which within a while after, was confirmed by Sir Rice, having taken a French man prisoner, by whom he understood as much; and that himself had ascried a number of men comming forward to his judgment, on the point of six thousand. This made the king suddenlie to prepare for battaile.[12] When on a

---

[11] See above p.55.

[12] The king had reached Thérouanne by 1 August 1513.

suddaine, a body of French horse with thirty-three banners displaid, appeared in sight, threatning wonders. But it was not long ere the English powring water on their wine, sone abated and appalled their courage, for their standard being overthrowne, away they all rann, casting away their speares and swordes, and cutting off the barbes of their horses to runn the lighter, which nimbleness of theirs makes them famous at this day, even in their owne stories; for notable *Huydors* and Runawayes.[13] In this battaile, called by themselves Journée des Esperons, or the Battaile of Spurres, Sir Rice tooke Duke Longuile prisoner. Soe saith Griffith Rice, Sir Rice Griffith his heire, in his petition to Queene Marie and Queene Elizabeth, yet extant; but master Camden in his remaines, gives the honour of that service to one Sir John Clarke, of Buckingham, whom the king (as he saith) rewarded for this particular act with a canton Azure, a Demy Ram saliant argent, two Fleurs de Lys, or in Chiefe, in addition to his paternal coate of armes; and on a conference had with Master Camden touching this point, I receaved for satisfaction, that undoubtedly Clarke was the man who took the person of the Duke; yet he verilie added, that then he served under Sir Rice, as well as other English gentlemen, who all bore testimonie to Sir Rice's magnanimous deportment, at the battle of Bosworth and elsewhere, soe as right the praise of the service was to redound to both; and soe Griffith Rice his petitions and his notes will agree; for *quidquid in membris laudis est, ad caput refertur* [whatever is praised in the limbs, is attributed to the head], and of everie brave exploit, performed by anie private gentleman of a companie, or common souldier, the principall glorie rests on the commaunders side: soe much for the reconciliation of this difference, which I take it, may hold well together without anie disparagement to eyther.[14] A fewe dayes after this discomfiture, the goodlie cittie of Terwin was rendered up to the king of England by the Lord Powntremy, captain general of the same. Then fell the king to a second resolution for the besieging of Tourney. The battaile was ordered as before; over the avantgarde the Earle of Shrewsburie was in chiefe, and rerewarde was conducted by the Lord Herbert, and the maine bodie by the king himself. First, the king commaunded Sir Rice ap Thomas to view one quarter of the towne, and the Earle of Essex another, who having taken a strict survey of the place, returned, making report to the king, howe all things stood.[15] Hereupon the towne was

---

[13] The battle of the Spurs took place on 16 August 1513. For the capture of the duc de Longueville, see above p.56.

[14] Cf. W. Camden, *Remaines of a Greater Worke, Concerning Britaine* (London, 1605; ed. R. D. Dunn, Toronto, 1984), p.162. For Henry Rice's acquaintance with Camden (died 1623), see above p.263.

[15] The siege of Tournai is less well reported by contemporaries, and the Life provides useful information about Sir Rhys's role, prior to the city's capture on 24 September 1513. The allusion to the capture of Joan of Arc, *La Pucelle*, in 1430 is a measure of the importance the English attached to

summoned by Garter, King of Armes; butt nothing could prevaile till the siege was laid and a batterie made, and then the cittie was yielded up by the Provost, with a summ of ten thousand pound sterling, for the redemption of their lawes, customes, and liberties; and soe we leave this stale maid to deplore the loss of her Pucellage, a thing she was soe loath to parte withall, though sollicited thereunto by a mightie monarch, a rare instance of chastitie. The king, on his return to England, forgot not the good services done by his followers; therefore, by way of reward, he gave Sir Griffith, sonne and heire of Sir Rice ap Thomas, *Officium reaptoris* [recte *receptoris*] *Dominii de Dynas*[16] [Office of receiver of the lordship of Dinas] in South Wales, with all fees and emoluments thereunto belonging; and in a while after he gave both to Sir Rice ap Thomas, and Sir Griffith (father and sonne).[17] *Officia seneshalli et cancellarii maneriorum, et dominiorum de Haverford-West et Rowse* [offices of steward and chancellor of the manors and lordships of Haverfordwest and Rhos], in the marches aforesaid, soe that nowe being possessed of all the prime offices in South Wales, and govenour of all Wales besides, wee may trulie affirme Sir Rice to be the greatest subject that ever was in those partes.[18] After this expedition, I doe not find that ever Sir Rice went abroad, wherein you may see he did nott *extremo actu deficere* [fail in his last act] (a misfortune that hath befalne the greatest commaunders that ever were) butt plaid his last parte most exactlie, for in this last service of his, you shall not read in all the English storie of anie more spoken of, more emploid, nor more honoured than he was, and if you will give credit to our Welch Bardes, he was sans-pareille, which drewe some envie upon him, even from the chiefest of the nobilitie of England, which made our Poete burst out, and say that he was '*Gwenwyn Lloegr, etc.*' [The Envy of England].[19]

The same poete, in his kowydd to Sir Rice, wherein he is whollie emploied about the late expedition to France, after labouring to give him the superioritie of all others in the siege of Terwin and Tourney, concludes his song with

the fall of Tournai.

[16] The *CR* editor adds a note: 'What office is here referred to, I have not been able to learn; there seems to have been a word after *Dynas*, which from the faintness of the manuscript can't be made out; perhaps we should read *Dynas fawr*, what is now called Dyne faur, in Carmarthenshire, the ancient residence of the Princes of South Wales, and the present justly admired seat of Lord Dynefaur, who enjoys it with a taste and a magnificence, suited to the beauties and the grandeur of the place, and every way worthy of his illustrious ancestors.' This is a rare inaccurate digression on the part of Richard Fenton. What is intended is the grant to Sir Gruffydd ap Rhys of the stewardship and receivership of the lordship of Dinas for life on 25 September 1514, albeit his tenure proved brief. See above p.57.

[17] The *CR* editor adds a note: 'Perhaps the offices were to be held jointly, or were granted to Sir Rice ap Thomas for life, with reversion to his son Sir Griffith Rice.' The grant was made to father and son for life and in survivorship on 16 May 1517: see above p.57.

[18] For an assessment of Sir Rhys in the last ten years of his life, see above pp.56–9.

[19] From Tudur Aled (*fl.*1480–1526), Jones *Tudur Aled*, I, 71. Whilst it is true that Sir Rhys did not campaign abroad after 1513, he accompanied Henry VIII to the Field of Cloth of Gold in 1520: see above p.58.

> Trecha un draw yn trychu'n trin
> Tair Brân ond Dûw ar Brenin.[20]

Which I take it to be thus Englished:

> Next after God and the king that day,
> Rice and his ravens did bear the sway.

Butt we must allow poetes their hyperboles. It sufficeth you doe him the honour, which, in justice, you cannot refuse him, even on the testimonie of the English historians themselves, to believe him for prowesse and deedes of armes to be equall with the best; and, as for us, we shall ever hold it a principall honour to our nation, that we have afforded such a spiritt, who was the terror of his enemies where-ever he came, who merited and received the loudest applauses of his countrie-men, and challenged the gratitude and esteeme of kings, who admitted him to drink deeply of the fountain of honour. For militarie conduct he is on all hands allowed to have had no superiour: and, when the sword of warr was returned to its scabbard (as I shall hereafter shewe)[21] during his civill administration, noe man held the ballance of the lawe with an evenner, or the sword of justice with a firmer, or more discreete hand. As a proofe howe terrible he was to his enimies, his name, as I was tould by a worthie gentleman that travayled in those partes, is yet used about Terwin as a bugg-beare or fire-abbras, such as a Talbott's was, in Henrie the Sixt's time, to affright the children from doing shrewd trickes.[22] Butt the eulogie and testimoniall given of his praise, when you understand under what roofe it is preserved,[23] you will easilie graunt to be *Palmare testimonium* [a testimony of excellence], and may well serve to eternize this man's fame, though all our bookes were barred of the light.

---

[20] The *CR* editor adds a note: 'Tudur Aled ai kant'. Jones *Tudur Aled*, I, 71:

> Trecha un draw'n trychu'n y drin,
> Tair bran, ond Duw, a'r Brenin!

[21] The *CR* editor adds a note: 'Here again my author adverts to a work he then had in contemplation, wherein he purposed to give a view of Sir Rice ap Thomas in his civil capacity, and which must have formed a most desirable companion to that he has here exhibited of his military life, had it been handed down to us. Every search has been made for such a performance, amongst those collections, where, if it ever existed, it was most likely to have been found but without success.'

[22] *Hall's Chronicle*, p.230; A. J. Pollard, *John Talbot and the War in France, 1427–1453* (London, 1983), pp. 1–2.

[23] The *CR* editor adds a note: 'The book of the Knights of the Garter is here alluded to, which (according to my author) was in his highness's collection at St James's Palace.' A testimonial to Sir Rhys's courage as a knight of the Garter in the service of Henry VII and Henry VIII, possibly of early-seventeenth-century date, in the Dynevor pedigree book of *c*.1900 (CRO, Dynevor, Add. 73) purports to have been copied from an entry in 'on of the king's bookes of the knights of the Garter in his Majesties Cabinet at St James'. This may be a note made in preparation for the writing of the Life itself.

Sir Rice ap Thomas, his dignified close of life – He dies full of honors and yeeres – His buriall – A breefe recorde of his alliances and his issue, as well legitimate as illegitimate.

Having brought our renowned Welchman to the end of his militarie career, and having consigned him in the full blaze of glorie, to the enjoyment of new offices and honors, proportionated to his great deservings and the high opinion entertained of him by his royall master, in the possession and discharge of which he carried himself with so much firmnesse, discretion, and temper, filling the judiciall chair with as much claim on fame as the war saddle (for of him it may trulie be said that he was '*tam marti quam mercurio*' [as much for Mars as for Mercury]) soe that it is yet a point undecided, whether he was a better souldier than a judge: let us now take a farewell view of him, in the last stage of his earthlie pilgrimage, making preparations for eternitie. Behold him then enjoy-ing, to as great an extent as it were possible for mortal, the *otium cum dignitate* [leisure with dignity], in a fair retreate, enriched with all the commodities needfull to supply the establishment of a man of his vast munificence, exalted rank, and unbounded swaye, associating with all who were celebrated for learning and pietie far and neere, who resorted to his castle[24] as to the court of a great monarch, to doe honour to him and themselves; behold him, I say, happy in the consciousness of having, by his justice and his perseverance, reformed the disorders of his countrie, and reduced a tumultuary people, split into various factions, into a respect for law and a love of subordination, with the toils of his station consequentlie abating, in proportion to his years and the necessity for repose, justlie venerated at home and abroad, with nothing to cloud the evening of his dayes, and darken the prospect beyond the grave! highly priviledged lot! and such was his! With courts and camps he seems not to have had much to doe, after his return from the affaire of Terwin and Tourney; from his attendance on the former, the important station he filled with soe much effect in his owne countrie, might well excuse him; and, from the latter he might well claim a dismission, which the best years of his life had been devoted to, and where he had left behinde him his valour and his discipline in soe manie young captaines of his owne rearing. Sir Rice having been trayned from his earliest youthe to the robuster exercises of the bodie nowe, his age being, as oure

---

[24] The *CR* editor adds a note: 'The Castle of Carew, in Pembrokeshire, his favourite residence, and where he chiefly spent the latter part of his life, at which time the Bishop of St David's resided at Lamphey Palace, a mile or two distant from Carew, between whom and Sir Rice there subsisted a constant intercourse and an inviolable friendship, circumstances which probably operated as the principal inducement for Sir Rice's preferring Carew to his other demesnes.' The reference may be to Edward Vaughan, bishop of St David's (1509–22); this might explain why Vaughan's building work at St David's Cathedral incorporated Sir Rice's device in its decoration. *DWB*, p.1001, and for Sir Rhys's links with St David's, see above p.80. The tag, *otium cum dignitate*, is Ciceronian: Cicero, *Pro Sestio*, 45.98.

greate poete expresses itt, a '*lustie winter*'[25] was ever watchfull to guarde againest that inertenesse with all its dire effectes, which a sudden passage from a lyfe of bustle and businesse to ease and retyrement, too often begetts in us, and to the last, therefore, kept up the spiritt of gymnastique discipline, in his servantes and followers haveinge sett dayes for a varietie of games and pastimes, which he often would attende in person to encourage and rewarde. The recreation he moste delighted in himselfe was that of horsemanshipp, in the knowlege of which he was reputed to excell everie man of his tyme, and in the practice of which he indulged himselfe with a passion unabated by yeeres. The supporte of his stables and his manage made one of the principall articles of his expensive and allmost princelie establishmente for his numerous stalls weare ever full of horses of the rarest breede, which he often had drawne out in martiall arraye, as if the ennimie weare att hande, it being his maxime, that peace was the best season to provyde for warre, soe that when itt came, it found him readie and prepared to meete it. His assistantes at these revewes and mocke battailes weare his olde fellowe souldiers, whoe, in manie a harde rencounter, bothe att home and in forraigne partes, hadd shared with him the daungers as well as the glorie of the daye, and nowe often mett together in such bloodlesse showes, to act over theire paste fieldes, when all the yonge gentrie of the countrie flocked thither as to a militarie schoole.[26] Nor, during all this provision for recreating and strengthening the bodie, was the wellfare of its immortall inmate overlooked, Sir Rice being as regular and exacte in his ghostlie as well as bodilie exercises; his fast friende and neighboure, the Bishop of St David's,[27] in his frequente visites to the castle, never failinge to supplie him with such spirituall compfortes as contributed to fytt him for that awfull journeye which, more from a consyderation of his age than anie particular pressinge warninges he then felt, he was persuaded in the run of nature he must shortlie sett oute upon, and for which, to make the necessarie preparationnes, some portion of hys everie daie was piouslie allotted. An exemplarie temperance in his dyett, a methodicall distribution of his tyme, and a discreete husbandinge of his vitall powres, had secured to Sir Rice a serenitie of mynde, and its allmost constaunt

[25] The *CR* editor adds a note:
'Therefore my age is as a *lusty winter*,
Frosty but kindly –
Shakespeare's As you like it.'
The first mention of this play is in 1600.

[26] Sir Rhys's special devotion to horsemanship is well attested: see above p.75.

[27] The *CR* editor adds a note: 'During the four last years of Sir Rice's life, Doctor Richard Rawlins was Bishop of that See, who succeeded Bishop Vaughan.' Rawlins was provided to the see on 11 March 1523, though it is surely with Vaughan that Rhys had the closer connection. Rawlins had no prior link with Wales, whereas Vaughan was a south Walian who had been a prebendary in St David's Cathedral (from 1504) before his consecration as bishop. Emden, *Oxford*, III, s.n.; *Cambridge*, s.n.

concomitaunte, helthe of bodie; norr doe I learne that his laste Glasse was hurryed by anie violente or painfull dyscase, butt was, bye the favoure of heavenn, sufferedd to runn oute graduallie and smoothelie, after a course of seventie and sixe yeeres.[28] His death was a publique losse and calamitie, and was so consydered and long lamented, leaveing suche a blanke in his countrie as it was nott easie to fill up. He was buried, as the tradition goes, first, in the Fryars at Carmarthen, but was afterwardes (as I have alreadie related in the proeme to this historie) moved and re-interred in the easterne isle of St Peter's church, where hys remaynes, together with those of his ladie, nowe reste under a statelie monument, which, to doe justice to his greate fame and honourable deservinges, should have beene '*Aere perennius*' [More lasting than bronze]; but, sorrie am I to saie, is made of a sorte of free-stone, of soe softe a graine, that itt alreadie beares evidente proofes of unfaithfullnesse to its truste; and in less than another centurie, will be likelie to lose all traces of what itt was at firste intended to recorde.[29] And nowe, having followed the heroe of mie storie from the cradle to the grave, ere I dismisse mie reeders, I shall give a breefe touche of his noble allyances and his hopeful progenie, to some of which, in the course of this narrative, I have had allreadie occasion to referr. His first wife was Eva, daughter and co-heiresse of Henrie ap Gwillim, of Coort Henrie, by which marriage his estates weere considerablie increased, and the long subsisteinge feudes betweene the twoe families weare, att lengthe, happilie extinguished.[30] The fruite of this union was one sonne, Sir Griffith Rice, whose birthe his mother survyved nott longe. To his second wife he matcht with Jonett, daughter of Thomas Mathewes, of an auntiente house in Glamorganshire, by whome he left noe issue.[31] Butt

---

[28] The *CR* editor adds a note: 'He died A.D. 1527, leaving his grandson then a youth of nineteen, to inherit his vast possessions, who was beheaded four years after, at the age of twenty-three.' For Sir Rhys's death in 1525, and his grandson's birth *c*.1508 and his execution in 1531, see above ch.4.

[29] The *CR* editor adds a note: 'My author's prediction has long been literally verified, as the monument he alludes to for above a century, I should suppose, has ceased to exhibit any more marks of the sculptor's art or original design, than were barely sufficient to distinguish the sex of the recumbent figures by. Of an inscription, not the faintest vestige now remains, and every endeavour to retrieve it has proved fruitless. It is to be regretted that, considering how much genealogy and history they contain, there never was a regular registry for monumental inscriptions established in every church, not merely for the gratification of the antiquarian and biographer; but, as it might essentially contribute to facilitate the investigation of disputed titles, and often settle property without driving the contending parties to seek for redress from an expensive and tedious litigation.' See above p.155; Horace, *Odes*, III, 30.1.

[30] See above p.63.

[31] The *CR* editor adds a note: 'Sir Rice ap Thomas seems to have made scarcely any distinction between his natural children and those born in wedlock, but what the law had previously settled, if we may judge by the laudable attention he shewed, in forming such honourable connections, and so ample a provision for them; an attention, I find, universal, in those days, in Wales, or with very slight shades of difference, in proportion to the degrees of sensibility and gallantry in different men. But, within this century, how is the system reversed! And of late so scandalous a neglect of children of a certain unhappy description, a neglect which disgraces humanity, has prevailed amongst gentlemen of birth, education, and, in other respects, perhaps, of nice feelings, insomuch that there

the children he had by diffrent concubynes weare verie numerouse; for of hym itt maie be saide, that, in his yonger dayes, under the standarde of Venus as well as thatt of Mars, *'militavit non sine gloria'* [he fought not without glory], and in the servyce of bothe, with him, it was butt *veni. vidi. vici.*[32] And, as moste of his illegittimate offspringe were matcht to, or became the founders of, houses of prime note in Southe Wales, and weare richlie endowed, itt maie nott be alltogether superfluouse or foraigne to oure purpose to enumerate as manie as weare publicklie acknowledged by their father, and maintayned with sutable respecte. By Gwenllian, sister to his counsellor and confidentiall secretarie, whoe, as well as her brother, might be styled *e secretis consiliis* [of secret councils]; he had issue Margerett, Ellen the elder, Ellen the yonger, Margarett the yonger, Mawd, William,[33] David the elder,[34] David the

have been instances of sons and daughters of that wretched class filling the most menial offices under the roofs of their own fathers; such is the fatal force of custom to stifle reflection and subdue nature. To confirm the just severity of this remark, I cannot forbear subjoining a few beautiful Latin lines on the death of an infant, born only to the inheritance of such neglect, by a gentleman, who, in his practice uncontaminated by the ruling fashion, exemplarily adhered to that humane principle which excited the indignation of his muse.

> His modo nate jaces sperato funere mersus
> Infausto vitam cui dedit atra dies;
> Lapsus es in superas, matris pudor, haud dolor, auras!
> Non tibi nascenti dextra ferebat opem:
> Nec partu gemuisse, neque orbam flesse Corinnam.
> Dicunt, et Prolem saepe negasse Patrem.
> Sis felix in morte nothus lis magna, Parentum!
> Sit tumulo tibi, quem vita negavit, amor.
> Carmina lusurae haec videant quaecunque Puelle
> Supprimere incipiens Fata precentur onus;
> Haec bona vel si Fata negent, miserabilis infans
> Vadat ut ad Stygias sic cito raptus aquas

[Here you lie, just born, brought to a hoped-for death, you, the unfortunate one, to whom black day gave life; you have slipped into the beyond, a cause of shame to your mother, not grief! Good fortune did not bring help to you when you were born. They say that Corinna did not lament your birth nor weep when bereft, and that a father often denies his offspring. May you be happy in death, bastard, a burden to your parents! May you find in your tomb the love which life denied you.

May any girls who are about to play who are about to play read these words and pray that the Fates prevent the conception of a child. Or if the Fates deny these good words, may the pitiable infant go to the Stygian waters to be quickly enveloped.]

See J.-L. Flandrin, *Families in Former Times* (Cambridge, 1979), pp.182ff.

[32] See Horace, *Odes*, III, 26.2 (*militavi non sine gloria*); Suetonius, *Divus Julius*, 37.2 (*veni, vidi, vici*).

[33] The *CR* editor adds a note: 'This William ap Rice was settled at Sandyhaven, on the banks of the harbour of Milford, and his name occurs amongst the earliest sheriffs of Pembrokeshire.' D. Miles, *Sheriffs of the County of Pembroke* (Haverfordwest, n.d.[*c*.1974]), p.17 (sheriff in 1557).

[34] The *CR* editor adds a note: 'David, the elder, married Alson, sole heiress of Arnold Martin, of Richardston, about five miles from St David's, whose son John married Catherine, sole heiress of John Perrot, Esq. of Scotsborough, near Tenby, in Pembrokeshire, and had great possessions. John ap Rice was sheriff of Pembrokeshire, A.D. 1582, as were several of his descendants afterwards.' Miles, *Sheriffs*, pp.21, 23; though pedigrees make John the grandson of Dafydd (Bartrum, *1400–1500*, IV, 646; IX, 1437).

yonger,[35] Thomas, and Philip. By Elizabeth Mortimer[36] one daughter, Jane. By Jenett, daughter of Meredydd Vychan of Talley, he had Gwenllian.[37] By Alice Kyffin, of Montgomerieshire (for he mighte well saye, *Quae regio in terris nostri non plena laboris* [which region of the earth is not full of our toil?]) a daughter, who died yonge. And, lastlie, by a daughter of Howell ap Jenkin, of Ynisymangwyn, in Merionethshire,[38] Anne, whome, itt is sayde, her father notyced above the rest, and had broughte up more under his owne eie, matcheinge her into one of the firste families of Pembrokshire. And nowe, gentle reader, havinge, to the utmost of mie abilitie, endeavoured to performe what I undertooke, I must leave thee with

> . . . Si quid novisti rectius istis
> Candidus imperti, si non, his utere mecum.[39]
> [If you know better than these precepts, share it openly: if not, join me in following these.]

---

[35] The *CR* editor adds a note: 'David, the younger, had Taliaris, in Carmarthenshire, now the seat of the Right Honourable Lord Robert Conway.' Jones, *Historic Carms. Homes*, pp.177–8. Robert, a younger son of Francis Seymour-Conway, Lord Conway of Ragley (War.) and earl of Hertford (created 1750), bought Taliaris from Sir Rhys's descendants in 1787. See also *CP*, VI, 509–10.

[36] The *CR* editor adds a note: 'Daughter of John Mortimer, Lord of Coedmor, near Cardigan. This was not the only Faux Pas which this lady had been guilty of, for Griffith Vaughan, of Corsygedol, when Governor of Cilgerran Castle, situated opposite to Coedmor, on the south side of the vale of Teifi, had a child by her, named Tudor, of whom was descended Doctor Theodore Price, formerly principal of Hart Hall, Oxford.' See above p.63 for Elizabeth Mortimer. For the Vaughan liaison (though with Gruffydd's son, William, rather than with Gruffydd himself), and her great-grandson, Dr Theodore Price, see Griffiths, *Principality of Wales*, p.222; *DWB*, pp.790–1.

[37] The *CR* editor adds a note: 'Who married Lewis Sutton, Esq. of Haythog, in Pembrokeshire'. They settled in Pembrokeshire, but 'Haythog' is Haydock in Cheshire: see above p.65. The Latin tag is from Virgil, *Aeneid*, I, 460.

[38] The *CR* editor adds a note: 'Or, as in some pedigrees she is called, Catherine, who married Henry Wirriott, Esq. of Orielton, whose daughter and sole heiress married Sir Hugh Owen, of Bodowen, in Anglesea, the first of that family who settled in Pembrokeshire'. Pedigrees make Sir Huw Owen the grandson of Henry Wirriot and Margaret, daughter of Sir Rhys ap Thomas (Bartrum, *1400–1500*, X, 1754; Dwnn, I, 247; see above p.64.

[39] Horace, *Epistles*, I, 6.67–8.

Appendix I

(From NLW MS 9098D: a fragment of the Life in a seventeenth-century hand, bound into 'A brife abstract, exposicion and true demonstracion of all parts and thinges belonginge to a Ship and the practique of Navigation', by 'H.M.'. The fragment is a single leaf of different dimensions to the manuscript and the writing is in a different hand from that of the work on navigation. Cf. above p.264 for the version published in 1796. . . . indicates where the copyist was unable to decipher the manuscript from which he was copying.)

Fees, commo . . . molumens[1] thereunto belonging within a while after he gave both to Sir Rice and Sir Griffith (father and son)[2] . . . seneshalli, cancellarii . . . Maneriorum and dominiorum de Haverford-West and Rowse in the Marches aforesaid: so that now being possessed of all the[3] . . . offices in South Wales[4] besides we may truly affirm Sir Rice to be the greatest subject that ever was in those parts.

After this expedition I do not find that ever Sir Rice went abroad, wherein you may see he did not ab entr[5] . . . actu deficere (a misfortune that hath befaln the greatest commanders, that ever were) but plaid his last part most exactly for in this service you shall not read in all the English story, of any more spoken of, more employed nor more trusted[6] than he was and [word deleted] if you will give our Welsh Bards credit, he was san[7] . . . drew some envy upon him ever[8] . . . chiefest of the nobility of England made our Poet burse out and[9] . . .

[1] 'commo[dities e]molumens' in *CR*.
[2] [officia] in *CR*.
[3] [prime] in *CR*.
[4] 'and governour of all Wales' (*CR*) is omitted by this copyist.
[5] [*extremo*] is preferred in *CR* version.
[6] [honoured] is preferred in the *CR* version.
[7] [sans-pareille, which] in *CR*.
[8] [even from the] in *CR*.
[9] [say that he was] in *CR*.

Gwenwyn Lloegr gan ein llygrwyr
godi nos o'r gwnod yn wyr
   Tudur Aled ai cant.[10]

[It is the envy of England, together with our corrupters,
That any of our blood be raised aloft as heroes.]

The same poet in his Cwydd . . . to Sir Rice, wherein he is wholly[11] . . .
about this matter labours to[12] . . . ority of all others where singing of the
taking of the Town of Terwin[13] he saith

Bronn Terwyn Bran ai Torres
a'r gwayw onn praft ar gwynn pres.[14]

[It was the raven that routed the hillside of Thérouanne
With his sturdy spear and cannon]

[ ] beginning at . . .[15]

---

[10] These two lines and the attributed author are omitted from the *CR* version. For a more accurate text, see Jones, *Tudur Aled*, I, 71:

Gwenwyn Lloegr, gan yn llygrwyr,
Godi neb o'n gwaed yn wŷr.

[11] [emploied] in *CR*.

[12] [give him the superioritie] in *CR*.

[13] The *CR* version includes 'and Tourney'.

[14] A quite different verse is given in the *CR* version. For an accurate text here, see Jones, *Tudur Aled*, I, 70:

Bron terwyn, – brân a'i torres,
A'r gwayw onn praff, a'r gwn pres.

[15] Such a phrase is absent from the *CR* version.

Appendix II

(From R. Fenton, *A Historical Tour Through Pembrokeshire* (London, 1811), pp. 253–67)

Now for the manner and setting foorthe of his shewes, with other civil respectes of entertainment, it is thus traditionallie given out, which I pray be pleased to accept by peece meals, as I have gathered the same from several discourses, and thereupon make your judgment both of worke and greatness of this man.[1] Sir Rice being at his castle of Carewe, in Pembrokeshire, made publication of a solemn just and turnament, with other marshall exercises, he went to hold for the honour of St George, patrone of that noble order of the Garter. The fame hereof being blowne abroad, manie worthie and valerouse gentlemen of his blood, some to do him honour, others to make triall of theire abilities in feates of armes, came unto him from all partes of Wales. The first that presented his service was his owne son Sir Griffith Rice, one of the knights of the Bath to Prince Arthur; then came Sir Thomas Perrott and Sir John Wogan, men of eminente note and his neere neighboures; likewise Arnold Butler, Richard Griffith, and John Morgan, old beaten souldiers and very expert commanders; Griffith Dunn, a brave man at arms, and one of Diana's champions against the scholars of Pallas at the coronation

---

[1] Fenton prefaces this excerpt from the Life thus: 'For the length of the following extract I may perhaps have occasion to apologize to my readers; but as Carew derives so much consequence from the ceremony that forms the subject of it, and as I found it would be impossible to have given a perfect idea of the splendor of the entertainments it commemorates without detail, I thought it would be doing it injustice to attempt to abridge it, or affect to give it in other words than those of the original MS it was first communicated in, through that most appropriate vehicle for materials illustrative of Welsh history, The Cambrian Register, a work I am happy to have this public opportunity of referring to as a most valuable accession to the literature of Wales, with a sincere hope that the Editor's intention of bringing out the third volume, which we have been for some time led to expect, is only suspended and not abandoned.' The third volume of *The Cambrian Register* did not appear until 1818.

of Henry the Eighth.[2] From Brecknockshire there came Vaughan of Tretowre, a grandchild to Roger Vaughan the marshall, beheaded by Jasper Earl of Pembroke, at his castle of Chepstowe. From Glamorgan and Monmouthshire came Jenkin Mansell, surnamed the Valiant, the same who procured the repeale of his father Phillip's attainder, slaine in the quarrell betweene the houses of Yorke and Lancaster, and Sir William Herbert, sonn to that thrice noble warrior Sir Richard Herbert beheaded at Banburie: all these weare of South Wales. Out of North Wales there repaired thither young —— Griffith son to Sir John Griffith lord of Lansadwrn, and young Wynn of Gwydir his kinsman, two hopefull gentlemen of good towardlinesse, and with them the lustie Robert Salisburie, a man much noted for his greate strength of bodie, a fast friend and companion to Sir Rice in manie of his warlike adventures. (He was afterwards knighted by Charles Brandon Duke of Suffolk, in the cheefe church of Roy, for his prowess and loftie courage.)

These men of prime ranke weare all lodged within the castle. Besides these manie more, to the number of five or six hundred, weare assembled and drawne together at that meeting, most of them of goode ranke and qualitie, to be spectators of those rare solemnities never before knowne in those partes, nor for ought I remember practised by anie of the order in their private heretofore. For them tentes and pavillions were pitched in the parke neere to the castle, wheare they quartered all the time, everie man according to his qualities, the place being furnished aforehand with all sortes of provisions for that purpose. This festivall and time of jollitie continued the space of five dayes.

On St George's eve, which was the first daie of their meeting, Sir Rice tooke a view of all the companie, choosing out five hundred of the tallest and ablest among them; those he divided into five troopes, a hundred to each troope, over whom he appointed captaines David the younger[3] and John, two of his brothers, Arnold Butler, Richard Griffith, and John Morgan, all tried men and readie in their profession.

The next being the daie after the eve, these five captaines drewe foorth theire forces into the field, excercising them in all pointes as if they had beene suddenlie to goe on some notable peece of service, in whiche delightfull shewe that whole dayes allowance was spent with the full contentation of all those noble gentlemen there present.

---

[2] Fenton adds: 'He was afterwards knighted in Brittany by Sir Edward Howard for his good service against the French.' This presumably refers to the expedition to harry the coast of Brittany which Howard, as lord admiral, commanded in 1513 and during which, towards the end of April, he was killed (Scarisbrick, *Henry VIII*, p.34). For Gruffydd Dwnn (*c*.1487–1543), see McFarlane, *Memling*, pp.54–5.

[3] Fenton adds: 'All our Welsh pedigrees prove this to be a common custom to give the same christian name to two sons, with the sole distinction of elder and younger. This David was called David Ceffil Cwtta, from a nag-tailed horse he rode, with which he performed wonderful exploits.' See above p.180, for Fenton's confusion with the elder Dafydd.

The third daie, St George's daie, the drummers beat upp, and trumpetes sounded, everie man with the summones betaking him to his charge: first the captaines ledd forthe theire companies in a militarie array, well armed at all pointes. Then followed Sir Rice on a goodlie courser, having two pages and a herauld on horseback before him richlie cladd, after whom the rest of the gentlemen followed, being all bravelie mounted in a most decent and seemlie manner. They passed on to the bishop's pallace at Lamphey, a mile or thereabouts distant from Carewe Castle. At theire comming thither they bidd goode morrowe to the bishoppe in the language of souldiers with arquebusses, musketts and callivers, and then dividing themselves they made a lane for Sir Rice to passe onward to the gates, which (as yett) weare not suffered to be opened. Upon his approache the bishoppe's subsidiaries (the businesse being so ordered among them aforehand) came out of the wickett, demanding what he was, why in armes, and the cause of his coming thither? To which Sir Rice made answeare, that he was one of St George's knightes, who ever shewed himself a trustie patrone and protector of martalistes, and therefore he held it most suitable to his profession, especiallie on the verie day (as that was) dedicated to the honour of that renowned Saint to appeare in harnesse and militarie equipage. Notwithstanding he willed the messenger to assure the bishopp that, as then, he was a man of peace, for he came thither to praie for the peace and rest of St George's soul, and for the welfare and prosperitie of his graciouse master, sole soveraine of that honourable order whereof himself was an unworthie companion; in which hartie and devoted excercise he earnestlie desired the bishopp would be pleased to come with him. 'Noe doubt', replied the messenger, 'but my lord besides the dutie of his calling will easilie assent to such piouse and religiouse notions, yet ere I give you admittance', said he, 'it is necessarie you change your habit, it being a thing ill becoming our scholasticall unmilitarie course of life, and the sanctimonie of this place, to conserte and join in devotion with the rough and all disturbing disciples of Mars. In the mean while I shall reporte unto my lord the summe of your desires.' Sir Rice hereupon passed by and rid up into the bishoppe's park, where he had a faire tent of purpose provided for him, over which was written – '*cedant arma togæ*'. There he alighted, and forthwith enrobed himself in St George's livery. After some small repose he walked on foote downe to the pallace, having a trumpetter before him and a herauld of armes, two pages carrying his traine, and the choicest of the gentlemen to be his associates, the rest during the time of the ceremonie he left behind him to cheere up and make merrie, for there was foisons and plentie both of wine and all other necessarie provision laid out in a readinesse for their solace and refreshment at the bishop's charge. Sir Rice drawing neare to the pallace, he caused the trumpet to sound the relay, to give notice of his approche, and then the gates were opened. The bishopp having with him the Abbott of Talley and the Prior of Carmarthen, all with rich capes, stood there to give him entrance. And soe some few compliments first passing between them, they walked forward in a solemn procession, *'canentes et supplicantes'*, twice or thrice round the court, and then to the chapel. There Sir Rice was desired to stay for awhile at the door till first the quire was placed and the bishopp had taken his seate. Within a while the herauld comes unto him and ushers him in; when they weare allmost in the middle of the chappel, they turned about, and made each of them two humble congés to the kinge's seate, and soe in like manner againe when Sir Rice went into his stall. Presentlie upon, the bishopp ascends to the high altar and reades divine service; after which much good musicke followed, manie new hymnes and anthemes they had made of purpose for that solemnitie, and there sange some for the long life, peace, and prosperitie of the kinge, others for the rest of St George's soule and his safe deliveraunce out of purgatorie. To be shorte, Sir Rice having done his offeringe, and all religiouse formes observed and ended, he took the bishopp, abbott, and prior along with him to dinner, and soe back againe he goes to Carewe in the same decent and comelie march that he sett forth. Drawing neare, the captaines saluted the castle with a brave volley of shott, and the like was returned them againe from the walles. That donn, they and their troopes passed into the parke, wheare each had his particular tente to entertaine his souldiers and friendes, a thing Sir Rice had a principall care of from the beginning.

When these weare gone and provided for, Sir Rice having reserved a greate companie of the better sorte for his guestes, he leads them to the castle with drummes, trumpetes, and other warlike musicke. Over the gate at the entrance was hung up a goodlie faire table, wherein was represented the species and pourtraiture of St George and St David embracing one another, with this mottoe –

NODO PLUS QUAM GORDIANO

In the front court which was the platea or common place wherein people did use to walke, two hundred tall men were arranged all in blewe coates, who made them a lane into another lesser courte, called *Pinacotheca*, in which the images, 'scutcheons, and coat armours of certaine of Sir Rice's ancestors stood and weare displayed, and soe they passed into the greate hall, which was a goodlie spaciouse roome richelie hanged with clothe of arras and tapestrie. At the upper end and under a plaine clothe of state of crimson velvet, was provided a cross-table for the king. On eache side downe the length of the halle, two other tables, the one for Sir Rice alone, the other for the rest of the gentlemen. Here everie man stood bare as in the kinge's presence; within a while after the trumpets sounded, and the herauld called for the kinge's service, whereupon all the gentlemen went presentlie downe to waite upon the sewer. The sewer for the time Sir Rice appointed his sonn Sir Griffith Rice, who had binn bredd up at coorte, and therefore had some advantage of the rest in point of curialitie and courtlinesse. Sir William Herberte, of Colebrooke, the carver, and young Griffith, of Penrhyn, the pocillator or cupbearer. When the kinge's meate was brought to the table, the bishop stood on the right side of the chaire, and Sir Rice on the left, and all the while the meate was a laying downe, the cornettes, hautboies, and other wind instrumentes weare not silent. After the table was served and all sett, the bishopp made his humble obejsance to the kinge's chaire, and then descended to saie grace, which donn, he returned againe to his former station. Muche pleasaunt discoorse passed betweene them for a time, which, ever and anon, was seasoned with a diversitie of musicke. When they saw theire tyme the table was voyded, and the meate removed to the sideboarde for the wayters. Then the kinge's chaire was turned, and soe everie man at libertie to putt on his hatt. The kinge's service being finished, Sir Rice went to his owne table, taking non else than the bishop along with him, whom he placed at the upper ende at a messe all alone, and himself at some distance sate him downe at another. All the gentlemen there present, for Sir Rice's more honour, were pleased to stand by and give him the looking on untill his first coorse was served; then Sir Griffith Rice, the king's sewer, his two fellow officers, and the rest of the gentlemen by the name of wayters, went to the kinge's reversion. The fare they had you will easilie believe was goode, being provided as for the king. Such cheere as they had was attended with much pleasaunt discourse, divers passages of mirth free of all offence, passed from one to the other. The kinge, queene, and prince's healthes were often drank among them, and the Bards and Prydidds, accompanied by the harp, sung manie a song in commemoration of the vertues and famouse atcheevements of those gentlemen's ancestors there present, a custom used long before by Achilles, '*qui in conviviis ingentium virorum facta canebat ad citharam*'.

By that time these conviviall merrimentes weare ended, the daie was well nigh spent, soe that they would fall to noe disportes for the rest of the afternoone, but onelie walke abroad and take the fresh aire of the parke; Sir Rice in the meane while betakes him to his privacie; but soon after he comes into the field, where he entertayned the gentlemen with some polemicall discourse, which was his proper element, most delectable to the hearers, who weare all of them professors of armes.

Hereupon having a fit opportunitie, Sir William Herbert steps forthe and makes challenge to all comers foure to foure at justs and turnamentes the next morning for the honoure of ladies. This challenge was presentlie accepted by Sir Griffith Rice. The appellant names for his assistantes Robert Salisburie,[4] Jenkin Mansell, and Vaughan of Tretown. The defendant, Sir Thomas Perrott, Sir William Wogan, and Sir Griffith Dwnn. The ordering of the whole businesse was referred to Sir Rice himselfe, whom they all jointlie desired to sit as judge. Sir Rice gave waie to the motion, and provided for them accordinglie. All parties agreed, and growing late besides, Sir Rice sawe it high tyme to go home, soe in they went, first to the chapel where they heard solemne service; then to supper, observing the same decorum and order at night that they had donn at dinner, for the kinge's table in all points, as likewise for the observation of those his civill lawes and complimentall shewes of hospitalitie.

Thus this daies pleasing labour or laboursome pleasure was ended. The first daie of this pompe and ceremonie and the third of theire meeting.

The next morning by sound of trumpette Sir Rice was summoned to play the judge's parte, which accordinglie he did. He had on that daie a fine gilt armour, two pages well provided on horseback before him, with a herauld and two trumpetters, himself mounted on a goodlie steede richlie barbed and trapped with four footmen, two on each side attending him. Two hundred tall men in blew coates, some before and some behinde him. In this manner he went into the parke where a tilt was made readie for the purpose, riding aboute the same twice or thrice for the well accommodating the enterprise then in hand. At one end of the tilt there was a tent for the appellants to rest them, at the other for the defendants. Sir Rice perceiving all thinges well ordered, he presentlie took him to the judgement seate. About the middle of the tilt over against the breaking place, his servaunts standing round about him, everie one having a halbert in his hand, and a good basket-hilt swoord at his side. When tyme served the trumpettes sounded, and then the appellants came in sight. The first that appeared was Sir William Herbert the challenger, having a trumpetter before him, and a page carrying his shield, without anie device, the mottoe, '*Et quæ non fecimus ipsi*'. The next was Robert Salisburie, who had for an impresse, a gyant running at a pygmie, with this mottoe, '*Pudet congredi cum homine vinci parato*'. Then came Jenkin Mansell the valiant, whose sentence was '*Perit sine adversario virtus*'. After followed Vaughan of Tretowne, who took this for his diction, '*Ingens gloria calcar habet*'. After these inceptors, or enterprisers, followed the noe lesse brave defendants, or propugnators.

---

[4] Fenton adds: 'Jenkin Mansell was son of Phillip Mansell, slain in the wars between the houses of York and Lancaster, and was attainted. He was married to Mary, daughter of Griffith ap Nicholas, of Newton (now Dynevaur) in the county of Carmarthen. This Jenkin procured a repeal of his father's attainder, and a restoration in blood and estate. Collins's Baronetage, vol. i. p.487.' See Arthur Collins, *Proceedings, Precedents and Arguments on Claims Concerning Baronies by writ and other Honours* (London, 1734). For Jenkin 'the Valiant', who secured the reversal in 1486, see *DWB*, p.611; see above p.62.

Theire manner was the same: Sir Griffith Rice had written on his 'scutcheon, '*Et vincere pulchrum*'. Sir Thomas Perrott in a more loftie language, made choice of this for his mottoe, '*Si non invenio singulos pares, pluribus simul objicior*'. Sir William Wogan meaning to do honour to his noble adversarie, took yet a more humble mottoe, which was this, '*Profuit hoc vincente capi*'. And Sir Griffith Dwnn, a man of an active spirit, used these wordes to expresse his inclination, '*Industrioso otium pæna*'. These gallant gentlemen in good order ridd twice or thrice about the tilt, and as they passed along, they, by theire pages, presented theire shieldes to the judge, which donn, both parties severed and tooke theire stand, the one at one end, the other at the other end of the tilt. Then the trumpettes sounded, whereupon the two first combattants putt theire launces into theire restes, and soe ranne each theire six coorses. In like sorte followed the reste, who charged the one the other with equall ardour ever and anon, deviding manie a shrewde counter buffe among them, and performing their devoirs with muche judgment and agilitie. Noe sooner had they made an ende with theire speares, but they fall to turney with theire swoordes all at once, which was a most delightfull spectacle to the standers by. This exercise was performed by them in the plaine fielde, and sound knockes you may be sure weare receaved and returned on both sides, butt noe harme at all done, for Sir Rice had taken order with the stickes to parte them, and prevent all cause of jarr, if anie the least occasion of it in that kind were offered. All which needed not more than to shewe Sir Rice's care for the preservation of love and amitie between those soe neere kin in blood, and who weare mett at that tyme for noe other end but to doe him honour, that care being taken aforehand among themselves not to esteeme of knockes valerouslie received and manfullie bestowed in the number of injuries, '*sed quicquid accideret, boni consulere*'.

Having performed theire devoirs both with sworde and speare, they mutuallie embraced eache other, and soe hand in hand they went to the judge to receave a definitive sentence of their activities. Sir Rice, whose office was to arbitrate the cause, after long deliberation with himself, grewe doubtfull in opinion, for some of them weare excellent at the speare, and some at the sworde; some who weare well with the speare, fell short with the sworde. This bredd much difficultie in the judgment, soe that Sir Rice, to drawe the thredd even when first he had commended them for theire heroicall deedes, and given a large testimonie of theire skill and valoure in the performaunce of them, concluded in the language of Virgil's Shepherd,

> Non nostrum inter vos tantas componere lites,
> Et vitulâ tu dignus, et hic, et quisquis amores,
> Aut metuet dulces, aut experietur amaros.

Willing them merrilie, as you may see by waie of caution, warilie to take heede of those saide dames whose honour that daye they had so faithfullie mayntayned.

Thus the emploiments and excercises of the morning ended, and soe in they went, first to hear divine service as they weare wont to doe, and then to dinner, where they wanted for nothing that mought give them all assurance of hartie wellcome. Robert Salisbury, Jenkin Mansell, and Vaughan of Tretowne, were appointed for this daye the honorarie officers of cupbearer, carver, and sewer, Sir Rice having a care in the matter of forme to grace them all equallie, and soe to stave off all cause of envie and other sinister interpretation. When they had dined they went to visit eache captaine in his quarter, wheare they found everie man in action, some wrestling, some hurling of the barr, some taking of the pike, some running at the quinteine,[5] everie man striving in a friendlie emulation to performe some act or other, worthie the name of souldier. With these and the like delightes the evening vanished.

At supper Sir Griffith Rice, in the presence of his father, made challenge to Sir William Herbert four to four at the ring next morning for a supper, which the loosers should pay at Carmarthen for theyre farewell at parting. Sir William forthwithe undertooke him, onelie wishing the young heirs of Penrhyn and Gwydyr mought be added to

---

[5] Fenton adds: 'A ludicrous and sportive way of tilting or running on horseback at some mark hung on high, moveable, and turning round, which, while the riders strike at with lances, unless they ride quickly off the versatile beam strikes upon their shoulders. Dr Watts in verbo quintena.

Sir H. Spelman, from being a spectator of it says, It is a piece of board fixed at one end of a turning beam, and a bag of sand at the other, by which means, striking at the board whirls round the bag and endangers the striker.

Minshew says, it was a sport used every fifth year among the Olympic games, or it was the last of the πενταθλοι used on the fifth or last day of the Olympics. It is supposed to be a Roman game, and left in this island ever since their time.

Dr Kennet in his Parochial Antiquities from Dr Plot, says, that at the village of Blackthorn, through which the Roman road lay, they use it at their weddings to this day on the common green with much solemnity and mirth. Mathew Paris mentioning this exercise thus expresses himself, "Eo tempore juvenes Londinenses, statuto pavone pro bravio, ad stadium quod quintena dicitur vires proprias, et equorum cursus sunt experti." M. Paris, sub initio, 1253 [translation below].

Strype in his History of London, vol.i. 1st part, p.249, delineates its figure thus: [followed by a line drawing].'

'Dr Watts' probably refers to Isaac Watts, the hymnologist, who also wrote *The Art of Reading and Writing in English* (London, 1721), and *Watt's Compleat Spelling-Book* (Dublin, 1737). For Sir Henry Spelman (c.1564–1641), author of a glossary of Latin and English terms, see *D.N.B.*, s.n. John Minsheu, a noted lexicographer (ibid., s.n.), offered his definition in *Ductor in Linguas* (London, 1617). The comment by Robert Plot, *The Natural History of Oxfordshire* (London, 1677), p.200, was adopted by White Kennett, *Parochial Antiquities* (London, 1695).

The quotation from Matthew Paris, *Chronica Majora*, ed. H. R. Luard (7 vols., Rolls Series, 1872–83), V, 367, is more accurately: 'Et eodem tempore [s.a. 1253], juvenes Londinenses, statuto pavone pro bravio, ad stadium quod quintena vulgariter dicitur, vires proprias et equorum cursus sunt experti' [At this time (1253) the youth of London, standing defiantly like a peacock, at the game commonly called quintena, put to the test their strength and the running of the horses.]; cf. Matthew Paris, *Historia Anglorum*, ed. F. Madden (3 vols., Rolls Series, 1866–9), III, 325, in almost identical words. The reference to a 'History of London' by John Strype (1643–1737) may well be to his edition of Stow's *Survey of London*, first published in 1720 in two volumes.

theire number, whom he sawe to be gentlemen of a faire expectation and clearlie spirited, and who had bore noe parte in all those activities, whiche indeede was not theyre faulte, for willinglie they would have bothe given some demonstration of theire youthfulle courage at the justs and turnaments, had nott Sir Rice in respect of theire greennesse (the eldest being not above sixteen yeares of age) persuaded the contrarie. The motion nowe being reasonable, and those two galliard younge spirrits besides forward of themselves, Sir Rice easilie gave his assent, the rather because on that excercise they weare not soe much to employe theire strength, as to shewe they weare gentlemen att armes, gracefull in behaviour, dexterouse and skillfull in running, and taking of the ring.

The next morning Sir Rice having taken his seat, the trumpettes weare commanded to sound, to which these rivall knightes obeyed, running eache of them theire six coorses withe such indifference, soe as to perplex the nicest judgment; but in the ende Sir Rice gave sentence against his sonn, a thinge agreed upon beforehand betweene him and his father; however the cause went, that soe he mought shewe his friendes the towne of Carmarthen before they went away, and what entertainment that place was able to afford, which at that tyme was thought to be verie good. Sir Griffith said noe more, but tould his father the decree should be obeyed, and soe to dinner they goe, observing the same order they had donn before, save onelie the changing of sewer, cupbearer, and carver, which offices that daie Sir Thomas Perrott, Sir William Wogan, and Sir Griffith Dwnn, did execute.

After dinner Sir Rice leades his noble guestes into the parke a hunting, where they killed divers buckes, all which he bestowed among them towards the furnishing out of theire festivall meeting at Carmarthen. To supper then they come, after which they had a comedie acted by some of Sir Rice his owne servauntes, with which these majesticall sightes and triumphes weare concluded. This meeting was for some yeares after called by the name of St George his Pilgrimage to St David's, wheare one thing is note worthie, that for the space of five dayes among a thousand people (for soe manie at the least weare thought to be assembled together at that tyme) there was not one quarrell, crosse worde, or unkind looke that happened betweene them, such care Sir Rice had taken for the well ordering of what he intended in commemoration of the famouse patrone and gloriouse soveraine of the Garter, whereof himselfe was an unworthie companion.

Earlie in the morning before they parted, the bishopp bestowed a sermon upon them, tending all to loyall admonitions, obedience to superiors, love and charitie one towards another. His text was out of Ecclesiastes, cap.x. verse 20, 'Curse not the king, no, not in thy thoughte, and curse not the rich in thy beddchamber, for a bird of the aire shall carry the voice, and that which hath winges will tell the matter.' After

the sermon was ended, and when the gentlemen came to take leave, Sir
Rice bestowed uppon divers of the choicest of them a ribband of true
blewe colour, which he desired them to weare for theire more honour. At
eache ribband there was a medaile, the impresse of which was that true
symbol of faith – 'Dextræ manus mutuo implicatæ', with this mottoe –
'Nec poterat ferrum'; which they kindlie accepted, and for manie yeares
wore for his sake, and soe giving them his thankes, he recommended
them to his sonn Sir Griffith Rice, who was ingaged to be their
symposiastes the night following.

Appendix III

(From *CR*, II (1797), 270–7. This text has been collated with that in CCL 4.30 (formerly Phillips MS 14416), a volume of *c*.1726 which belonged to Richard Fenton, who used it as the basis of the *CR* version. The text has also been compared with four copies in NLW, Dynevor A 94b–f, which are couched in virtually identical terms, though with some rearrangement of paragraphs.)

OBJECTIONS against RICE GRIFFITH in his Indictment, with the ANSWERS thereunto.

1st. That Rice Griffith lying at Islington,[1] in the countie of Middlesex, did there plott and conspire with Edward Floyd, and William Hughes, two of his servants, for the deposing of Henry the 8th. and putting his crowne upon the head of James the 5th. king of Scotland.

2d . . . That there was att that tyme in Wales, a prophecie which gave encouragement to this their practice, (vizt.) *James of Scotland with the red hand, and the raven,* (being Rice his creast)[2] should conquer England.

3rd . . . That Rice Griffith did divers tymes imploy Edward Floyd, his clerk, to one James ap Griffith, prisoner at the Tower. There persuading him to come into this conspiracie, and that he would receive the sacrament of the eucharist in token of a secure[3] and faithfull covenant between them for the performance of the premises.

---

[1] CCL 4.30, marginal note: 'In a copy of the Attainder *Penes me* it is called *Iseldon* F'. This manuscript belonged to Richard Fenton, who in 1797 evidently possessed a copy of the parliamentary act of attainder against Rhys ap Gruffydd.

[2] The phrase is omitted from CCL 4.30 and was probably inserted in the course of preparing the manuscript for publication.

[3] 'future' in CCL 4.30.

4th . . . That the said Rice to convey himself secretlie into Scotland, did mortgage his lordships of Carewe and Narberth, to one Robert White, citizen and clothier of London, for two thousand pounds.

5th . . . That the said Rice tooke upon him a new name, (vizt.) Rice ap Griffith Fitzurian, to the intent that under this faire pretence, and title, he might more worthily obteyne the principallitie of Wales, which was the marke he assigned at after the conquest.

The Answeare to the First [4]

Rice Griffith stood charged with these objections in the year 1531, being about the 19th of James the 5th. and the 23d. of Henry the 8th. at which tyme (and so for the space of 5 or 6 years before) there was a most firme league of amity and friendshippe betwixt these two kings. Insomuch that Henry the 8th. to regaine his nephew's good opinion, and to remove all former unkindnesses chieflie occasioned by the Duke of Albanie in the time of his government, did then absolutelie refuse to breake the peace with Scotland in favor of the Earl of Angus, though the same Earl earnestlie laboured for that purpose. This James the 5th. took so well at Henry the 8th. his handes, that presently after he sent his ambassadours into England to treate for the contynuance of a peace betweene them, during their naturall lives, which in the yeare following was concluded to the great contentment of both nations. So that theise kings standing uppon such faire terms the one with the other, Rice Griffith had no ground in that kinde to build a conspiracie upon, and so consequentlie must needes be innocent of theise accusations laid to his charge, for James the 5th. was known to have a heart so full of honor, that he would scorn to enterteyne such a motion, as might tend [to][5] the destruction of his uncle, under the colour of friendship.

Iff James the 5th, who was for his years a most valiant [and][5] wise prince, had aym'd at a business of that high nature, as the conquest of this kingdom, without question hee would have been well advised in his undertakinges: First, by examining his own strength at home, and making preparations thereafter; secondlie, by labouring a partie in

[4] The copy of the Objections in CCL 4.30 is immediately followed by this comment: 'This Sir R. ap Ths. at Blackheath did take prisoner the Lord Audley, general of the Cornish Rebells; afterward in H.8 tyme before Terwin and Tornay at the Battle of Spurres he took the Duke Longuevill prisoner.' Cf. NLW, Dynevor A 94c, where a marginal note in identical terms is added to another copy. In NLW, Dynevor A 94d, the Answer to the first Objection begins: 'There were three Pregnant wittnesses, when Rice Griffith was questioned uppon theise heades (Common Report, Probable Circumstances, and undoubted truth); who, though they could not preserve him in his life and fortunes, yett they held him upright in the worldes opinion, by recommending his Innocencie to future tymes after this manner.'
[5] Inserted in CCL 4.30.

England, and trying the affections there, of men more eminent and powerfull then Rice Griffith was (but at that time having newlie taken the government of his kingdome upon himselfe) he found his strength so devided, and his power so weakened with civil broils, happening amongst his peeres, during his minoritie, that he was wholie taken upp in quietting and appeazing those[6] home-bred discontents, having no leasure to looke abroad for the enlarging of his dominions. Besides there was noe Englishman of note knowne or suspected at that time to[7] favor the Scottish cause, or likelie to have sided with them in such an attempt. It could never be prooved that Rice Griffith did ever speake, send, or write unto James the 5th. to offer him his service and assistance, for the deposing of Henry the 8th. or that James the fifth did employ any minister of his to corrupt and withdraw Rice Griffith from his allegiance.

As for Rice Griffith himself he was verie young, being not above three and twentie yeares of age when he lost his head, and therefore not likelie to apprehend so great an enterprize.

He was wholie given to his booke, and retired in the course of his life, neither ambitious of honor, nor hunting after wordlie preferment. Hee lived in a plentiefull fortune, and in grace and favor with the king, so that he had no reason to bee either discontented or disloyal.

Sir Rice ap Thomas (this Rice his grandfather) received [inn][5] Henry the 7th. at Milford Haven, and attended him with four thousand men, never leaving him till Richard the third was slaine in the fielde, for which service he had the spoile of king Richard's tent. Hee was made chiefe governor of all Wales,[8] afterwards advanced to the order of the garter, and lastlie, for the good service be [*sic*] did against those of the Cornish Rebellion, he was made knight banneret att Blackheath. His son, Sir Griffith Rice, (this Rice's father) received likewise a marke of this king's favor, for he was made knight of the Bath to Prince Arthure; and this Rice himself was offered the earldome of Essex by Henry the 8th.[9] but he houlding himselfe unworthie of

---

[6] 'those' omitted from CCL 4.30.

[7] 'to' omitted from CCL 4.30. In NLW, Dynevor A 94d, this paragraph runs as follows: 'All histories, both English and Scottish make honourable mention of James the 5th as of a most valiant and wise Prince; and therefore it is not probable he would ayme at a busines of that high nature, as the conquest of this kingdome, but uppon sound advice and most mature deliberation: First, by making preparations of his owne; Secondly by labouring a partie in England and trying the affections there of men more eminent and powerfull then Rice Griffith was: but att that tyme there was no forces raised in Scotland for such a designe; neither was there any Englishman of note knowne or suspected to have any correspondencie with that King, or likelie to have sided with him in such an attempt.'

[8] 'high chamberlaine of all Wales' in NLW, Dynevor A 94b.

[9] The remainder of this sentence is replaced in NLW, Dynevor A 94b as follows: 'But all the perswasions of the Earles of Oxford, Darby and Sussex his halfe brothers could not make him accept of it, the refusall whereof (humillitie and lack of ambition being, as it seemes, a fault in him) turned afterwardes to his ruyn;...' Edward Stanley (1509–72), earl of Derby from 1521, John de

so high a title, humblie refused the same. Theise graces and favours
summ'd upp together, sure it cannot be that Rice Griffith should be so
degenerate or unthankfull, as to entertayn any ignoble or disloyal
thought against that lyne; which alwaies looked upon him, and his, with
the eye of favour.[10]

As concerning Rice Griffith's lying at Islington (making that place as
his adversaries would inforce, the sceane of his disloyaltie) it was well
known he had neither been there, nor about London, at that time, but
upon command: for the king had then sent for him to make answer
touching certain affraies between the Lord Ferrars, and the Lady
Katherine Howard, the said Rice his wife, wherein (Rice being absent)
there were slain 5 or 6 of the Lord Ferrars his servants and three or four
of the said Rice his servants.

There are named in this objection to be of conspiracie with Rice
Griffith, but two of his servants, a poor council, God wot, and a weak
strength to undergoe so great a designe; whereof the one falslie
answering[11] him, was (as I shall hereafter prove) both pardoned and
rewarded: the other acquitting him was condemned and executed. So
that here appears (and we have just cause to believe it) a treason rather
purposed and intended by a servant against his master, than by a subject
towards his sovereign.

The Answer to the second

There was no such prophecye knowne in Wales, untill about the time
Rice was questioned, and therefore 'tis likelye his adversaries did then
invent it, to give a better colour to their mischievous designs.[12]

I cannot finde in anie Scottish historye, nor learne from any of that
nation, that James the 5th had any such eminent marke about him, as
that one of his hands upp to the wrist should be as redd, as iff it had been
dip'd in blood: but admitt we itt were so – Sure I am we have no warrant
to repose any confidence in such predictions, the most of them ever vain
and failing, and therefore not to be regarded.

Vere (1499–1526), earl of Oxford from 1513, and Henry Radcliffe (c.1507–57), earl of Sussex from
1542, were each married to a sister of Catherine Howard, daughters of Thomas Howard, second
duke of Norfolk, and were therefore Rhys ap Gruffydd's brothers-in-law by marriage. Oxford
married Anne Howard in 1512, Radcliffe married Elizabeth Howard before 21 May 1524, and
Derby married Dorothy Howard before 21 February 1530. *CP*, IV, 209–11; X, 244–5; XII, part 1,
520–2. For this intriguing possibility, see above p.246.

[10] The following sentence is added to this paragraph in NLW, Dynevor A 94b: 'The truth is, hee
never gave any occation of offence at all to the King; but he had a verie great estate, hee was
powerfull in freindes, rich in possessions, and with envy could not looke uppon and endure.'

[11] 'accusing' in CCL 4.30.

[12] 'devises' in CCL 4.30.

It was a common thing (it seems)[13] in Henrie the 8th his tyme, to make prophecies upon the bodyes and cognizances of noblemen and others, and to divine the good or ill that should befall them, by the letters of their names, to the utter ruyne and destruction of many noble houses and worthie families in this kingdome. To prevent which inconveniencies in future tymes, the high court of parliament, held in the 33rd of the said king's reigne, made it felony for any man to print, write, speak, sing, or declare any such prophecie: so that if Rice Griffith had lived to have been tryed in that sessions, (having no greater matter laid to his charge then a bare prophecy, as more he had not; his adversaries making that the very basis, and foundation of their practice) no question he had been quitted, by act of parliament.

When Rice Griffith had declined the Earldom of Essex (though it were with an humble acknowledgment of his owne unworthiness) yet his adversaries made other construction thereof to the king, by possessing him with an opinion that Rice his high aspiring thoughts could not be [so][5] satisfy'd, there being at that tyme in Wales[14] a prophecie, which gave his hopes far fairer promises; hereupon certaine sparcles of jelousie were kindled in the king's heart, which not long after (and that upon a mere trifle) burst out into a flame. The king one daie at Wandsworth hawking at the brooke, his faulcon being seized of a fowle, there came by accident a raven, that put his faulcon from the quarrey, whereat the king chafed exceedinglie. One standing by (as malice is ever watchful to do mischief) stepps to the king, and whispered[15] him in the eare, saying, Sir, you see how preremptorie this raven is growne, and therefore it is high tyme to pull him down, thereby to secure your majestie, and to[16] prevent his insolencies. These words (the king's heart alreadie full of suspition) amazed him straight as a presage of his own fortune: so that from that time forward he was never att peace [with himself][5], till he had removed (as he thought) the disturber of his peace: and this is a storie of the Earl of Nottinghame's, the only man of note now living[17], who came nearest those times; which may serve to shewe how maliciouslie Rice Griffith[18] was prosecuted by his adversaries to his undeserved destruction.

---

[13] This paragraph is preceded by the following in NLW, Dynevor A 94b: 'If a Prophecie may make a man a Traitor, twere an easie matter for one malitiouslie minded to coyne such a one, as would quicklie fetch off any mans heade, and father itt upon Merlin or some such like. Divinity affordes us no warrant that wee should Beleeve in such propheties.'

[14] 'in Wales' omitted from CCL 4.30.
[15] 'whispers' in CCL 4.30.
[16] 'to' omitted from CCL 4.30.
[17] 'living' omitted from CCL 4.30.
[18] 'Griffith' omitted from CCL 4.30.

The Answer to the third

Of this Edward Floyd[19], the Ladie Katherine Howard did take much pains to be trulie informed; who, knowing in her own heart her husband's innocencie, and fearing the ruyne of herself and children, left no stone unmoved whereby this practice might be discovered. Att [at][5] length (by the help of her friends, and God's direction) shee found out, that this man was corrupted with a reward of ffive hundred[20] marks, to betraye his maister, and this also was prooved by divers others: soe that I hope no credit shall be given to him in this case.[21]

James ap Griffith[22] (to whom this Floyd did often of himself repaire, not sent by Rice, as is suggested) was apprehended by the said Rice, for counterfeating the great seal, and by him sent up to the lords of the councell, and so committed to the Tower; so that it had been meere madnes in Rice to put his life into that man's hands, whose life at that time by his means was questioned.

James ap Griffith, and Edward Floyd, (the one's heart full of revenge, the other[23] of corruption and treachery) did oftentymes meet and consult by what means they might lay matter of treason to Rice his charge, and (as fitting for their purpose at that time) they called to mind an unfortunate blank of Rice's, which had long layne in the hands of James ap Griffith, and was gotten upon this occasion. James ap Griffith, a man of mean estate, having his chiefest stay of living from the said Rice, and being on a tyme verie famillier together, desired the said Rice his letter to a gentleman in North Wales, for a farm, which was then to be lett, which the said Rice granted him; but never a clerk being present to write the letter, the said James persuaded Rice to subscribe to a blanck, and that Edward Floyd, his clerk, should indite[24] the letter according to his meaning. In this blanck by them was set downe matter enough for the indictment, and they two onlie gave in evidence against Rice, being both of them condemned with him, but afterwards pardoned, and hee

---

[19] CCL 4.30, marginal note: 'Edward Floyd being ashamed of his villanie fled his Countrey and was never heard of afterwards.' Cf. NLW, Dynevor A 94c: 'Edward Floyd, being ashamed of his villaine, fled his Country, and was never hard off after-wardes.'

[20] '500' in CCL 4.30.

[21] 'also' in place of 'case' in CCL 4.30.

[22] CCL 4.30, marginal note: 'James ap Griffith (a man banished for divers treasons and excepted in all pardons) did confess beyond Seas to divers of his acquaintance this damnable practise of his against Rice and being sore troubled in conscience he returned home with intent to acknowledge his offence and to submitt himself to my grandfather. But he (my grandfather not enduring to heare of him) retirid himself into Cardiganshire where he died most miserably. There are some yet alive will affirm this from my grandfather's mouth.' The writer was evidently Henry Rice, and his grandfather Gruffydd Rice; James ap Gruffydd ap Hywel may have returned from exile after the accession of Mary I (1553): Williams, *Y Cymmrodor*, XVI(1902), 93. Cf. NLW, Dynevor A 94c, in identical terms.

[23] 'others' in CCL 4.30.

[24] 'write' in place of 'indite' in CCL 4.30.

with Wm. Hughes, one of his chamber, executed; who took it upon their deathes they were both innocent of the treasons laid to their charge, which no doubt deserveth due consideration.

The Answer to the fourth

Rice Griffith had so great an estate att that tyme, that he might have commaunded greater sums of money uppon his credit, without mortgaging of lands: for the inventory of his goods, jewels, and plate, upon his attainer, amounted to thirtie thousand pounds[25], besides an estate of a thousand pound[26] land a yeare old rent of assize.

If Rice Griffith would have gone for Scotland, it is likelie he would have made better preparations for his journey, then is sett down in this objection: for he might well assure himself, that whatsoever he left behind him (upon notice given to the state of his flight) would have been seized uppon for the king.

If James the 5th had intended to invade this kingdom, Rice Griffith could have done him better service in his own countrie of Wales, where he had both a great fortune, and many powerful friends to assist him, than by going over into Scotland, to offer his particular service, where he could be of no use, more than a private soldier, bringing with him neither men, money, nor munition, and so no way capable of that great rewards,[27] which his adversaries would persuade the world he looked after.

The Answer to the fift

It can be no new name that is of a thousand years standing, and so long this name hath continued in Rice his house, if wee may believe either heraldrie, tradition, or those who are well read in antiquities: so that his adversaries were driven to a very narrow straight, to find matter of treason against him, when to owne his owne name, was laid to his charge as a treason.

Vrian[28] Rheged, whose posteritie was called by the name of Fitzvrian[29], and from whome Rice Griffith lyneallie descended, lived about eleaven hundred[30] years ago, in Kinge Arthure's tyme, and was

---

[25] '£30,000' in CCL 4.30.
[26] 'pounds' in CCL 4.30.
[27] 'reward' in CCL 4.30.
[28] 'Urian' in CCL 4.30.
[29] 'Fitzurian' in CCL 4.30.
[30] '1100' in CCL 4.30.

married to his half-sister, Margaret le Fay, daughter and heire to Gorolus[31], Duke of Cornwall: this Vrian[28] was, as some say, King of Scotland; others will have him to bee but a prince of a place, called Rheged, in Scotland; and some do affirme he was a great lord in Wales, and a knight of King Arthure's table. Thus our writers do varie; but bee hee what hee will (for of times so far distant, we have little truth or certaintie) sure I am, that this[32] Rice Griffith could not be so blind in his understanding, as to think he could thence derive to himselfe any manner of clayme to the principalitie of Wales; so that I am persuaded, no answere is so poore, but will easilie[33] satisfie this, and the rest of theise objections.[34]

Queene Elizabeth, whom it most concerned (for if any such treason had been intended against her father, her expectation of a crown had been frustrated) was with theise reasons so well satisfied[35] of the extreame and hard measure[36] offered to Rice Griffith, that she never looked upon any of his children, but as upon spectacles of infinite sufferance: insomuch that she would often say, she was indebted both to justice and her father's honor, till she had repaired them. But my grandfather, and father after him, met with hereditarie enemies at court, and thus stands our case.

---

[31] 'Gurlas' in CCL 4.30.

[32] 'this' omitted from CCL 4.30.

[33] 'easilie' omitted from CCL 4.30.

[34] The following paragraph is inserted in NLW, Dynevor A 94b and f: 'If Rice Griffith should have done the King of Scottes any meritoriouse service in the conquering of this kingdome, without question hee would have looked for his reward in some other kinde; ffor itt is not liklie (James the 5th overcoming) that Rice should long hould the Principality of Wales, the inheritance and right of the Kinges children.'

[35] 'so well satisfied' repeated in CCL 4.30.

[36] 'measures' in CCL 4.30.

Appendix IV

(From NLW, Dynevor A 94i. Other versions, with minor differences, including an occasional variation in the ordering of paragraphs, are in ibid., h, j and k. This list of claims about the role of James ap Gruffydd ap Hywel and Edward Lloyd in the attainder of Rhys ap Gruffydd in 1531 was probably compiled *c*.1576 for Gruffydd Rice.)

f.1. Certayne things that is to be alledged to the points of the Indictmente of Rees Griffythe Esquire.[1]

In primis, James Griffithe ap Howell was nere kynsmane to Rees Griffithe beinge a mann but of foure Marks Lands but by reason that he was a kynsmane to the sayd Rees Griffithe he had onlie his Lyvinge from the said Rees Griffythe.[2] And the said James beinge very great with him, upon a time desyred to have the sayd Rees Griffythe his letter to a gent' of North Wales for a farme that was upon his hands to be letten. Att whose request the sayd Rees Griffythe graunted him his lettre. And for that ther was never a clerke presente the said James perswadyd the said Rees Griffythe to put his hande to a blanke in which blanke Edwarde lloyd beinge clerke to the sayd Rees Griffithe should wrytt in the effecte of his whole minde in which letter the sayd James and Edward Lloyd did devyse certaine tresons.

Item that James Griffythe ap Hoell was prisoned in the Towre for counterfetinge of the kings majesties great seale of England at which time Rees Griffithe was sent for to London by the kynge for that ther had byn many affrayes made betwene the Lord fferrise and the Lady Katherin Haward wyffe to the said Rees Griffythe, the sayd Rees

---

[1] This document appears to be supplementary to Gruffydd Rice's petition, *c*.1576, to secure the reversal of his father's attainder: see above p.123.

[2] James was the son of Sir Rhys ap Thomas's sister, Sage. For his alleged role in Rhys ap Gruffydd's attainder, see above pp.101–11.

Griffyth not being at home in which affrayes ther was kylled fyve or sixe of the Lord fferryseis servaunts and three or iiii of the saide Rees Griffithis servaunts. And for this cause Rees Griffythe was sent for by the kynge.

Item that the said Rees Griffythe ley at Islyngtone havinge with him Edwarde Lloyd his clerke and William Hughes his chamberlyne, the said Edwarde Lloyd being a nere kynsmane to James Griffythe ap Hoell,[3] as it is to be supposed dyd often and sundrie tymes repayer to the Towre of London to the sayd James his kynsman when he and the said James often tymes consulted togeather howe and by what meanes they might best devyse some matter of treasons agaynst the sayd Rees Griffythe beinge promysed as the common report went by the adversaries of the sayd Rees Griffythe that in layinge treason to the sayd Rees Griffyth, the sayd James should have his pardone. And so the said Edward lloyd, and the said James, for the consyderacon before mencioned, and as it was commonlie reported a pece of mony being given to them besydes, was the onely occasion that they layd theis treasons in the Indictment mencioned agaynst him. And this the Lady Katerin Haward wyffe to the saide Rees Griffithe with a greatt number more in her lyffe tyme dyd declare to be true.

Item that when in the sayd Indictment yt is mencioned of three severalle Lordshippes, that the sayd Rees Griffethe should have sold or pledge to borowe greate somes of mony upon, yt was never harde by anye mann that ever he sold or pledged any of his lands, but the same beinge devysed by Edward Lloide and James Griffythe ap Hoell who were his aunsers and as I have hard by credable reports ther was none that gave anye Evydens agaynst [f.1*v*.] the said Rees Griffythe, but the sayd Edward and James. And beinge contempned themselves togeather with the saide Rees Griffythe, but afterward they the sayd Edwarde and James havinge their pardons and noue put to death but the sayd Rees Gryffethe and one William Hughes, who toke upon theire deathes that they were never giltie of the sayd tresons, wherupon they were condempned. Thus all things beinge well consydered I hope the Queenes Majestie will have consyderation therof.[4]

Item that the sayd Rees Griffyth was most bounde of all others to serve the kings majestie, for that his graundfather Sir Rees ap Thomas knyghte was preferred by the kinges Majestie and his most noble father Kinge Henrie the Seventhe to the noble order of the garter with other great offices that he had at theire Majesties handes in Walles. And thus is the holle consyderacion that is humbly desired may be considered at the Quenes Majesties hands and that it will please your Lordshipe to be so

---

[3] Llwyd and Hughes were not identified as Rhys ap Gruffydd's household officials at the time of the latter's trial in 1531. Nor was Llwyd's kinship with James ap Gruffydd ap Hywel alleged. See above pp.101ff.

[4] This probably refers to Queen Elizabeth I.

good Lord as to be a meane to my lord tresorer withe your Lordshipe, as to reed overe the whole Indictment throwlye and then to consyder of yt, as yt shall plese god to put in your noble harte.[5]

Also James Griffythe ap Hoell was apprehendyd by the said Rees Griffythe after that he had counterfeyeted the great Seall of England and sente up to the kings Majestie and the counsell wheruppon he was comytted to the Tower, and therfore your Lordship may judge whether he bare any malise to the sayd Rees Gr' ye or noe, he beinge the apprehender of him and the sender up of him.

---

[5] The lord referred to here may be Gruffydd Rice's kinsman, Thomas Radcliffe, earl of Sussex, the lord chamberlain, and the treasurer is likely to have been William Cecil, Lord Burghley, treasurer of England from July 1572 until his death in 1598. See above p.123.

Sources

A. *Original Sources: Unpublished*

Archives Départementales du Nord, Lille
   recette générale

British Library, London
   Additional MSS
   Cotton MSS
   Egerton MSS
   Egerton Rolls
   Harleian MSS
   Stowe MSS

Cambridge University Library MSS

Cardiff Free Central Library MSS

Carmarthen Record Office
   Cawdor MSS
   Dynevor MSS

College of Arms, London
   Box 36
   H.8
   I.2 and 9
   M.6 *bis* and 8

Durham University Library
   Church Commission Deposit, Durham Bishopric Estate Papers,
      Miscellaneous

National Library of Wales, Aberystwyth
   Bronwydd Deeds

Duchy of Cornwall MSS
Dynevor MSS
Llanstephan MSS
Mostyn MSS
National Library MSS
Pedigree Boxes
Peniarth MSS
Slebech Papers

Public Record Office, London

C1	Chancery, Early Chancery Proceedings
C54	Chancery, Close Rolls
C65	Chancery, Parliament Rolls
C66	Chancery, Patent Rolls
C67	Chancery, Pardon Rolls
C82	Chancery, Warrants for the Great Seal, Series II
C266	Chancery, Files, Cancelled Letters Patent
CP40	Common Pleas, Plea Rolls
DL5	Duchy of Lancaster, Entry Books of Decrees and Orders
DL29	Duchy of Lancaster, Ministers' Accounts
DL37	Duchy of Lancaster, Chancery Rolls
DL43	Duchy of Lancaster, Rentals and Surveys
E28	Exchequer, Treasury of Receipt, Council and Privy Seal
E30	Exchequer, Treasury of Receipt, Diplomatic Documents
E36	Exchequer, Treasury of Receipt, Miscellaneous Books
E101	Exchequer, King's Remembrancer, Various Accounts
E159	Exchequer, King's Remembrancer, Memoranda Rolls
E315	Exchequer, Augmentations, Miscellaneous Books
E326	Exchequer, Augmentations, Ancient Deeds, Series B
E357	Exchequer, Lord Treasurer's Remembrancer, Escheators' Accounts
E404	Exchequer, Exchequer of Receipt, Writs and Warrants for Issues
E405	Exchequer, Exchequer of Receipt, Rolls of Receipts and Issues
KB9	King's Bench, Ancient Indictments
KB27	King's Bench, Plea Rolls
LR1	Auditors of Land Revenue, Enrolments
PROB	Prerogative Court of Canterbury, Wills
PSO1	Privy Seal Office, 1
Req2	Court of Requests, Proceedings
SC2	Special Collections, Court Rolls
SC6	Special Collections, Ministers' Accounts
SC11	Special Collections, Rentals and Surveys, Rolls

SC12   Special Collections, Rentals and Surveys, Portfolios
SP1   State Papers, Henry VIII
Stac2   Star Chamber, Proceedings

Westminster Abbey MSS

Worcester Record Office MSS

B. *Original Sources: Published*

Acts of the Privy Council of England
Allen, P. S. and H. M. (eds.), *Letters of Richard Fox, 1456–1527* (Oxford, 1929)
Anderson, W. E. K. (ed.), *The Journals of Sir Walter Scott* (Oxford, 1972)
Anstis, J., *The Register of the Most Noble Order of the Garter* (2 vols., London, 1724).

Bacon, F., *The History of the Reign of King Henry the Seventh*, ed. R. Lockyer (London, 1971)
Baker, J. H. (ed.), *The Reports of John Spelman*, Vol.I (Selden Society, 93, 1977 for 1976)
Ballinger, J. (ed.), *The History of the Gwydir Family* (Cardiff, 1927)
Bayne, C. G. (ed.), *Select Cases in the Council of Henry VII* (Selden Society, 75, 1958)
Birch, W. de Gray (ed.), *A Descriptive Catalogue of the Penrice and Margam Manuscripts*, 4th series, part 2 (London, 1904)
Brewer, J. S. and Bullen, W. (eds.), *Calendar of Carew Manuscripts* (London, 1871)
Buchon, J. A. (ed.), *Chroniques de Jean Molinet*, Vol. II (Collections des Chroniques Nationales Françaises, Paris, 1828)

Calendars of Ancient Deeds
Calendars of State Papers, Domestic
Calendars of State Papers, Spanish
Calendars of the Close Rolls
Calendars of the Papal Registers
Calendars of the Patent Rolls
Camden, W., *Britannia* (London, 1610)
Camden, W., *Remaines of a Greater Worke, Concerning Britaine* (London, 1605; ed. R. D. Dunn, Toronto, 1984)
Campbell, W. (ed.), *Materials for a History of the Reign of Henry VII* (2 vols., RS, 1877)
Case, J., *Sphera Civitatis* (Oxford, 1588)
Cavendish, George, *The Life and Death of Cardinal Wolsey*, ed. R. S. Sylvester (EETS, 243, 1959 for 1957)

Caxton, W., *The Chronicles of England* (London, 1480)

Chrimes, S. B. and Brown, A. L. (eds.), *Select Documents of English Constitutional History, 1307–1485* (London, 1961)

Cicero, *De Officiis*, transl. W. Miller (London, 1913)

Cicero, *Pro Sestio*, transl. R. Gardner (London, 1958)

Clark, G. T. (ed.), *Cartae et alia Munimenta quae ad Dominium de Glamorgancia pertinent* (6 vols., Cardiff, 1893–1910)

Coss, P. R. (ed.), *The Langley Cartulary* (Dugdale Society, 32, 1980)

Davis, N. (ed.), *Paston Letters and Papers of the Fifteenth Century* (2 vols., Oxford, 1971–6)

Delfius, Pontus Heuterus, *Rerum Burgundicarum Libri Sex* (Antwerp, 1584); *Libri Sex* (Antwerp, 1583)

Denholm-Young, N. (ed.), *Vita Edwardi Secundi* (London, 1957)

Devon, F. (ed.), *Issues of the Exchequer, Henry III–Henry VI* (Record Commission, 1837)

Dugdale, W., *Monasticon Anglicanum* (6 vols. in 8, London, 1846)

Dwnn, Lewys, *Heraldic Visitations of Wales*, ed. S. R. Meyrick (2 vols., Llandovery, 1846)

Ellis, H. (ed.), *Holinshed's Chronicles*, Vol. III (London, 1808)

Ellis, H. (ed.), *Hall's Chronicle of the Union of the Two Noble and Illustre Famelies of Lancastre and York, 1548* (London, 1809)

Ellis, H. (ed.), *John Hardyng's Chronicle . . . with the continuation by Richard Grafton* (London, 1812)

Ellis, H. (ed.), *Original Letters illustrative of English History*, 1st series, Vol.I (London, 1825)

Ellis, H. (ed.), *Three Books of Polydore Vergil's English History* (Camden Society, 1st series, 29, 1844)

Fabyan, Robert, *The New Chronicles of England and France*, ed. H. Ellis (London, 1811)

Garlick, R. and Mathias, R. (eds.), *Anglo-Welsh Poetry, 1480–1980* (Bridgend, 1984)

Griffiths, R. A., 'The Cartulary and Muniments of the Fort family of Llanstephan', *BBCS*, XXIV, part 3 (1971), 311–84

Gupitza, J. (ed.), *The Romance of Guy of Warwick* (EETS, extra series, 25–6, 1875–6)

Hales, J. W. and Furnivall, F. J. (eds.), *Bishop Percy's Folio Manuscript* (London, 1868)

Halliwell, J. O. (ed.), *Percy Society Publications*, XX (1847)

Hamilton, W.D. (ed.), *A Chronicle of England . . . by Charles Wriothesley*, Vol. I (Camden Society, 2nd series, 11, 1875)

Harding, John, *The Chronicle from the Firste Begynnyng of Englande, 2 parts* (London, 1543), with A Continuation, f.122

Harries, L. (ed.), *Gwaith Huw Cae Llwyd ac Eraill* (Cardiff, 1953)

Harvey, J. H. (ed.), *William Worcestre: Itineraries* (Oxford, 1969)

Hay, D. (ed.), *The Anglica Historia of Polydore Vergil, AD 1485–1537* (Camden Society, 74, 1950)

Historical Manuscripts Commission, Vol. X (1885)

Historical Manuscripts Commission, Report on Manuscripts in the Welsh Language (2 vols., London, 1898–1905)

Historical Manuscripts Commission, Various Collections, Vol. II (London, 1903)

Historical Manuscripts Commission, Calendar of the Manuscripts of the Marquess of Salisbury, part 2 (London, 1906); part 13 (London, 1915)

Horace, *Odes*, ed. and transl. K. Quinn (London, 1980)

Horace, *Satires, Epistles and Ars Poetica*, ed. H. R. Fairclough (London, 1942)

Horrox, R. and Hammond, P.W. (eds.), *British Library, Harleian Manuscript 433* (4 vols., London, 1979–83)

Howard de Walden, Lord (ed.), *Banners, Standards and Badges from a Tudor Manuscript in the College of Arms* (De Walden Library, 1904)

Isaacson, R. F. (ed.), *The Episcopal Registers of the Diocese of St David's, 1397–1518* (2 vols., London, 1917–20)

Ives, E. W. (ed.), *Letters and Accounts of William Brereton of Malpas* (Lancashire and Cheshire Record Society, 1976)

James, T. B. (ed.), *The Port Book of Southampton, 1509–10*, Vol. II (Southampton Record Society, 33, 1990)

Jones, E. D. (ed.), *Lewys Glyn Cothi (Detholiad)* (Cardiff, 1984)

Jones, F., *Report on the Welsh Manuscripts contained in the College of Arms* (London, n.d.)

Jones, F., *A Catalogue of Welsh Manuscripts in the College of Arms* (Harleian Society, new series, VII, 1988)

Jones, H. Ll. and Rowlands, E. I. (eds.), *Gwaith Iorwerth Fynglwyd* (Cardiff, 1975)

Jones, J. and Davies, W. (eds.), *The Poetical Works of Lewis Glyn Cothi* (Oxford, 1837)

Jones, J. G. (ed.), *The History of the Gwydir Family and Memoirs* (Llandysul, 1990)

Jones, J. G. (ed.), *Gwaith Tudur Aled* (2 vols., Cardiff, 1926)

Jones, T. (ed.), *Ystoryaeu Seint Greal*: Rhan I, *Y Keis* (Cardiff, 1992)

Juvenal and Persius, transl. G. G. Ramsay (London, 1957)

Kingsford, C. L. (ed.), *Chronicles of London* (Oxford, 1905)

Kipling, G. (ed.), *The Receyt of the Ladie Kateryne* (EETS, 296, 1990)

Leadam, J. S. (ed.), *Select Cases before the King's Council in the Star Chamber*, Vol. II (1509–44) (Selden Society, 25, 1910)

Leclerc, J. (ed.), *Opera omnia Erasmi Roterodami*, Vol. II (*Adagia*) (Louvain, 1704)

Leland, John, *De Rebus Britannicis Collectanea* (6 vols., London, 1715)

Letters and Papers, Foreign and Domestic, of the Reign of Henry VIII (23 vols. in 38, London, 1862–1932)

Lewis, E. A., 'Materials illustrating the history of Dynevor and Newton from the earliest times to the close of the reign of Henry VIII', *WWHR*, I (1910–11); II (1911–12)

Lewis, E. A., *An Inventory of the Early Chancery Proceedings concerning Wales* (Cardiff, 1937)

Lloyd, T. D. (ed.), *Baronia de Kemeys* (Cambrian Archaeological Society, 1861)

Maxwell-Lyte, H. (ed.), *Documents and Extracts illustrating the History of the Honour of Dunster* (Somerset Record Society, 33, 1918)

Merrick, Rice, *Morganiae Archaiographia*, ed. B. Ll. James (South Wales Record Society, 1, 1983)

Merriman, R. B. (ed.), *Life and Letters of Thomas Cromwell* (2 vols., Oxford, 1902)

Morris, W. H., 'A Kidwelly town rental of the early 16th century (temp. Henry VII)', *Carms. Antiquary*, XI (1975), 55–87

Myers, A. R. (ed.), *English Historical Documents*, Vol. III (1327–1485) (London, 1969)

Nichols, J. G. (ed.), *The Chronicle of Calais* (Camden Society, old series, 35, 1846)

Nicolas, N. H. (ed.), *Testamenta Vetusta* (2 vols., London, 1826)

Nicolas, N. H. (ed.), *Privy Purse Expenses of Henry the Eighth* (London, 1827)

'Objections against Rhys ap Gruffydd', *Cambrian Register*, II (1797), 270–7

Ocland, Christopher, *Anglorum Praelia, ab anno . . . 1327 . . . usque ad annum . . . 1558* (London, 1580)

Owen, H., *Calendar of the Public Records relating to Pembrokeshire* (3 vols., Cymmrodorion Record Series, 7, 1911–18)

Paris, Matthew, *Historia Anglorum*, ed. F. Madden (3 vols., RS, 1866–9)

Paris, Matthew, *Chronica Majora*, ed. H. R. Luard (7 vols., RS, 1872–83)

'Parochialia . . . by Edward Llwyd', *Arch. Camb.*, supplementary Vol. III (1911)

Parry, T. (ed.), *Gwaith Dafydd ap Gwilym* (Cardiff, 1952)

Piccolomini, Aeneas Sylvius, *I Commentarii*, ed. L. Tokaro (2 vols., Milan, 1984)

Plautus, *Works*, Vol. I (*Aulularia*), transl. P. Nixon (London, 1921)

Plutarch, *Lives*, transl. B. Perrin (11 vols., London, 1914–43)

Pronay, N. and Cox, J. (eds.), *The Crowland Chronicle Continuations, 1459– 1486* (London, 1986)

Pugh, T. B. (ed.), *The Marcher Lordships of South Wales, 1415–1536: Select Documents* (Cardiff, 1963)

Raine, J. (ed.), *Testamenta Eboracensia* (6 vols., Surtees Society, 1836– 1902)

Records of the Honourable Society of Lincoln's Inn (2 vols., London, 1896)

Reusnerus, Elias, *Genealogia Imperatorum, Regum, Principum, Comitum, Baronum et Dynasticarum Germanorum . . .* (Frankfurt, 1612)

Richards, W. L. (ed.), *Gwaith Dafydd Llwyd o Fathafarn* (Cardiff, 1964)

Roberts, T. (ed.), *Gwaith Dafydd ab Edmwnd* (Bangor, 1914)

Rotuli Parliamentorum (6 vols., London, 1767)

Rowlands, E. I. (ed.), *Gwaith Lewys Môn* (Cardiff, 1975)

Seneca, *Moral Essays*, Vol. III (*De Beneficiis*), transl. J. W. Basore (London, 1948)

Shakespeare, William, *King Henry V*, ed. J. H. Walter (Arden edn., London, 1954)

Shakespeare, William, *King Richard III*, ed. A. Hammond (Arden edn., London, 1981)

Shakespeare, William, *Romeo and Juliet*, ed. B. Gibbons (Arden edn., London, 1980)

Sheppard, J. B. (ed.), *Christ Church Letters* (Camden Society, 2nd series, 19, 1877)

'A short view of the long life of . . . Rice ap Thomas', *Cambrian Register*, I (1796), 49–144

Smet, J.-J. (ed.), *Recueil des Antiquités de Flandre, par le Président Ph. Wielant* (Recueil des Chroniques de Flandre, Vol. IV, Brussels, 1865)

Smith, L. T. (ed.), *The Itinerary in Wales of John Leland* (London, 1906)

Smyth, J., *The Lives of the Berkeleys*, ed. J. Maclean (3 vols., London, 1893)

Sneyd, C. A. (ed.), *A Relation, or rather a True Account of the Island of England* (Camden Society, 1st series, 37, 1847)

Speed, John, *The History of Great Britain . . .* (1st edn., London, 1611; ?2nd edn., London, 1625)

Statutes of the Realm (11 vols., Record Commission, 1810–28; reprinted, 1963)

Stow, John, *A Survey of London*, ed. C. L. Kingsford (2 vols., Oxford, 1908; reprinted, 1971)

Strype, John, *Ecclesiastical Memorials*, Vol. II, part 2 (Oxford, 1822)

Suetonius, *Lives of the Caesars*, transl. J. C. Ralfe (2 vols., London, 1920)

Tacitus, *Histories and Annals*, transl. C. H. Moore and J. Jackson (4 vols., London, 1943–51)

Tanner, J. R. (ed.), *Constitutional Documents of the Reign of James I* (Cambridge, 1952)

Thomas, A. H. and Thornley, I. D. (eds.), *The Great Chronicle of London* (London, 1935)

Trevelyan, W. C. (ed.), 'Account of Henry the Eighth's expedition into France, AD 1513', *Archaeologia*, XXVI (1836)

Virgil, *Aeneid*, transl. R. Fairclough (2 vols., London, 1918–20)

Virgil, *Eclogues*, ed. H. E. Gould (London, 1983)

Warner, G. F. and Gilson, J. P., *Catalogue of the Western Manuscripts in the Old Royal and King's Collections* (4 vols., London, 1921)

Williams, I. and J. Ll. (eds.), *Gwaith Guto'r Glyn* (Cardiff, 1939)

Williams, J. M. and Rowlands, E. I. (eds.), *Gwaith Rhys Brydydd a Rhisiart ap Rhys* (Cardiff, 1976)

Willis-Bund, J. W. (ed.), *The Black Book of St David's* (London, 1902)

Woodhouse, P., *Democritus his Dreame, or the Contention between the Elephant and the Flea* (1605), ed. A. B. Grosart (Manchester, 1877)

C. *Secondary Sources*

Alexander, M. V. C., *The First of the Tudors* (London, 1981)

Allen, E., 'The tomb of the earl of Richmond in St David's Cathedral', *Arch. Camb.*, 5th series, XIII (1896), 315–20

Allen, E., 'The arms of Sir Rhys ap Thomas, K.G.', *Arch. Camb.*, 5th series, XIV (1897), 80–2

Anglo, S., *Spectacle, Pageantry and Early Tudor Policy* (Oxford, 1969)

Anglo, S. (ed.), *Chivalry in the Renaissance* (Woodbridge, 1990)

Antonovics, A. V., 'Henry VII, king of England, "By the Grace of Charles VIII of France" ', in R. A. Griffiths and J. Sherborne (eds.), *Kings and Nobles in the Later Middle Ages* (Gloucester, 1986), pp.169–84

Arthurson, I., 'The rising of 1497: a revolt of the peasantry?', in J. Rosenthal and C. Richmond (eds.), *People, Politics and Community in the Later Middle Ages* (Gloucester, 1987), pp.1–18

Arthurson, I., 'The king's voyage into Scotland: the war that never was', in D. Williams (ed.), *England in the Fifteenth Century* (Woodbridge, 1987), pp.1–22

Ashmole, E., *The Institutions, Laws and Ceremonies of the Most Noble Order of the Garter* (2 vols., London, 1672; 1 vol., Baltimore, 1971)

Ballard, M., 'An expedition of English archers to Liège in 1467, and the Anglo-Burgundian marriage alliance', *Nottingham Medieval Studies*, XXXIV (1990), 152–75

Barber, R. and Barker, J., *Tournaments* (Woodbridge, 1989)

Barnes, P. M., 'The Chancery *Corpus Cum Causa* file, 10–11 Edward IV', in R. F. Hunnisett and J. B. Post (eds.), *Medieval Legal Records* (London, 1978), pp.430–76

Barnwell, E. L., 'Notes on the Perrot family', *Arch. Camb.*, 3rd series, XII (1866), 64–72

Bartrum, P. C., *Welsh Genealogies, AD 300–1400* (8 vols., Cardiff, 1974)

Bartrum, P. C. *Welsh Genealogies, 1400–1500* (18 vols., Aberstwyth, 1983)

Bennett, M., *The Battle of Bosworth* (Gloucester, 1985)

Bennett, M., *Lambert Simnel and the Battle of Stoke* (Gloucester, 1987)

Berger, T. L. and Bradford Jnr., W. C., *An Index of Characters in English Printed Drama to the Restoration* (Englewood, Col., 1975)

Bernard, G. W. (ed.), *The Tudor Nobility* (Manchester, 1992)

Bindoff, S. T. (ed.), *History of Parliament: The Commons, 1509–1558* (3 vols., London, 1982)

Binns, J. W., *Intellectual Culture in Elizabethan and Jacobean England: The Latin Writings of the Age* (Leeds, 1991)

Bowen, D. J., 'Marwnad Syr Gruffudd ap Rhys', *BBCS*, XXV (1972), 31–2

Bowen, D. J., 'Dafydd ab Edmwnt ac Eisteddfod Caerfyrddin', *Barn*, rh. 142 (Awst 1974), 441–8

Bowen, E. G. and Gresham, C. A., *History of Merioneth*, Vol. I (Dolgellau, 1967)

Burke, P., 'Tacitism', in T. A. Dorey (ed.), *Tacitus* (London, 1969), pp.149–71

Busch, W., *England under the Tudors*, Vol. I: *King Henry VII* (London, 1895)

Carlton, C., *Charles I* (London, 1983)

Carr, A. D., *Owen of Wales* (Cardiff, 1991)

Carr, G., *William Owen Pughe* (Cardiff, 1983)

Cary, M. (and H. H. Scullard), *A History of Rome* (3rd edn., London, 1975)

Charles, B. G., *Non-Celtic Place Names in Wales* (London, 1935)

Charles, B. G., *George Owen of Henllys* (Aberystwyth, 1973)

Chrimes, S. B., 'The landing place of Henry of Richmond, 1485', *WHR*, II (1964–5), 173–80

Chrimes, S. B., *Henry VII* (London, 1972)

Chrimes, S. B., Ross, C. D. and Griffiths, R. A. (eds.), *Fifteenth-Century England, 1399–1509* (Manchester, 1972)

Clark, G. T., *Limbus Patrum Morganiae et Glamorganiae* (London, 1886)

Cockayne, G. E., *The Complete Peerage of England, Scotland and Ireland, Great Britain and the United Kingdom* (12 vols. in 13, London, 1910–59)

Collins, A., *Proceedings, Precedents and Arguments on Claims Concerning Baronies by Writ and other Honours* (London, 1734)

Colvin, H. M. *et al.*, *The History of the King's Works: The Middle Ages* (3 vols., London, 1963)

Colvin, H. M. *et al.*, *The History of the King's Works*, Vol. IV, part 2 (London, 1982)

Condon, M. M., 'Ruling élites in the reign of Henry VII', in C. Ross (ed.), *Patronage, Pedigree and Power in Later Medieval England* (Gloucester, 1979), pp.109–42

Condon, M. M., 'An anachronism with intent? Henry VII's Council Ordinance of 1491/2', in R. A. Griffiths and J. Sherborne (eds.), *Kings and Nobles in the Later Middle Ages* (Gloucester, 1986), pp.228–53

Cosgrove, A. (ed.), *A New History of Ireland*, Vol. II: *Medieval Ireland, 1169–1534* (Oxford, 1987)

Cross, F. L. and Livingstone, E. A. (eds.), *The Oxford Dictionary of the Christian Church* (2nd edn., Oxford, 1974)

Cruickshank, C. G., *Army Royal: Henry VIII's Invasion of France, 1513* (Oxford, 1969)

Davies, C. S. L., 'Bishop John Morton, the Holy See and the accession of Henry VII', *EHR*, CII (1987), 2–30

Davies, J. D., 'Weobley Castle', *Arch. Camb.*, 5th series, IV (1887), 13–23

Davies, M. B., 'Suffolk's expedition to Montdidier, 1523', *Bulletin of the Faculty of Arts, Fouad I University, Cairo*, VII (1944), 33–43

Davies, M. B., 'The "Enterprize" of Paris and Boulogne, 1544', *Bulletin of the Faculty of Arts, Fouad I University, Cairo*, XI, part 1 (1949), 37–95

Davis, G. R. C., *Medieval Cartularies of Great Britain* (1st edn., London, 1951)

Dickinson, W. C., *Scotland from the Earliest Times to 1603* (3rd edn., Oxford, 1977)

Dictionnaire de la langue française du seizième siècle, Vol. I (Paris, 1925)

Donaldson, G., *Scotland, James V to James VII* (Edinburgh and London, 1965)

Dorey, T. A. (ed.), *Tacitus* (London, 1969)

Dunning, R. W., 'Patronage and promotion in the later medieval Church', in R. A. Griffiths (ed.), *Patronage, the Crown and the Provinces in Later Medieval England* (Gloucester, 1981), pp.167–82

Edwards, R., *The Itinerary of King Richard III, 1483–1485* (London, 1983)

Elton, G. R., *Policy and Police* (Cambridge, 1972)

Elton, G. R., *Reform and Dissent* (Cambridge, 1973)

Emden, A. B., *A Biographical Register of the University of Oxford to 1500* (3 vols., Oxford, 1957–9)

Emden, A. B., *A Biographical Register of the University of Cambridge to 1500* (Cambridge, 1963)

'The epytaphye of Sir Gryffyth Apryse', *Anglia*, XXXI (1908), 347–50

Evans, G. E., 'The seal of Sir Rhys ap Thomas, 1494', *TCASFC*, XXVI (1936), 15–17

Evans, H. T., *Wales and the Wars of the Roses* (Cambridge, 1915)

Fenton, R., *A Historical Tour through Pembrokeshire* (London, 1811; 2nd edn., 1903)

Flandrin, J.-L., *Families in Former Times* (Cambridge, 1979)

Folz, R., *The Concept of Empire in Western Europe from the Fifth to the Fourteenth Century* (London, 1969)

Foster, J., *Alumni Oxonienses, 1500–1714* (4 vols., Oxford, 1892)

Fox, L. (ed.), *English Historical Scholarship in the Sixteenth and Seventeenth Centuries* (Oxford, 1956)

Frank, J., *The Beginning of the English Newspaper, 1620–1660* (Cambridge, Mass., 1961)

Französisches Etymologisches Wörterbuch (Basle, 1948–)

Fussner, F. S., *The Historical Revolution: English Historical Writing and Thought, 1580–1640* (London, 1962)

Gairdner, J., *History of the Life and Reign of Richard the Third* (London, 1878)

Geiriadur Prifysgol Cymru (Cardiff, 1950–)

Goodman, A. E., *The Wars of the Roses* (London, 1981)

Gransden, A., *Historical Writing in England*, Vol. II (London, 1982)

Green, F., 'The Wogans of Pembrokeshire', *WWHR*, VI (1916), 169–232

Green, V., *The History and Antiquities of the City and Suburbs of Worcester* (2 vols., London, 1796)

Gregory, D., *The History of the Western Highlands and Isles of Scotland* (2nd edn., Edinburgh, 1881; reprinted 1975)

Griffiths, R. A., 'The rise of the Stradlings of St Donat's', *Morgannwg*, VII (1963), 15–47

Griffiths, R. A., 'Gruffydd ap Nicholas and the rise of the House of Dinefwr', *NLWJ*, XIII (1964), 256–68

Griffiths, R. A., 'Gruffydd ap Nicholas and the fall of the House of Lancaster', *WHR*, II (1965), 213–31

Griffiths, R. A., *The Principality of Wales in the Later Middle Ages*, Vol. I: *South Wales, 1277–1536* (Cardiff, 1972)

Griffiths, R. A., 'Wales and the March', in S. B. Chrimes, C. D. Ross and R. A. Griffiths (eds.), *Fifteenth-Century England, 1399–1509* (Manchester, 1972), pp.145–72

Griffiths, R. A., 'The sense of dynasty in the reign of Henry VI', in C. D. Ross (ed.), *Patronage, Pedigree and Power in Later Medieval England* (Gloucester, 1979), pp.13–36

Griffiths, R. A., *The Reign of King Henry VI* (London, 1981)

Griffiths, R. A., *King and Country: England and Wales in the Fifteenth Century* (London, 1991)

Griffiths, R. A., 'A tale of two towns: Llandeilo Fawr and Dinefwr in the Middle Ages', in H. James (ed.), *Sir Gâr: Studies in Carmarthenshire History* (Carmarthen, 1991), pp.205–26

Griffiths, R. A. (ed.), *Boroughs of Medieval Wales* (Cardiff, 1978)

Griffiths, R. A. (ed.), *Patronage, the Crown and the Provinces in Later Medieval England* (Gloucester, 1981)

Griffiths, R. A. and Thomas, R. S., *The Making of the Tudor Dynasty* (Gloucester, 1985)

Griffiths, R. A. and Sherborne, J. (eds.), *Kings and Nobles in the Later Middle Ages* (Gloucester, 1986)

Gunn, S. J., 'The régime of Charles, duke of Suffolk, in north Wales and the "reform of Welsh government", 1509–25', *WHR*, XII, no.4 (1985), 461–94

Gunn, S. J., *Charles Brandon, Duke of Suffolk, c.1484–1545* (Oxford, 1988)

Gunn, S. J., 'Chivalry and the politics of the early Tudor court', in S. Anglo (ed.), *Chivalry in the Renaissance* (Woodbridge, 1990), 107–28

Gunn, S. J., 'The courtiers of Henry VII', *EHR*, CVIII (1993), 23–49

Guy, J., *Tudor England* (Oxford, 1988)

Gwyn, P., *The King's Cardinal* (London, 1990)

Hampton, W. E., 'The White Rose under the first Tudors: Part 3, Richard de la Pole, "The king's dreaded enemy" ', *Ricardian*, VII, no.99 (1987), 525–40

Harris, B. J., *Edward Stafford, Third Duke of Buckingham, 1478–1521* (Stanford, Calif., 1986)

Hasler, P. W., *History of Parliament: The Commons, 1558–1603* (3 vols., London, 1981)

Hay, D., *Polydore Vergil* (Oxford, 1952)

Hearder, H. and Loyn, H. R. (eds.), *British Government and Administration: Studies presented to S. B. Chrimes* (Cardiff, 1974)

Heymann, F. G., *John Zizka and the Hussite Revolution* (Princeton, 1969)

Hodges, G., *Ludford Bridge and Mortimer's Cross* (Logaston, Herefs., 1989)

Holmes, G. A., *The Estates of the Higher Nobility in Fourteenth-Century England* (Cambridge, 1957)

Hore, H. F., 'Note on the history of mayors and bailiffs of Tenby', *Arch. Camb.*, 2nd series, IV (1853), 121–6

Horrox, R., *Richard III: A Study of Service* (Cambridge, 1989)

Horrox, R. (ed.), *Richard III and the North* (Hull, 1986)

Howard, M., *The Early Tudor Country House: Architecture and Politics, 1490–1550* (London, 1987)

Howatson, M. C., *The Oxford Companion to Classical Literature* (2nd edn., Oxford, 1989)

Howells, B. E. (ed.), *Pembrokeshire County History*, Vol. III: *Early Modern Pembrokeshire 1536–1815* (Haverfordwest, 1987)

Hunnisett, R. F., and Post, J. B. (eds.), *Medieval Legal Records* (London, 1978)

Hunt, A. Leigh, *The Capital of the Ancient Kingdom of East Anglia* (London, 1870)

Ives, E. W., 'Court and County Palatine in the reign of Henry VIII: the case of Sir William Brereton of Malpas', *THSLC*, CXXIII (1972), 1–38

Ives, E. W., *Anne Boleyn* (Oxford, 1986)

Ives, E. W., Knecht, R. J. and Scarisbrick, J. J. (eds.), *Wealth and Power in Tudor England* (London, 1978)

James, H. (ed.), *Sir Gâr: Studies in Carmarthenshire History* (Carmarthen, 1991)

James, M. E., *Society, Politics and Culture* (Cambridge, 1986)

James, T., *Carmarthen* (Carmarthen, 1980)

Jansen, S. L., *Political Protest and Propaganda under Henry VIII* (Woodbridge, 1991)

Jarman, A. O. H. and Hughes, G. R. (eds.), *A Guide to Welsh Literature*, Vol. II (Swansea, 1979)

Jenkins, R. T. and Ramage, H. M., *A History of the Honourable Society of Cymmrodorion* (London, 1951)

Johnson, P. A., *Duke Richard of York, 1411–1460* (Oxford, 1988)

Jones, D., 'Sir Rhys ap Thomas: a study in family history and Tudor politics', *Arch. Camb.*, 5th series, IX (1892), 81–101

Jones, E. W., 'Wales and Bosworth Field: selective historiography', *NLWJ*, XXI (1979), 43–75

Jones, F., 'Sir Rhys ap Thomas: the blood of the raven', *TCASFC*, XXIX (1939), 29–33

Jones, F., 'Sir Rhys ap Thomas and the Knights of St John', *Carms. Antiquary*, II (1945–57), 70–4

Jones, F., 'The trail of a fugitive', *Carmarthenshire Historian*, 7 (1970), 7–19

Jones, F., 'Lloyd and Mears of Plas Llanstephan', *Carms. Antiquary*, XIV (1978), 42–60

Jones, F., 'Knights of the Holy Sepulchre', *Journal of the Historical Society of the Church in Wales*, XXVI (1979), 11–33

Jones, F., 'The Annals of Muddlescwm', *Carms. Antiquary*, XXI (1985), 11–26

Jones, F., *Historic Carmarthenshire Homes and their Families* (Carmarthen, 1987)

Jones, F., 'Annals of an old manor house: Green Castle', *Carms. Antiquary*, XXVII (1991), 3–20

Jones, J. G., 'Bishop Lewis Bayly and the Wynns of Gwydir, 1616–27', *WHR*, VI (1973), 404–23

Jones, M. (ed.), *Gentry and Lesser Nobility in Later Medieval Europe* (Gloucester, 1986)

Jones, M. K., 'Richard III and the Stanleys', in R. Horrox (ed.), *Richard III and the North* (Hull, 1986), pp.27–50

Jones, M. K. and Underwood, M. G., *The King's Mother* (Cambridge, 1991)

Jones, T., *The History of the County of Brecknock* (4 vols. in 2, Brecknock, 1909–11)

Jones, T., 'A Welsh chronicler in Tudor England', *WHR*, I (1960), 1–18

Kennett, W., *Parochial Antiquities* (London, 1695)

Kibre, P., 'Lewis of Caerleon, doctor of medicine, astronomer and mathematician (d.1494)', *Isis*, XLIII, part 1 (1952), 100–8

King, D. J. C. and Perks, J. C., 'Carew Castle, Pembs.', *Archaeological Journal*, CXIX (1962), 270–307

Knecht, R. J., *Francis I* (London, 1982)

Knowles, M. D., *The Religious Orders in England*, Vol. III (Cambridge, 1959)

Laws, E., *Little England beyond Wales* (London, 1880)

Lees-Milne, J. and Brocklehurst, C., *Cotehele House, Cornwall*, revised edn., M. Trinick (National Trust, 1979)

Le Neve, J., *Fasti Ecclesiae Anglicanae, 1300–1541*, ed. B. Jones (12 vols., London, 1962–7)

Levine, M., *Tudor Dynastic Problems, 1460–1571* (London, 1973)

Lewis, C., 'The literary tradition of Morgannwg', in T. B. Pugh (ed.), *Glamorgan County History*, Vol. III: *The Middle Ages* (Cardiff, 1971), pp.449–554

Lewis, J. M., *Carreg Cennen Castle* (new edn., Cardiff, 1990)

Lloyd, H. A., *The Gentry of South-west Wales, 1540–1640* (Cardiff, 1968)

Lloyd, H. W., 'Sir Rhys ap Thomas and his family, illustrated by the poems of contemporary bards', *Arch. Camb.*, 4th series, IX (1878), 200–16

Lloyd, J. E., *Owen Glendower* (Oxford, 1931)

Lloyd, J. E. (ed.), *History of Carmarthenshire* (2 vols., Cardiff, 1935–9)

Lloyd, J. E. and Jenkins, R. T. (eds.), *The Dictionary of Welsh Biography down to 1940* (London, 1959)

Lowe, D. E., 'The Council of the Prince of Wales and the decline of the Herbert family during the reign of Edward IV', *BBCS*, XXVII (1977–8), 278–96

Lowe, D. E., 'Patronage and politics: Edward IV, the Wydevills and the Council of the Prince of Wales, 1471–83', *BBCS*, XXIX (1980–2), 545–73

McConica, J., *The History of the University of Oxford*, Vol. III: *The Collegiate University* (Oxford, 1986)

McFarlane, K. B., 'A business-partnership in war and administration, 1421–1445', *EHR*, LXXVIII (1963), 290–308

McFarlane, K. B., *Hans Memling* (Oxford, 1971)

McFarlane, K. B., *England in the Fifteenth Century* (London, 1981)

McKisack, M., *Medieval History in the Tudor Age* (Oxford, 1971)

Maclagan, M., 'Genealogy and heraldry in the sixteenth and seventeenth centuries', in L. Fox (ed.), *English Historical Scholarship in the Sixteenth and Seventeenth Centuries* (Oxford, 1956)

Magnusson, M., *The Clacken and the Slate* (London, 1974)

Marks, R. and Payne, A., *British Heraldry* (London, 1978)

Maxwell-Lyte, H., *A History of Dunster* (2 vols., London, 1909)

Melville, H., *The Ancestry of John Whitney* (New York, 1896)

Mendyk, S. A. E., *'Speculum Britanniae': Regional Study, Antiquarianism and Science in Britain to 1700* (Toronto, 1989)

Meyrick, S. R., *The History and Antiquities of the County of Cardigan* (Brecon, 1907)

Miles, D., *Sheriffs of the County of Pembroke* (Haverfordwest, n.d. (*c*.1974))

Mitchell, R. J., 'English students at Padua, 1460–75', *TRHS*, 4th series, XIX (1936), 101–18

Morgan, D. A. L., 'The individual style of the gentleman', in M. Jones (ed.), *Gentry and Lesser Nobility in Later Medieval Europe* (Gloucester, 1986), pp.15–35

Morgan, G. B., *Historical and Genealogical Memoirs of the Morgan Family . . .* (2 vols. in 1, London, 1891–5)

Morgan, O. M., *A History of Wales* (Liverpool, 1911)

Morgan, P., *The Eighteenth Century Renaissance* (Llandybïe, 1981)

New Catholic Encyclopaedia (17 vols., New York, 1967)

Nicholson, R., *Scotland: The Later Middle Ages* (Edinburgh, 1974)

Nicolas, N. H., *History of the Battle of Agincourt* (2nd edn., London, 1832)

Odlozilik, O., *The Hussite King* (Rutgers, N. J., 1965)

Owen, D. H. (ed.), *Settlement and Society in Wales* (Cardiff, 1989)

Owen, H., *Old Pembrokeshire Families* (London, 1902)

Owen, H. and Blakeway, J. B., *A History of Shrewsbury* (2 vols., London, 1825)

Parry, C., 'Survey and excavation at Newcastle Emlyn Castle', *Carms. Antiquary*, XXIII (1987), 11–27

Pennant, T., *The Journey to Snowdon* (London, 1781)

Phillips, J. R. S. (ed.), *The Justices of the Peace in Wales and Monmouthshire, 1541 to 1689* (Cardiff, 1975)

Pollard, A. J., *John Talbot and the War in France, 1427–1453* (London, 1983)

Portal, E. M., 'The Academ Roial of King James I', *PBA*, VII (1915–16), 189–208

Pugh, T. B., 'Henry VII and the English nobility', in G. W. Bernard (ed.), *The Tudor Nobility* (Manchester, 1992), pp.49–105

Pugh, T. B. (ed.), *Glamorgan County History*, Vol. III: *The Middle Ages* (Cardiff, 1971)

Radford, C. A. R., *The Bishop's Palace, Lamphey, Pembrokeshire* (London, 1948)

Rees, D., *The Son of Prophecy* (London, 1985)

Rees, D., 'Neuadd Wen: changing patterns of tenure', in H. James (ed.), *Sir Gâr: Studies in Carmarthenshire History* (Carmarthen, 1991), pp.43–52

Rees, D., 'The Gower estates of Sir Rhys ap Thomas', *Gower*, XLIII (1992), 31–41

Rees, D., *Sir Rhys ap Thomas* (Llandysul, 1992)

Rees, W., *A History of the Order of St John of Jerusalem in Wales and the Welsh Border* (Cardiff, 1947)

'Rhyderwen (Rhyd Owen), Llanarthney', *TCASFC*, XI (1916–17), illustrations opposite pp.38, 54, 58

Roberts, E. P., *Dafydd Llwyd o Fathafarn* (Caernarfon, 1981)

Roberts, M., *Gustavus Adolphus* (2 vols., London, 1953–8)

Robinson, W. R. B., 'Early Tudor policy towards Wales: the acquisition of lands and offices in Wales by Charles Somerset, earl of Worcester', *BBCS*, XX, part 4 (1964), 421–38

Robinson, W. R. B., 'The marriages of knighted Welsh landowners, 1485–1558', *NLWJ*, 25 (1987–8), 387–98

Rosenthal, J., *Patriarchy and Families of Privilege in Fifteenth-Century England* (Philadelphia, 1991)

Rosenthal, J. and Richmond, C. (eds.), *People, Politics and Community in the Later Middle Ages* (Gloucester, 1987)

Roskell, J. S., *The Commons in the Parliament of 1422* (Manchester, 1954)

Roskell, J. S., *The Commons and their Speakers in English Parliaments, 1376–1523* (Manchester, 1965)

Ross, C. D., *Edward IV* (London, 1974)

Ross, C. D., *Richard III* (London, 1981)

Ross, C. D., 'Rumour, propaganda and public opinion during the Wars of the Roses', in R. A. Griffiths (ed.), *Patronage, the Crown and the Provinces in Later Medieval England* (Gloucester, 1981), pp.15–32

Ross, C. D. (ed.), *Patronage, Pedigree and Power in Later Medieval England* (Gloucester, 1979)

Rowlands, E. I., 'Terwyn a Thwrnai', *NLWJ*, IX (1955–6), 295–300

Rowlands, E. I., 'The continuing tradition', in A. O. H. Jarman and G. R. Hughes (eds.), *A Guide to Welsh Literature*, Vol. II (Swansea, 1979), pp.298–321

Rowlands, E. I., 'Tudur Aled', in A. O. H. Jarman and G. R. Hughes (eds.), *A Guide to Welsh Literature*, Vol. II (Swansea, 1979), pp.322–37

Royal Commission on Ancient and Historical Monuments, County of Carmarthen (London, 1917); *County of Merioneth* (London, 1921); *County of Pembrokeshire* (London, 1925); *An Inventory of the Historic Monuments in Herefordshire*, Vol. I: *South-West* (London, 1931); *An Inventory of the Ancient Monuments in Caernarvonshire*, Vol. III (London, 1964)

Russell, J. G., *The Field of Cloth of Gold* (London, 1969)

Sadie, S. (ed.), *New Grove Dictionary of Music and Musicians* (20 vols., London, 1980)

Saer, D. R., *The Harp in Wales in Pictures* (Cardiff, 1991)

Scarisbrick, J. J., *Henry VIII* (London, 1968)

Schmitt, C. B., *John Case and Aristotelianism in Renaissance England* (Kingston and Montreal, 1983)

Shaw, W. A., *The Knights of England* (2 vols., London, 1906)

Siddons, M. P., *The Development of Welsh Heraldry*, Vol. I (Aberystwyth, 1991)

Smallwood, T. M., '*The Prophecy of the Six Kings*', *Speculum*, 60 (1985), 571–92

Smyth, A. P., *Warlords and Holy Men: Scotland, AD 80–1000* (London, 1984)

Somerville, R., *History of the Duchy of Lancaster*, Vol. I (London, 1953)

Spurrell, W., *Carmarthen and its Neighbourhood* (2nd edn., Carmarthen, 1879)

Spurrell, W. G., *The History of Carew* (Carmarthen, 1921)

Starkey, D., *The Reign of Henry VIII: Personalities and Politics* (London, 1985)

Stephen, L. and Lee, S. (eds.), *The Dictionary of National Biography* (63 vols., London, 1885–1900; reprinted Oxford, 1921–2)

Stephens, M. (ed.), *The Oxford Companion to the Literature of Wales* (Oxford, 1986)

Stone, L., *The Crisis of the Aristocracy, 1558–1641* (Oxford, 1965)

Stone, L., *The Family, Sex and Marriage in England, 1500–1800* (London, 1977)

Sturge, C., *Cuthbert Tunstal* (London, 1938)

Thomas, W. G., *Weobley Castle* (London, 1971)
Tilley, M. P., *A Dictionary of the Proverbs in England in the Sixteenth and Seventeenth Centuries* (Ann Arbor, 1950)
Trevelyan, G. M., *History of England* (3rd edn., London, 1945)
Tucker, M. J., *The Life of Thomas Howard, Earl of Surrey and Second Duke of Norfolk, 1443–1524* (The Hague, 1964)
Tucker, N., 'Bodrhyddan and the families of Conwy, Shipley-Conwy and Rowley-Conwy', *Flintshire Historical Society Publications*, XIX (1961), 61–85

Vaughan, R., *Philip the Good* (London, 1970)
Vaughan, R., *Charles the Bold* (London, 1973)
Virgoe, R., 'The recovery of the Howards in East Anglia, 1485–1509', in E. W. Ives, R. J. Knecht and J. J. Scarisbrick (eds.), *Wealth and Power in Tudor England* (London, 1978), pp.1–20

Wagner, A., *English Genealogy* (3rd edn., Chichester, 1983)
Walker, R. F., 'Carew Castle', *Arch. Camb.*, CV (1956), 81–95
Warnicke, R. M., *The Rise and Fall of Anne Boleyn* (Cambridge, 1989)
Wedgwood, J. C., *History of Parliament, 1439–1509* (2 vols., London, 1936–8)
Weightman, C., *Margaret of York, Duchess of Burgundy, 1446–1503* (Gloucester, 1989)
Welsby, P. A., *Launcelot Andrewes, 1555–1626* (London, 1958)
Williams, C. H., 'The rebellion of Humphrey Stafford in 1486', *EHR*, XLIII (1928), 181–9
Williams, D. (ed.), *England in the Fifteenth Century* (Woodbridge, 1987)
Williams, D. H., 'The White Monks in Powys, I', *Cistercian Studies*, XI (1976), 73–101
Williams, G., 'Rice Mansell of Oxwich and Margam (1487–1559)', *Morgannwg*, VI (1962), 33–51
Williams, G., 'Local and national history in Wales', *WHR*, V (1970), 45–66
Williams, G., 'Prophecy, poetry and politics in medieval and Tudor Wales', in H. Hearder and H. R. Loyn (eds.), *British Government and Administration: Studies presented to S. B. Chrimes* (Cardiff, 1974), pp.69–86
Williams, G., *The Welsh Church from Conquest to Reformation* (2nd edn., Cardiff, 1976)
Williams, G., *Harri Tudur a Chymru: Henry Tudor and Wales* (Cardiff, 1985)
Williams, G., *Recovery, Reorientation and Reformation: Wales, c.1415–1642* (Oxford and Cardiff, 1987)

Williams, G. A., 'The bardic road to Bosworth: a Welsh view of Henry Tudor', *Transactions of the Honourable Society of Cymmrodorion* (1986), pp.7–31

Williams, G. J., 'Eisteddfod Caerfyrddin', *Y Llenor*, V (1926), 94–102

Williams, I., *Cywyddau Dafydd ap Gwilym a'i Gyfoeswyr* (2nd edn., Cardiff, 1935)

Williams, J., *A History of Wales* (London, 1869)

Williams, P., *The Council in the Marches of Wales under Elizabeth I* (Cardiff, 1958)

Williams, S., 'The Lord Mayor's show in Tudor and Stuart times', *Guildhall Miscellany*, I, no.10 (1959), 3–18

Williams, W. Ll., 'A Welsh insurrection', *Y Cymmrodor*, XVI (1902), 1–94

Williams-Jones, K., 'Another "Indenture of the Marches", March 1490', *BBCS*, XXIV, part 1 (1970), 93–4

Wright, F. A. (ed.), *Lemprière's Classical Dictionary* (new edn., London, 1879)

Young, A. R., *Tudor and Jacobean Tournaments* (London, 1987)

Young, A. R., *English Tournament Imprese* (New York, 1988)

D. *Unpublished Theses*

Allan, A., 'Political propaganda employed by the House of York in England in the mid-fifteenth century' (University of Wales Ph.D. thesis, 1981)

Davies, A. E., 'Gwaith Deio ab Ieuan Du a Gwilym ab Ieuan Hen' (University of Wales MA thesis, 1979)

Davies, E. R. Ll., 'Noddwyr y Beirdd yn Sir Gaerfyrddin' (University of Wales MA thesis, 1976)

Grace, F. R., 'The life and career of Thomas Howard, third Duke of Norfolk (1473–1554)' (University of Nottingham MA thesis, 1961)

Griffith, W. P., 'Welsh students at Oxford and Cambridge and the Inns of Court during the sixteenth and early seventeenth centuries' (University of Wales Ph.D. thesis, 1981)

Griffiths, R. A., 'Royal government in the southern counties of the Principality of Wales, 1422–1485' (University of Bristol Ph.D. thesis, 1962)

Headley, M. G., 'Barddoniaeth Llawdden a Rhys Nanmor' (University of Wales MA thesis, 1938)

Howells, B. E., 'Studies in the social and agrarian history of medieval and early modern Pembrokeshire' (University of Wales MA thesis, 2 vols., 1956)

Jones, M. K., 'The Beaufort family and the war in France, 1421–50' (University of Bristol Ph.D. thesis, 1982)

Lloyd, J. M., 'The rise and fall of the House of Dinefwr (the Rhys family), 1430–1530' (University of Wales MA thesis, 1963)

Turvey, R. K., 'The Perrot family and their circle in south-west Wales during the later Middle Ages' (University of Wales Ph.D. thesis, 1988)

Vokes, S. E., 'The early career of Thomas Howard, earl of Surrey and third duke of Norfolk, 1474–*c.*1525' (University of Hull Ph.D. thesis, 1988)

Williams, J. M., 'The Stanley family of Lathom, *c.*1450–1504: a political study' (University of Manchester MA thesis, 1979)

Index

Aberbrân (Brecs.), 223 and n.46
Aberglasney (Carms.), 48, 89, 115
Abergwili (Carms.), 165 and n.31
Abermarlais (or Llansadwrn) (Carms.), 16,
  28, 31, 32, 61, 74–5, 77 n.134, 82, 95, 114,
  116, 158 n.5, 164 and n.27, 173 n.7, 175–6,
  190, 196 and n.13, 248–9, 252 n.65, 274;
  manor of, receiver, steward and surveyor of,
  114–15
Aberystwyth, borough of, 113; castle of, 23–4,
  35, 60, constable of, 27, 35–6, 49, 89; church
  of, 77–8
Abigail, 203
Abner, 157 and n.1
'Academ Roial', 141
Achelous, River (Greece), 149 and n.6
Achilles, 253, 277
Acts of Union, of Wales and England, 6, 110,
  139
admirals, 66, 126, 129–30, 141, 248 and n.48,
  259, 274 n.2
advowsons, 113 and n.6
Aeron, River (Cards.), 78
affinities, see retinues
Agesilaus, 175 and nn.16,17
Agincourt, battle of (1415), 196 n.11, 223 n.46
Agrippa Posthumus, 172
Ajax, 150 and n.9
Albany, John Stewart, duke of (d. 1536), 284
Alba, see Scotland
Albania, 141, 153 n.22
Alcibiades, 181 and n.36
Alcock, John, bishop of Worcester (d. 1500),
  36
Alexander, 19
Alexander the Bey, see Scanderbeg, Castriota
Alnwick, castle of, 30
Alvard, Thomas, 97
André, Bernard, 236 n.13

Andrewes, Lancelot, bishop of Winchester (d.
  1626), 139–40, 143 n.20, 154 n.27, 164 and
  n.26
Àngle (Pembs.), 113, 119–20, 125, 129
Anglesey, county of, 4 n.3, 82, 270 n.38
Angoulême (France), 259
Angus, Archibald Douglas, earl of (d. 1557),
  284
Anjou (France), 238
Anne Boleyn, Queen, marchioness of
  Pembroke (d. 1536), 102, 104, 109–10, 121;
  mother of, 104
Anne Neville, Queen (d. 1485), 218 n.32
Anne, duchess of Brittany (d. 1514), 238 and
  n.20
Antalcidas, 175 and n.17
Antigonus, king of Macedonia, 177 n.25
Antigonus Pyrrhus, 174 and n.14, 177
antiquarianism, 127, 130–1, 136, 139–41, 147,
  155, 268 n.29, 289
Antiquaries, Society of, 141
Appleyard, Sir Nicholas, 69
Aragon, king of, see Ferdinand II
Arc, Joan of, 263 n.15
Ardres (France), 58
Ariosto, 175 n.19
Aristotle, Politics of, 230 and n.69
arms, coats of, 10 n.10, 74, 80–1, 103, 127,
  136, 263, 265, 276, 283; College of, 127,
  139; seals of, 90, 114, 136
Artaxerxes, king of Persia, 258 and n.81
Arthur, King, 82–3, 85, 102–3, 154, 159, 289–
  90
Arthur, prince of Wales (d. 1502), 4, 46, 49–
  51, 57, 65, 66, 70, 74, 79, 115, 123, 247 and
  n.46, 252 n.64, 259, 273, 285; council of, 46;
  death of, 51–2, 71, 86, 105, 246 n.42;
  household of, 51 and n.31, 65–6, 105; wife
  of, see Catherine of Aragon
Arthur's Stone (Herefs.), 176 and n.21